2016 ALMANAC of Puerto Ricans in the United States

Centro Press

Printed in the United States of America

Library of Congress Cataloging-in-Publication Data
Names: Hinojosa, Jennifer, editor. | Vargas-Ramos, Carlos, editor.
Title: Almanac of Puerto Ricans in the United States, 2016 / Jennifer Hinojosa and Carlos Vargas-Ramos, editors.
Description: New York, NY : Centro Press, Center for Puerto Rican Studies, 2017. | Includes bibliographical references and index.
Identifiers: LCCN 2017002040 | ISBN 9781945662072 (pbk. : alk. paper)
Subjects: LCSH: Puerto Ricans--United States--Statistics. | Puerto Ricans--United States--Social conditions--Statistics. | Puerto Ricans--United States--Economic conditions--Statistics.
Classification: LCC E184.P85 A59 2017 | DDC 305.868/7295073--dc23
LC record available at https://lccn.loc.gov/20170020

Centro Press
Center for Puerto Rican Studies
Hunter College, CUNY
695 Park Avenue, E-1429
New York, NY 10065
centrops@hunter.cuny.edu
http://centropr.hunter.cuny.edu

CONTENTS

INTRODUCTION 5

REPORTS

United States 12

New York 24

Florida 35

New Jersey 46

Pennsylvania 57

Massachusetts 68

Connecticut 79

Illinois 90

California 101

Texas 112

Ohio 123

Virginia 134

Georgia 145

North Carolina 156

Introduction

The Puerto Rican population in the United States continues to grow and disperse throughout the U.S., particularly in the southern region. The combination of Puerto Rico's declining economy, which led many Puerto Ricans to flee the island for better economic opportunities in the U.S. mainland, the internal migration of Puerto Ricans from the Northeast and Midwest to the southern states, and general population growth have all resulted in a changing geography for Puerto Ricans in the United States.

This almanac provides a portrait of a heterogeneous Puerto Rican population in the United States, punctuated by the geographic dispersion of a highly mobile group. The overall picture that emerges from the data suggests that inter-state mobility and geographic dispersion correlates with better socioeconomic indicators for stateside Puerto Ricans.

Between 2000 and 2014, the Puerto Rican population in the United States grew from about 3.4 million to almost 5.3 million. With this increase, 60 percent of people who identified as Puerto Rican resided in the United States mainland, compared to 39 percent (3.4 million) in Puerto Rico. The changing geography of Puerto Ricans in the United States was apparent in 2014. In previous decades, New York remained the only state with more than one million Puerto Ricans. As of 2014, Florida's Puerto Rican population also exceeded one million. It is also anticipated that before the next decennial census in 2020, Florida will become the state with the largest share of the Puerto Rican population in the United States.

Using the 2014 American Community Survey (one-year estimates), this almanac compiles demographic, economic, and social data about the Puerto Rican population in the United States and in states with the largest proportion of Puerto Ricans: New York (1,095,858); Florida (1,006,542); New Jersey (468,200); Pennsylvania (423,755); Massachusetts (308,028); Connecticut (301,182); Illinois (211,626); California (207,565); Texas (177,448); Ohio (108,174); Virginia (92,319); Georgia (89,462); and North Carolina (89,212). These 13 states contained more than 86 percent of the Puerto Rican population in the United States. In addition, settlement patterns for both the overall Puerto Rican population and the recent Puerto Rican arrivals (between 2006 and 2014) are mapped to observe the spatial location within each state. Boundaries illustrating congressional districts are presented by the incumbent political party, county, and census tract geographies. The overall Puerto Rican population (represented in red dots) and recent Puerto Rican migrants (represented in black dots), who arrived in selected states from Puerto Rico during the previous year between 2006 and 2014, are mapped to establish their settlement patterns. In all, the Puerto Rican population shows great demographic, economic, and social variations within and between the selected states.

THE BROAD GEOGRAPHY OF PUERTO RICAN SETTLEMENT

Between 2000 and 2014, notable Puerto Rican population growth was apparent in the following states: North Carolina, Texas, Georgia, Virginia, and Florida, all of which are located in the U.S. south. Puerto Rican population growth was also seen in Pennsylvania and Ohio, both states of traditional settlement for Puerto Ricans. On the other hand, Puerto Rican population declined in the following states: New York, New Jersey, Illinois, and California. Lastly, Puerto Ricans in Connecticut and Massachusetts showed no population growth or decline, instead the population remained steady between 2000 and 2014.

DEMOGRAPHIC

Demographic characteristics described in this analysis include age, educational attainment, and language proficiency. Median age is an indicator of age distribution. Puerto Ricans are a relatively young population. Puerto Ricans in the United States had a median age (28.9 years) ten years lower than in Puerto Rico (38.9 years) and nine years lower than for the total U.S. population (37.7 years). Relative to the other groups in the U.S., Puerto Ricans in the United States had a lower median age than non-Hispanic whites (43.1 years) and non-Hispanic blacks (33.7 years). Relative to Hispanics in the United States overall, Puerto Ricans had a higher median age of about six months (28.4 years for Hispanics).

Puerto Ricans in New York and New Jersey appeared to be an older population than Puerto Ricans in the Sunbelt states (except for Florida). Puerto Ricans in Florida (32.2 years), New York (31.9 years), and New Jersey (29.9 years) had a higher median age than Puerto Ricans in Georgia (27 years), Virginia (27.3 years), Massachusetts (26.8 years), Connecticut (26.4 years), Ohio (26.3 years), Pennsylvania (25.5 years), and North Carolina (25.3 years). Puerto Ricans in Texas and Illinois (28 years) closely hewed to the median age for stateside Puerto Ricans overall (28.9 years).

Another demographic indicator of age used in this report is the percentage of population that is 62 years of age or older. At least 9.9 percent of the Puerto Rican population in the United States occupied this age category, a much lower rate compared to Puerto Ricans in Puerto Rico (21%). Puerto Ricans in New York (13.6%), Florida (12.3%), New Jersey (10.6%), and California (10.3%) had a higher percentage of Puerto Ricans aged 62 years or higher compared to Puerto Ricans in the U.S. overall. On the other hand, Puerto Ricans in Virginia (5.6%), Ohio (6%), Georgia (6.4%), Pennsylvania (6.5%), Massachusetts (7%), North Carolina and Texas (7.1%), and lastly Connecticut (7.8%) had a relatively lower percentage of their population over 61 years of age.

EDUCATION

Puerto Rican educational attainment overall is relatively lower than it is for non-Hispanic groups. As of 2014, the nation's educational attainment profile among those aged 25 years and older was as follows. Nationally, 22.6 percent of stateside Puerto Ricans age 25 and older had an educational attainment of less than a high school degree, followed by 29.7 percent with a high school education; 30 percent with some college experience or an associate's degree; and lastly 17.6 percent who had earned a bachelor's degree or higher. Relative to other groups in the U.S., Puerto Ricans in the U.S. had greater proportions of those with less than a high school education, compared to non-Hispanic whites (8%) and non-Hispanic blacks (15.5%), but lower than all Latinos (34.7%). Stateside Puerto Ricans had higher rates of those with a high school degree than the total U.S. population (27.7%), Hispanics overall (27.2%), and non-Hispanic whites (28.2%), but lower than non-Hispanic blacks (31.7%). The proportion of college graduates among Puerto Ricans in the U.S. was lower than for non-Hispanic whites (33.6%) and non-Hispanic blacks (19.7%). On the other hand, stateside Puerto Ricans had a greater proportion of college graduates than Hispanics in the U.S. overall (14.4%). Puerto Ricans in Puerto Rico (24.1%) had a higher rate of higher educational attainment.

Educational attainment varied by state. Puerto Ricans were more likely to have higher educational attainment (some college or associate's and bachelor's degree or higher) in Texas, Florida, Illinois, California, Georgia, North Carolina, and Virginia. Lower educational attainment profile was evident among Puerto Ricans in Connecticut, Ohio, Pennsylvania, New Jersey, and New York.

The proportion of Puerto Ricans in the U.S. with less than a high school degree was highest in Massachusetts (36.6%), followed by Pennsylvania (30.5%), New York (28.5%), Connecticut (26.5%), and Ohio (25.9%), compared with the national rate of 22.6 percent. On the other hand, Puerto Ricans in Florida (18.1%), California (15%), and Texas (11.3%), North Carolina (11.9%), Georgia (10.5%), and Virginia (7.7%) had lower rates of Puerto Ricans without a high school education. New Jersey (22.6%) and Illinois (22.4%) had similar rates to the national average (22.6%).

The proportion of Puerto Ricans with some college experience or an associate's degree was highest in Texas (41.4%) compared to the Puerto Rican national rate of 30 percent and 21.6 percent in Puerto Rico. Again, Puerto Ricans in the Sunbelt states showed higher rates of some college or associate's degree. For example, 40.9 percent of Puerto Ricans in North Carolina, 39.4 percent in California, 37.7 percent in Virginia, 34.1 percent in Florida, and lastly 33.5 percent in Georgia had at least some college or an associate's degree.

Puerto Ricans in the U.S. South and California were more likely to hold a bachelor's degree or higher compared to Puerto Ricans in Northeast and Midwest. For example, Puerto Ricans in Virginia (34.1%) nearly doubled the national rate (17.6%) of those with a bachelor's degree or higher. Other states like Georgia (32%), Texas (27.5%), California (24.5%), and North Carolina (22.4%) also had higher rates. In contrast, Pennsylvania (9.4%), Massachusetts (10.4%), and Connecticut (11.6%) had the lowest rates of Puerto Ricans earning a bachelor's degree or more. The rates in Florida and Illinois closely resembled the national rate of 17.7 percent of Puerto Ricans with a bachelor's degree or more.

The proportions of Puerto Rican females with a bachelor's degree or higher was 19.5 percent. These rates were higher in the Sunbelt states: Georgia (35.2%), Virginia (33.8%), Texas (31.8%), North Carolina (28.7%), and California (25.2%) compared to Pennsylvania, Connecticut, Massachusetts, Ohio, and New York, which had notably lower proportions of college education. Nationally, at least 15.6 percent of Puerto Rican males earned a bachelor's degree or higher, this is at least 4 percentage points lower than Puerto Rican females. However, similarly to Puerto Rican women, more Puerto Rican men were likely to have a bachelor's degree or higher in Virginia (34.5%), Georgia (29.5%), California (23.8%), Texas (23.4%), and Florida (16.7%) than in states in the Northeast and Midwest.

LANGUAGE

The majority of Puerto Ricans in the U.S. are bilingual, with more than 60 percent speaking both English and Spanish. This ability to speak more than one language did not detract from speaking English at least very well. The overwhelmingly majority of Puerto Ricans (83%) did so. This rate of English proficiency was higher among non-Hispanic blacks and non-Hispanic whites, in the order of 95 percent or above. Puerto Ricans' bilingualism is higher than that of non-Hispanic blacks and whites, and comparable to that of Hispanics overall. However, more Puerto Ricans reported speaking only in English than Hispanics overall.

Generally, Puerto Ricans in the Northeast and Florida, like Massachusetts (72.8%), Connecticut (67.1%), New Jersey and New York (62.9%), and Pennsylvania (62.5%) had a larger proportion of speaking a language other than English and higher proportions of people reporting speaking English less than "very well." At least 39 percent of Puerto Ricans reported speaking only English at home, a rate higher than Hispanics overall (26.5%) in the U.S. Puerto Ricans reported speaking only English at home ranged from 27.2 percent in Massachusetts to 58.2 percent in California. States with the highest proportion of Puerto Ricans speaking only English included: California (58.2 %), Georgia (51.9%), Virginia (48.6%), North Carolina (48.2%), Ohio (45.3%), Illinois (40.3%), and Texas (39.7%). On the other hand, lower rates of speaking English only at home included: Pennsylvania (37.5%), New York and New Jersey (37.1%), Connecticut (32.9%), Florida (28.9%), and Massachusetts (27.2%). Notably, Puerto Ricans in the Sunbelt states and Ohio reported higher rates of the population who "speak English only," whereas Puerto Ricans in the Northeast and Midwest showed lower rates. Higher rates of bilingualism among the Puerto Rican population appeared to correspond with the large presence of Hispanic and Puerto Rican communities in the Northeast and some states in the south (Florida and Texas).

EMPLOYMENT STATUS

Puerto Rican participation in the labor force is comparable to the participation of the population as a whole and that of non-Hispanic blacks and non-Hispanic whites. However, the distribution of that participation differs for Puerto Ricans when compared to other groups in the United States. The national labor force participation rate for stateside Puerto Ricans was 62.4 percent in 2014, a rate comparable to non-Hispanic whites (62.5%), non-Hispanic blacks (62%), but lower than for Latinos as a whole (67.1%). Stateside Puerto Rican labor force participation rate was 18.7 percentage points higher than in Puerto Rico (43.7%). Labor force participation differed strikingly across the selected states. Among the Sunbelt states, Texas (72.8%), North Carolina (72.6%), Virginia (70.3%), California (70%), and Georgia (67.2%) had the highest labor force participation rates for Puerto Ricans. On the other hand, Florida (61.2%) had comparable Puerto Rican labor force participation rates in the U.S. Some Northeast and Midwest states – such as Ohio (67.1%), New Jersey (65.9%), Illinois (65.8%), and Connecticut (64.6%) – also remained above the national average (62.4%), but lower when compared to Puerto Ricans in the Sunbelt states. The remaining states, New York (55.3%) and Pennsylvania (58.1%), had the lowest labor force participation rates.

In terms of the distribution of the labor force participation in 2014, 7.2 percent of the U.S. civilian labor force was unemployed. Stateside Puerto Ricans had the second highest unemployment rate (11.6%) after non-Hispanic blacks (13.3%), and followed by Latinos overall (8.4%) and non-Hispanic whites (5.8%). Overall, employment status varied among Puerto Ricans in the selected states. Unemployment rates were higher for Puerto Ricans in Pennsylvania (17%), Massachusetts (16.5%), and Connecticut (14.8%). On the other hand, Puerto Ricans in Texas (8.2%), Georgia (8.7%), Virginia (9.8%), and North Carolina (11.1%) had lower unemployment rates. Stateside Puerto Rican unemployment rate was at least 7 percentage points lower compared to the 18.9 percent rate in Puerto Rico.

Labor force participation often distinguishes between civilians and the population serving in the armed forces. Nationally, the Puerto Rican rate of service in the armed forces was 0.8 percent, twice the rate of service of non-Hispanic whites (0.4%), non-Hispanic blacks (0.4%), and Latinos (0.4%) overall. The rates of Puerto Ricans serving in the armed forces were higher in North Carolina (5.7%), Virginia (4.1%), Georgia (3.7%), and Texas (3.2%). For Puerto Ricans, the large presence of military bases in these states contributed to their above-average representation in the armed forces.

In the management, business, science, and arts occupation sector, non-Hispanic whites (41.4%) were represented above the national average (36.9%), while Latinos (20.4%) showed the lowest representation. Puerto Ricans in Puerto Rico (31.3%), stateside Puerto Ricans (28.1%), and non-Hispanic blacks (28.7%) had similar rates within this occupational sector; however, they were lower than the national average (36.9%).

In 2014, Puerto Ricans in the United States were most represented in "management, science, business, and arts" (28.1%) occupations, followed by "sales and office" (27.4%), "service" (23.4%), "production, transportation, and material moving" (13.7%), and "natural resources, construction, and maintenance" (7.4%) occupations. Both Puerto Rican males and females in the United States represented a larger proportion in the "management, science, business, and art" occupations. However, Puerto Rican females had a higher rate of employment in these occupations (33.1%) than Puerto Rican males (23.4%). Puerto Ricans in some Sunbelt states showed higher rates of employment in these occupations. For example, a large proportion of Puerto Rican males in Virginia (41.6%), California (34.7%), and Texas (31.8%) worked in the management, science, business, and art occupations whereas Puerto Rican females showed even higher rates in Texas (46.9%), Virginia (42.1%), and California (41.5%).

INCOME AND EARNINGS

Puerto Ricans had consistently lower income and earnings across the board, relative to the population as a whole and to non-Hispanic whites, in particular. In 2014, the median household income in the United States was $53,657. The median household income for stateside Puerto Ricans was $39,322, higher than that of non-Hispanic blacks ($35,434), yet notably lower than that of non-Hispanic whites ($59,622) and that of Hispanic households overall ($42,748). For Puerto Ricans in the U.S., median household income ranged from $24,983 in Massachusetts to $68,393 in Virginia. In addition to Virginia, California ($60,273), Texas ($53,565), New Jersey ($46,889), Illinois ($44,991), and Florida ($40,465) were among the selected states with the highest median household income for Puerto Ricans. Puerto Ricans in the remaining states showed significantly lower median household income than the Puerto Rican national average. These states included, in addition to Massachusetts, Connecticut ($29,323), Pennsylvania ($30,385), Ohio ($34,862), North Carolina ($37,238), and New York ($33,906).

In the United States, the mean earnings of full-time and year-round male workers were $66,829 and $49,172 for female workers, an estimated difference of $17,600 in 2014. Mean earnings of Puerto Rican males ($50,756) were higher than non-Hispanic black males ($47,755) and Latinos ($43,214), but they were lower than for non-Hispanic white males ($74,773). Across all racial and ethnic groups, the mean earnings for full-time, year-round women were lower than for males in the United States. However, similarly to Puerto Rican males in the U.S., Puerto Rican females had higher mean earnings ($42,263) than non-Hispanic black females ($41,520) and Latinas overall ($36,293), but lower than non-Hispanic white females ($52,638).

Mean earnings of stateside Puerto Rican men, working full-time and year-round, were higher than women by $8,500 in 2014. However, there was great variation across the different states. Puerto Rican women made at least $20,000 more than other Puerto Rican women in Virginia, $16,000 more in Georgia, $14,000 more in North Carolina, $10,000 more in Florida, and, lastly, $8,500 more in both Ohio and New Jersey. Smaller disparities were evident in states of traditional settlement. Stateside Puerto Rican women did not appear to be translating greater educational attainment and higher management jobs into higher earnings in the U.S. South and California.

Mean earnings for Puerto Rican men ranged from $43,027 in Massachusetts to $69,680 in Virginia. As for Puerto Rican women, mean earnings ranged from $35,096 in Florida to $54,608 in California. Puerto Rican men had higher earnings in Virginia ($69,680), California ($62,132), Georgia ($56,304), New Jersey ($55,051), Texas ($52,203), New York ($52,111), and North Carolina ($51,336). States with lower mean earnings for Puerto Rican men included: Massachusetts ($43,027), Pennsylvania ($44,929), Ohio ($45,521), Florida ($45,500), Illinois ($47,490), and Connecticut ($50,423). Mean earnings for full-time, year-round Puerto Rican women workers were higher in California ($54,608), Virginia ($49,393), Texas ($46,635), New Jersey ($46,412), New York ($46,389), Illinois ($44,701), and Connecticut ($42,813) compared to the national mean earnings of $42,263 for Puerto Rican women in the United States. Puerto Rican women had lower earnings in Florida ($35,096), Ohio ($36,970), North Carolina ($36,716), Pennsylvania ($37,810), Massachusetts ($39,543), and Georgia ($40,374). In sum, paradoxically, considering that in general Northeast states workers typically will have higher earnings than those in the South, Puerto Ricans comparable earnings are the opposite among the selected states.

POVERTY RATES

Puerto Ricans as a population group have stood out for decades for exhibiting high rates of poverty. This pattern persists in 2014. The overall family poverty rate in the United States was 11.3 percent in 2014. Stateside Puerto Ricans (22.7%), non-Hispanic blacks (22.9%), and Latino groups (21.7%) showed twice the rate of poverty than the national average. For non-Hispanic white families, the poverty rate was 7.1 percent, the lowest across all groups in the United States. The poverty rates among Puerto Rican families in the U.S. were about half as high as in Puerto Rico (42.8%) in 2014. High poverty rates among Puerto Rican families were reported in Pennsylvania (34.3%), Massachusetts (34.2%), Connecticut (31.8%), Ohio (29%), and New York (25.8%). Puerto Rican households in North Carolina (22.2%) and Illinois (20.5%) reported similar poverty rates to that the average for all Puerto Ricans in the United States. Puerto Rican families with lower poverty rates than the average stateside Puerto Ricans were reported in Georgia (12.2%), California and Virginia (12.5%), Texas (15.2%), New Jersey (17.3%), and Florida (18%).

In 2014 the poverty rate for female-headed households overall (without a husband present in the household) was 30.5 percent in the United States as a whole. Stateside Puerto Ricans female-headed households had a poverty rate of 42.4 percent, followed by 40 percent for all Hispanic female-headed households and 36.8 percent of non-Hispanic black households. In contrast, non-Hispanic white female-headed householders had the lowest poverty rate (23.5%). As high as the rate of poverty is for stateside Puerto Rican female-headed households was, yet it was 17 percentage points lower than for those in Puerto Rico (59.6%). As troublesome, about half (49.7%) of stateside Puerto Rican female-headed householders with children under 18 years old lived in poverty and was substantially higher for those Puerto Rican households in Puerto Rico (69.7%). Ohio (57.6%), Connecticut (50.5%), Pennsylvania (50.4%), Massachusetts (46.8%), and New York (43.6%) reported higher poverty rates for Puerto Rican female-headed householders than the average stateside Puerto Ricans (42.4%). On the other hand, Puerto Rican female-headed householders in California (27.7%), Virginia (29.4%), New Jersey (34%), Texas (34.5%), Florida (35.8%), and Illinois (39.9%) showed lower rates of poverty than the Puerto Rican national average yet substantially higher than similar rates for other groups.

The average poverty rate among stateside Puerto Rican children was 33.4 percent; this was at least 11.7 percentage points higher than the national average among children under 18 years of age. Child poverty rates among Puerto Rican children in Puerto Rico were even more staggering with an average of 58.7 percent. Nationally, non-Hispanic black children (38.5%) had the highest poverty rates followed by Puerto Ricans (33.4%), Latinos (32.1%), and non-Hispanic white children (13%). Child poverty rates among Puerto Rican children ranged widely between the selected states in 2014. Poverty rates for Puerto Rican children ranged from 46 percent in Massachusetts to 19 percent in Virginia; thus, a Puerto Rican child in the former state was more than twice as likely to be poor than in the latter. Again, child poverty rates were evident across the selected states, regardless of region. For example, child poverty among Puerto Rican children in New Jersey (26.8%), Illinois (31.5%), North Carolina (31%), and Florida (30.8%) showed comparable rates to the Puerto Rican national average.

HOUSING

The homeownership rate for Hispanics has been consistently low. This is even more so for Puerto Ricans in the United States. At least 63.1 percent of the nation's total population owned the home they lived in and the remaining 36.9 percent were renters in 2014. Only the non-Hispanic white population (71%) and Puerto Ricans in Puerto Rico (68.7%) had higher homeownership rate than the average for the United States (63.1%). Hispanics overall (45%) showed the second highest percentage of homeownership followed by non-Hispanic blacks (41.4%), while stateside Puerto Ricans (36%) showed the lowest rate of homeownership. Puerto Ricans in Georgia (48.6%), Florida and Texas (47.1%), and Virginia (46.6%) showed higher rates of homeownership among Puerto Rican households when compared to the Puerto Rican national level, though these homeownership rates were still below the U.S. national average. On the other hand, less than a quarter (23.6%) of Puerto Ricans in New York were homeowners, where the cost of housing is among the highest in the nation. This was the lowest homeownership rate relative to Puerto Ricans in other states. Pennsylvania Puerto Ricans had similar rates to the national average of Puerto Ricans homeownership rates.

Compared to other groups in the U.S., the median value of owner-occupied housing for stateside Puerto Ricans was $175,900, lower than for the U.S. total population ($181,200), a difference of $5,300. The median value of owner-occupied housing for Puerto Ricans in the selected states ranged from $103,100 in Ohio to $377,100 in California. This discrepancy in home values may be affected largely by lower costs in states such as the South and Midwest, and medium to high home values in the Northeast and West Coast states.

Puerto Rican household's median monthly owner cost associated with a mortgage was $1,545 in the United States and $873 in Puerto Rico. The median monthly owner cost compared to other groups ranged from $1,117 in Ohio to $2,165 in New York. Puerto Ricans in Pennsylvania (43.7%), followed by those in Connecticut (43.5%), New Jersey (42.2%), Florida (41.7%) who owned a home paid more than 30 percent of their income in monthly owner costs.

HEALTH INSURANCE CONVERAGE

Puerto Ricans in the U.S. had the second highest rates of health insurance coverage in the U.S. (88.5%), after non-Hispanic whites (94.5%). Latinos overall had the lowest health insurance coverage (76.5%). More than half (51.6%) of Puerto Ricans in the United States were covered by private health insurance, 43.5 percent with public coverage, and the remaining 11.5 percent reported being without any health insurance coverage.[1] Puerto Ricans in Puerto Rico showed contrasting proportions, whereby 62.9 percent reported coverage with public health insurance followed by 38 percent with private health insurance and the remaining 5.5 percent without health insurance coverage. Florida (17.9%), Texas (15.3%), North Carolina (13.9%), Georgia (13.2%), and Pennsylvania (12.3%) showed higher rates of Puerto Ricans without any health insurance coverage compared to the national level. As such, these states (except for Pennsylvania) are considered as "non-expansion" states under the Affordable Care Act (ACA). On the other hand, Massachusetts (68.1%), Connecticut (57.4%), Ohio (49.2%), and New York (48.8%) were among the leading states for Puerto Ricans with the highest public health insurance coverage than the national average of 43.5 percent. Lastly, Virginia (72.6%), Georgia (65.7%), Texas (64.1%), California (63.8%), North Carolina (60.5%), and New Jersey (57.5%) were among the leading states of Puerto Ricans covered with a private health insurance.

CONCLUSION

Puerto Ricans in selected states and Puerto Rico are distinct socially, economically, and demographically. Large socioeconomic disparities characterize Puerto Ricans in those selected states.

Demographically, median age was used to analyze Puerto Rican's age structure across states of the Sunbelt region and Northeast and Midwest regions. In all, Puerto Ricans are generally younger compared to the overall U.S. population. Generally, Puerto Ricans in selected states showed a larger median age gap relative to the overall population (Pennsylvania, Connecticut, Ohio, North Carolina, Massachusetts, and Virginia). On the other hand, Puerto Ricans in New Jersey, Illinois, Florida, Georgia, California, New York, and Texas showed a narrow median age gap relative to each state's overall population.

Educationally, Puerto Ricans tended to have lower rates of educational attainment than the population as a whole. But Puerto Ricans in the Sunbelt states showed relatively higher educational attainment (with a bachelor's degree or higher) than Puerto Ricans in states of traditional settlement (Northeast and Midwest) and comparable rates relative to that state's overall population. Puerto Ricans in the Northeast and Midwest showed higher educational attainment disparity not only relative to Puerto Ricans in the Sunbelt states, but to a higher degree compared to that state's overall population. Thus, achieving high educational attainment represents an obstacle for Puerto Ricans in states of Northeast and Midwest regions. Puerto Ricans in Sunbelt states showed a narrower gap in higher educational attainment relative to each state's overall population. Furthermore, Georgia was the only state among those analyzed in this almanac in which Puerto Ricans showed higher rates of those who obtained a bachelor's degree or more than the comparable rate for that state's population as a whole. In all, Puerto Ricans in the U.S. South and California have greater educational attainment than Puerto Ricans in states of traditional settlement.

Economically, median household income and poverty rates (among all households, female-headed households, and children) were analyzed. The effects of low median household income and high poverty rates continue to plague Puerto Rican households and children in the Northeast and Midwest. Puerto Ricans in the U.S. South region and California showed comparable or higher median household income to each state's overall population. Overall, Puerto Ricans in the Sunbelt states had higher median household incomes than Puerto Ricans in the Northeast and Midwest states. This data shows that geographic dispersion is related to better economic indicators for stateside Puerto Ricans.

Poverty—especially poverty among female-headed households—continues to be a recurrent problem among stateside Puerto Ricans. As with low median household incomes as an indicator of socioeconomic progress among Puerto Ricans, households in states in the Northeast and Midwest regions also had higher poverty rates relative to Puerto Rican households in the South and California, and to each state's overall population. Puerto Rican households in the Sunbelt states had lower poverty rates than Puerto Ricans in the Northeast and Midwest states. Moreover, Puerto Rican households in states of traditional settlement, like in the Northeast and Midwest, continued to face poverty disparities, higher than each state's overall population.

Puerto Rican female-headed householders with children under 18 years of age showed higher poverty rates in the Northeast and Midwest selected states relative to Puerto Rican female-headed householders with children under 18 years of age in the U.S. South and California (with the exception of North Carolina). Poverty rate disparities were even higher between Puerto Rican female-headed householders (with children under 18 years of age) relative to each state's overall female-headed households (with children under 18 years of age) in the Northeast and Midwest states, as well as in Georgia and Florida. However, Puerto Rican female-headed householders (with children under 18 years old) in the Sunbelt states showed lower poverty rates relative to that state's overall population (except in Georgia and Florida). Poverty rates among stateside Puerto Rican children, under 18 years of age were higher, by at least 11.7 percentage points, than the national average (21.7%).

Occupational location in the labor force Puerto Ricans in the United States differed across the selected states. Puerto Ricans in the Sunbelt states showed comparable rates of occupational attainment within the "management, business, science, and arts occupations" with each state's overall population (except for Florida and North Carolina). On the other hand, Puerto Ricans in states of traditional settlement showed the opposite, whereby rates within the "management, business, science, and art occupations" were lower compared to the general population. In contrast, Puerto Ricans in states of traditional settlement, females had higher rates of employment in the "management, business, science, and arts" occupational sector than Puerto Rican males; however, their rates were not comparable to each state's overall population.

In 2014, stateside Puerto Rican homeownership rates was less than half that of the nation's overall population. Puerto Ricans in states of traditional settlement had even lower rates of homeownership relative to that state's overall population. On the other hand, Puerto Ricans in the Sunbelt states showed comparable homeownership rates relative to each state's overall population.

Data presented in this almanac contribute to identify and understand present-day socioeconomic conditions and settlement patterns of Puerto Ricans in the United States. More importantly, this almanac sheds light on Puerto Rican socioeconomic conditions beyond states of traditional settlement but in the areas of recent population growth like: Florida, Texas, Virginia, North Carolina, California, and Georgia. In fact, Puerto Ricans communities are increasingly growing to other parts of the nation and well beyond the Northeast and Midwest with diverse human and financial capital.

These data show relatively improved economic conditions for Puerto Ricans in many of the Sunbelt states. What is not clear from these data is whether the more robust socioeconomic characteristics Puerto Ricans in these states exhibit are the result of those Sunbelt states providing better economic opportunities for Puerto Ricans of any background or because Puerto Ricans in those states may be different ("select") relative to Puerto Ricans elsewhere. In other words, do Puerto Ricans who move to those Sunbelt states improve their socioeconomic situation because those states provide better opportunities for improvement? Or are Puerto Ricans settling in those states already better off than Puerto Ricans elsewhere even before settling in those states, showing off such differences in states' profiles? Alternatively, are Puerto Ricans with increased human capital able to exploit it with greater returns in those states than they might in states of traditional settlement? However, these are questions and avenues for further research.

In all, this almanac provides a more detailed profile of the economic, social, and geographic conditions of Puerto Ricans in the top 13 states, in the nation, and in Puerto Rico.

[1] Percentages do not add up to 100 because individuals may have more than one insurance coverage.

Puerto Ricans in the United States, 2014

Between the years 2000 and 2014 the Puerto Rican population in the United States grew from about 3.4 million to almost 5.3 million. According to U.S. Census Bureau estimates, Puerto Ricans accounted for 1.6% of the U.S. population in 2014, up from 1.2% in 2000. Despite Puerto Ricans' proportional growth among the total U.S. population, their proportional representation among all Hispanics or Latinos remained fairly stable, dropping marginally from 9.6% in 2000 to 9.5% in 2014. Approximately 1.8 million more Puerto Ricans resided in the U.S than in Puerto Rico.

Graph 1.A: Latino Population the United States, 2014

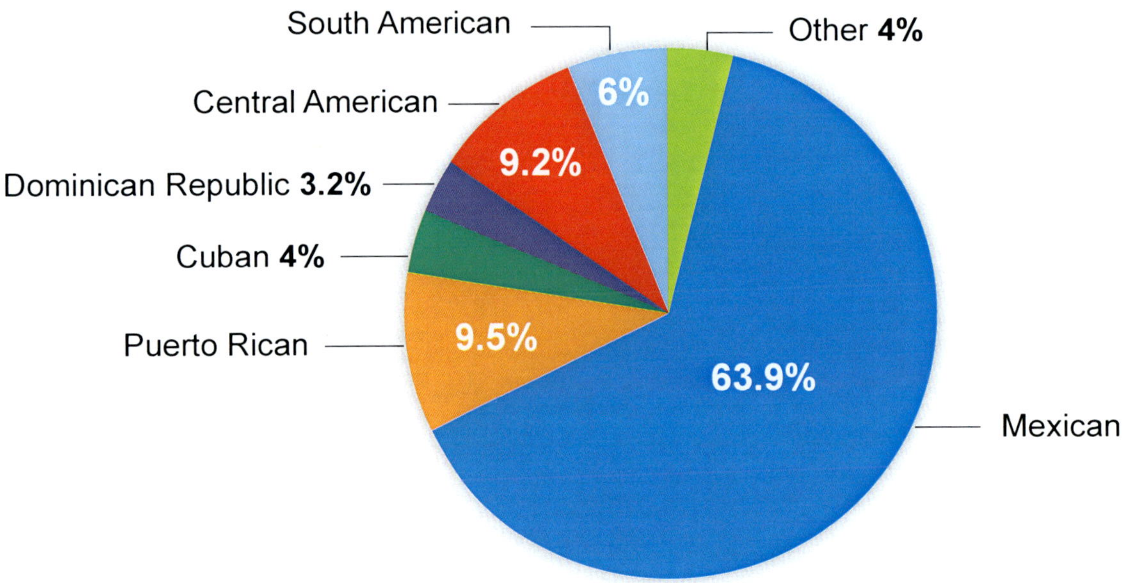

Table 1. Puerto Rican and Latino Population in the United States

	2000		2010		2014	
Total	281,421,906	100%	308,745,538	100%	318,857,056	100%
Not Hispanic or Latino	246,116,088	87.5%	258,267,944	83.7%	263,577,604	82.7%
Hispanic or Latino	35,305,818	12.5%	50,477,594	16.3%	55,279,452	17.3%
Mexican	20,640,711	7.3%	31,798,258	10.3%	35,320,579	11.1%
Puerto Rican	3,406,178	1.2%	4,623,716	1.5%	5,266,738	1.7%
Cuban	1,241,685	0.4%	1,785,547	0.6%	2,046,805	0.6%
Dominican Republic	764,945	0.3%	1,414,703	0.5%	1,760,354	0.6%
Central American	1,686,937	0.6%	3,998,280	1.3%	5,097,021	1.6%
South American	1,353,562	0.5%	2,769,434	0.9%	3,320,848	1.0%
Other	6,211,800	2.2%	4,087,656	1.3%	2,467,107	0.8%

Sources: U.S. Census Bureau, Census 2000 Summary File 1, 2010 Census. Summary File 1, and 2014 American Community Survey 1-Year Estimates.

Puerto Ricans accounted for 1.6% of the total U.S. population in 2014, up from 1.2% in 2000 and 1.5% in 2010. Puerto Ricans in the U.S. represented just fewer than 10% of the total Hispanic or Latino population in the U.S. Although Mexicans accounted for close to two-thirds (63.9%) of the Hispanic or Latino population, Puerto Ricans were the next largest national origin group accounting for 9.5% of the Hispanic or Latino population in 2014.

Puerto Ricans in the U.S. had a median age of 28.9 years, over a decade lower the 38.9 median age of those in Puerto Rico. However, Puerto Ricans in the U.S. and in Puerto Rico had a

Graph 2.A: Puerto Rican Education Attainment, 25 years and over, 2014

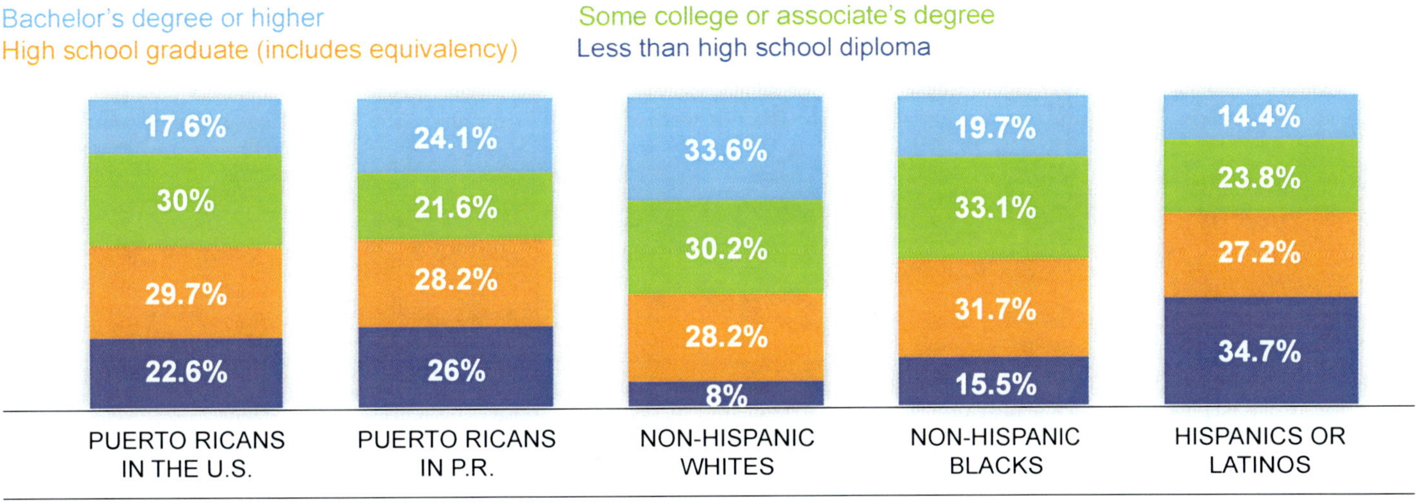

Table 2. Age, Education, and Language, 2014

	Puerto Ricans in the U.S.	Puerto Ricans in P.R.	Non-hispanic Whites	Non-Hispanic Blacks	Hispanics or Latinos
TOTAL POPULATION	5,266,738	3,404,122	197,409,353	39,267,149	55,279,452
Median age (years)	28.9	38.9	43.1	33.7	28.4
62 years and over	9.9%	21%	22.4%	13.1%	8.2%
EDUCATIONAL ATTAINMENT Population 25 years and over					
Less than high school diploma	22.6%	26%	8%	15.5%	34.7%
High school graduate (includes equivalency)	29.7%	28.2%	28.2%	31.7%	27.2%
Some college or associate's degree	30%	21.6%	30.2%	33.1%	23.8%
Bachelor's degree or higher	17.6%	24.1%	33.6%	19.7%	14.4%
Male, BA degree or higher	15.6%	19.6%	34%	17.2%	13.1%
Female, BA degree or higher	19.5%	28.1%	33.3%	21.8%	15.6%
LANGUAGE SPOKEN AT HOME AND ABILITY TO SPEAK ENGLISH Population 5 years and over					
English only	38.8%	5.3%	94.6%	92.5%	26.5%
Language other than English	61.2%	94.7%	5.4%	7.5%	73.5%
Speak English less than "very well"	17.3%	78.8%	1.6%	2.4%	31.8%

Source: U.S. Census Bureau, 2014 American Community Survey 1-Year Estimates.
* Puerto Ricans only.

median age lower than non-Hispanic whites in the U.S. (43.1 years). Compared to the median age of non-Hispanic blacks (33.7 years), Puerto Ricans in the U.S. had a lower median age by almost five years. Among other Hispanics or Latinos in the U.S., Puerto Ricans actually had a higher median age by about six months (28.4 years for Hispanics or Latinos).

Almost one in ten (9.9%) Puerto Ricans in the U.S. were age 62 and older. On the other hand, 21% of Puerto Ricans in Puerto Rico and 22.4% of non-Hispanic whites in the U.S were 62 and older which were about twice as high as Puerto Ricans in the U.S. Compared to Puerto Ricans in the U.S., Non-Hispanic blacks also had a higher proportion of individuals age 62 and older (13.1%). Hispanics or Latinos in the U.S. had a lower proportion aged 62 and older (8.2%) compared to Puerto Ricans in the U.S.

English fluency indicators for stateside Puerto Ricans compared to those of all Hispanics or Latinos in the U.S. demonstrated higher levels of fluency among stateside

Table 3. Employment and Occupations, 2014

	Puerto Ricans in the U.S.	Puerto Ricans in P.R.	Non-Hispanic Whites	Non-Hispanic Blacks	Hispanics and Latinos
EMPLOYMENT STATUS					
Population 16 years and over					
In labor force	62.4%	43.7%	62.5%	62%	67.1%
Civilian labor force	61.6%	43.7%	62.2%	61.6%	66.8%
Employed	54.4%	35.4%	58.6%	53.4%	61.1%
Unemployed	11.6%	18.9%	5.8%	13.3%	8.4%
Not in labor force	37.6%	56.3%	37.6%	56.3%	37.5%
Armed Forces	0.8%	0%	0.4%	0.4%	0.4%
OCCUPATION					
Civilian employed population 16 years and over					
Male	1,058,918	516,762	50,657,284	7,414,019	13,622,730
Management, business, science, and arts	23.4%	23.9%	37.9%	23.1%	16.7%
Service occupations	22.5%	23%	12.3%	22.5%	21.7%
Sales and office occupations	19.6%	21.3%	17.6%	18.7%	14.6%
Construction and maintenance	13.8%	18%	15.5%	10.4%	25.5%
Production, transportation, and moving	20.7%	13.7%	16.7%	25.4%	21.6%
Female	999,105	456,356	45,323,203	8,823,764	10,343,448
Management, business, science, and arts	33.1%	39.7%	45.3%	33.4%	25.2%
Service occupations	24.4%	16.6%	18%	27.7%	31.9%
Sales and office occupations	35.7%	38.3%	31.5%	31%	31.3%
Construction and maintenance	0.6%	0.6%	0.7%	0.6%	2.1%
Production, transportation, and moving	6.2%	4.8%	4.5%	7.2%	9.5%
CLASS OF WORKER					
Civilian employed population 16 years and over					
Private wage and salary workers	82%	69%	79.1%	78.2%	83.8%
Government workers	14.8%	22.5%	14.2%	18.3%	9.8%
Self-employed workers in own not incorporated business	3.1%	8.3%	6.5%	3.4%	6.2%
VETERAN STATUS					
Civilian population 18 years and over					
Civilian veteran	6%	3.3%	9.6%	7.4%	3.1%

Source: U.S. Census Bureau, 2014 American Community Survey 1-Year Estimates.
* Puerto Ricans only.

Puerto Rican Population by States in the U.S., 2014

The majority of Puerto Ricans in the U.S. resided in New York (20.8%) and Florida (18.9%). Florida joined New York in 2014 as the only other state with over a million Puerto Ricans. Although Puerto Ricans were most concentrated in the Northeast (New Jersey, Pennsylvania, Massachusetts and Connecticut in particular), they were also present out west in California (207,256) and Midwestern states like Illinois (208,043) and Ohio (106,135). In the south Texas (181,599), Virginia (98,254), Georgia (87,927), and North Carolina (89,160) had significant Puerto Rican populations. Overall, Puerto Ricans were concentrated in the northeast and Florida, but as visible in the attached maps, were dispersed throughout much of the U.S.

STATE	Puerto Rican Population	Percent	Latino Population	Percent	Total Population	Percent
New York	1,107,487	20.8%	3,668,399	6.6%	19,746,227	6.2%
Florida	1,005,424	18.9%	4,789,830	8.7%	19,893,297	6.2%
New Jersey	488,949	9.2%	1,649,784	3.1%	8,938,175	2.8%
Pennsylvania	439,818	8.3%	784,562	1.5%	12,787,209	4%
Massachusetts	306,062	5.8%	681,824	1.3%	6,745,408	2.1%
Connecticut	293,997	5.5%	512,795	1%	3,596,677	1.1%
Illinois	208,043	3.9%	14,534,449	3.9%	12.880,580	4%
California	207,256	3.9%	2,095,495	27.1%	38,802,500	12.2%
Texac	181,599	0.6%	9,962,643	18.8%	26,956,958	8.5%
Ohio	106,135	2%	379,542	0.7%	11,593,163	3.6%
Virginia	98,254	1.8%	687,265	1.3%	8,326,289	2.6%
North Carolina	89,160	1.7%	896,717	1.6%	9,943,964	3.1%
Georgia	87,927	1.7%	848,697	1.7%	10,097,343	3.2%
Wisconsin	62,672	1.2%	355,292	0.7%	5,757,564	1.8%
Maryland	52,507	1%	133,485	1%	5,976,407	1.9%
Michigan	46,468	0.9%	515,724	0.9%	9,909,877	3.1%
Hawaii	43,221	0.8%	457,109	0.3%	1,419,561	0.4%
Arizona	40,013	0.8%	1,977,026	3.7%	6,731,484	2.1%
Rhode Island	39,266	0.7%	139,832	0.3%	1,055,173	0.3%
Washington	35,701	0.7%	411,536	1.6%	7,061,530	2.2%
Other States	379,003	7.1%	7,863,188	14.2%	90,636,670	28.4%
Total	**5,319,961**	**100%**	**52,963,800**	**100%**	**318,857,056**	**100%**

Sources: U.S. Census Bureau 2014 American Community Survey 5-Year Estimates
Notes: Total counts for populations may differ depending on whether the estimates are derived from the five-year estimates or the one-year estimates of the American Community Survey.

PUERTO RICAN POPULATION BY STATE, 2014

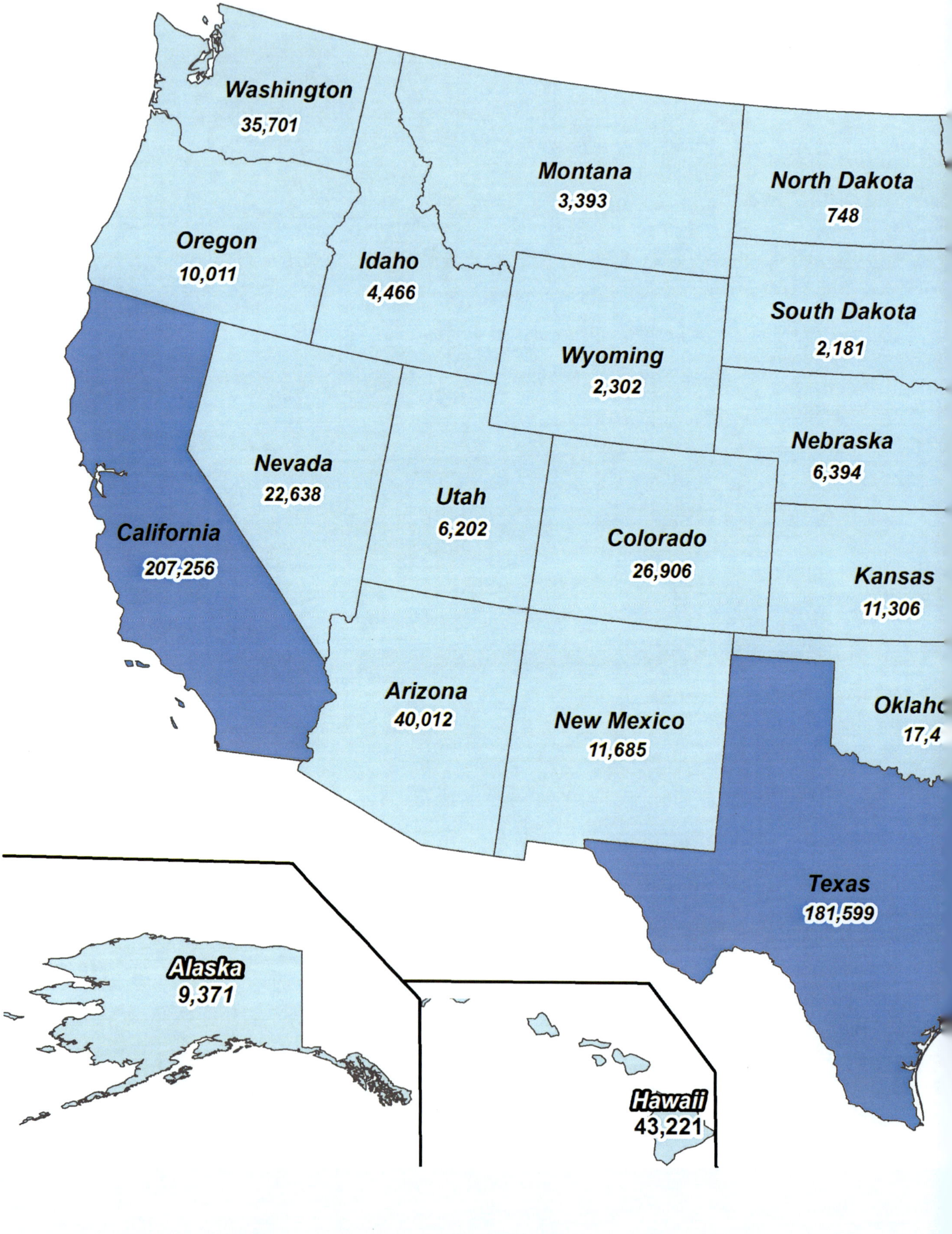

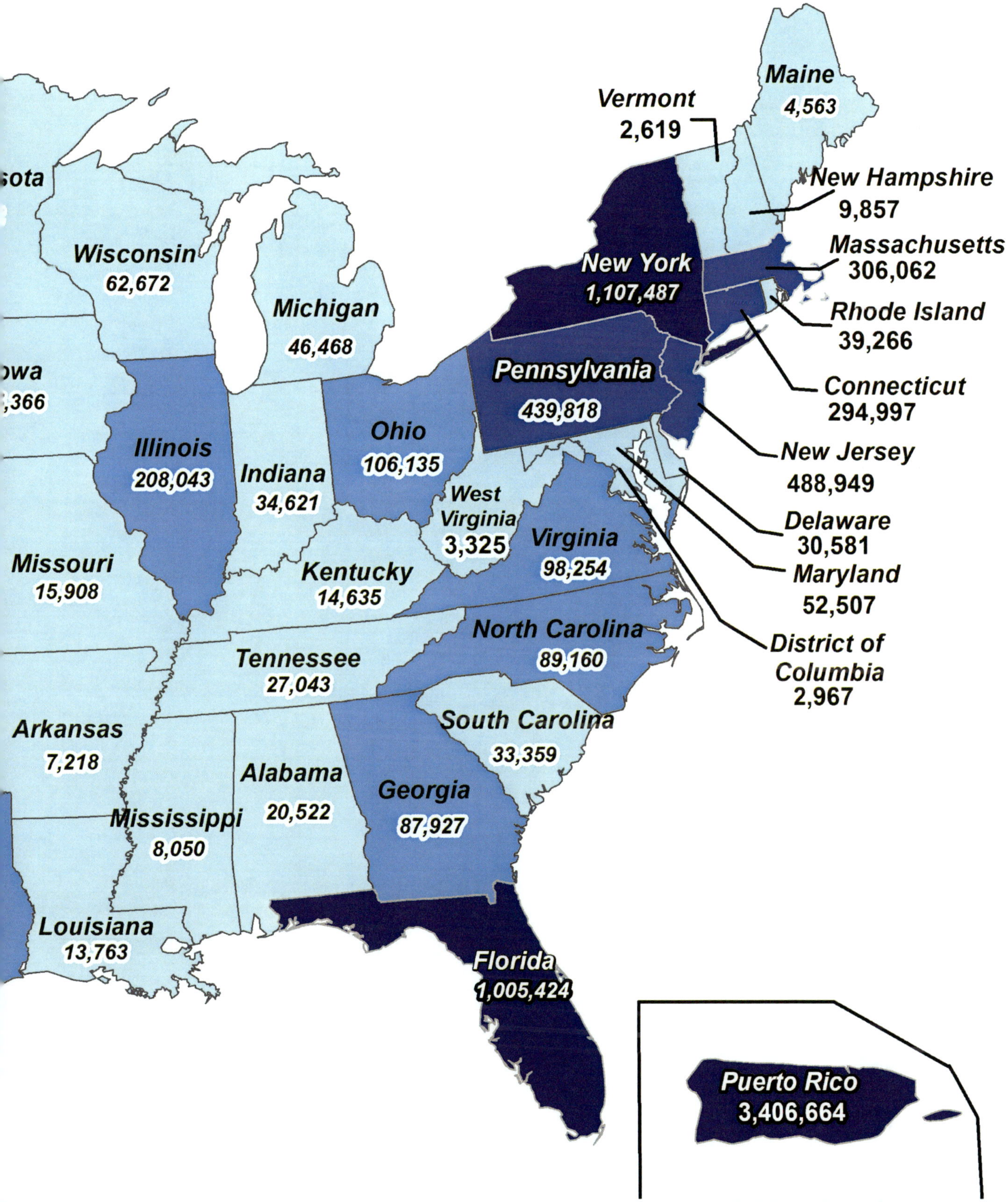

sota
Wisconsin
62,672
Michigan
46,468
owa
,366
Illinois
208,043
Indiana
34,621
Ohio
106,135
Pennsylvania
439,818
New York
1,107,487
Vermont
2,619
Maine
4,563
New Hampshire
9,857
Massachusetts
306,062
Rhode Island
39,266
Connecticut
294,997
New Jersey
488,949
Delaware
30,581
Maryland
52,507
District of Columbia
2,967
West Virginia
3,325
Virginia
98,254
Missouri
15,908
Kentucky
14,635
North Carolina
89,160
Tennessee
27,043
South Carolina
33,359
Arkansas
7,218
Alabama
20,522
Georgia
87,927
Mississippi
8,050
Louisiana
13,763
Florida
1,005,424
Puerto Rico
3,406,664

PUERTO RICAN POPULATION AS PERCENTAGE OF HISPANIC AND LATINO POPULATION BY STATE, 2014

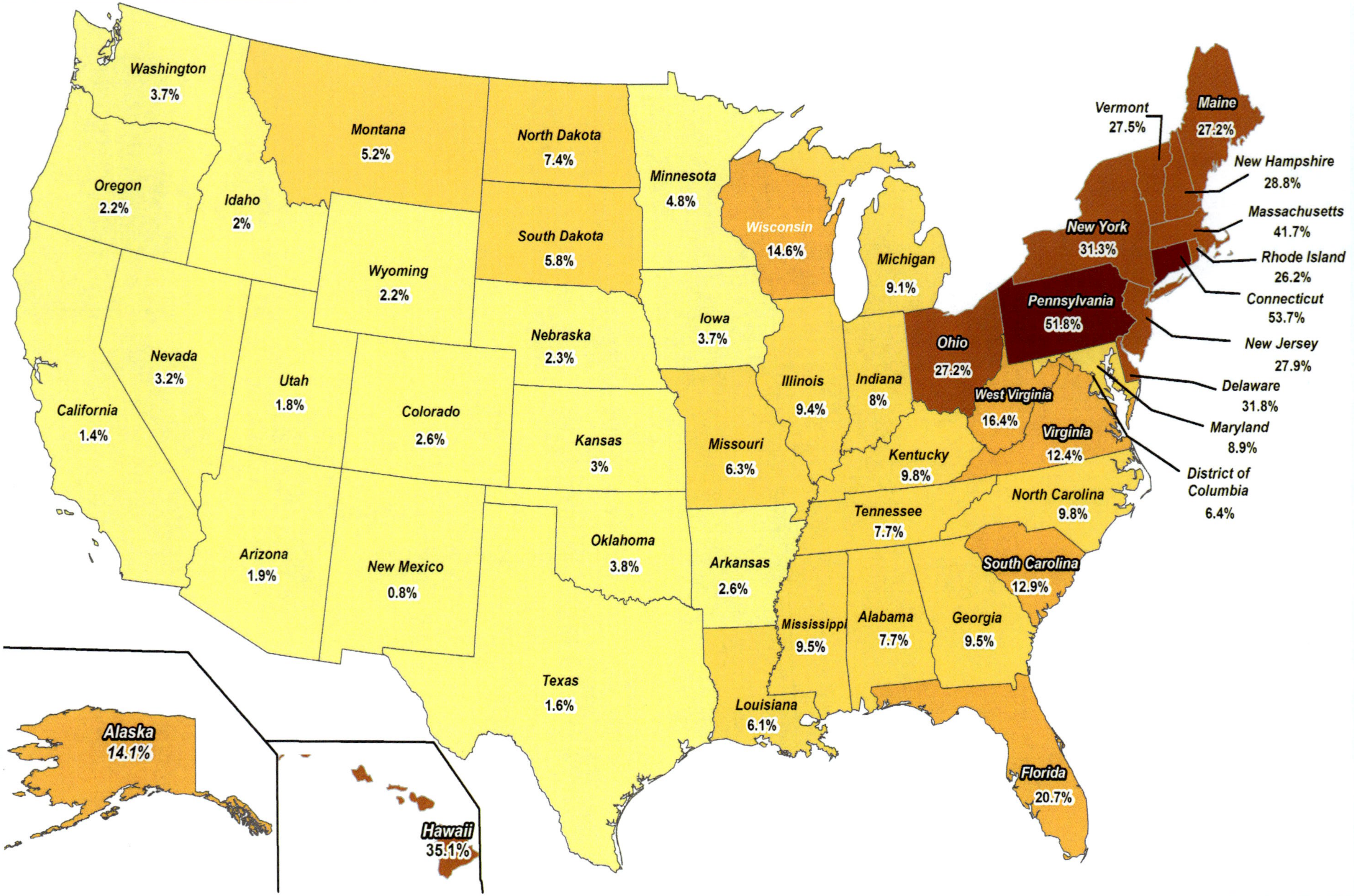

Puerto Ricans. Only 17.3% of Puerto Ricans in the U.S. reported speaking English less than "very well", compared to 31.8% of all Hispanic or Latino individuals in the U.S. A higher proportion of Puerto Ricans in the U.S. (38.8%) reported speaking only English in the home than Hispanics or Latinos overall (26.5%).

Higher educational attainment among Puerto Ricans in the U.S. fell behind that of non-Hispanic whites, non-Hispanic blacks, and Puerto Ricans in Puerto Rico. Only 17.6% of Puerto Ricans in the U.S. held a bachelor's degree or higher — lower than non-Hispanic whites (33.6%), non-Hispanic blacks (19.7%), and Puerto Ricans in Puerto Rico (24.1%). However, the proportion of Puerto Ricans in the U.S. with a bachelor's degree or higher was more than the 14.4% proportion among all Hispanics or Latinos in the U.S. Educational attainment counting individuals with some college experience or an associate's degree was 30% among Puerto Ricans in the U.S., similar to non-Hispanic whites (30.2%) and slightly below non-Hispanic blacks (33.1%), but 6.2 percentage points over the rate among Hispanics or Latinos in the U.S (23.8%).

Table 4. Income and Earnings, 2014

	Puerto Ricans in the U.S.	Pueto Ricans in Puerto Rico	Non-Hispanic Whites	Non-Hispanic Blacks	Hispanics and Latinos
INCOME IN THE PAST 12 MONTHS (IN 2013 INFLATION-ADJUSTED DOLLARS)					
Households	1,635,808	1,175,297	80,656,787	14,032,393	14,693,205
Median household income (dollars)	$39,322	$18,710	$59,622	$35,434	$42,748
With earnings	76.9%	54.7%	75.6%	75.6%	87.1%
Mean earnings (dollars)	$61,065	$36,407	$84,153	$52,772	$58,731
With Social Security income	24.1%	43.2%	34.2%	26.6%	17.6%
Mean Social Security income (dollars)	$13,727	$12,159	$18,889	$14,250	$14,069
With Supplemental Security Income	12.6%	0.4%	4.4%	10%	6.2%
Mean Supplemental Security Income (dollars)	$8,780	$10,025	$9,895	$8,828	$8,537
With cash public assistance income	6.9%	8.1%	2%	4.9%	3.9%
Mean cash public assistance income (dollars)	$3,441	$2,316	$3,016	$3,017	$3,557
With retirement income	10.1%	15.6%	21.1%	15.8%	7.9%
Mean retirement income (dollars)	$20,452	$15,387	$24,872	$21,614	$19,905
With Food Stamp/SNAP benefits	31.5%	39.7%	9%	28.2%	22.4%
Families	111,4628	83,0807	51,723,163	8,618,827	11,251,003
Median family income (dollars)	$44,499	$22,220	$74,706	$42,915	$44,873
Married-couple family	53.9%	56.1%	79.7%	43.8%	61.8%
Median income (dollars)	$67,129	$29,417	$84,594	$68,045	$56,042
Male householder, no spouse present	10.2%	9.5%	6.1%	10%	11.8%
Median income (dollars)	$37,513	$17,797	$50,453	$36,910	$39,412
Female householder, no husband present	35.9%	34.4%	14.2%	46.2%	26.4%
Median income (dollars)	$23,957	$13,554	$37,683	$27,237	$25,974
Individuals	5,266,738	3,404,122	197,409,353	39,267,149	55,279,452
Per capita income (dollars)	$18,457	$10,960	$34,393	$19,393	$16,716
Mean earnings (dollars) for full-time, year-round workers:					
Male	$50,756	$32,512	$74,773	$47,755	$43,214
Female	$42,263	$29,166	$52,638	$41,520	$36,293

Source: U.S. Census Bureau, 2014 American Community Survey 1-Year Estimates.
* Puerto Ricans only.

Generally, educational attainment indicators placed Puerto Ricans in the U.S. above overall Hispanics or Latinos educational attainment indicators in the U.S., but below those of non-Hispanic whites and non-Hispanic blacks. Comparisons between Puerto Ricans in the U.S. and those in Puerto Rico reveal a greater rate of higher educational attainment for Puerto Ricans in Puerto Rico (24.1%) along with a greater proportion of the population without a high school diploma (26%).

The labor force participation rate for Puerto Ricans in the U.S. (62.4%) did not differ much from non-Hispanic whites (62.5%) and non-Hispanic blacks (62%), and was 4.7 percentage points lower the labor participation rate among all Hispanics or Latinos (67.1%). However, the labor force participation rate for Puerto Ricans in the U.S. was 18.7 percentage points above the labor force participation rate of those in Puerto Rico (43.7%).

The employment rate among Puerto Ricans in the U.S. was almost 20 percentage points higher (54.4%) than among those in Puerto Rico (35.4%). Among other populations in the U.S., non-Hispanic whites (5.8%) and Hispanics or Latinos overall (8.4%) had lower unemployment indicators than Puerto Ricans in the U.S. (11.6%). However, Puerto Ricans in the U.S. had a lower unem-

Graph 4.A: Mean Earnings for Full-Time Year-Round Puerto Rican Workers, 2014

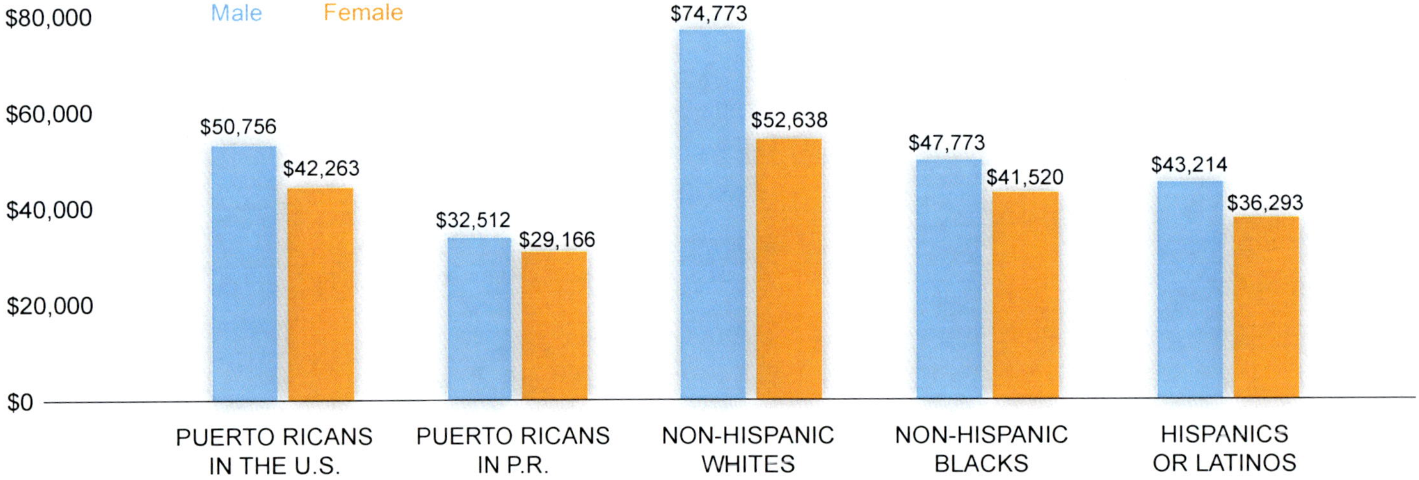

Graph 4.B: Puerto Rican Purchasing Power, in Billions, 2014

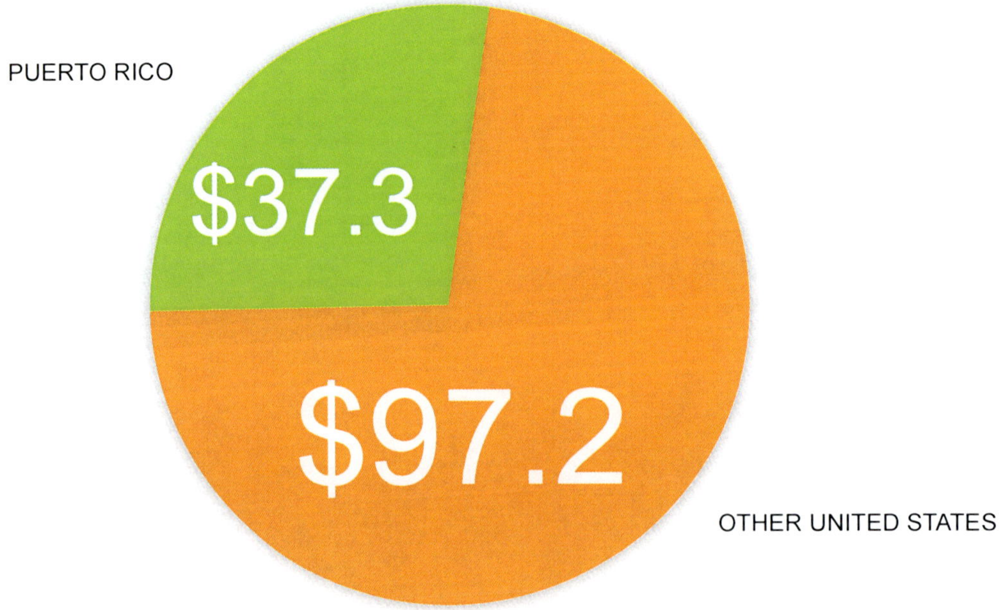

Graph 5.A: Poverty Rates, 2014

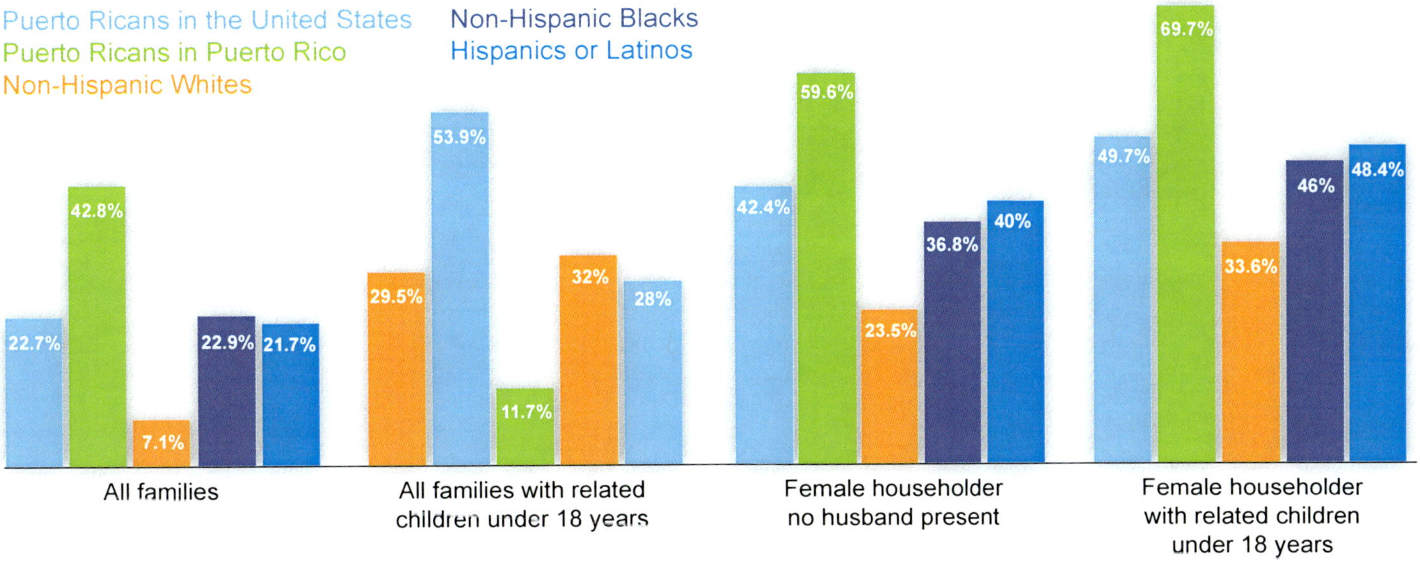

Table 5. Poverty, 2014

	Puerto Ricans in the U.S.	Puerto Ricans in P.R.	Non-Hispanic Whites	Non-Hispanic Blacks	Hispanics and Latinos
POVERTY RATES					
All families	22.7%	42.8%	7.1%	22.9%	21.7%
With related children under 18 years	29.5%	53.9%	11.7%	32%	28%
With related children under 5 years only	24.6%	57.1%	12.8%	33.8%	24.7%
Married-couple family	9.7%	30.9%	3.7%	8%	14.3%
With related children under 18 years	11.3%	35.5%	5%	10.6%	18.2%
With related children under 5 years only	5.9%	33.9%	4.6%	10.4%	13%
Female householder, no husband present, family	42.4%	59.6%	23.5%	36.8%	40%
With related children under 18 years	49.7%	69.7%	33.6%	46%	48.4%
With related children under 5 years only	49.4%	75.7%	42.9%	47.8%	48.8%
All people	26.2%	46.6%	10.8%	26.9%	24.1%
Under 18 years	33.4%	58.7%	13%	38.5%	32.1%
Related children under 18 years	33.1%	58.6%	12.6%	38.2%	31.8%
Related children under 5 years	34.7%	62.8%	14.6%	43.1%	33.9%
Related children 5 to 17 years	32.4%	57.3%	11.9%	36.5%	31%
18 years and over	22.8%	43.2%	10.3%	22.8%	20.3%
18 to 64 years	22.8%	43.8%	11.2%	23.6%	20.4%
65 years and over	22.4%	41%	7.3%	17.8%	19.4%
People in families	23.6%	44.6%	7.5%	24.5%	22.5%
Unrelated individuals 15 years and over	38.5%	58%	23.3%	36.2%	35%

Source: U.S. Census Bureau, 2014 American Community Survey 1-Year Estimates.
* Puerto Ricans only.

ployment rate than non-Hispanic blacks (13.3%) and those in Puerto Rico (18.9%).

Proportionately, representation in the Armed Forces of Puerto Ricans in the U.S. (0.8%) was double that of non-Hispanic whites (0.4%), non-Hispanic blacks (0.4%), and Hispanics or Latinos overall (0.4%). Although the proportion of veterans among Puerto Ricans in the U.S. (6%) was lower than that of non-Hispanic whites (9.6%) and non-Hispanic blacks (7.4%), it was almost double that of Hispanics or Latinos in the U.S. overall (3.1%).

Median household earnings for Puerto Ricans in the U.S. were $39,322 — more than double the median household earnings for those in Puerto Rico ($18,710). However, Puerto Rican household earnings in the U.S. were below those of non-Hispanic white households ($59,622) and all Hispanic or Latino households overall ($42,748).

Puerto Ricans in the U.S. earned less on a per-capita basis ($18,457) than non-Hispanic whites ($34,393) and non-Hispanic blacks ($19,393). Compared to all Hispanics or Latinos in the U.S., Puerto Ricans in the U.S. earned $1,741 more ($16,716) on a per-capita basis.

The purchasing power of Puerto Ricans in the U.S. was $97. 2 billion, more than double that of Puerto Ricans in Puerto Rico ($37.3 billion). An estimated 1.8 million more Puerto Ricans were living in the U.S. than in Puerto Rico, and on a per-capita basis, Puerto Ricans in the U.S. earned $7,497 more than Puerto Ricans in Puerto Rico. Purchasing power is defined simply as per capita income multiplied by the population. This difference in earnings indicates that Puerto Ricans in the U.S. represented a substantial potential market for investment, tourism, and trade with Puerto Rico.

Poverty indicators revealed that proportionately less Puerto Rican families in the U.S. (22.7%) lived in poverty than in Puerto Rico (42.8%). However, a proportion of Puerto Rican families in the U.S three times as high as that of non-Hispanic whites (7.1%) lived in poverty. Puerto Rican families in the U.S. had similar poverty levels of non-Hispanic black families (22.9%) and all Hispanic and Latino families (21.7%).

Households with a female householder and children under 18 years of age proved particularly vulnerable to poverty. Among Puerto Rican families in the U.S., 49.7% — almost half — of this particular demographic segment lived in poverty — a rate slightly above that of non-Hispanic blacks (46%) and Hispanics or Latinos (48.4%). In Puerto Rico, 69.7% of households with a female householder and children under 18 lived in poverty. These are alarmingly high rates of poverty by any measure or comparative context.

In 2014, 6.9% of Puerto Rican households in the U.S. received cash public assistance income, which was a lower

Table 6. Housing and Health Insurance, 2014

	Puerto Ricans in the U.S.	Puerto Ricans in P.R.	Non-Hispanic Whites	Non-Hispanic Blacks	Hispanics and Latinos
HOUSING					
Owner-occupied housing units	36%	68.7%	71%	41.4%	45%
Monthly owner costs as a percentage of household income in the past 12 months					
Less than 30 percent	62.8%	52.6%	72%	59.4%	59.2%
30 percent or more	37.2%	47.4%	28%	40.6%	40.8%
Owner-occupied housing units					
Median value (dollars)	$175,900	$119,500	$185,300	$124,700	$159,600
Median selected monthly owner costs with a mortgage (dollars)	$1,545	$873	$1,444	$1,311	$1,429
HEALTH INSURANCE COVERAGE					
Civilian noninstitutionalized population					
With private health insurance	51.6%	38%	74.9%	52.7%	45.3%
With public coverage	43.5%	62.9%	31.4%	42.4%	35.5%
No health insurance coverage	11.5%	5.5%	8.1%	13.5%	23.5%

Source: U.S. Census Bureau, 2014 American Community Survey 1-Year Estimates.
* Puerto Ricans only.

proportion than those in Puerto Rico (8.1%). However, the proportion of non-Hispanic whites (2%), non-Hispanic blacks (4.9%), and Hispanics or Latinos overall (3.9%) that received public assistance income were all below that of Puerto Ricans in the U.S. Cash public assistance income averaged $3,441 for Puerto Ricans in the U.S. and $2,316 for Puerto Ricans in Puerto Rico.

Participation in the Supplementary Nutrition Assistance Program (SNAP) among Puerto Ricans in the U.S. was 31.5%, 8.2 percentage points lower that of Puerto Ricans in Puerto Rico (39.7%). However, compared to rates of non-Hispanic whites (9%), non-Hispanic blacks (28.2%), and Hispanics or Latinos (22.4%), the rates of Puerto Ricans in the U.S. using SNAP were significantly higher.

Housing is a primary determinant of the cost of living. In general, the United States has a higher cost of home ownership than Puerto Rico. The median value of owner-occupied housing for Puerto Ricans in the U.S. was $175,900 — $55,500 more than the median value of owner-occupied homes in Puerto Rico ($119,500). However, compared to the value of non-Hispanic white owner-occupied homes ($185,300) the difference in owner-occupied home values was much less drastic. Compared to the values of owner-occupied home values among non-Hispanic blacks ($124,700) and all Hispanics or Latinos ($159,600), stateside Puerto Rican owner-occupied homes had higher values. Little over one in three (36%) of Puerto Ricans in the U.S. owned the home they lived. In Puerto Rico, the percentage of Puerto Rican owner-occupied homes was more than double that in the U.S. at 68.7%.

Proportionately, more Puerto Ricans in the U.S. lacked health insurance coverage (11.5%) than in Puerto Rico (5.5%). A greater proportion of Puerto Ricans in the U.S. received public health insurance coverage (43.5%) than non-Hispanic whites (31.4%) and Hispanics or Latinos (35.5%). However, Puerto Ricans in the U.S. had a similar proportion of public health insurance coverage as non-Hispanic blacks (42.4%). Both Puerto Ricans in the U.S. and non-Hispanic blacks, despite having higher rates of public insurance coverage, had proportions of people without any health insurance coverage (11.5% and 13.5%, respectively), more than twice as higher as non-Hispanic whites (5.5%).

Puerto Ricans in New York, 2014

In 2014, New York continues to be the state with the most Puerto Ricans in the United States with an estimated population of 1.1 million Puerto Ricans. The Puerto Rican population continues to be 5.5% of the New York population in 2014 when compared to the years 2000 and 2010. Puerto Ricans represent 30% of the total Latino population in the state.

Graph 1.A: Latino Population New York, 2014

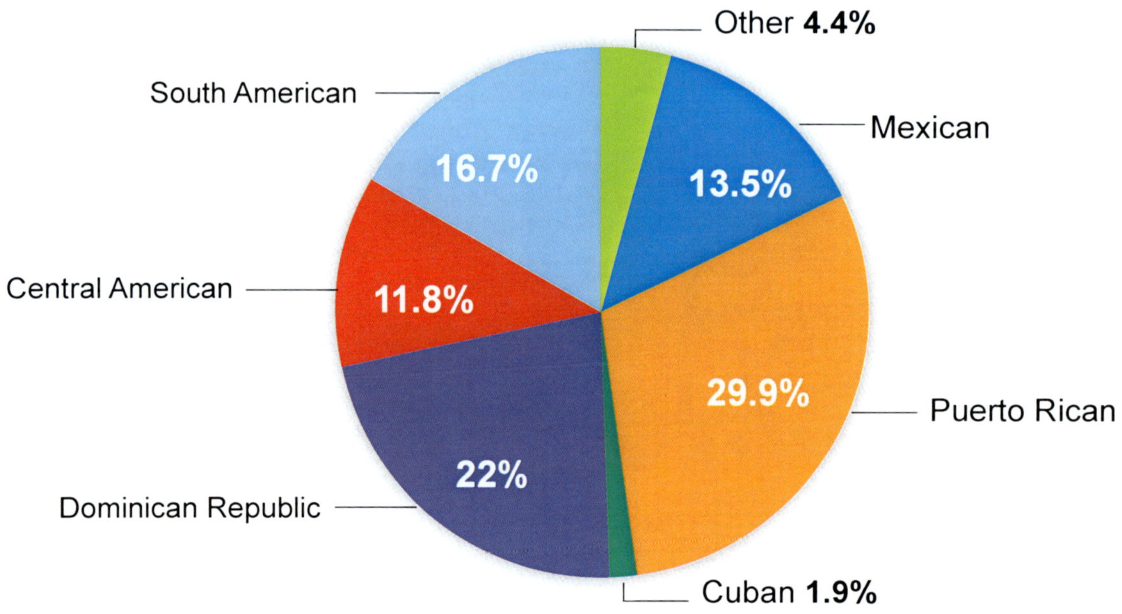

Table 1. Puerto Rican and Latino Population in New York

	2000		2010		2014	
Total	18,976,457	100%	19,378,102	100%	19,746,227	100%
Not Hispanic or Latino	16,108,874	84.9%	15,961,180	82.4%	16,075,938	81.4%
Hispanic or Latino	2,867,583	15.1%	3,416,922	17.6%	3,670,289	18.6%
Mexican	260,889	1.4%	457,288	2.4%	494,290	2.5%
Puerto Rican	1,050,293	5.5%	1,070,558	5.5%	1,095,858	5.5%
Cuban	62,590	0.3%	70,803	0.4%	69,566	0.4%
Dominican Republic	455,061	2.4%	674,787	3.5%	806,078	4.1%
Central American	181,875	1%	353,589	1.8%	431,369	2.2%
South American	318,387	1.7%	513,417	2.6%	612,031	3.1%
Other	538,488	2.8%	276,480	1.4%	161,097	0.8%

Sources: U.S. Census Bureau, Census 2000 Summary File 1, 2010 Census. Summary File 1, and 2014 American Community Survey 1-Year Estimates.

In general, Puerto Ricans in the United States showed substantial improvement in socioeconomic well-being relative to Puerto Ricans in Puerto Rico. The data supported a view of labor market integration where Puerto Ricans' occupational distribution was very similar stateside and Puerto Ricans in Puerto Rico.

New York has one of the most diverse Latino populations in the country. The Latino population in New York grew from 15.1% of the state's total population in 2000 to 18.6% in 2014. After Puerto Ricans (29.9% of total Latino population), Dominicans (22%), Mexicans (13.5%), Ecuadorian (7.6%), and Salvadorans (5.2%) constitute the next largest groups.

Graph 2.A: Puerto Rican Education Attainment, 25 years and over, 2014

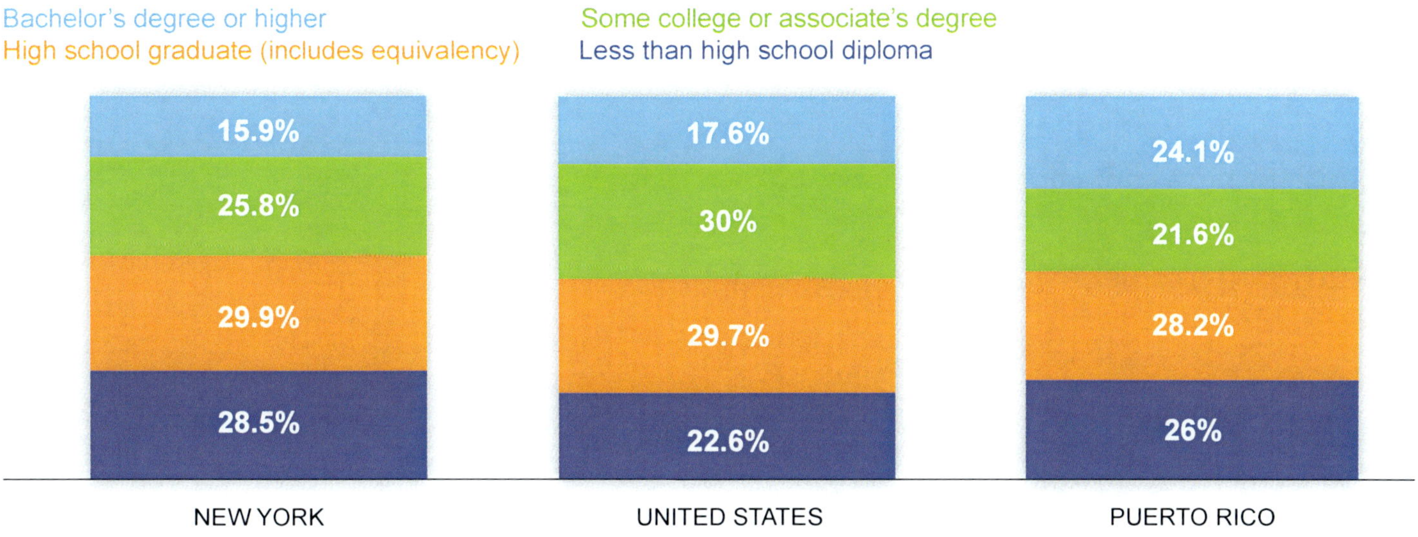

Table 2. Age, Education, and Language, 2014

Puerto Ricans	New York	United States	Puerto Rico*
TOTAL POPULATION	1,095,858	5,266,738	3,404,122
Median age (years)	31.9	28.9	38.9
62 years and over	13.6%	9.9%	21%
EDUCATIONAL ATTAINMENT			
Population 25 years and over			
Less than high school diploma	28.5%	22.6%	26%
High school graduate (includes equivalency)	29.9%	29.7%	28.2%
Some college or associate's degree	25.8%	30%	21.6%
Bachelor's degree or higher	15.9%	17.6%	24.1%
Male, bachelor's degree or higher	13.4%	15.6%	19.6%
Female, bachelor's degree or higher	18%	19.5%	28.1%
LANGUAGE SPOKEN AT HOME AND ABILITY TO SPEAK ENGLISH			
Population 5 years and over			
English only	37.1%	38.8%	5.3%
Language other than English	62.9%	61.2%	94.7%
Speak English less than "very well"	17%	17.3%	78.8%

Source: U.S. Census Bureau, 2014 American Community Survey 1-Year Estimates.
* Puerto Ricans only.

The median age of Puerto Ricans in New York for the year 2014 was 31.9 years, which is 3 years older than for stateside Puerto Ricans (28.9 years), but 7 years younger than the 38.9 years median age for Puerto Ricans in Puerto Rico. These differences in the age structure were evident in the percent of the population older than 62 years of age: 13.6% of Puerto Ricans in New York were 62 years of age or older, a higher percent than stateside Puerto Ricans (9.9%) in this age group.With 21% of the population 62 years of age or older Puerto Ricans in Puerto Rico had a significantly higher proportion of the population in this age group. Though New York received a large proportion of Puerto Ricans in the large migration flow in the 1950s decade, the age structure of the Puerto Ricans in New York was younger than the comparable age cohort in the island.

Puerto Ricans in New York had similar English-fluency indicators than Puerto Ricans in the U.S as a whole. In New York, 37.1% of the population speaks only English at home, while nationally 38.8% of Puerto Ricans do so. Similarly, 61.2% of Puerto Ricans nationally speak a language other than English at home, while 62.9% of Puerto Ricans in New York do so. Only about one in six stateside Puerto Ricans declared they speak English less than "very well".

Puerto Ricans residing in Puerto Rico had a significantly higher proportion of individuals 25 years of age or older

Table 3. Employment and Occupations, 2014

Puerto Ricans	New York	United States	Puerto Rico*
EMPLOYMENT STATUS			
Population 16 years and over			
In labor force	55.3%	62.4%	43.7%
Civilian labor force	55.2%	61.6%	43.7%
Employed	48.5%	54.4%	35.4%
Unemployed	12%	11.6%	18.9%
Not in labor force	44.7%	37.6%	56.3%
OCCUPATION			
Civilian employed population 16 years and over			
Male	198,105	1,058,918	516,762
Management, business, science, and arts	23.1%	23.4%	23.9%
Service occupations	26.9%	22.5%	23%
Sales and office occupations	21.2%	19.6%	21.3%
Construction and maintenance	12.3%	13.8%	18%
Production, transportation, and moving	16.4%	20.7%	13.7%
Female	202,756	999,105	456,356
Management, business, science, and arts	32.8%	33.1%	39.7%
Service occupations	25.9%	24.4%	16.6%
Sales and office occupations	36.6%	35.7%	38.3%
Construction and maintenance	0.5%	0.6%	0.6%
Production, transportation, and moving	4.2%	6.2%	4.8%
CLASS OF WORKER			
Civilian employed population 16 years and over			
Private wage and salary workers	78.2%	82%	69%
Government workers	18.3%	14.8%	22.5%
Self-employed workers in own not incorporated business	3.3%	3.1%	8.3%
VETERAN STATUS			
Civilian population 18 years and over			
Civilian veteran	3.8%	6%	3.3%

Source: U.S. Census Bureau, 2014 American Community Survey 1-Year Estimates.
* Puerto Ricans only.

Puerto Rican Population by Counties in New York, 2014

Puerto Ricans accounted for 5.5% of New York State's total 19.6 million population in 2014. One in four Puerto Ricans in New York State lives in Bronx County (296,633), compared to one in five of the total Latino population, and just over one in fourteen of the total New York State population. The four other counties — Kings, Queens, New York, and Richmond — accounted for another 39.7% of the Puerto Rican population in New York State. New York City's five boroughs accounted for two-thirds of the Puerto Rican population in New York State. Westchester and Suffolk counties account for another 10.2% of the Puerto Rican population. Puerto Ricans also have a presence in other urban areas of the state, such as Monroe county (Rochester), Erie county (Buffalo) and Albany, as well as exurban areas (Rockland county) and rural areas (Onondaga county). When compared to Latinos overall, the geographic distribution of Puerto Ricans was nearly identical with 67.5% of the Latino population living in the New York City boroughs. However, less than half the overall population of the state (42.6%) lived in the New York City boroughs. Latinos, generally and Puerto Ricans in particular are a decidedly urban population.

COUNTY	Puerto Rican Population	Percent	Latino Population	Percent	Total Population	Percent
Bronx County	296,633	26.6%	767,506	21.6%	1,413,566	7.2%
Kings County	176,183	15.8%	506,015	14.2%	2,570,801	13.1%
Queens County	116,374	10.4%	634,930	17.8%	2,280,602	11.6%
New York County	109,500	9.8%	416,166	11.7%	1,618,398	8.3%
Suffolk County	64,760	5.8%	261,177	7.3%	1,500,373	7.7%
Westchester County	49,039	4.4%	219,725	6.2%	962,319	4.9%
Richmond County	39,959	3.6%	83,366	2.3%	471,522	2.4%
Monroe County	39,938	3.6%	57,682	1.6%	748,076	3.8%
Nassau County	33,050	3%	207,996	5.8%	1,350,601	6.9%
Erie County	31,007	2.8%	44,600	1.3%	920,694	4.7%
Orange County	29,614	2.7%	70,307	2%	374,518	1.9%
Rockland County	14,228	1.3%	52,289	1.5%	318,186	1.6%
Dutchess County	11,804	1.1%	32,858	0.9%	297,388	1.5%
Onondaga County	10,409	0.9%	20,281	0.6%	467,846	2.4%
Albany County	8,591	0.8%	16,336	0.5%	306,124	1.6%
Other Counties	83,260	7.4%	168,410	4.7%	3,993,316	20.4%
Total	**1,114,349**	**100%**	**3,559,644**	**100%**	**19,594,330**	**100%**

Sources: U.S. Census Bureau and 2014 American Community Survey 5-Year Estimates
Notes: Total counts for populations may differ depending on whether the estimates are derived from the five-year estimates or the one-year estimates of the American Community Survey

PUERTO RICAN POPULATION BY COUNTIES IN NEW YORK, 2014

PUERTO RICAN POPULATION

1 dot = 500

'06-'14 PUERTO RICAN ARRIVALS

1 dot = 100

BOUNDARIES

County

City/Towns

Census Tracts

CONGRESSIONAL DISTRICT

Republican

Democrat

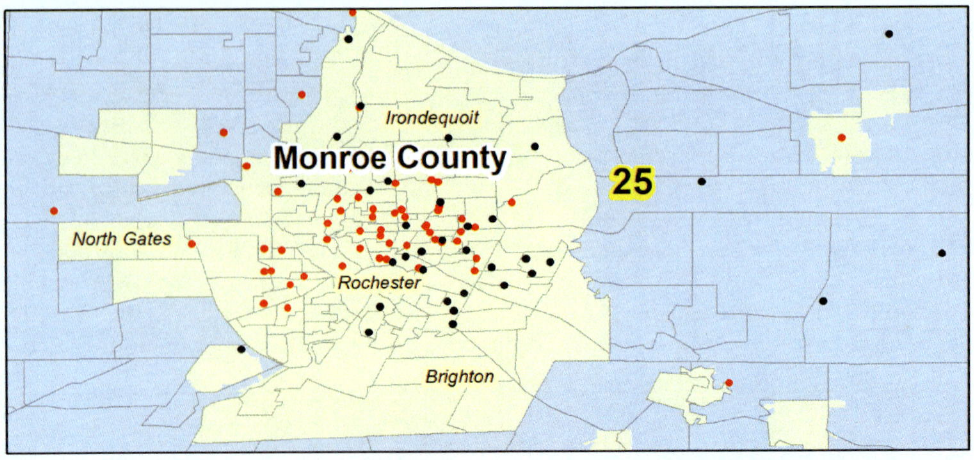

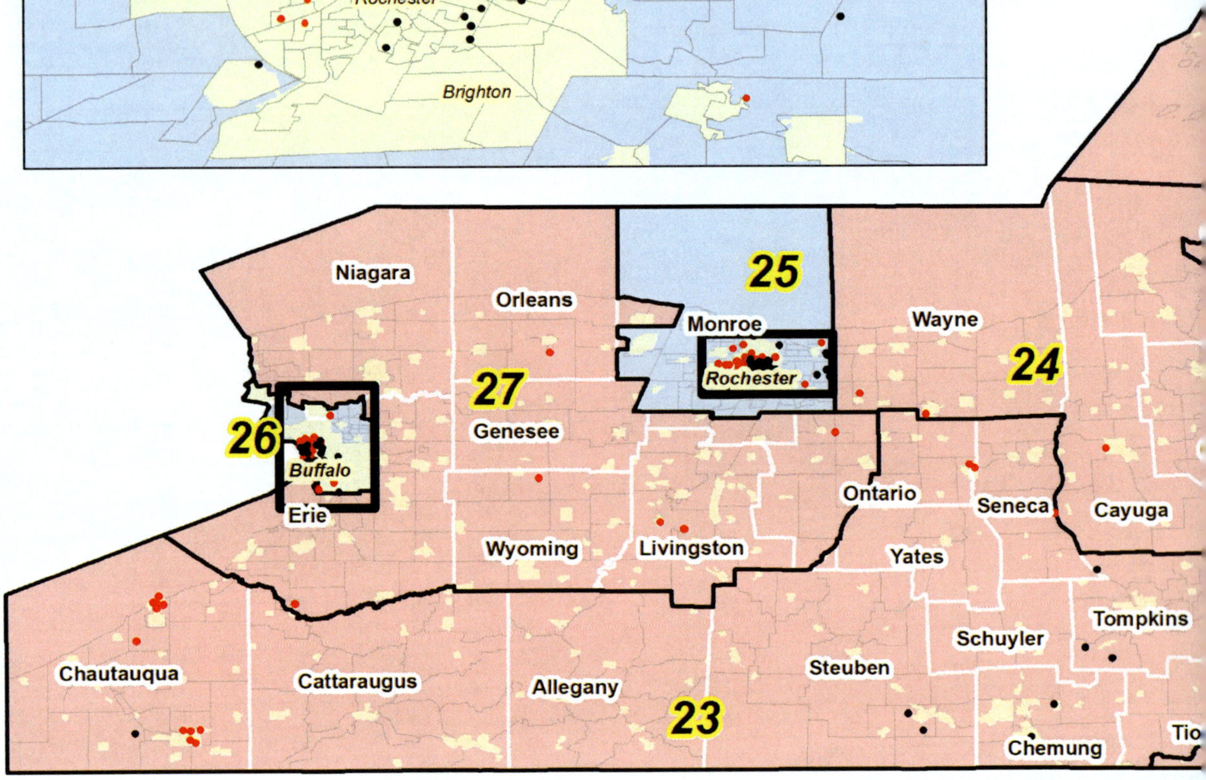

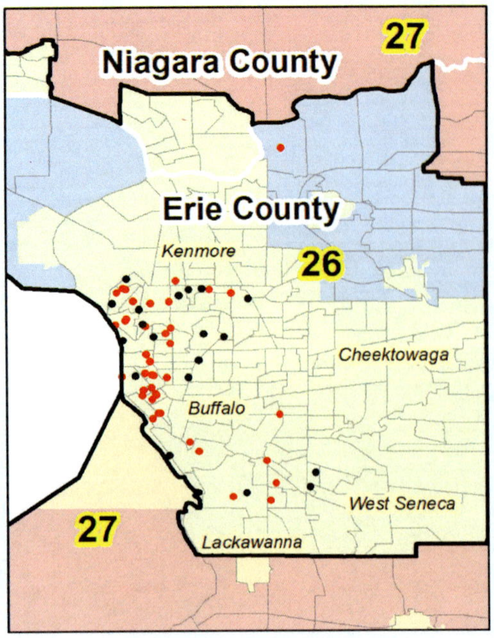

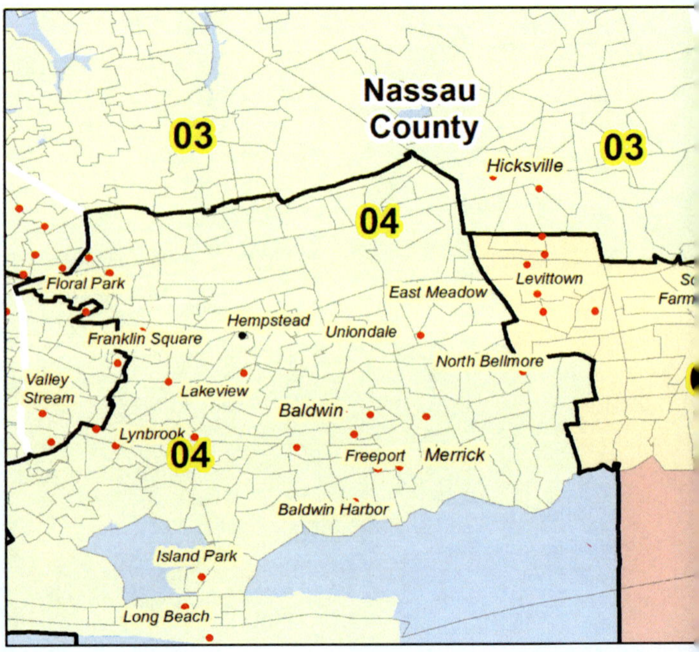

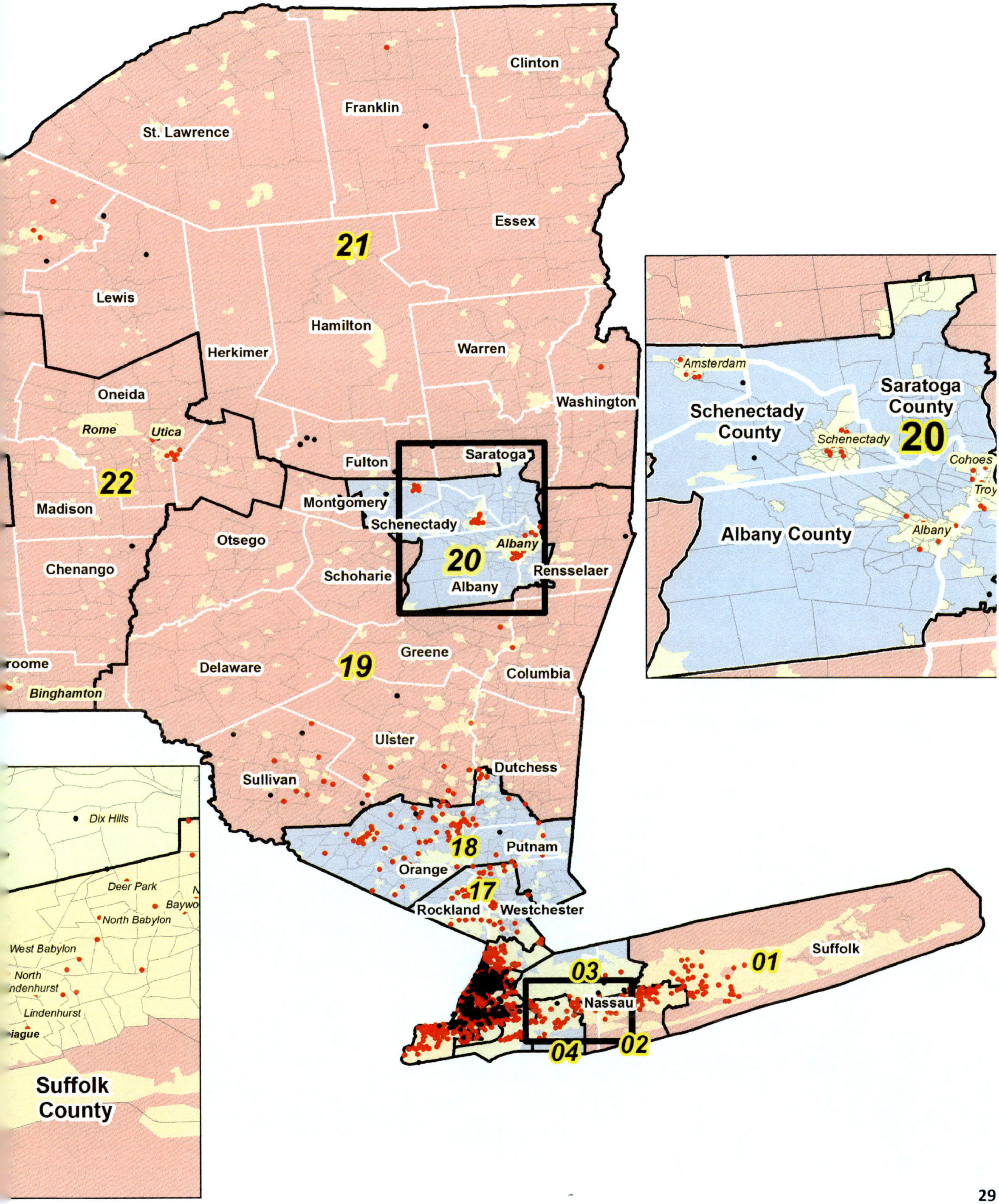
Clinton
Franklin
St. Lawrence
Essex
21
Lewis
Hamilton
Warren
Herkimer
Oneida
Washington
Rome
Utica
Fulton
Saratoga
22
Madison
Montgomery
Schenectady
Otsego
Albany
20
Chenango
Schoharie
Albany
Rensselaer
Greene
roome
Delaware
19
Columbia
Binghamton
Ulster
Dutchess
Sullivan
18
Putnam
Orange
17
Rockland
Westchester
Suffolk
01
03
Nassau
02
04
Amsterdam
Schenectady County
Saratoga County
Schenectady
20
Cohoes
Troy
Albany County
Albany
Dix Hills
Deer Park
Baywo
North Babylon
West Babylon
North
ndenhurst
Lindenhurst
iague
Suffolk County

PUERTO RICAN POPULATION BY COUNTIES IN NEW YORK, 2014

PUERTO RICAN POPULATION

1 dot = 500

'06-'14 PUERTO RICAN ARRIVALS

1 dot = 100

BOUNDARIES

County

City/Towns

Census Tracts

CONGRESSIONAL DISTRICT

Republican

Democrat

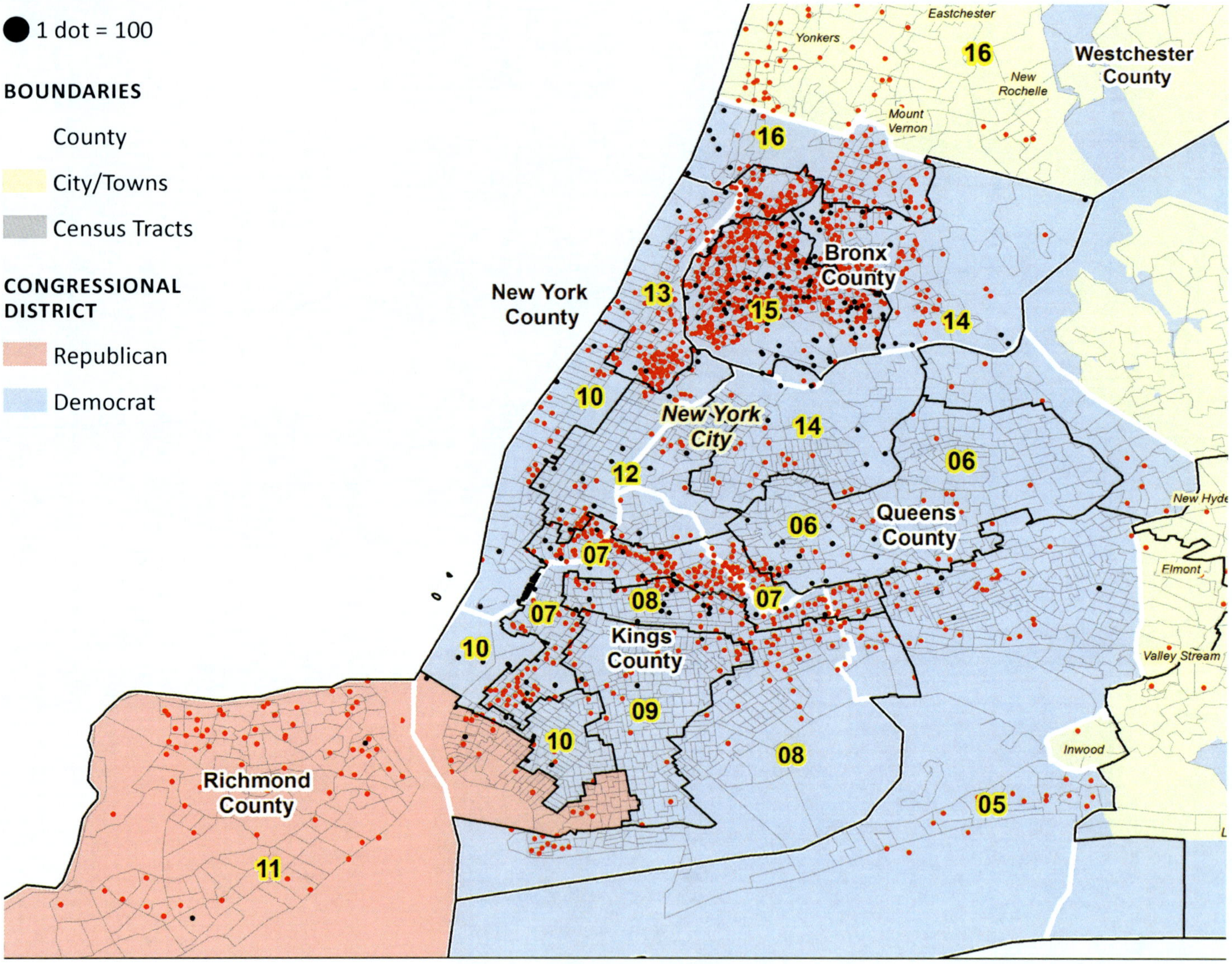

with bachelor's or graduate degrees than stateside Puerto Ricans, whether they reside in New York or elsewhere. The most pronounced difference was found among women: 28% of Puerto Rican women in Puerto Rico had earned bachelor's or graduate degrees when compared to residents in New York, where 18% had completed similar degrees, or the U.S. overall where 19.5% had completed similar degrees. For Puerto Rican men, the differences were 6.2 and 4 percentage points, respectively.

The data by major occupational category indicated that the structure of Puerto Rican employment in New York was similar to that of other stateside Puerto Ricans and those in Puerto Rico with two notable exceptions. Though 23.1% of Puerto Rican men were employed in managerial occupations in New York and elsewhere, Puerto Rican women in New York had a lower representation in this category; 32.8% of Puerto Rican women in New York were in managerial occupations, compared to 33.1% of stateside Puerto Ricans and 39.7% Puerto Ricans in Puerto Rico. The underrepresentation of women in managerial occupations clearly challenges the notion of Puerto Ricans in New York having an overrepresentation in professional occupations. However, Puerto Rican women in New York and the U.S. are overrepresented in service occupations when compared to Puerto Rico.

The employment rate of Puerto Ricans in New York was lower (48.5%) than other stateside Puerto Ricans (54.4%), but much higher than Puerto Ricans in Puerto Rico (35.4%). New York Puerto Ricans participated more actively in the labor

Table 4. Income and Earnings, 2014

Puerto Ricans	New York	United States	Puerto Rico*
INCOME IN THE PAST 12 MONTHS (IN 2013 INFLATION-ADJUSTED DOLLARS)			
Households	374,519	1,635,808	1,175,297
Median household income (dollars)	33,906	39,322	18,710
With earnings	67.2%	76.9%	54.7%
Mean earnings (dollars)	63,726	61,065	36,407
With Social Security income	28.4%	24.1%	43.2%
Mean Social Security income (dollars)	13,434	13,727	12,159
With Supplemental Security Income	17.5%	12.6%	0.4%
Mean Supplemental Security Income (dollars)	9,032	8,780	10,025
With cash public assistance income	8.7%	6.9%	8.1%
Mean cash public assistance income (dollars)	3,715	3,441	2,316
With retirement income	11.7%	10.1%	15.6%
Mean retirement income (dollars)	21,616	20,452	15,387
With Food Stamp/SNAP benefits	36.9%	31.5%	39.7%
Families	235,976	1,114,628	830,807
Median family income (dollars)	42,655	44,499	22,220
Married-couple family	43.6%	53.9%	56.1%
Median income (dollars)	76,179	67,129	29,417
Male householder, no spouse present	10.8%	10.2%	9.5%
Median income (dollars)	37,409	37,513	17,797
Female householder, no husband present	45.6%	35.9%	34.4%
Median income (dollars)	23,449	23,957	13,554
Individuals	1,095,858	5,266,738	3,404,122
Per capita income (dollars)	$19,289	$18,457	$10,960
Mean earnings (dollars) for full-time, year-round workers:			
Male	$52,111	$50,756	$32,512
Female	$46,389	$42,263	$29,166

Source: U.S. Census Bureau, 2014 American Community Survey 1-Year Estimates.
* Puerto Ricans only.

force and had a lower unemployment rate when compared to Puerto Ricans in Puerto Rico but had worse off indicators when compared to other U.S.-based Puerto Ricans. The disparity in unemployment was equally significant. In 2014, the unemployment rate in Puerto Rico stood at 18.9% of those in the labor force. In contrast, the unemployment rate for Puerto Ricans in New York was 12.2%, slightly higher than the overall rate for stateside Puerto Ricans of 11.6%.

Besides better employment opportunities, an important factor inducing migration to the United States from Puerto Rico or interstate mobility among Puerto Ricans is differences in earnings. Given that stateside Puerto Rican are concentrated in the Northeast, where earnings are higher than in the South, the average earnings of full-time, year-round stateside Puerto Ricans of $50,756 for men and $42,263 for women were lower than in New York of $52,111 and $46,389, respectively. Earnings for Puerto Ricans in New York were also substantially higher than for Puerto Ricans in Puerto Rico where full-time, year-round men in 2014 earned $32,512 and women earned $29,166.

Household and family incomes are important indicators of economic well-being. These indicators were similar for stateside Puerto Ricans, including those in New York, but doubled that of Puerto Ricans in Puerto Rico. Median household income was $33,906 for Puerto Ricans in New York and $39,322 for other stateside Puerto Ricans, but less than half

Graph 4.A: Mean Earnings for Full-Time Year-Round Puerto Rican Workers

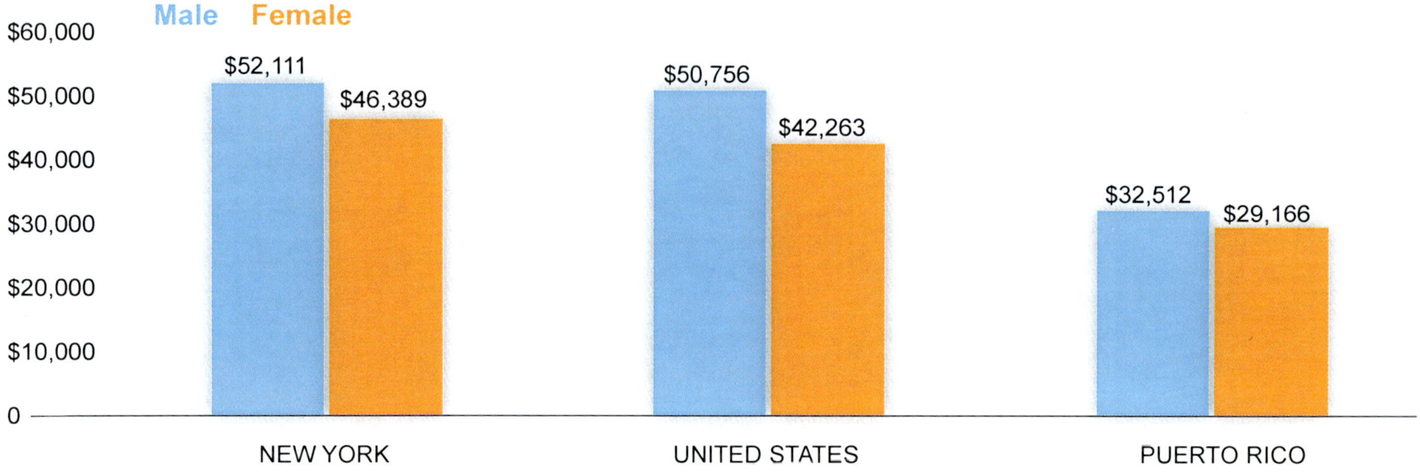

Graph 4.B: Puerto Rican Purchasing Power in Billions of Dollars, 2014

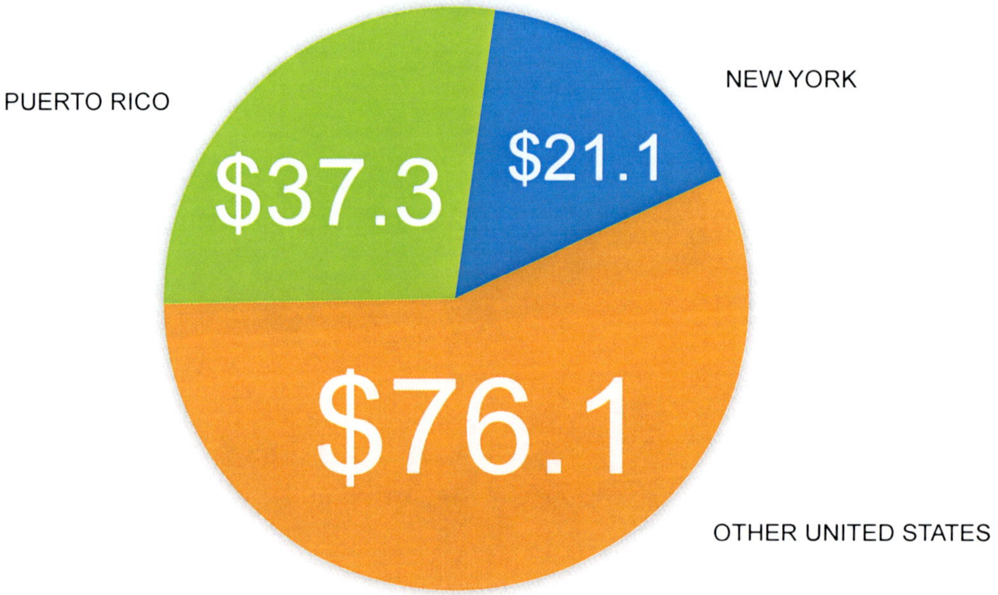

Graph 5.A: Poverty Rates, 2014

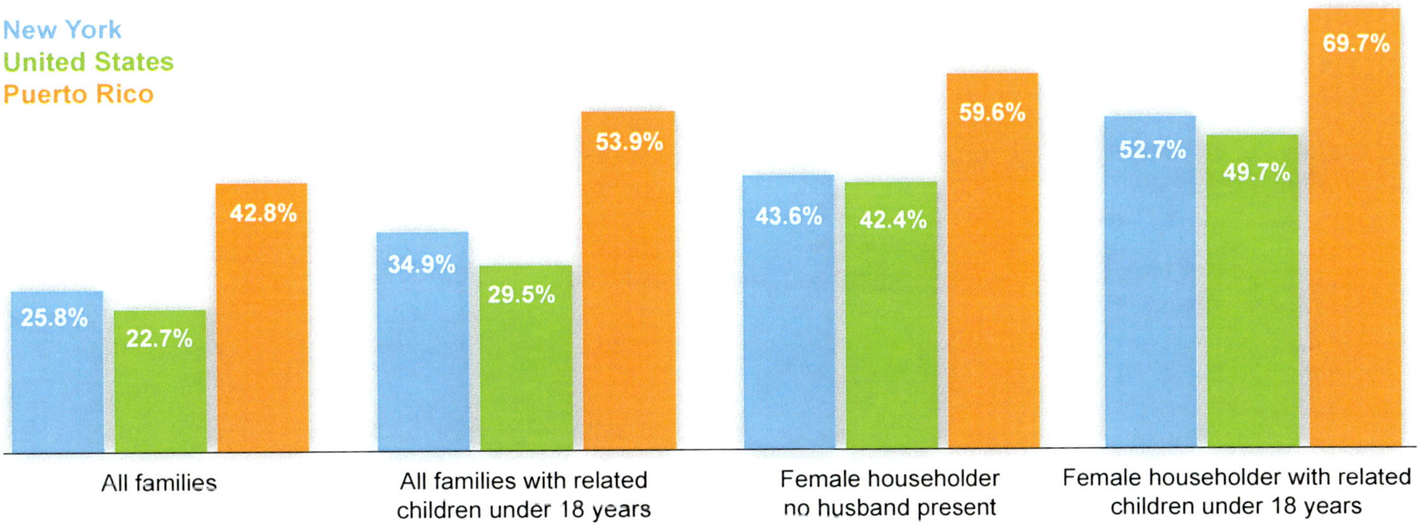

Table 5. Poverty, 2014

Puerto Ricans	New York	United States	Puerto Rico*
POVERTY RATES			
All families	25.8%	22.7%	42.8%
With related children under 18 years	34.9%	29.5%	53.9%
With related children under 5 years only	27.9%	24.6%	57.1%
Married-couple family	8.4%	9.7%	30.9%
With related children under 18 years	9.8%	11.3%	35.5%
With related children under 5 years only	5.7%	5.9%	33.9%
Female householder, no husband present, family	43.6%	42.4%	59.6%
With related children under 18 years	52.7%	49.7%	69.7%
With related children under 5 years only	49.8%	49.4%	75.7%
All people	29.2%	26.2%	46.6%
Under 18 years	38.1%	33.4%	58.7%
Related children under 18 years	37.8%	33.1%	58.6%
Related children under 5 years	36.9%	34.7%	62.8%
Related children 5 to 17 years	38.1%	32.4%	57.3%
18 years and over	25.8%	22.8%	43.2%
18 to 64 years	25.3%	22.8%	43.8%
65 years and over	28.7%	22.4%	41%
People in families	26.3%	23.6%	44.6%
Unrelated individuals 15 years and over	41.5%	38.5%	58%

Source: U.S. Census Bureau, 2014 American Community Survey 1-Year Estimates.
* Puerto Ricans only.

those levels for Puerto Ricans in the island at $18,710. These differences were also evident in the per capita income. In 2014, per capita income for Puerto Ricans in New York was $19,289 and $18,457 for stateside Puerto Ricans, but only $10,960 for Puerto Ricans in Puerto Rico.

From an economic perspective, stateside Puerto Ricans represented 72.3% of the $134.5 billion total purchasing power of the entire Puerto Rican community in the year 2014. Purchasing power was defined simply as per capita income multiplied by the Puerto Rican population. Stateside Puerto Ricans had more than double the total purchasing power of Puerto Ricans in Puerto Rico of $37.3 billion. Puerto Ricans in New York, had $21.1 billion in purchasing power which represented a significant potential market for trade, investments, tourism in general and medical tourism in particular, and other economic activities in the island.

In 2014, the proportion of households that received cash public assistance income was 8.7% for Puerto Ricans in New York, 6.9% for other stateside Puerto Ricans, and 8.1% Puerto Ricans in Puerto Rico. In other words, by staying in Puerto Rico a higher proportion of Puerto Ricans would have received public assistance income when compare to the majority of states, and at a comparable proportion than in New York State. In addition, the differences in the amount that the households received by public assistance were higher for stateside Puerto Ricans ($3,441) and Puerto Ricans in New York ($3,715) when compared to the amount received by Puerto Ricans in Puerto Rico ($2,316). The proportion of Puerto Rican households in New York receiving benefits from the Supplemental Nutrition Assistance Program (SNAP) was 36.9% in 2014, five percentage points higher than the 31.5% rate for Puerto Rican households in other parts of the U.S. and three percentage points lower than the 39.7% for Puerto Ricans in Puerto Rico.

The poverty rate for all Puerto Rican families was 25.8% in New York, 22.7% in the U.S. overall, and 42.8% in Puerto Rico. Though stateside Puerto Ricans' rates where about half or lower than poverty rates in Puerto Rico, families with female householder, no husband present and children under 18 years of age exhibited much higher incidence of poverty than the average family. For Puerto Rican female-headed families with children the rates were 52.7% in New York, 49.7% for the rest of the U.S., and 69.7% in Puerto Rico. These are inordinately high poverty rates by any measure or comparative context.

Housing is a primary determinant of the cost of living. In general, the Northeast has higher cost of home ownership than the South or other parts of the country. The median value of owner-occupied housing for Puerto Ricans in New York was $312,700, compared to $175,900 for other stateside Puerto Ricans, and $119,500 for Puerto Ricans in Puerto Rico. The median monthly owner cost with a mortgage was $2,165 for Puerto Ricans in New York, and $1,545 for other stateside Puerto Ricans. A comparable cost was $873 for Puerto Ricans in Puerto Rico. These relative prices and ownership costs were reflected in ownership rates. Puerto Ricans in New York had lower rates of home ownership than stateside Puerto Ricans. The Census data revealed that Puerto Ricans in New York had a 23.6% rate of owner-occupied housing units, while the comparable rate for stateside Puerto Ricans was 36%. The home ownership rate for Puerto Ricans in Puerto Rico was much higher, at 68.7%.

Table 6. Housing and Health Insurance, 2014

Puerto Ricans	New York	United States	Puerto Rico*
HOUSING			
Owner-occupied housing units	23.6%	36%	68.7%
Monthly owner costs as a percentage of household income in the past 12 months			
Less than 30 percent	58%	62.8%	52.6%
30 percent or more	42%	37.2%	47.4%
Owner-occupied housing units			
Median value (dollars)	$312,700	$175,900	$119,500
Median selected monthly owner costs with a mortgage (dollars)	$2,165	$1,545	$873
HEALTH INSURANCE COVERAGE			
Civilian noninstitutionalized population			
With private health insurance	50.8%	51.6%	38%
With public coverage	48.8%	43.5%	62.9%
No health insurance coverage	8.3%	11.5%	5.5%

Source: U.S. Census Bureau, 2014 American Community Survey 1-Year Estimates.
* Puerto Ricans only.

Puerto Ricans in Florida, 2014

In 2014, for the first time, the Puerto Rican population exceeded one million in Florida. Florida joined New York as the only other state with more than one million Puerto Ricans. The Puerto Rican population grew from 3% of the Florida population in 2000 to 5.1% in 2014. One out of every five Latinos in Florida is Puerto Rican.

Graph 1.A: Latino Population Florida, 2014

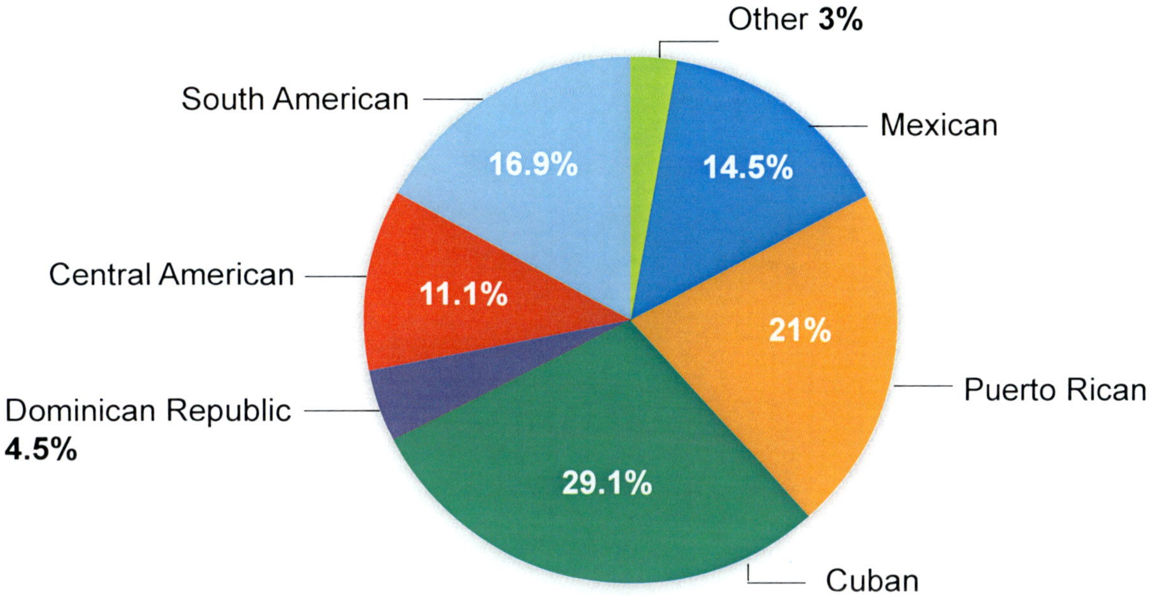

Table 1. Puerto Rican and Latino Population in Florida

	2000		2010		2014	
Total	15,982,378	100%	18,801,310	100%	19,893,297	100%
Not Hispanic or Latino	13,299,663	83.2%	14,577,504	77.5%	15,104,427	75.9%
Hispanic or Latino	2,682,715	16.8%	4,223,806	22.5%	4,788,870	24.1%
Mexican	363,925	2.3%	629,718	3.3%	693,483	3.5%
Puerto Rican	482,027	3%	847,550	4.5%	1,006,542	5.1%
Cuban	833,120	5.2%	1,213,438	6.5%	1,392,605	7%
Dominican Republic	70,968	0.4%	172,451	0.9%	216,202	1.1%
Central American:	202,772	1.3%	432,665	2.3%	530,143	2.7%
South American	301,236	1.9%	674,542	3.6%	807,465	4.1%
Other	428,667	2.7%	253,442	1.3%	142,430	0.7%

Sources: U.S. Census Bureau, Census 2000 Summary File 1, 2010 Census. Summary File 1, and 2014 American Community Survey 1-Year Estimates.

However, the data supports a view of labor market integration, where Puerto Ricans' occupational distribution is very similar among stateside Puerto Ricans and those in Puerto Rico and is contrary to an overrepresentation of professionals or brain drain argument. The data also suggests that higher welfare benefits in the U.S. are likely not a significant factor inducing migration.

Florida has one of the most diverse Latino populations in the country. The Latino population in Florida grew from 16.8% of the state's total population in 2000 to 24.1% in 2014. Cubans (29.1% of the Latino population) and Puerto Ricans (21%) comprised half the Latino population of Florida. Mexicans (14.5%), Colombians (7.3%), and Dominicans (4.5%) were the next largest single national origin Latino populations.

Graph 2.A: Puerto Rican Education Attainment, 25 years and over, 2014

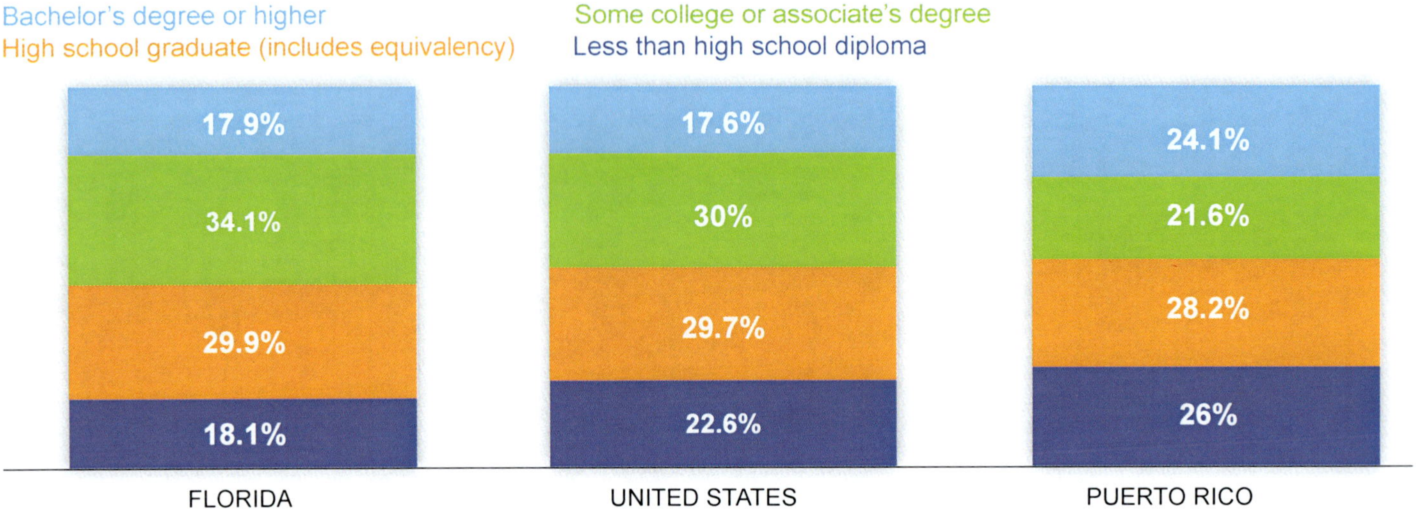

Table 2. Age, Education, and Language, 2014

Puerto Ricans	Florida	United States	Puerto Rico*
TOTAL POPULATION	1,006,542	5,266,738	3,404,122
Median age (years)	32.2	28.9	38.9
62 years and over	12.30%	9.9%	21%
EDUCATIONAL ATTAINMENT			
Population 25 years and over			
Less than high school diploma	18.1%	22.6%	26%
High school graduate (includes equivalency)	29.9%	29.7%	28.2%
Some college or associate's degree	34.1%	30%	21.6%
Bachelor's degree or higher	17.9%	17.6%	24.1%
Male, bachelor's degree or higher	16.7%	15.6%	19.6%
Female, bachelor's degree or higher	19.1%	19.5%	28.1%
LANGUAGE SPOKEN AT HOME AND ABILITY TO SPEAK ENGLISH			
Population 5 years and over			
English only	28.9%	38.8%	5.3%
Language other than English	71.1%	61.2%	94.7%
Speak English less than "very well"	20.9%	17.3%	78.8%

Source: U.S. Census Bureau, 2014 American Community Survey 1-Year Estimates.
* Puerto Ricans only.

The median age of Puerto Ricans in Florida (32.2 years) is 3.3 years older than the median age of stateside Puerto Ricans (28.9 years) and 6.7 years younger than the 38.9 year median age in Puerto Rico. These differences in median age are evident in the percent of the population 62 years or older in 2014. Florida had a slightly higher population proportion aged 62 and older than stateside Puerto Ricans overall, 12.3% and 9.9%, respectively. However, the proportion of Floridian Puerto Ricans aged 62 and older is considerably below that of Puerto Rico's population (21%). The Puerto Rican population in Florida is not significantly older than in other parts of the country, and was significantly younger than the comparable age cohort in the island. Puerto Ricans in Florida have lower English-fluency indicators than Puerto Ricans in the U.S. as a whole. In Florida, 28.9% of Puerto Ricans speak only English at home, while 38.8% of Puerto Ricans in the U.S. overall do so. Similarly, while 71.1% of Puerto Ricans in Florida speak a language other than English at home, only 61.2% of stateside Puerto Ricans do so. About one in five (20.9%) Florida Puerto Ricans declare they speak English at a less than "very well" fluency level, compared to almost one in six of all stateside Puerto Ricans (17.3%).

Table 3. Employment and Occupations, 2014

Puerto Ricans	Florida	United States	Puerto Rico*
EMPLOYMENT STATUS			
Population 16 years and over			
In labor force	61.2%	62.4%	43.7%
Civilian labor force	60.9%	61.6%	43.7%
Employed	54.9%	54.4%	35.4%
Unemployed	10%	11.6%	18.9%
Not in labor force	38.8%	37.6%	56.3%
Armed Forces	0.3%	0.8%	0%
OCCUPATION			
Civilian employed population 16 years and over			
Male	216,575	1,058,918	516,762
Management, business, science, and arts	23.2%	23.4%	23.9%
Service occupations	22.8%	22.5%	23%
Sales and office occupations	20.8%	19.6%	21.3%
Construction and maintenance	15.3%	13.8%	18%
Production, transportation, and moving	17.8%	20.7%	13.7%
Female	193,256	999,105	456,356
Management, business, science, and arts	31.6%	33.1%	39.7%
Service occupations	23.6%	24.4%	16.6%
Sales and office occupations	40.1%	35.7%	38.3%
Construction and maintenance	0.8%	0.6%	0.6%
Production, transportation, and moving	3.9%	6.2%	4.8%
CLASS OF WORKER			
Civilian employed population 16 years and over			
Private wage and salary workers	85.7%	82%	69%
Government workers	10.8%	14.8%	22.5%
Self-employed workers in own not incorporated business	3.5%	3.1%	8.3%
VETERAN STATUS			
Civilian population 18 years and over			
Civilian veteran	6.9%	6%	3.3%

Source: U.S. Census Bureau, 2014 American Community Survey 1-Year Estimates.
* Puerto Ricans only.

One of the assertions commonly made in the media is that Puerto Ricans in Florida are more educated than Puerto Ricans in other parts of the country and Puerto Rico. Data on the educational attainment of Florida Puerto Ricans do not support this assertion. Puerto Ricans in Florida have a signicantly lower population proportion 25 years and older with bachelor's or graduate degrees (17.9%) than those in Puerto Rico (24.1%). Among all Puerto Ricans in the U.S. this proportion of bachelor's and graduate degree holders aged 25 and older was 17.6%, only slightly below Florida indicators.

The most pronounced difference was found among women: 28.1% of women in Puerto Rico had earned bachelor's or graduate degrees, a significantly higher proportion than Puerto Rican women in Florida (19.1%) and Puerto Rican women throughout the U.S. (19.5%). For men, the differences were 3 and 4 percentage points, respectively.

More than one in four Puerto Ricans in Florida (27.2%) worked in the management, business, science, and arts sector; however, this rate was lower than in Puerto Rico (31.3%) and marginally lower than the rate for all stateside Puerto Ricans (28.1%). As a whole this contradicts the notion that Floridian Puerto Ricans were overrep-

Table 4. Income and Earnings, 2014

Puerto Ricans	Florida	United States	Puerto Rico*
INCOME IN THE PAST 12 MONTHS (IN 2013 INFLATION-ADJUSTED DOLLARS)			
Households	305,143	1,635,808	1,175,297
Median household income (dollars)	$40,465	$39,322	$18,710
With earnings	80.2%	76.9%	54.7%
Mean earnings (dollars)	$54,257	$61,065	$36,407
With Social Security income	27.8%	24.1%	43.2%
Mean Social Security income (dollars)	$15,274	$13,727	$12,159
With Supplemental Security Income	8.3%	12.6%	0.4%
Mean Supplemental Security Income (dollars)	$8,015	$8,780	$10,025
With cash public assistance income	4.1%	6.9%	8.1%
Mean cash public assistance income (dollars)	$2,402	$3,441	$2,316
With retirement income	11.7%	10.1%	15.6%
Mean retirement income (dollars)	$19,627	$20,452	$15,387
With Food Stamp/SNAP benefits	25.4%	31.5%	39.7%
Families	220,178	1,114,628	830,807
Median family income (dollars)	$43,164	$44,499	$22,220
Married-couple family	64.1%	53.9%	56.1%
Median income (dollars)	$55,093	$67,129	$29,417
Male householder, no spouse present	9.4%	10.2%	9.5%
Median income (dollars)	$37,319	$37,513	$17,797
Female householder, no husband present	26.5%	35.9%	34.4%
Median income (dollars)	$26,005	$23,957	$13,554
Individuals	1,006,542	5,266,738	3,404,122
Per capita income (dollars)	$17,570	$18,457	$10,960
Mean earnings (dollars) for full-time, year-round workers:			
Male	$45,500	$50,756	$32,512
Female	$35,096	$42,263	$29,166

Source: U.S. Census Bureau, 2014 American Community Survey 1-Year Estimates.
* Puerto Ricans only.

Puerto Rican Population by Counties in Florida, 2014

Puerto Ricans accounted for about 5 percent of Florida's total population and were most concentrated in the metropolitan areas of Orlando (Orange, Osceola, and Seminole counties), Tampa (Hillsborough County), Miami (Miami-Dade County), and Ft. Lauderdale (Broward County). Over 50% of the Puerto Rican population in Florida resided in or around these major urbanized areas. About one in six Puerto Ricans in Florida (17.7%) lived in Orange County compared to about one in twenty of all Floridians (6.2%). The Puerto Rican presence in Miami-Dade County was 10.8% compared to 37.5% for Latinos, indicating that more than one in three Latinos in Florida lives in Miami-Dade. Outside of these major urban areas, Puerto Ricans were also found in Polk and Pinellas counties, between Orlando and Tampa along the I-4 corridor.

COUNTY	Puerto Rican Population	Percent	Latino Population	Percent	Total Population	Percent
Orange County	165,699	17.7%	337,871	7.5%	1,200,241	6.2%
Hillsborough County	101,479	10.8%	328,820	7.3%	1,279,668	6.6%
Miami-Dade County	101,253	10.8%	1,696,171	37.5%	2,600,861	13.4%
Broward County	81,978	8.8%	480,080	10.6%	1,815,269	9.4%
Osceola County	80,438	8.6%	138,512	3.1%	289,449	1.5%
Palm Beach County	40,315	4.3%	271,524	6%	1,359,074	7%
Polk County	40,193	4.3%	115,072	2.5%	617,323	3.2%
Seminole County	37,731	4%	78,917	1.7%	432,135	2.2%
Volusia County	28,587	3.1%	58,558	1.3%	498,981	2.6%
Lee County	27,527	2.9%	122,812	2.7%	647,554	3.3%
Pinellas County	24,683	2.6%	78,298	1.7%	925,030	4.8%
Duval County	23,760	2.5%	71,540	1.6%	880,750	4.5%
Pasco County	23,370	2.5%	59,716	1.3%	472,745	2.4%
Brevard County	20,114	2.1%	48,070	1.1%	548,891	2.8%
Marion County	17,086	1.8%	38,444	0.9%	334,771	1.7%
Lake County	15,996	1.7%	39,764	0.9%	305,010	1.6%
St. Lucie County	12,316	1.3%	48,603	1.1%	283,988	1.5%
Hernando County	9,987	1.1%	19,011	0.4%	173,792	0.9%
Other Counties	109,389	10.9%	541,104	11.3%	5,065,721	25.5%
Total	**1,005,389**	**100%**	**4,789,830**	**100%**	**19,893,297**	**100%**

Sources: U.S. Census Bureau and 2014 American Community Survey 5-Year Estimates
Notes: Total counts for populations may differ depending on whether the estimates are derived from the five-year estimates or the one-year estimates of the American Community Survey

PUERTO RICAN POPULATION BY COUNTIES IN FLORIDA, 2014

PUERTO RICAN POPULATION

1 dot = 500

'06-'14 PUERTO RICAN ARRIVALS

1 dot = 500

BOUNDARIES

County

City/Towns

Census Tracts

CONGRESSIONAL DISTRICT

Republican

Democrat

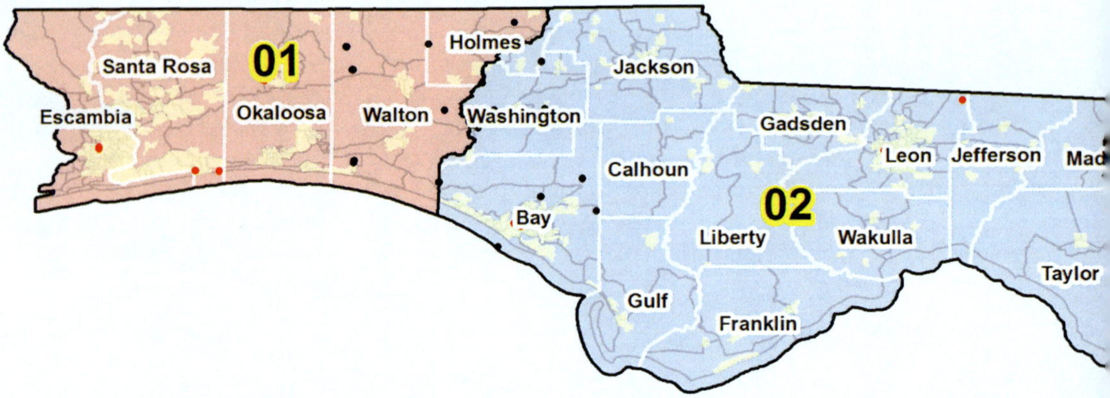

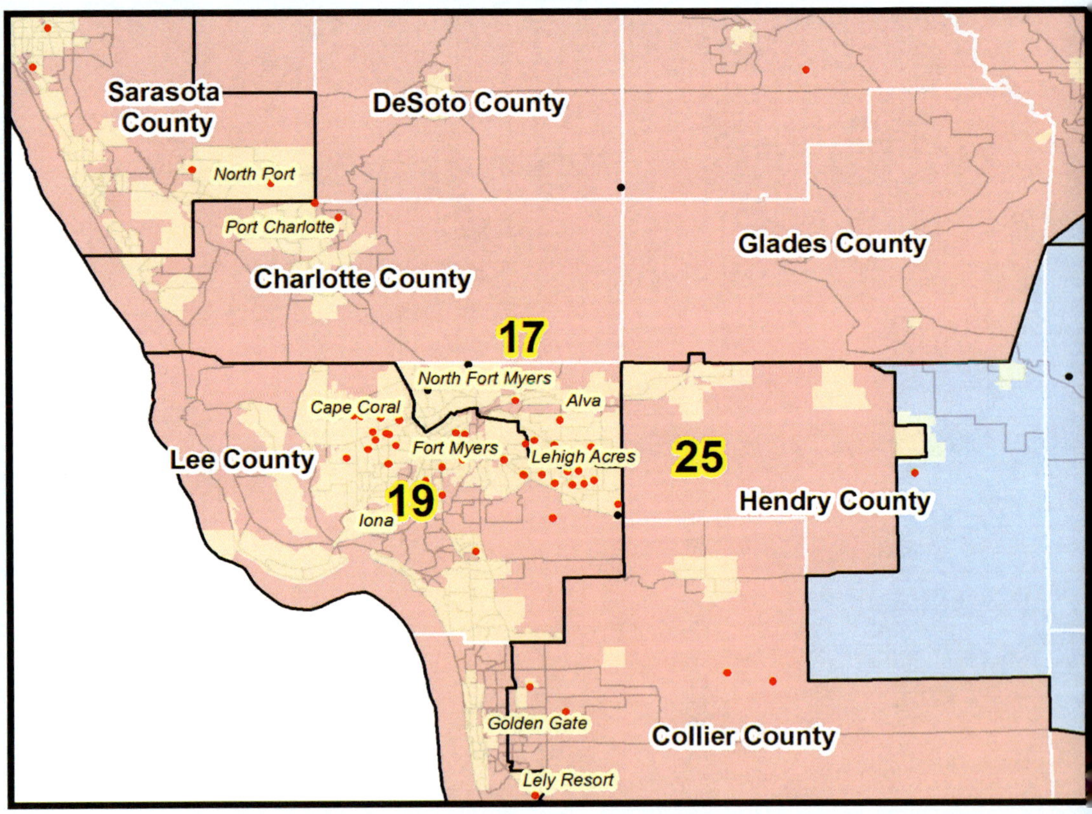

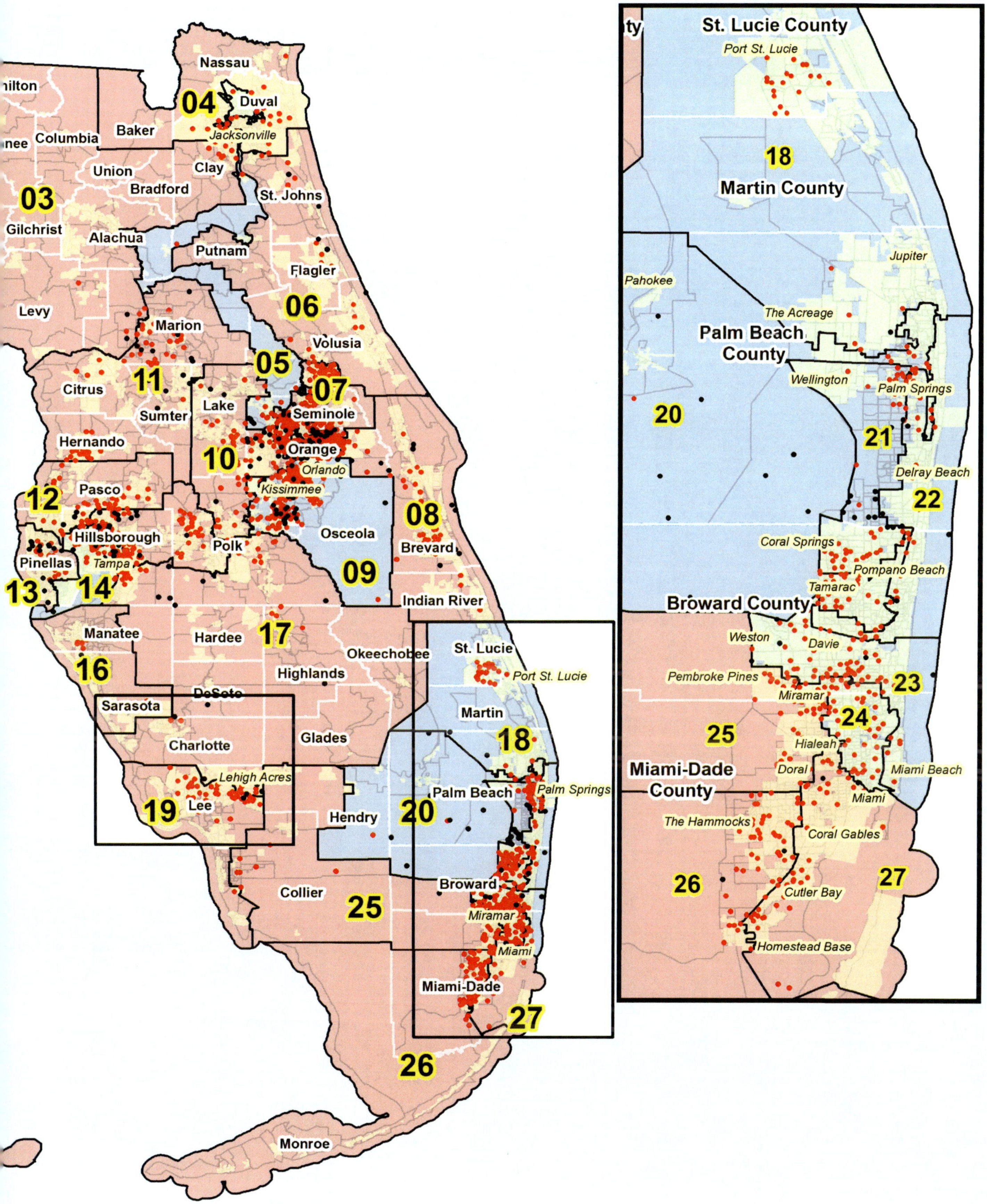

Nassau
04
Duval
Jacksonville
Baker
Columbia
Union
Bradford
Clay
St. Johns
03
Gilchrist
Alachua
Putnam
Flagler
Levy
06
Marion
Volusia
05
11
07
Citrus
Lake
Seminole
Sumter
Hernando
10
Orange
Orlando
Pasco
12
Kissimmee
08
Osceola
Hillsborough
Polk
Brevard
Pinellas
Tampa
09
13
14
Indian River
Manatee
Hardee
17
St. Lucie
Okeechobee
16
Highlands
Port St. Lucie
DeSoto
Sarasota
Martin
Charlotte
Glades
18
Lehigh Acres
Palm Beach
Palm Springs
19
Lee
Hendry
20
Broward
Collier
25
Miramar
Miami
Miami-Dade
27
26
Monroe
St. Lucie County
Port St. Lucie
Martin County
Jupiter
Pahokee
The Acreage
Palm Beach County
Wellington
Palm Springs
21
Delray Beach
22
Coral Springs
Pompano Beach
Tamarac
Broward County
Weston
Davie
Pembroke Pines
23
Miramar
24
Hialeah
Miami-Dade County
Doral
Miami Beach
The Hammocks
Coral Gables
Cutler Bay
Homestead Base

PUERTO RICAN POPULATION BY COUNTIES IN FLORIDA, 2014

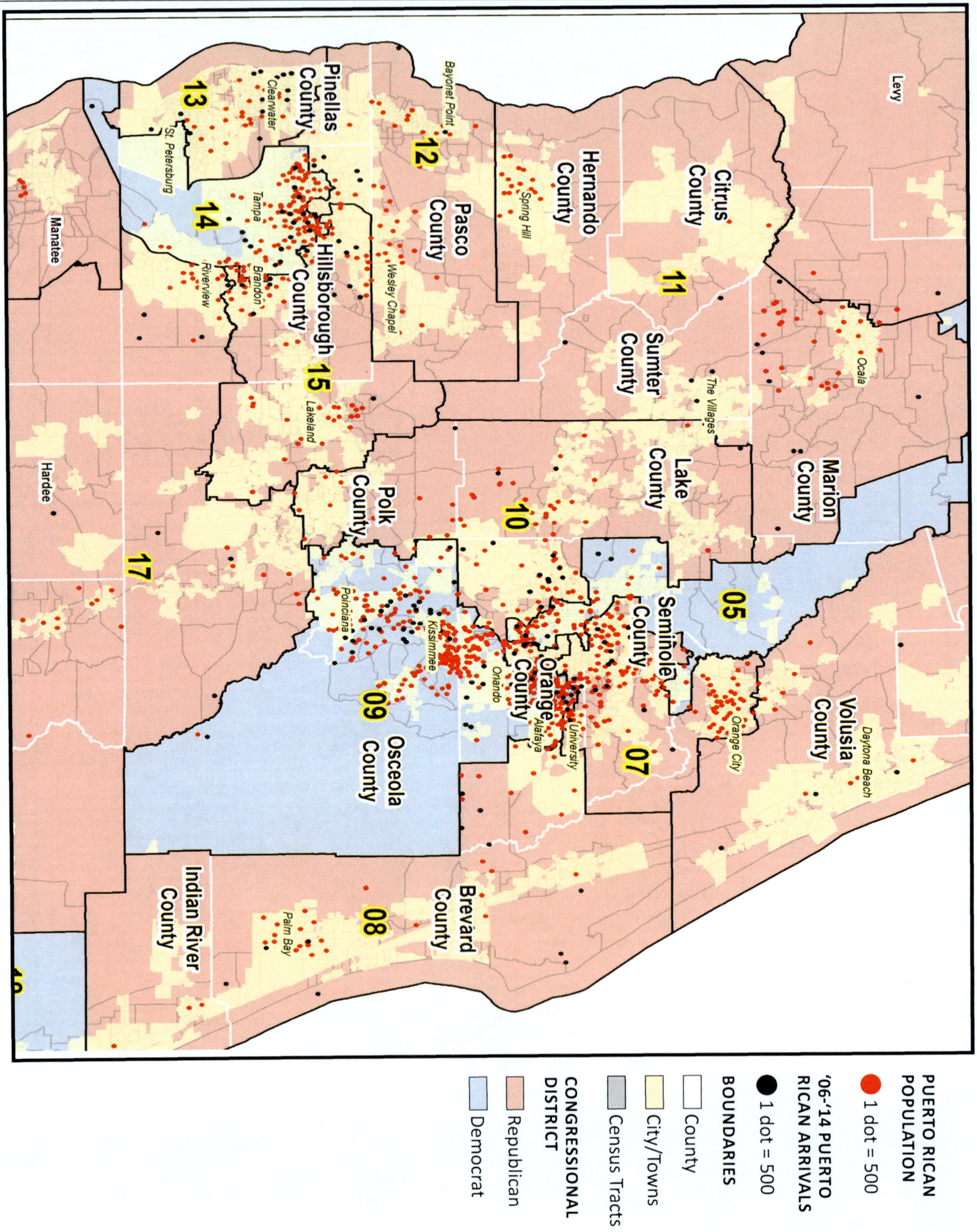

resented in the higher wage managerial sector, and is particularly evident in the case of Puerto Rican women. Only 31.6% of Puerto Rican women in Florida work in the management sector, which is less than the average stateside rate (33.1%) and considerably less than the rate in Puerto Rico (39.7%).

Employment rates among Florida Puerto Ricans mirrored that of stateside Puerto Ricans at 54.9% and 54.4%, respectively. Labor force participation among Florida Puerto Ricans, 61.2%, was slightly lower than the stateside Puerto Rican average of 62.4%. Both figures were close to 20 percentage points higher than Puerto Rico's labor force participation of 43.7%. Furthermore, the unemployment rate in Florida, 10%, was slightly below the stateside Puerto Rican average of 11.6%, and considerably below the 18.9% unemployment rate in Puerto Rico.

Besides better employment opportunities, an important factor inducing migration to the United States from Puerto Rico or interstate mobility among Puerto Ricans within the United States are differences in earnings. Given that stateside Puerto Ricans are concentrated in the Northeast, where earnings are higher than in the South, the average earnings of full-time, year-round workers for all stateside Puerto Rican men ($50,756) and women ($42,263) are higher than in Florida ($45,500 and $35,096, respectively). However, earnings for Puerto Ricans in Florida are substantially higher than for those in Puerto Rico, where full-time, year-round men earned $32,512 and women earned $29,166 in 2014.

Graph 4.A: Mean Earnings for Full-Time Year-Round Puerto Rican Workers, 2014

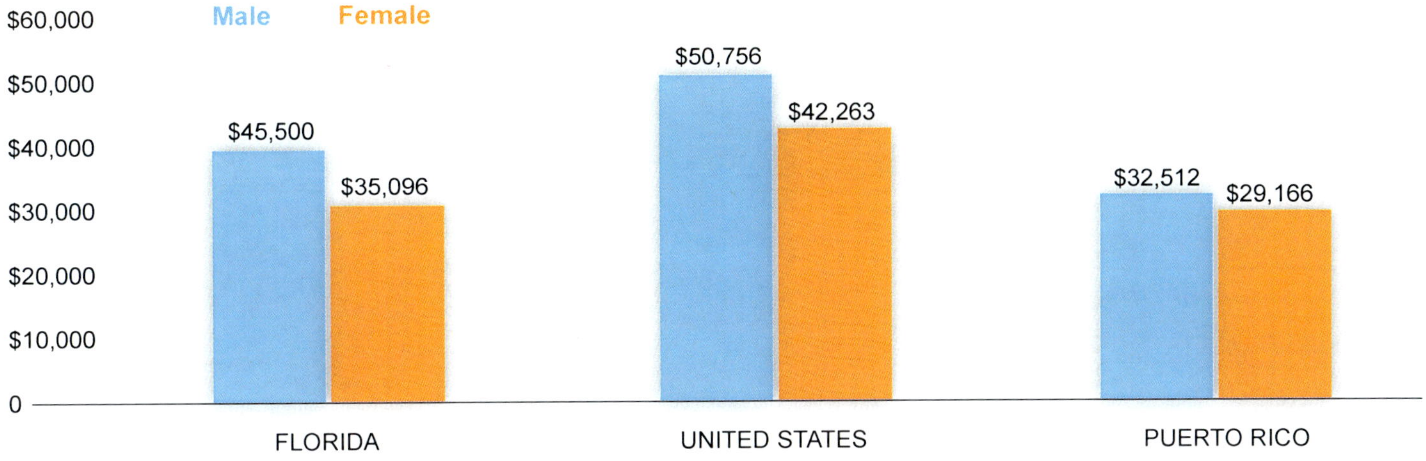

Graph 4.B: Puerto Rican Purchasing Power in Billions of Dollars, 2014

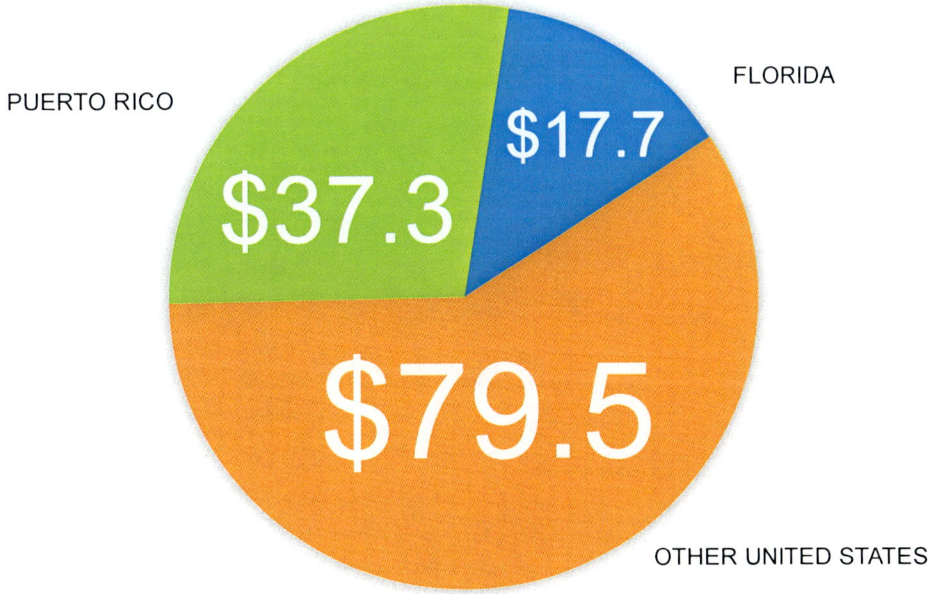

Household and family incomes are important indicators of economic well-being. These indicators are similar for stateside Puerto Ricans, including those in Florida, but double that of the island. Median household income was $40,465 for Puerto Ricans in Florida and $39,322 for other stateside Puerto Ricans, but less than half those levels for the island at $18,710. These differences are also evident in per capita income. In 2014, per

Graph 5.A: Poverty Rates, 2014

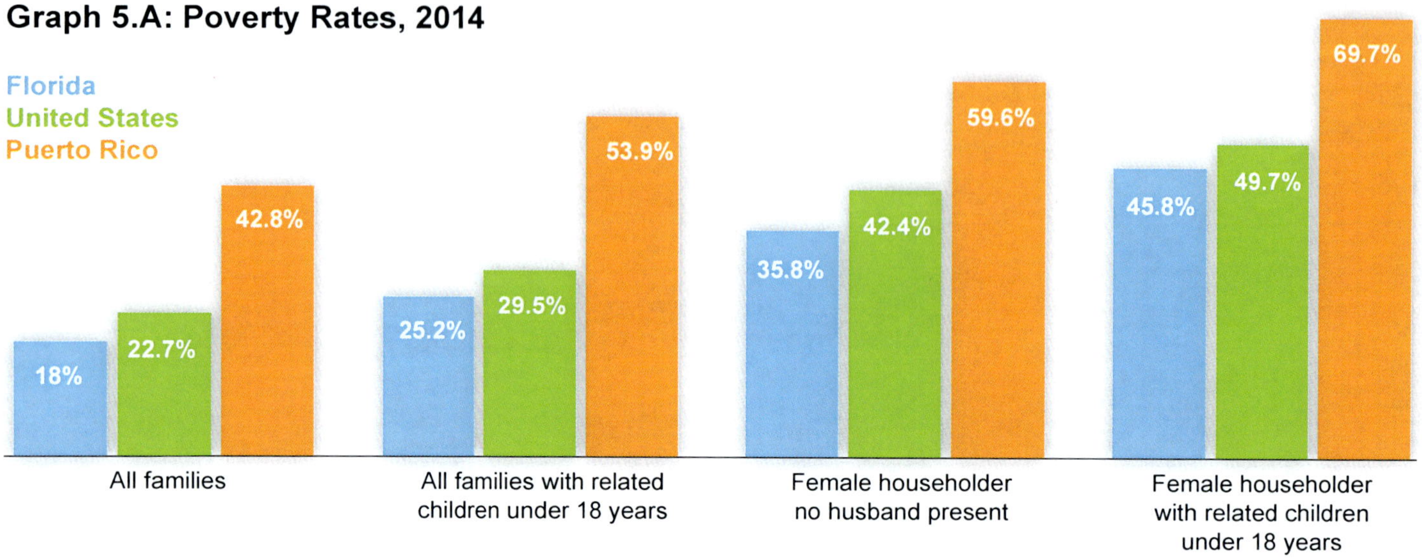

Table 5. Poverty, 2014

Puerto Ricans	Florida	United States	Puerto Rico*
POVERTY RATES			
All families	18%	22.7%	42.8%
With related children under 18 years	25.2%	29.5%	53.9%
With related children under 5 years only	18.4%	24.6%	57.1%
Married-couple family	10.5%	9.7%	30.9%
With related children under 18 years	13.1%	11.3%	35.5%
With related children under 5 years only	6.7%	5.9%	33.9%
Female householder, no husband present, family	35.8%	42.4%	59.6%
With related children under 18 years	45.8%	49.7%	69.7%
With related children under 5 years only	37.3%	49.4%	75.7%
All people	22.5%	26.2%	46.6%
Under 18 years	30.8%	33.4%	58.7%
Related children under 18 years	30.5%	33.1%	58.6%
Related children under 5 years	33.1%	34.7%	62.8%
Related children 5 to 17 years	29.6%	32.4%	57.3%
18 years and over	19.2%	22.8%	43.2%
18 to 64 years	20.1%	22.8%	43.8%
65 years and over	13.7%	22.4%	41%
People in families	20.1%	23.6%	44.6%
Unrelated individuals 15 years and over	35.7%	38.5%	58.6%

Source: U.S. Census Bureau, 2014 American Community Survey 1-Year Estimates.
* Puerto Ricans only.

capita income for Puerto Ricans in Florida was $17,570 and $18,457 for other stateside Puerto Ricans, but only $10,960 for the island.

From an economic perspective, stateside Puerto Ricans represent 72.1% of the $134.5 billion total purchasing power of the entire Puerto Rican community. Purchasing power is defined simply as per capita income multiplied by the Puerto Rican population. Stateside Puerto Ricans have nearly double the total purchasing power of Puerto Ricans in Puerto Rico of $37.3 billion. Puerto Ricans in Florida, with their proximity to Puerto Rico and $17.7 billion in purchasing power, represent a significant potential market for trade, investments, tourism in general and medical tourism in particular, and other economic activities in the island.

In 2014, the proportion of households receiving cash public assistance income was 4.1% for Puerto Ricans in Florida, 6.9% for other stateside Puerto Ricans, and 8.1% in Puerto Rico. In addition, the difference in the amount households received in public assistance is only slightly higher for stateside Puerto Ricans ($3,441) while cash public assistance income in Florida of $2,402 was only marginally higher ($2,316) than in Puerto Rico. The proportion of Puerto Rican households in Florida receiving benefits from the Supplemental Nutrition Assistance Program (SNAP) was 25.4% in 2014, six percentage points lower than the overall 31.5% rate for Puerto Rican households in the U.S. and fifteen percentage points lower than the 39.7% rate in Puerto Rico.

The poverty rate for all Puerto Rican families was 18% in Florida, 22.7% in the U.S. overall, and 42.8% in Puerto Rico. Though stateside Puerto Ricans' poverty rates were about half or lower than poverty rates in Puerto Rico, families with a female householder and no husband present with children under 18 years of age exhibited a much higher incidence of poverty than the average family. For Puerto Rican female-headed families with children the rates were 45.8% in Florida, 49.7% for all stateside Puerto Ricans, and 69.7% in Puerto Rico. These are inordinately high poverty rates by any measure or comparative context.

Housing is a primary determinant of the cost of living. In general, the South has a lower cost of home ownership than the Northeast or other parts of the country. The median value of owner-occupied housing for Puerto Ricans in Florida was $145,200, compared to $175,900 for other stateside Puerto Ricans, and $119,500 in Puerto Rico. The median monthly owner costs with a mortgage are $1,247 for Puerto Ricans in Florida, and $1,545 for other stateside Puerto Ricans. A comparable cost is $873 in Puerto Rico. These relative prices and ownership costs are reflected in ownership rates. Puerto Ricans in Florida have higher rates of home ownership than stateside Puerto Ricans. The Census data reveals that Puerto Ricans in Florida have a 47.1% rate of owner-occupied housing units, while the comparable rate for stateside Puerto Ricans is 36%. The home ownership rate in Puerto Rico is much higher, at 68.7%.

Table 6. Housing and Health Insurance, 2014

Puerto Ricans	Florida	United States	Puerto Rico*
HOUSING			
Owner-occupied housing units	47.1%	36%	68.7%
Monthly owner costs as a percentage of household income in the past 12 months			
Less than 30 percent	58.3%	62.8%	52.6%
30 percent or more	41.7%	37.2%	47.4%
Owner-occupied housing units			
Median value (dollars)	$145,200	$175,900	$119,500
Median selected monthly owner costs with a mortgage (dollars)	$1,247	$1,545	$873
HEALTH INSURANCE COVERAGE			
Civilian noninstitutionalized population			
With private health insurance	50%	51.6%	38%
With public coverage	38.8%	43.5%	62.9%
No health insurance coverage	17.9%	11.5%	5.5%

Source: U.S. Census Bureau, 2014 American Community Survey 1-Year Estimates.
* Puerto Ricans only.

Puerto Ricans in New Jersey, 2014

In 2014, New Jersey was the third state with the most Puerto Ricans in the United States, behind the Puerto Rican population in Florida and New York. In 2014, the Puerto Rican population in New Jersey (468,200) was 5.2% of the total population. This represents an increase when compared to the years 2000 (4.4%) and 2010 (4.9%).

Graph 1.A: Latino Population New Jersey, 2014

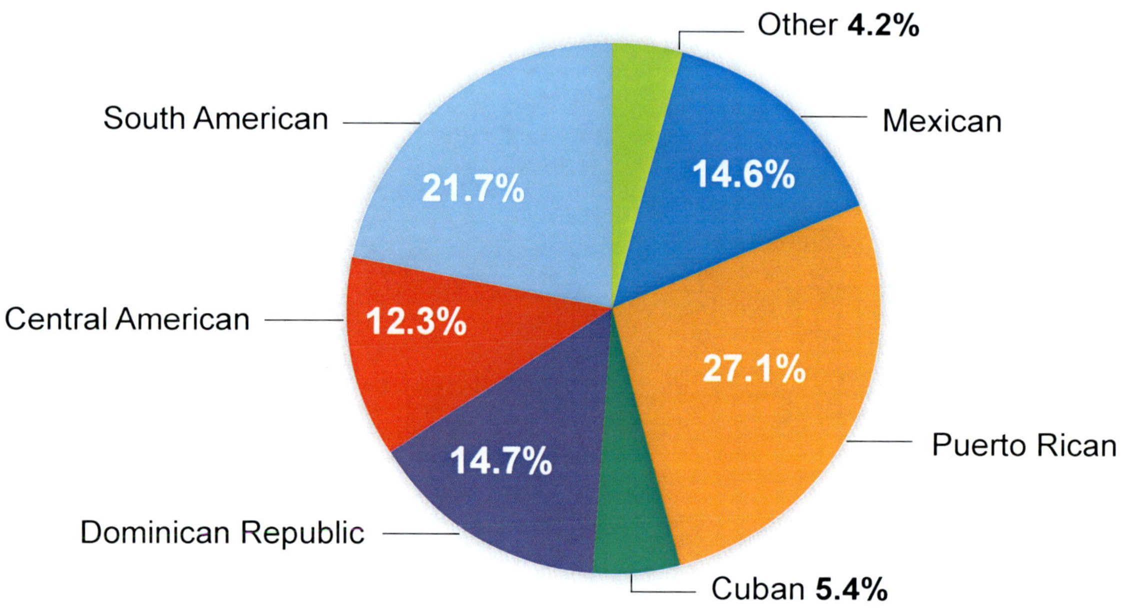

Table 1. Puerto Rican and Latino Population in New Jersey

	2000		2010		2014	
Total	8,414,350	100%	8,791,894	100%	8,938,175	100%
Not Hispanic or Latino	7,297,159	86.7%	7,236,750	82.3%	7,209,003	80.7%
Hispanic or Latino	1,117,191	13.3%	1,555,144	17.7%	1,729,172	19.4%
Mexican	260,889	3.1%	217,715	2.5%	252,206	2.8%
Puerto Rican	366,788	4.4%	434,092	4.9%	468,200	5.2%
Cuban	77,337	0.9%	83,362	0.9%	92,810	1%
Dominican Republic	102,630	1.2%	197,922	2.3%	255,013	2.9%
Central American	80,497	1%	176,611	2%	213,210	2.4%
South American	177,017	2.1%	325,179	3.7%	375,622	4.2%
Other	209,993	2.5%	120,263	1.4%	72,111	0.8%

Sources: U.S. Census Bureau, Census 2000 Summary File 1, 2010 Census. Summary File 1, and 2014 American Community Survey 1-Year Estimates.

New Jersey has one of the most diverse Latino populations in the country. The Latino population in New Jersey grew from 13.3% of the state's total population in 2000 to 19.4% in 2014. Puerto Ricans were 27.1% of total Latino population. After Puerto Ricans, Dominicans (14.7%), Mexicans (14.6%), Colombians (6.9%), and Ecuadorians (6.7%) constitute the next largest groups.

The median age of Puerto Ricans in New Jersey for 2014 was 29.9, one year older than the average for stateside Puerto Ricans of 28.9 years, and 9 years younger than the 38.9 median age in Puerto Rico. Similarly, 10.6% of Puerto Ricans in New Jersey were 62 years of age or older, a slightly higher proportion than stateside Puerto Ricans (9.9%) in this age group. With 21% of the population 62

Graph 2.A: Puerto Rican Education Attainment, 25 years and over, 2014

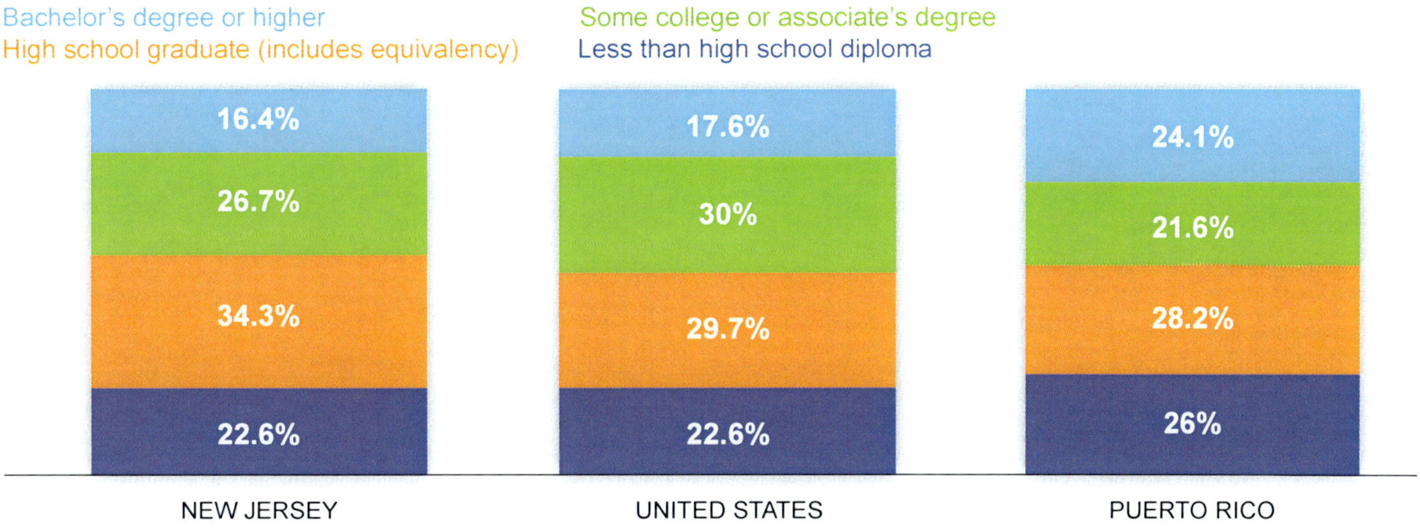

Table 2. Age, Education, and Language, 2014

Puerto Ricans	New Jersey	United States	Puerto Rico*
TOTAL POPULATION	468,200	5,266,738	3,404,122
Median age (years)	29.9	28.9	38.9
62 years and over	10.6%	9.9%	21%
EDUCATIONAL ATTAINMENT			
Population 25 years and over			
Less than high school diploma	22.6%	22.6%	26%
High school graduate (includes equivalency)	34.3%	29.7%	28.2%
Some college or associate's degree	26.7%	30%	21.6%
Bachelor's degree or higher	16.4%	17.6%	24.1%
Male, bachelor's degree or higher	13.9%	15.6%	19.6%
Female, bachelor's degree or higher	18.8%	19.5%	28.1%
LANGUAGE SPOKEN AT HOME AND ABILITY TO SPEAK ENGLISH			
Population 5 years and over			
English only	37.1%	38.8%	5.3%
Language other than English	62.9%	61.2%	94.7%
Speak English less than "very well"	16.3%	17.3%	78.8%

Source: U.S. Census Bureau, 2014 American Community Survey 1-Year Estimates.
* Puerto Ricans only.

years of age or older Puerto Rico, had a significantly higher proportion of the population in this age group.

In New Jersey, 37.1% of Puerto Ricans reported speaking only English at home, compared to the 38.8% average among stateside Puerto Ricans. About one in six Puerto Ricans in New Jersey (16.3%) identified as speaking English less than "very well"; this figure, though lower, was not very different than the stateside average of 17.3%.

Puerto Ricans in New Jersey had a much lower proportion, 16.4%, of individuals 25 years of age or older with bachelor's or higher degrees, than the 24.1% in Puerto Rico. Despite the lower rate of higher educational attainment, a higher proportion of Puerto Ricans in New Jersey had attained at least a high school diploma (77.4%) than in Puerto Rico (74%). New Jersey Puerto Ricans had a higher population proportion with just a high school diploma (34.3%) when compared to stateside Puerto Ricans (29.7%). There is a notable disparity of about ten percentage points between New Jersey Puerto Rican females holding a bachelor's degree or higher (18.8%) and females in Puerto Rico (28.1%). Educational attainment figures among Puerto Ricans in New Jersey were slightly lower than all stateside Puerto Ricans.

Table 3. Employment and Occupations, 2014

Puerto Ricans	New Jersey	United States	Puerto Rico*
EMPLOYMENT STATUS			
Population 16 years and over			
In labor force	65.9%	62.4%	43.7%
Civilian labor force	65.8%	61.6%	43.7%
Employed	59.2%	54.4%	35.4%
Unemployed	10%	11.6%	18.9%
Not in labor force	34.1%	37.6%	56.3%
Armed Forces	0.1%	0.8%	0%
OCCUPATION			
Civilian employed population 16 years and over			
Male	106,264	1,058,918	516,762
Management, business, science, and arts	21.1%	23.4%	23.9%
Service occupations	23.2%	22.5%	23%
Sales and office occupations	20.2%	19.6%	21.3%
Construction and maintenance	14%	13.8%	18%
Production, transportation, and moving	21.6%	20.7%	13.7%
Female	94,911	999,105	456,356
Management, business, science, and arts	35.8%	33.1%	39.7%
Service occupations	23%	24.4%	16.6%
Sales and office occupations	35%	35.7%	38.3%
Construction and maintenance	0.3%	0.6%	0.6%
Production, transportation, and moving	5.9%	6.2%	4.8%
CLASS OF WORKER			
Civilian employed population 16 years and over			
Private wage and salary workers	82.4%	82%	69%
Government workers	14.6%	14.8%	22.5%
Self-employed workers in own not incorporated business	2.8%	3.1%	8.3%
VETERAN STATUS			
Civilian population 18 years and over			
Civilian veteran	3.7%	6%	3.3%

Source: U.S. Census Bureau, 2014 American Community Survey 1-Year Estimates. * Puerto Ricans only.

Besides education, it is also important to examine the occupational distribution of Puerto Ricans in various regions of the country and the island. The data by major occupational category indicated that the structure of Puerto Rican employment in New Jersey was similar to that of other stateside Puerto Ricans and those in Puerto Rico. However, there is a striking contrast in the occupational distribution between men and women. In 2014, 35.8% of women in New Jersey were employed in management, business, science, and arts occupations compared to 21.1% of men. These are typically the highest compensation and benefits occupations. The proportion of women in the higher occupational strata in New Jersey of 35.8% was slightly higher than for other stateside women of 33.1%, but the proportion for men in New Jersey was slightly lower (21.1%) than for stateside Puerto Ricans (23.4%). Similarly, women were overwhelmingly overrepresented in sales and office occupations, while men were overrepresented in production, transportation, and moving, and construction and maintenance occupations.

The employment status of Puerto Ricans in New Jersey was four percentage points higher than for stateside Puerto Ricans overall, but they also participated more actively in the labor force and had a lower unemploy ment rate when compared to Puerto Ricans in the U.S. as a whole

Table 4. Income and Earnings, 2014

Puerto Ricans	New Jersey	United States	Puerto Rico*
INCOME IN THE PAST 12 MONTHS (IN 2013 INFLATION-ADJUSTED DOLLARS)			
Households	145,808	1,635,808	1,175,297
Median household income (dollars)	$46,889	$39,322	$18,710
With earnings	80.4%	76.9%	54.7%
Mean earnings (dollars)	$72,239	$61,065	$36,407
With Social Security income	25%	24.1%	43.2%
Mean Social Security income (dollars)	$14,183	$13,727	$12,159
With Supplemental Security Income	9.4%	12.6%	0.4%
Mean Supplemental Security Income (dollars)	$7,923	$8,780	$10,025
With cash public assistance income	6.5%	6.9%	8.1%
Mean cash public assistance income (dollars)	$2,885	$3,441	$2,316
With retirement income	8.9%	10.1%	15.6%
Mean retirement income (dollars)	$20,431	$20,452	$15,387
With Food Stamp/SNAP benefits	23.9%	31.5%	39.7%
Families	104,535	1,114,628	830,807
Median family income (dollars)	$54,355	$44,499	$22,220
Married-couple family	55.4%	53.9%	56.1%
Median income (dollars)	$85,225	$67,129	$29,417
Male householder, no spouse present	10.6%	10.2%	9.5%
Median income (dollars)	$45,840	$37,513	$17,797
Female householder, no husband present	34%	35.9%	34.4%
Median income (dollars)	$28,142	$23,957	$13,554
Individuals	468,200	5,266,738	3,404,122
Per capita income (dollars)	$21,401	$18,457	$10,960
Mean earnings (dollars) for full-time, year-round workers:			
Male	$55,051	$50,756	$32,512
Female	$46,412	$42,263	$29,166

Source: U.S. Census Bureau, 2014 American Community Survey 1-Year Estimates.
* Puerto Ricans only.

and those in Puerto Rico. The employment rate of stateside and New Jersey Puerto Ricans (54.4% and 59.2%, respectively) was between 19 and 23.8 percent points higher than the similar rate in Puerto Rico of 35.4%. The disparity in unemployment was equally significant. In 2014, the unemployment rate among New Jersey Puerto Ricans stood at 10% of those in the labor force. In contrast, the unemployment rate for Puerto Ricans in Puerto Rico was 18.9%, considerably higher than the rate among New Jersey Puerto Ricans and all stateside Puerto Ricans (11.6%).

The average earnings of full-time, year-round of Puerto Ricans in New Jersey of $55,501 and $46,412 were higher than for stateside Puerto Ricans of $50,756 for men and $42,263 for women. Earnings for Puerto Ricans in New Jersey were also substantially higher than for Puerto Rico where full-time, year-round working men in 2014 earned $32,512 and women earned $29,166.

Household and family income are important indicators of economic well-being. These indicators were higher for Puerto Ricans in New Jersey than for stateside Puerto Ricans, and more then doubled that of the island. Median household income was $46,889 for Puerto Ricans in New Jersey and $39,322 for other stateside Puerto Ricans, and $18,710 for the island. These differences were also evident in per capita income. In 2014, per capita income for Puerto Ricans in New Jersey was $21,401 and $18,457 for other stateside Puerto Ricans, and $10,960 for the island.

Graph 4.A: Mean Earnings for Full-Time, Year-Round Puerto Rican Workers, 2014

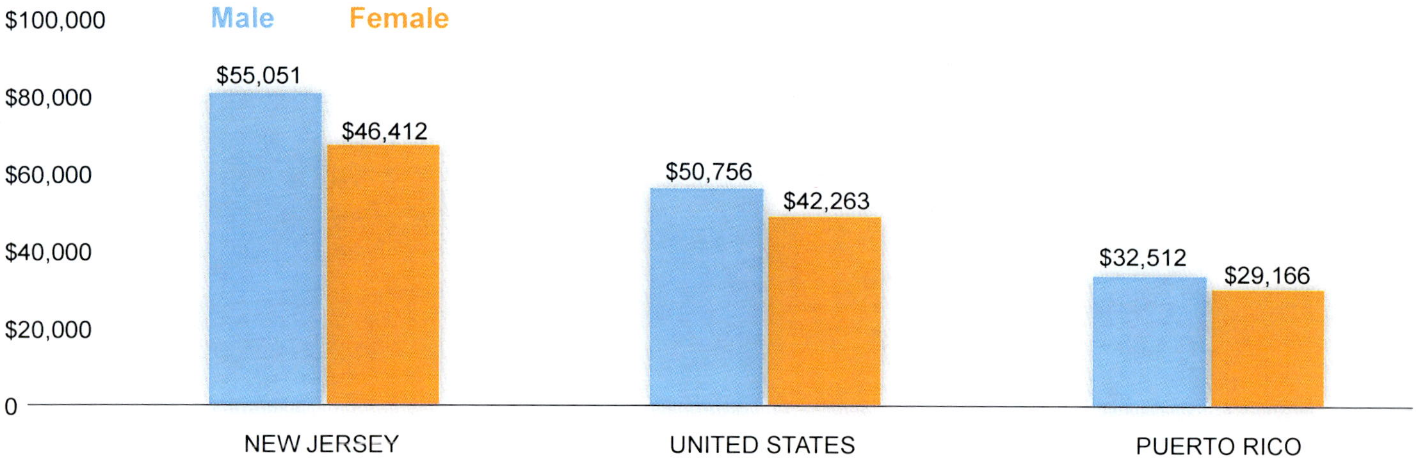

Graph 4.B: Puerto Rican Purchasing Power, in Billions, 2014

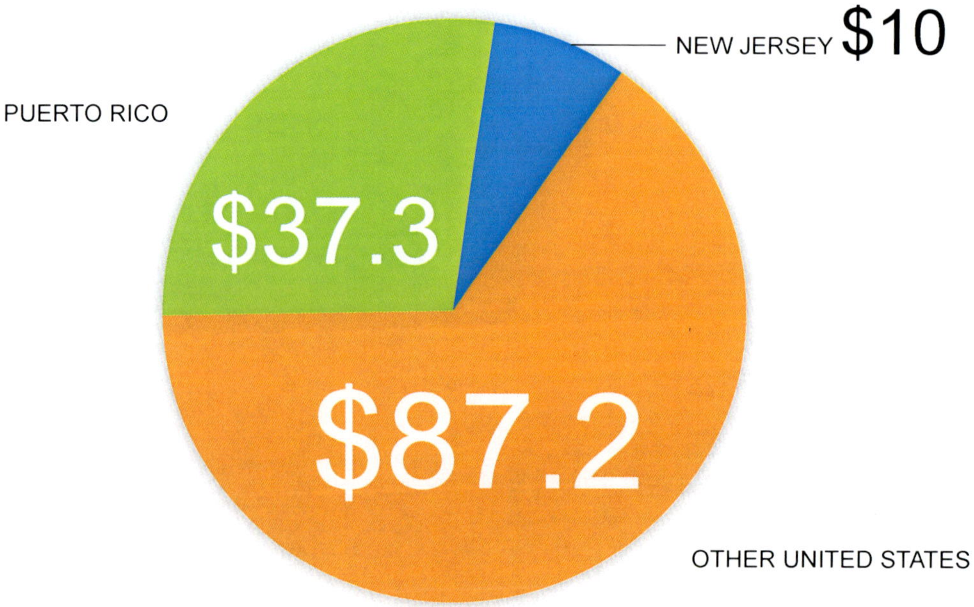

Puerto Rican Population by Counties in New Jersey, 2014

The nearly half million Puerto Ricans in New Jersey accounted for about five percent of New Jersey's population, with over half (57.3%) living in the NYC metropolitan region (consisting of Hudson, Essex, Middlesex, Passaic, Bergen, and Union counties). Puerto Ricans were disproportionately present in New Jersey's most urban counties, such as Hudson, Essex, Middlesex, Passaic, and Union, when compared the total population of New Jersey. Outside of the NYC metropolitan region, most Puerto Ricans in New Jersey were present in the urban areas to the south of New Jersey within the Philadelphia metropolitan region in Camden County (9.5%), Cumberland County (5.3%), and Atlantic County (4.5%). Puerto Ricans were underrepresented in the four middle counties of New Jersey (Burlington Mercer, Monmouth, and Ocean).

COUNTY	Puerto Rican Population	Percent	Latino Population	Percent	Total Population	Percent
Hudson County	58,396	12.7%	279,712	17%	654,878	7.4%
Essex County	56,891	12.4%	168,373	10.2%	789,616	8.9%
Middlesex County	48,037	10.4%	158,164	9.6%	824,046	9.3%
Camden County	43,538	9.5%	76,956	4.7%	512,632	5.8%
Passaic County	42,526	9.2%	194,313	11.8%	505,403	5.7%
Bergen County	30,155	6.6%	160,193	9.7%	920,456	10.4%
Union County	27,417	6%	157,092	9.5%	545,236	6.1%
Cumberland County	24,224	5.3%	44,369	2.7%	157,429	1.8%
Atlantic County	20,583	4.5%	48,865	3%	275,325	3.1%
Monmouth County	18,451	4%	63,488	3.8%	629,702	7.1%
Mercer County	17,591	3.8%	58,733	3.6%	369,526	4.2%
Ocean County	16,700	3.6%	50,206	3%	581,413	6.6%
Burlington County	14,732	3.2%	31,743	1.9%	450,155	5.1%
Morris County	11,594	2.5%	60,488	3.7%	497,103	5.6%
Somerset County	8,161	1.8%	44,972	2.7%	328,704	3.7%
Gloucester County	7,596	1.7%	15,120	0.9%	289,705	3.3%
Sussex County	3,782	0.8%	10,105	0.6%	146,888	1.7%
Cape May County	2,596	0.6%	6,504	0.4%	96,286	1.1%
Warren County	2,573	0.6%	8,293	0.5%	107,624	1.2%
Hunterdon County	2,323	0.5%	7,213	0.4%	126,746	1.4%
Salem County	1,927	0.4%	4,882	0.3%	65,501	0.7%
Total	**459,793**	**100%**	**1,649,784**	**100%**	**8,874,374**	**100%**

Sources: U.S. Census Bureau and 2014 American Community Survey 5-Year Estimates
Notes: Total counts for populations may differ depending on whether the estimates are derived from the five-year estimates or the one-year estimates of the American Community Survey

PUERTO RICAN POPULATION BY COUNTIES IN NEW JERSEY, 2014

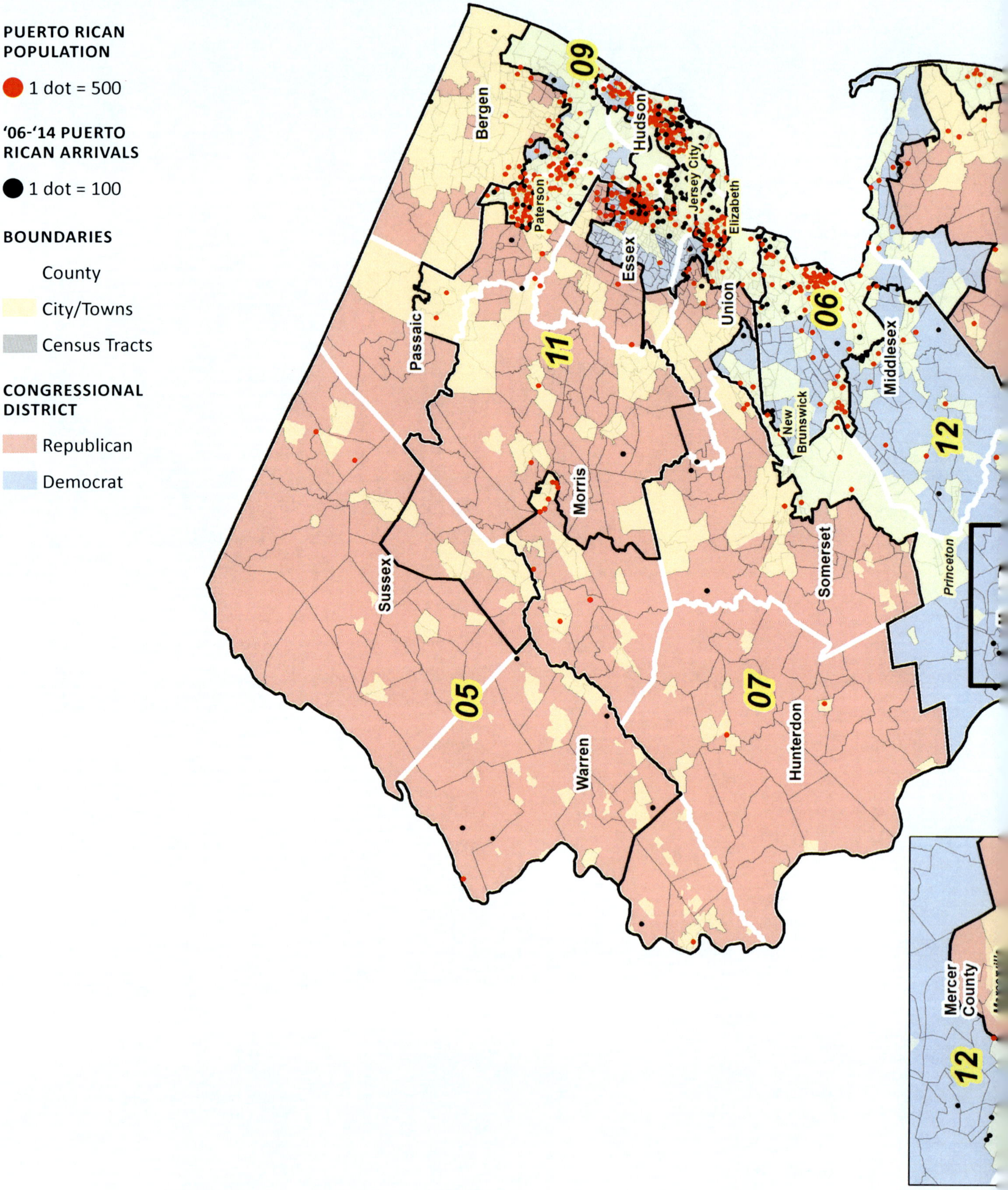

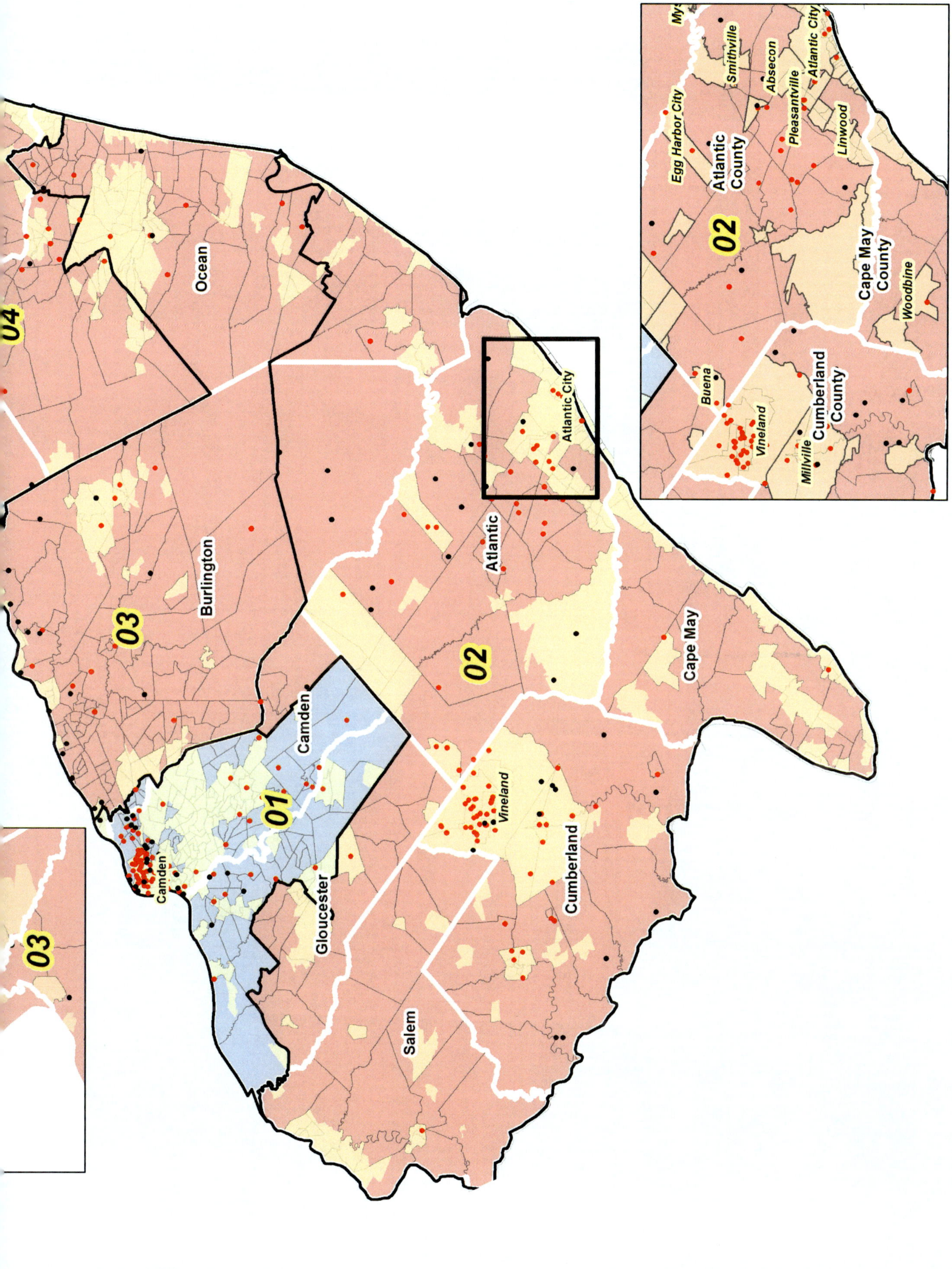
Ocean
04
Burlington
03
Camden
01
Camden
Gloucester
Salem
Cumberland
Vineland
02
Atlantic
Atlantic City
Cape May
Egg Harbor City
Smithville
Absecon
Pleasantville
Atlantic City
Linwood
Atlantic County
02
Cape May County
Woodbine
Buena
Vineland
Cumberland County
Millville
03

PUERTO RICAN POPULATION BY COUNTIES IN NEW JERSEY, 2014

PUERTO RICAN POPULATION

1 dot = 500

'06-'14 PUERTO RICAN ARRIVALS

1 dot = 100

BOUNDARIES

County

City/Towns

Census Tracts

CONGRESSIONAL DISTRICT

Republican

Democrat

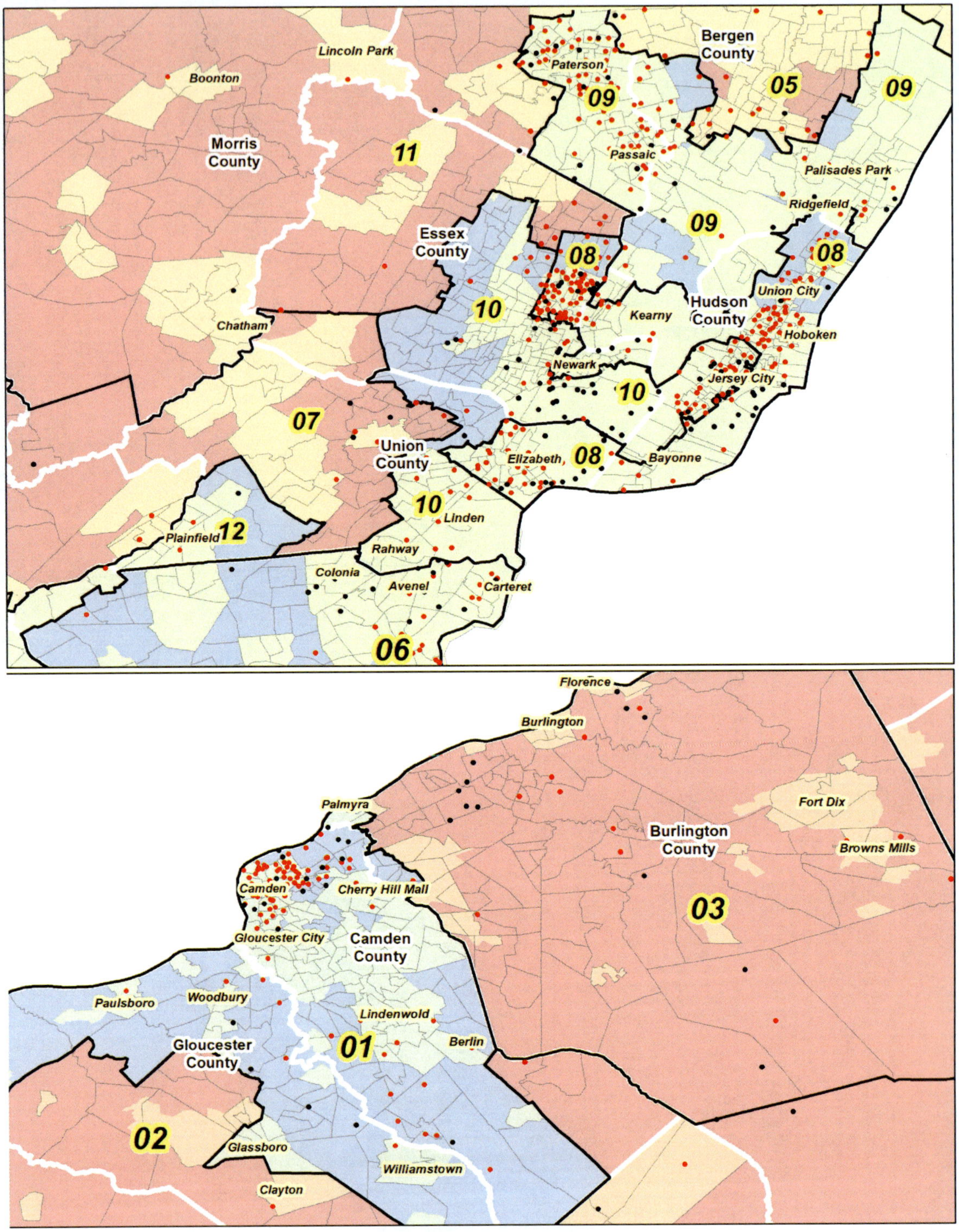

Graph 5.A: Poverty Rates, 2014

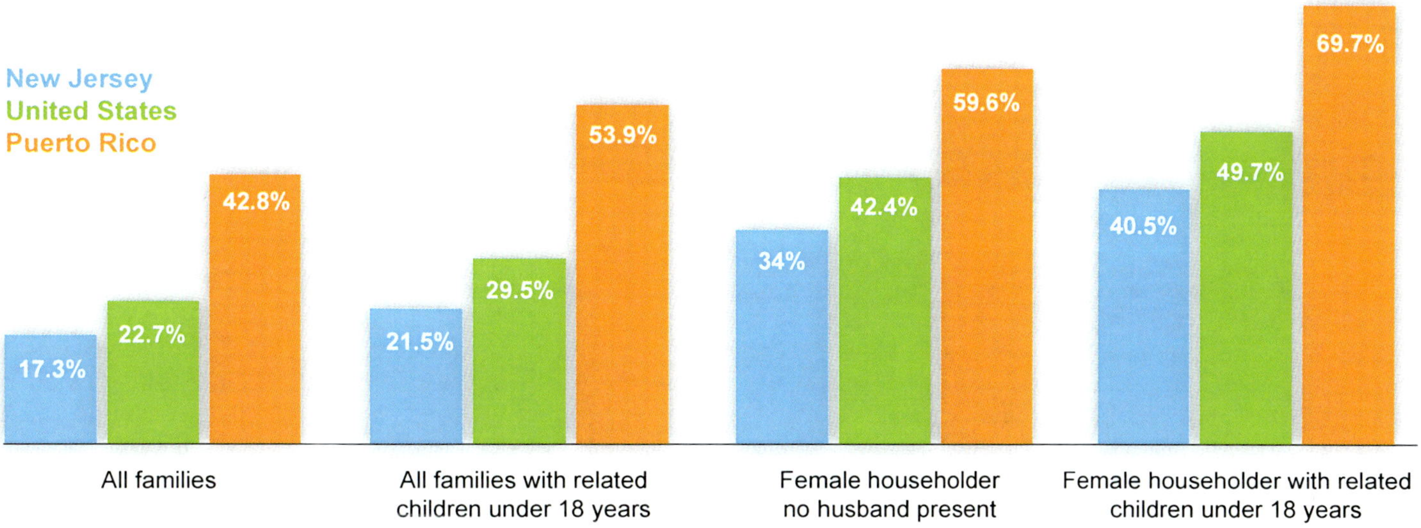

Table 5. Poverty, 2014

Puerto Ricans	New Jersey	United States	Puerto Rico*
POVERTY RATES			
All families	17.3%	22.7%	42.8%
With related children under 18 years	21.5%	29.5%	53.9%
With related children under 5 years only	23.8%	24.6%	57.1%
Married-couple family	6.4%	9.7%	30.9%
With related children under 18 years	6%	11.3%	35.5%
With related children under 5 years only	N	5.9%	33.9%
Female householder, no husband present, family	34%	42.4%	59.6%
With related children under 18 years	40.5%	49.7%	69.7%
With related children under 5 years only	52.8%	49.4%	75.7%
All people	19.8%	26.2%	46.6%
Under 18 years	26.8%	33.4%	58.7%
Related children under 18 years	26.5%	33.1%	58.6%
Related children under 5 years	29.8%	34.7%	62.8%
Related children 5 to 17 years	25.1%	32.4%	57.3%
18 years and over	16.7%	22.8%	43.2%
18 to 64 years	16.2%	22.8%	43.8%
65 years and over	20.5%	22.4%	41%
People in families	17.9%	23.6%	44.6%
Unrelated individuals 15 years and over	31.3%	38.5%	58.6%

Source: U.S. Census Bureau, 2014 American Community Survey 1-Year Estimates.
* Puerto Ricans only. N= No Observations.

Puerto Ricans in New Jersey had $10.0 billion in purchasing power and represented a significant potential market for trade, investments, tourism in general and medical tourism in particular, and other economic activities in the island. From an economic perspective, stateside Puerto Ricans represented 72.3% of the $134.5 billion total purchasing power of the entire Puerto Rican community in the year 2014. Purchasing power was defined simply as per capita income multiplied by the Puerto Rican population.

In 2014, the proportion of households that received cash public assistance income of 6.5% was not much different for Puerto Ricans in New Jersey than a comparable rate of 6.9% for other stateside Puerto Ricans, but lower than the 8.1% in Puerto Rico. In addition, the differences in the amount that the households received by public assistance were higher for stateside Puerto Ricans ($3,441) than for Puerto Ricans in New Jersey ($2,885). The proportion of Puerto Rican households in New Jersey receiving benefits from the Supplemental Nutrition Assistance Program (SNAP) was 23.9% in 2014, 7.6 percentage points lower than the 31.5% rate for Puerto Rican households in other parts of the U.S. and 15.8 percentage points lower than the 39.7% for Puerto Rico.

The poverty rate for all Puerto Rican families in New Jersey was 17.3% - lower than the 22.7% average for all stateside Puerto Ricans, and the 42.8% rate in Puerto Rico. These disparities in poverty widened in specific, more vulnerable subgroups. Among Puerto Rican households with a female householder and no husband present, the poverty rate in New Jersey was 34%, alarmingly high, but almost half of Puerto Rico's poverty rate in the same subgroup of 59.6%. In female led households with children under 18 years, the poverty rate among New Jersey Puerto Ricans was 40.5% — alarmingly high, but close to 30 percentage points below Puerto Rico's 69.7% poverty rate for the same population subgroup. Despite the substantial differences in poverty rates, the rates seen in the aforementioned subgroups are egregiously high in whatever context or comparison.

Housing is a primary determinant of the cost of living. In general, the Northeast has higher cost of home ownership than the South or other parts of the country. The median value of owner-occupied housing for Puerto Ricans in New Jersey was $254,000, compared to $175,900 for other stateside Puerto Ricans, and $119,500 in Puerto Rico. The median monthly owner costs with a mortgage was $2,117 for Puerto Ricans in New Jersey, and $1,545 for other stateside Puerto Ricans. A comparable cost was $873 in Puerto Rico. These relative prices and ownership costs were reflected in ownership rates. Puerto Ricans in New Jersey had lower rates of home ownership than Puerto Ricans in Puerto Rico. The Census data evealed that Puerto Ricans in New Jersey had a 38.7% rate of owner-occupied housing units, while the comparable rate for stateside Puerto Ricans was 36%. The home ownership rate in Puerto Rico was much higher, at 68.7%.

Table 6. Housing and Health Insurance, 2014

Puerto Ricans	New Jersey	United States	Puerto Rico*
HOUSING			
Owner-occupied housing units	38.7%	36%	68.7%
Monthly owner costs as a percentage of household income in the past 12 months			
Less than 30 percent	57.8%	62.8%	52.6%
30 percent or more	42.2%	37.2%	47.4%
Owner-occupied housing units			
Median value (dollars)	$254,000	$175,900	$119,500
Median selected monthly owner costs with a mortgage (dollars)	$2,117	$1,545	$873
HEALTH INSURANCE COVERAGE			
Civilian noninstitutionalized population			
With private health insurance	57.5%	51.6%	38%
With public coverage	36.3%	43.5%	62.9%
No health insurance coverage	11.3%	11.5%	5.5%

Source: U.S. Census Bureau, 2014 American Community Survey 1-Year Estimates.
* Puerto Ricans only.

Puerto Ricans in Pennsylvania, 2014

In 2014, Pennsylvania was the fourth state with most Puerto Ricans in the U.S. (423,755), accounting for 8% of all Puerto Ricans in the U.S. The Puerto Rican population in Pennsylvania was 3.3% of the state's total population. This represents an increase when compared to the years 2000 (1.9%) and 2010 (2.9%). Puerto Ricans represented half of the Latinos in the state in 2014.

Graph 1.A: Latino Population Pennsylvania 2014

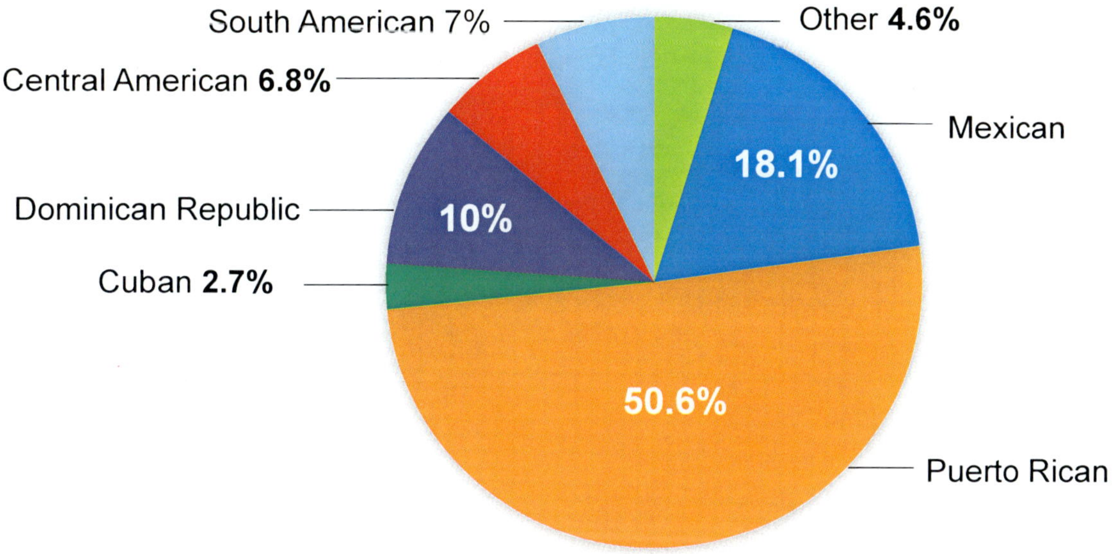

Table 1. Puerto Rican and Latino Population in Pennsylvania

	2000		2010		2014	
Total	12,281,054	100%	12,702,379	100%	12,787,209	100%
Not Hispanic or Latino	11,886,966	96.8%	11,982,719	94.3%	11,949,722	93.5%
Hispanic or Latino	394,088	3.2%	719,660	5.7%	837,487	6.6%
Mexican	55,187	0.4%	129,568	1%	151,830	1.2%
Puerto Rican	228,557	1.9%	366,082	2.9%	423,755	3.3%
Cuban	10,363	0.1%	17,930	0.1%	22,325	0.2%
Dominican Republic	12,186	0.1%	62,348	0.5%	83,820	0.7%
Central American	9,845	0.1%	35,453	0.3%	56,737	0.4%
South American	18,268	0.1%	48,126	0.4%	58,583	0.5%
Other	59,691	0.5%	60,153	0.5%	40,437	0.3%

Sources: U.S. Census Bureau, Census 2000 Summary File 1, 2010 Census. Summary File 1, and 2014 American Community Survey 1-Year Estimates.

The Latino population in Pennsylvania doubled from 3.2% of the state's total population in 2000 to 6.6% in 2014. Puerto Ricans grew from 228,557 to 423,755, an 85% rate of growth. In 2014 Puerto Ricans were the largest national origin Latino group with 50.6% of total Latino population, followed by Mexicans (18.1%) and Dominicans (10%).

Puerto Ricans in Pennsylvania are on average much younger than other stateside Puerto Ricans and those in the island. The median age of Puerto Ricans in Pennsylvania for the year 2014 was 25.5 years, 3.4 years lower than the median for stateside Puerto Ricans (28.9 years) and 13.4 years lower than the 38.9 median age in

Graph 2.A: Puerto Rican Education Attainment, 25 years and over, 2014

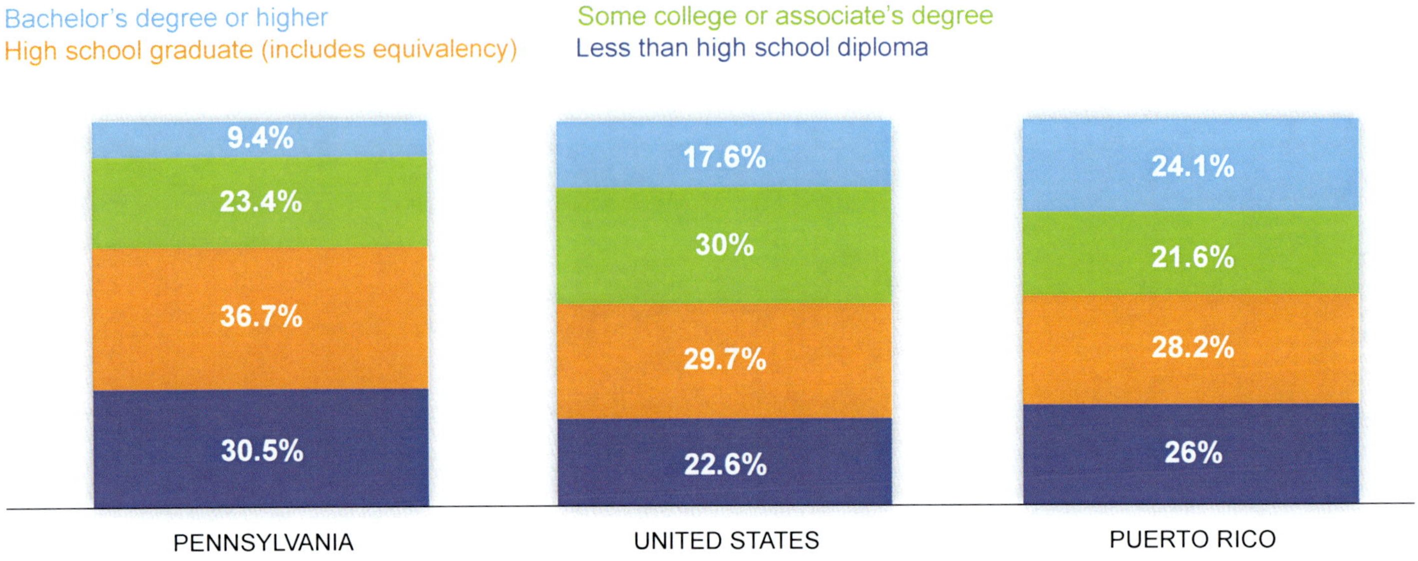

Table 2. Age, Education, and Language, 2014

Puerto Ricans	Pennsylvania	United States	Puerto Rico*
TOTAL POPULATION	423,755	5,266,738	3,404,122
Median age (years)	25.5%	28.9%	38.9%
EDUCATIONAL ATTAINMENT			
Population 25 years and over			
Less than high school diploma	30.5%	22.6%	26%
High school graduate (includes equivalency)	36.7%	29.7%	28.2%
Some college or associate's degree	23.4%	30%	21.6%
Bachelor's degree or higher	9.4%	17.6%	24.1%
Male, bachelor's degree or higher	7.1%	15.6%	19.6%
Female, bachelor's degree or higher	11.6%	19.5%	28.1%
LANGUAGE SPOKEN AT HOME AND ABILITY TO SPEAK ENGLISH			
Population 5 years and over			
English only	37.5%	38.8%	5.3%
Language other than English	62.5%	61.2%	94.7%
Speak English less than "very well"	22.1%	17.3%	78.8%

Source: U.S. Census Bureau, 2014 American Community Survey 1-Year Estimates. * Puerto Ricans only.

Puerto Rico. These differences in the age structure were evident in the percent of the population older than 62 years of age: 6.5% of Puerto Ricans in Pennsylvania were 62 years of age or older, which is a lower percentage than for all stateside Puerto Ricans (9.9%). With 21% of the population 62 years of age or older, Puerto Rico had a significantly higher proportion of the population in this age group.

In Pennsylvania, 37.5% of the Puerto Ricans reported speaking only English at home, a figure close to 38.8% of Puerto Ricans across all states. However, a higher proportion of Puerto Ricans in Pennsylvania claimed to speak English less than "very well" (22.1%) than all stateside Puerto Ricans (17.3%).

Overall, Puerto Ricans in Pennsylvania had lesser educational attainment indicators than both stateside and island Puerto Ricans. Puerto Ricans in Pennsylvania had a lower proportion of individuals 25 years of age or older with bachelor's or graduate degrees (9.4%) than all stateside Puerto Ricans (17.7%), and Puerto Ricans in Puerto Rico (24.1%). While there is a pronounced difference in higher educational attainment, this difference is most pronounced difference

Table 3. Employment and Occupations, 2014

Puerto Ricans	Pennsylvania	United States	Puerto Rico*
EMPLOYMENT STATUS			
Population 16 years and over			
In labor force	58.1%	62.4%	43.7%
Civilian labor force	58.1%	61.6%	43.7%
Employed	48.2%	54.4%	35.4%
Unemployed	17%	11.6%	18.9%
Not in labor force	41.9%	37.6%	56.3%
Armed Forces	0%	0.8%	0%
OCCUPATION			
Civilian employed population 16 years and over			
Male	69,295	1,058,918	516,762
Management, business, science, and arts	14.3%	23.4%	23.9%
Service occupations	20.9%	22.5%	23%
Sales and office occupations	15.7%	19.6%	21.3%
Construction and maintenance	12.2%	13.8%	18%
Production, transportation, and moving	36.9%	20.7%	13.7%
Female	69,020	999,105	456,356
Management, business, science, and arts	25.5%	33.1%	39.7%
Service occupations	29.1%	24.4%	16.6%
Sales and office occupations	30.3%	35.7%	38.3%
Construction and maintenance	0.5%	0.6%	0.6%
Production, transportation, and moving	14.7%	6.2%	4.8%
CLASS OF WORKER			
Civilian employed population 16 years and over			
Private wage and salary workers	87.4%	82%	69%
Government workers	10%	14.8%	22.5%
Self-employed workers in own not incorporated business	2.6%	3.1%	8.3%
VETERAN STATUS			
Civilian population 18 years and over			
Civilian veteran	3.2%	6%	3.3%

Source: U.S. Census Bureau, 2014 American Community Survey 1-Year Estimates.
* Puerto Ricans only.

among men. Only 7.1% of Puerto Rican males in Pennsylvania earned a bachelor's degree or higher compared to 15.6% among all stateside Puerto Rican males and 19.6% of Puerto Rican males in Puerto Rico. Similarly, the proportion of Puerto Rican women in Pennsylvania with a bachelor's degree or higher (11.6%) was lower than the average for Puerto Rican stateside women (19.5%) and that of Puerto Rican women in Puerto Rico (28.1%).

The data by major occupational category indicate that the structure of Puerto Rican employment in Pennsylvania in 2014 was different from that of other stateside Puerto Ricans and those in Puerto Rico. In Pennsylvania, the proportion of male (14.3%) and female (25.5%) Puerto Ricans working in the management, business, science, and arts sector was lower than in stateside Puerto Ricans (23.4% and 33.1%, respectively) and in Puerto Rico (23.9% and 39.7%, respectively). Puerto Ricans in Pennsylvania were more present in the production, transportation and material moving occupations (25.8%). In terms of industries, their greater representation in manufacturing industries was twice the average rate (17.6%) than for all Puerto Ricans in the United States (8.4%).

The employment rate of Puerto Ricans in Pennsylvania (48.2%) was lower than the stateside Puerto Rican average (54.4%). Puerto Ricans in Pennsylvania had a lower rate of labor force participation (58.1%) than other

Table 4. Income and Earnings, 2014

Puerto Ricans	Pennsylvania	United States	Puerto Rico*
INCOME IN THE PAST 12 MONTHS (IN 2013 INFLATION-ADJUSTED DOLLARS)			
Households	120,553	1,635,808	1,175,297
Median household income (dollars)	$30,385	$39,322	$18,710
With earnings	72.1%	76.9%	54.7%
Mean earnings (dollars)	$49,487	$61,065	$36,407
With Social Security income	24.5%	24.1%	43.2%
Mean Social Security income (dollars)	$10,920	$13,727	$12,159
With Supplemental Security Income	21.7%	12.6%	0.4%
Mean Supplemental Security Income (dollars)	$9,064	$8,780	$10,025
With cash public assistance income	12.1%	6.9%	8.1%
Mean cash public assistance income (dollars)	$3,162	$3,441	$2,316
With retirement income	6.6%	10.1%	15.6%
Mean retirement income (dollars)	17,114	20,452	15,387
With Food Stamp/SNAP benefits	45.2%	31.5%	39.7%
Families	83,608	1,114,628	830,807
Median family income (dollars)	$31,819	$44,499	$22,220
Married-couple family	42.2%	53.9%	56.1%
Median income (dollars)	$56,412	$67,129	$29,417
Male householder, no spouse present	8.9%	10.2%	9.5%
Median income (dollars)	$31,586	$37,513	$17,797
Female householder, no husband present	48.9%	35.9%	34.4%
Median income (dollars)	$20,488	$23,957	$13,554
Individuals	423,755	5,266,738	3,404,122
Per capita income (dollars)	$13,559	$18,457	$10,960
Mean earnings (dollars) for full-time, year-round workers:			
Male	$13,559	$18,457	$10,960
Female	$37,810	$42,263	$29,166

Source: U.S. Census Bureau, 2014 American Community Survey 1-Year Estimates. * Puerto Ricans only.

Puerto Rican Population by Counties in Pennsylvania, 2014

Most Puerto Ricans in Pennsylvania are settled in the eastern part of the state. In 2014, one out of three Puerto Ricans in Pennsylvania (32.7%) resided in Philadelphia County. Lehigh and Berks Counties each accounted for about 10% of Pennsylvania's Puerto Rican population and neighboring Lancaster County accounted for another 8.1%. These four counties together accounted for more than half of Pennsylvania Puerto Ricans. Census data revealed Puerto Rican clustering around the urban centers of southeastern Pennsylvania including Philadelphia (Philadelphia County), Reading (Berks County), and Allentown (Lehigh County). Allegheny County accounted for 9.6% of the total population, but only 1.4% of Pennsylvania Puerto Ricans indicating the sharpest underrepresentation around Pittsburgh and the western areas of the state. Over half of Philadelphia's Latino population was Puerto Rican and geographic placement of all Latinos closely mirrored that of Puerto Ricans.

COUNTY	Puerto Rican Population	Percent	Latino Population	Percent	Total Population	Percent
Philadelphia County	133,044	32.7%	201,575	25.7%	1,546,920	12.1%
Lehigh County	41,196	10.1%	71,984	9.2%	354,537	2.8%
Berks County	39,627	9.8%	72,707	9.3%	413,016	3.2%
Lancaster County	32,835	8.1%	48,984	6.2%	526,839	4.1%
Northampton County	19,562	4.8%	33,782	4.3%	299,225	2.3%
York County	14,949	3.7%	26,767	3.4%	438,052	3.4%
Monroe County	12,312	3%	23,410	3%	168,342	1.3%
Bucks County	12,069	3%	28,853	3.7%	626,205	4.9%
Dauphin County	11,460	2.8%	20,680	2.6%	269,946	2.1%
Montgomery County	11,171	2.7%	36,590	4.7%	809,372	6.3%
Lebanon County	9,991	2.5%	14,110	1.8%	135,184	1.1%
Chester County	7,424	1.8%	34,542	4.4%	506,422	4%
Delaware County	6,955	1.7%	18,273	2.3%	560,775	4.4%
Erie County	6,035	1.5%	10,186	1.3%	280,132	2.2%
Luzerne County	5,856	1.4%	25,629	3.3%	320,392	2.5%
Lackawanna County	5,737	1.4%	12,021	1.5%	214,023	1.7%
Allegheny County	5,687	1.4%	21,344	2.7%	1,229,172	9.6%
Other Counties	30,427	7.5%	83,125	10.6%	4,060,175	31.8%
Total	**406,337**	**100%**	**784,562**	**100%**	**12,758,729**	**100%**

Sources: U.S. Census Bureau and 2014 American Community Survey 5-Year Estimates
Notes: Total counts for populations may differ depending on whether the estimates are derived from the five-year estimates or the one-year estimates of the American Community Survey. Counties with less than 1% of the total Puerto Rican population were omitted.

PUERTO RICAN POPULATION BY COUNTIES IN PENNSYLVANIA, 2014

PUERTO RICAN POPULATION

1 dot = 100

'06-'14 PUERTO RICAN ARRIVALS

1 dot = 100

BOUNDARIES

County

City/Towns

Census Tracts

CONGRESSIONAL DISTRICT

Republican

Democrat

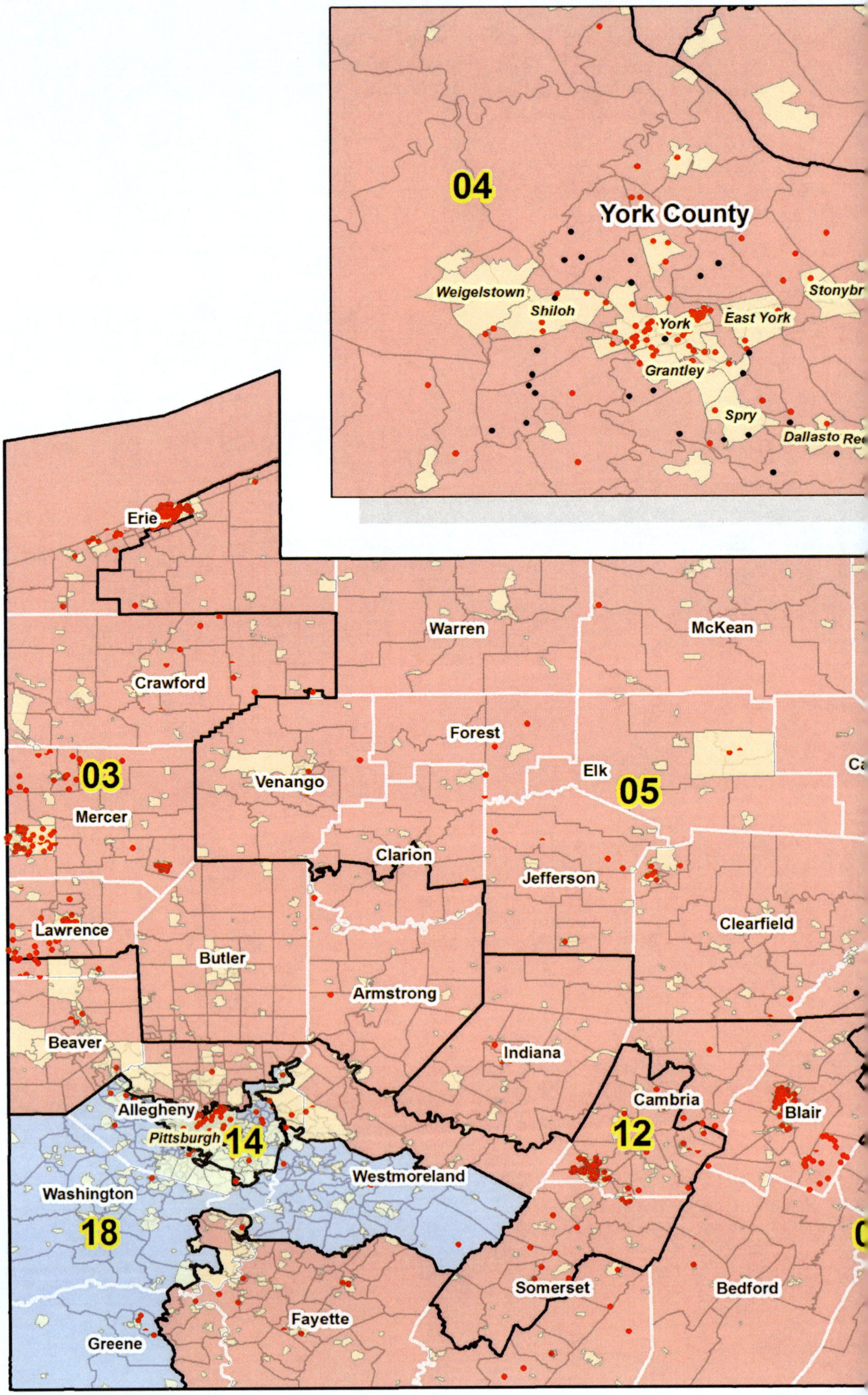

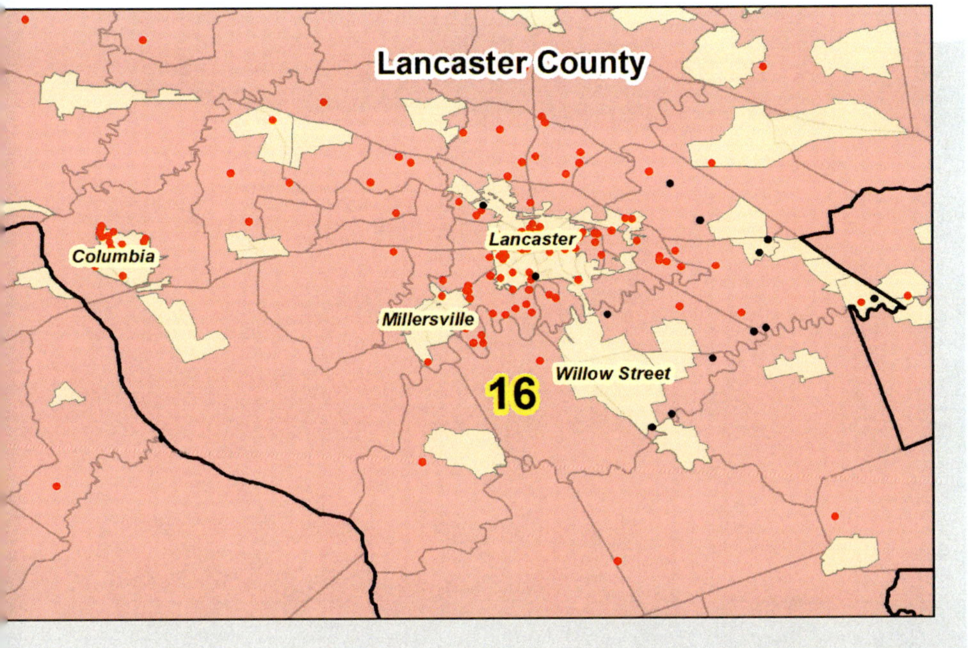
Lancaster County
Columbia
Lancaster
Millersville
Willow Street
16

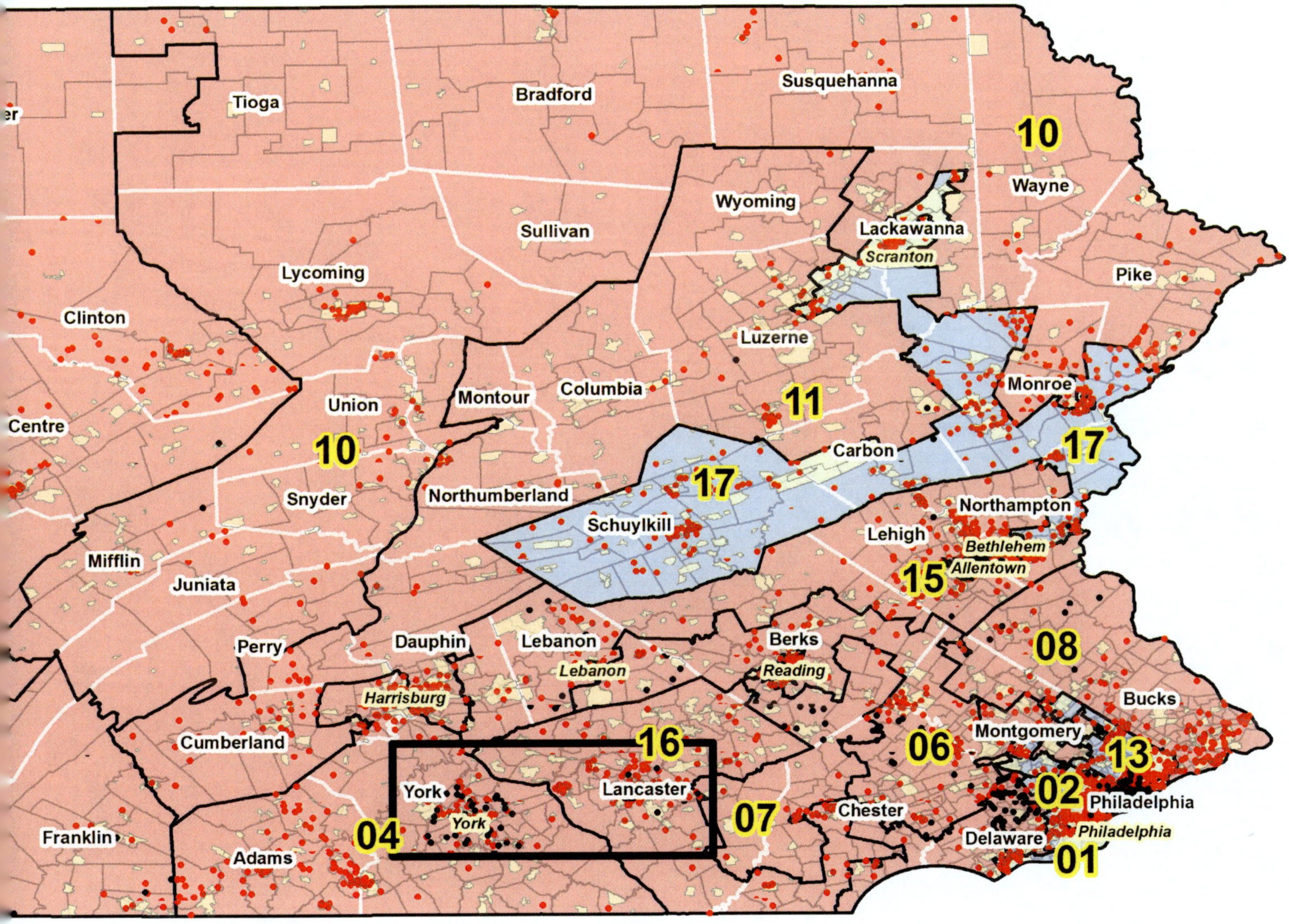
Tioga
Bradford
Susquehanna
10
Wayne
Wyoming
Sullivan
Lackawanna
Scranton
Pike
Lycoming
Clinton
Luzerne
Monroe
Union
Montour
Columbia
11
Centre
10
Carbon
17
17
Snyder
Northumberland
Northampton
Schuylkill
Lehigh
Bethlehem
Mifflin
Allentown
15
Juniata
08
Perry
Dauphin
Lebanon
Berks
Lebanon
Reading
Bucks
Harrisburg
Montgomery
16
13
Cumberland
06
02
York
Lancaster
Philadelphia
07
Chester
York
Franklin
04
Delaware
Philadelphia
Adams
01

PUERTO RICAN POPULATION BY COUNTIES IN PENNSYLVANIA, 2014

PUERTO RICAN POPULATION

1 dot = 100

'06-'14 PUERTO RICAN ARRIVALS

1 dot = 100

BOUNDARIES

County

City/Towns

Census Tracts

CONGRESSIONAL DISTRICT

Republican

Democrat

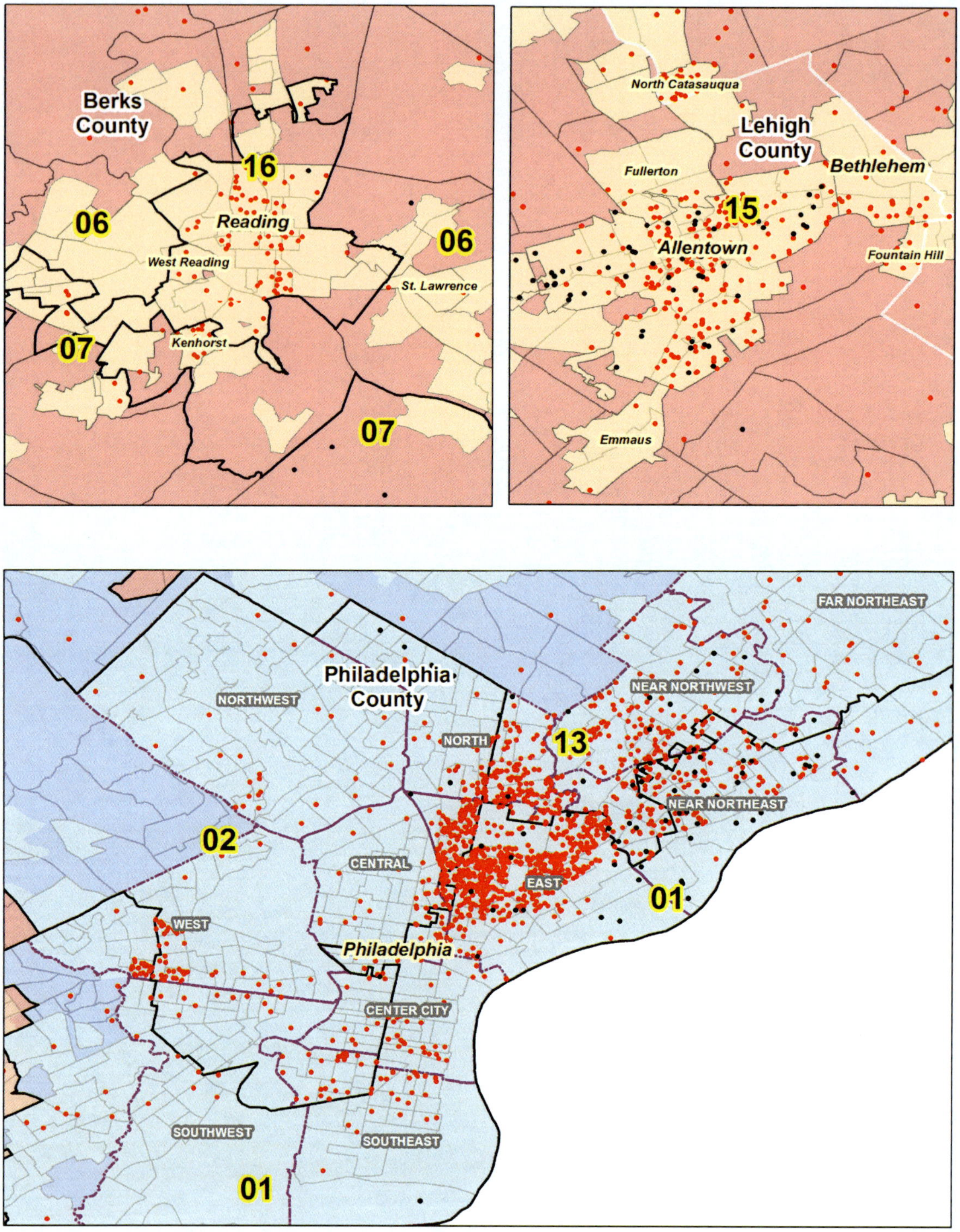

stateside Puerto Ricans (62.4%) and a substantially higher unemployment rate at 17%. The employment rates of Pennsylvania and stateside Puerto Ricans (48.2% and 54.4%, respectively) were between 12.8 and 19 percentage points higher than the rate in Puerto Rico (35.4%). In 2014, the unemployment rate among Pennsylvania Puerto Ricans was 17%, closer to the rate in Puerto Rico of 18.9%, than the stateside Puerto Rican average of 11.6%.

The average earnings of full-time, year-round Puerto Rican in Pennsylvania of $44,929 for men and $37,810 for women, were lower than the average earnings of full-time, year-round stateside of Puerto Ricans men and women, $50,756, and $42,263, respectively. Despite earning less than the stateside Puerto Rican average, Puerto Ricans in Pennsylvania earned significantly more than the average earnings of full-time, year-round Puerto Rican workers in Puerto Rico of $32,512 for men and $29,166 for women. In all cases, the average earnings for women were less than men's.

Household and family incomes are important indicators of economic well-being. These indicators were lower for Puerto Ricans in Pennsylvania than for stateside Puerto Ricans, and higher than on the island. Median household income was $30,305 for Puerto Ricans in Pennsylvania and $39,322 for other stateside Puerto Ricans, but lower for the island at $18,710. There were also significant differences in the per capita income.

Graph 4.A: Mean Earnings for Full-Time Year-Round Puerto Rican Workers, 2014

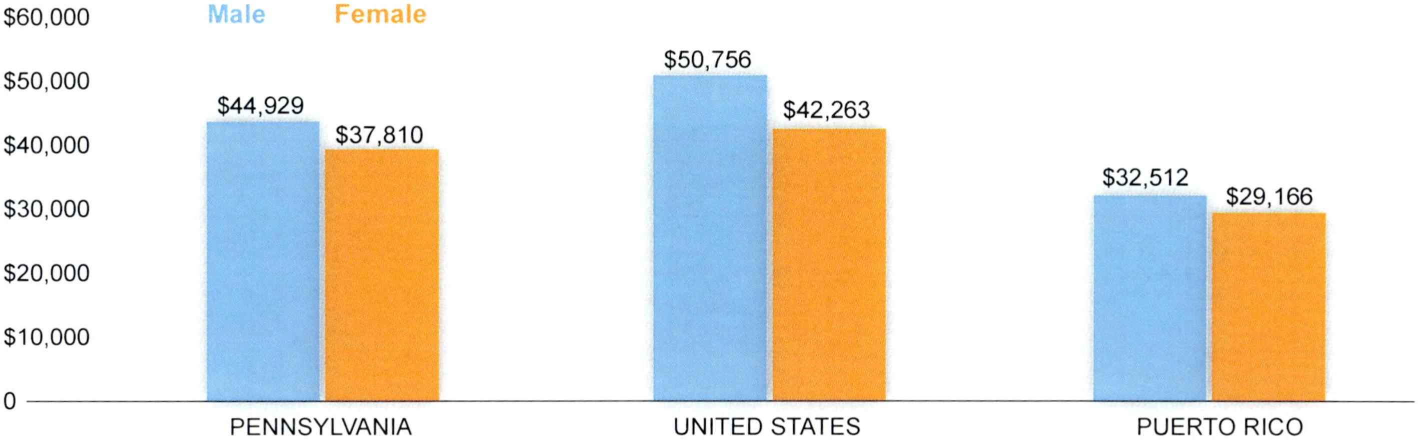

Graph 4.B: Puerto Rican Purchasing Power, in Billions, 2014

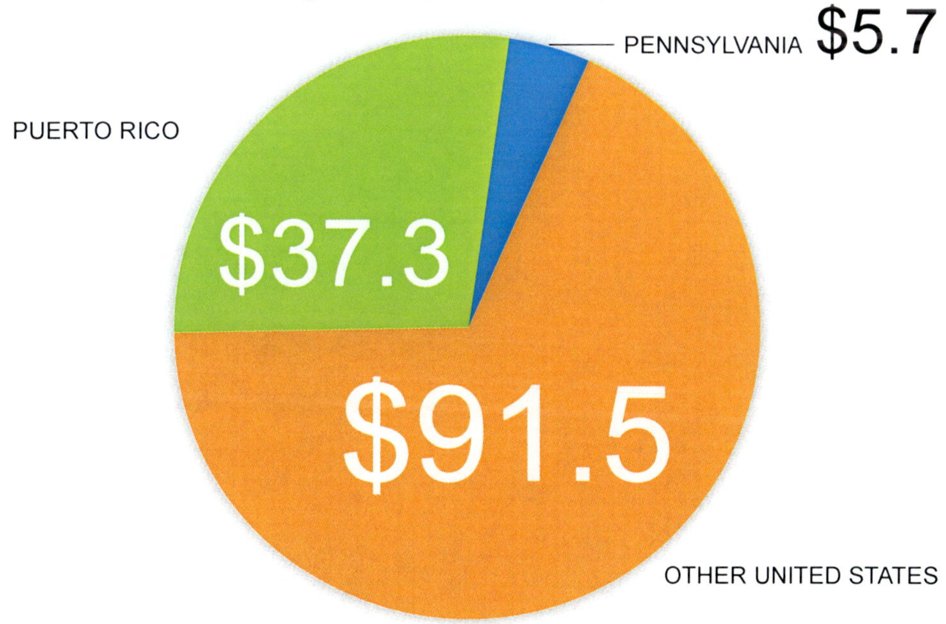

Graph 5.A: Poverty Rates, 2014

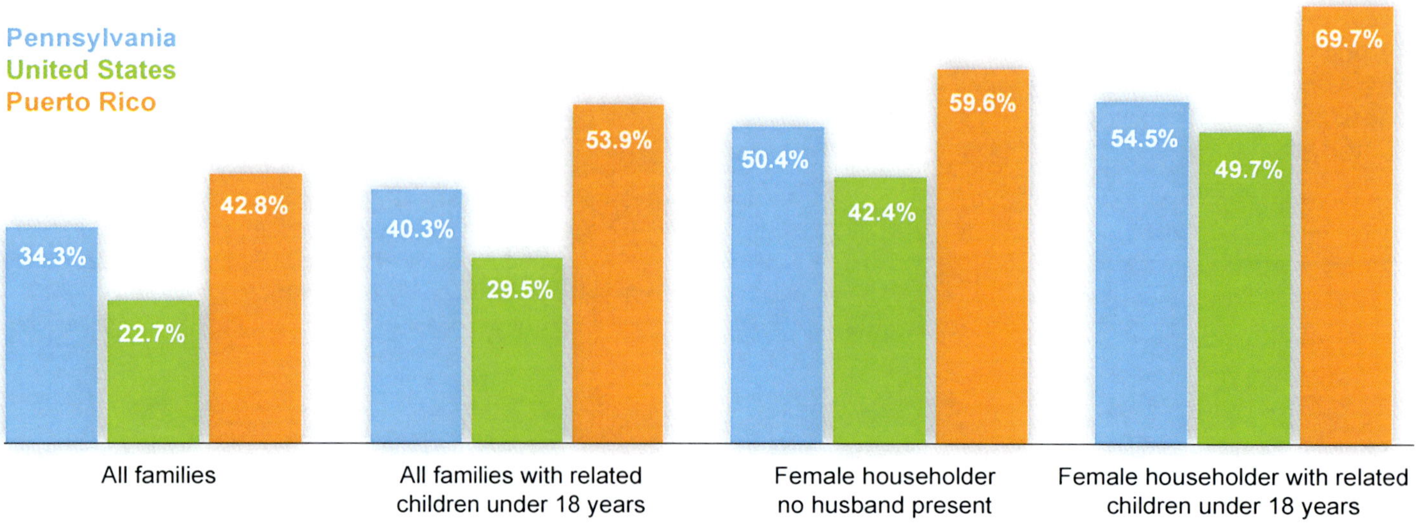

Table 5. Poverty, 2014

Puerto Ricans	Pennsylvania	United States	Puerto Rico*
POVERTY RATES			
All families	34.3%	22.7%	42.8%
With related children under 18 years	40.3%	29.5%	53.9%
With related children under 5 years only	34.8%	24.6%	57.1%
Married-couple family	17%	9.7%	30.9%
With related children under 18 years	17.6%	11.3%	35.5%
With related children under 5 years only	10.9%	5.9%	33.9%
Female householder, no husband present, family	50.4%	42.4%	59.6%
With related children under 18 years	54.5%	49.7%	69.7%
With related children under 5 years only	48.9%	49.4%	75.7%
All people	36.8%	26.2%	46.6%
Under 18 years	43.8%	33.4%	58.7%
Related children under 18 years	46.4%	33.1%	58.6%
Related children under 5 years	46.4%	34.7%	62.8%
Related children 5 to 17 years	42.5%	32.4%	57.3%
18 years and over	32.8%	22.8%	43.2%
18 to 64 years	32.6%	22.8%	43.8%
65 years and over	34.6%	22.4%	41%
People in families	35.3%	23.6%	44.6%
Unrelated individuals 15 years and over	44.2%	38.5%	58%

Source: U.S. Census Bureau, 2014 American Community Survey 1-Year Estimates. * Puerto Ricans only.

In 2014, per capita income for Puerto Ricans in Pennsylvania of $13,559, was 33% lower than the $18,457 for other stateside Puerto Ricans, but higher than in Puerto Rico ($10,960).

Puerto Ricans in Pennsylvania possessed $5.7 billion in purchasing power, approximately six percent of the $97.2 billion generated by all stateside Puerto Ricans. This purchasing power represented a significant market for economic activities in Puerto Rico including investment, tourism, and trade. Purchasing power was defined simply as per capita income multiplied by the Puerto Rican population.

The poverty rate for Puerto Rican families was 34.3% in Pennsylvania, 22.7% for all stateside Puerto Rican families, and 42.8% in Puerto Rico. Though stateside Puerto Ricans' rates of poverty where about half or lower than poverty rates in Puerto Rico, families with a female householder and no husband present with children under 18 years of age exhibited a much higher incidence of poverty than the Puerto Rican family average family. For Puerto Rican female-headed families with children the poverty rates were 54.5% in Pennsylvania, 49.7% for the rest of the U.S., and 69.7% in Puerto Rico. These are inordinately high poverty rates by any measure or comparative context.

In 2014, the proportion of households that received cash public assistance income was 12.1% for Puerto Ricans in Pennsylvania, 6.9% for other stateside Puerto Ricans, and 8.1% in Puerto Rico. In addition, the amount of money that the households received by public assistance were higher for stateside Puerto Ricans ($3,441) and Puerto Ricans in Pennsylvania ($3,162) when compared to the amount received in Puerto Rico ($2,316). The proportion of Puerto Rican households in Pennsylvania receiving benefits from the Supplemental Nutrition Assistance Program (SNAP) was 45.2% in 2014, 13.7 percentage points higher than the 31.5% rate for Puerto Rican households in the U.S. as a whole and 5.5 percentage points higher than the 39.7% for Puerto Rico.

Housing is a primary determinant of the cost of living. The median value of owner-occupied housing for Puerto Ricans in Pennsylvania was $116,000, compared to $175,900 for other stateside Puerto Ricans, and $119,500 in Puerto Rico. The median monthly owner costs with a mortgage was $1,216 for Puerto Ricans in Pennsylvania, and $1,545 for other stateside Puerto Ricans. A comparable cost was $873 in Puerto Rico. These relative prices and ownership costs, along with income, were reflected in ownership rates. Census data revealed that Puerto Ricans in Pennsylvania had a 36.0% rate of owner-occupied housing units, the same percentage than stateside Puerto Ricans. The home ownership rate in Puerto Rico was much higher, at 68.7%. Among Puerto Ricans in Pennsylvania, housing costs were relatively higher than for other Puerto Ricans in the United States in terms of the gross rent paid as a percentage of their household income: 63% of Puerto Ricans in the state paid more than 30% of the income in rent, compared to 59.6% of Puerto Ricans in the United States as a whole. However, the median gross rent these Pennsylvania Puerto Ricans paid ($820) was substantially lower than Puerto Ricans in the United States overall ($942).

Table 6. Housing and Health Insurance, 2014

Puerto Ricans	Pennsylvania	United States	Puerto Rico*
HOUSING			
Owner-occupied housing units	36%	36%	68.7%
Monthly owner costs as a percentage of household income in the past 12 months			
Less than 30 percent	56.3%	62.8%	52.6%
30 percent or more	43.7%	37.2%	47.4%
Owner-occupied housing units			
Median value (dollars)	$116,000	$175,900	$119,500
Median selected monthly owner costs with a mortgage (dollars)	$1,216	$1,545	$873
HEALTH INSURANCE COVERAGE Civilian noninstitutionalized population			
With private health insurance	42.2%	51.6%	38%
With public coverage	51.6%	43.5%	62.9%
No health insurance coverage	12.3%	11.5%	5.5%

Source: U.S. Census Bureau, 2014 American Community Survey 1-Year Estimates.
* Puerto Ricans only.

Puerto Ricans in Massachusetts, 2014

In 2014, Massachusetts was the fifth state with most Puerto Ricans in the United States. In 2014, the Puerto Rican population in Massachusetts was 4.6% of the state's total population. This represents an increase when compared to the years 2000 (3.1%) and 2010 (4.1%). Puerto Ricans were the largest national origin group among Latinos, accounting for 42% of Latinos in the state.

Graph 1.A: Latino Population Massachusetts 2014

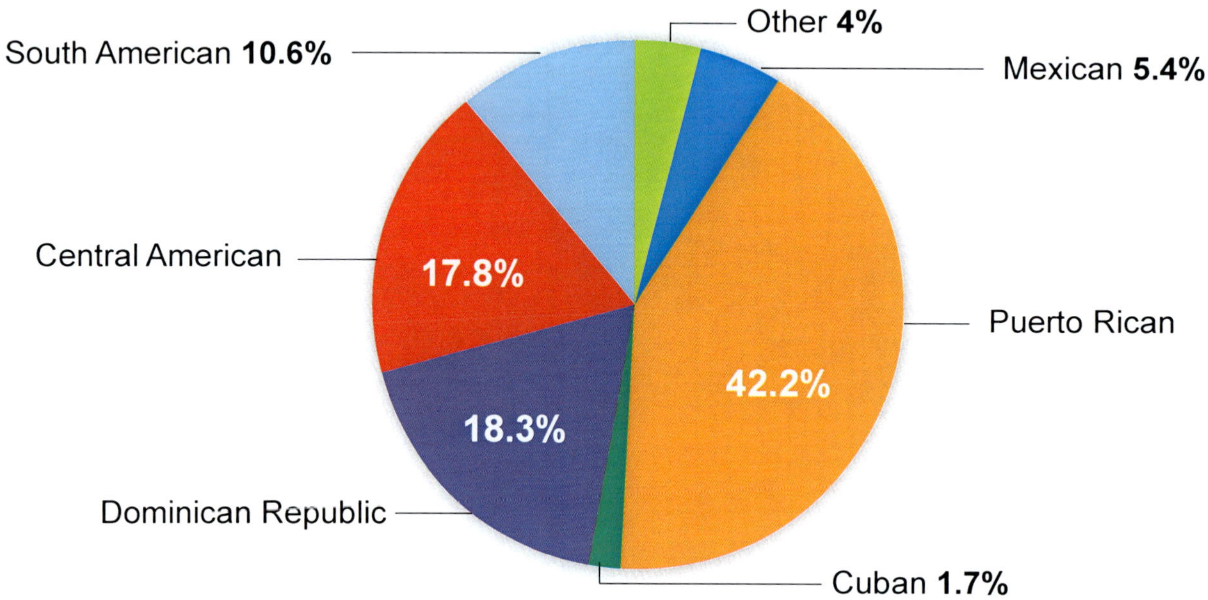

Table 1. Puerto Rican and Latino Population in Massachusetts

	2000		2010		2014	
Total	6,349,097	100%	6,547,629	100%	6,745,408	100%
Not Hispanic or Latino	5,920,368	93.3%	5,919,975	90.4%	6,015,314	89.2%
Hispanic or Latino	428,729	6.8%	627,654	9.6%	730,094	10.8%
Mexican	22,288	0.4%	38,379	0.6%	39,223	0.6%
Puerto Rican	199,207	3.1%	266,125	4.1%	308,028	4.6%
Cuban	8,867	0.1%	11,306	0.2%	12,313	0.2%
Dominican Republic	49,913	0.8%	103,292	1.6%	133,321	2%
Central American	38,317	0.6%	96,958	1.5%	130,265	1.9%
South American	28,036	0.4%	54,398	0.8%	77,683	1.2%
Other	82,101	1.3%	57,196	0.9%	29,261	0.4%

Sources: U.S. Census Bureau, Census 2000 Summary File 1, 2010 Census. Summary File 1, and 2014 American Community Survey 1-Year Estimates.

Massachusetts has one of the most diverse Latino populations in the country. The Latino population in Massachusetts grew from 6.8% of the state's total population in 2000 to 10.8% in 2014. Puerto Ricans constitute the largest national-origin Latino group (42.2% of total Latino population), followed by Dominicans (18.3%). Central Americans accoutned for 17.8% of the Latino population. The Puerto Rican population in Massachusetts grew by more than 40%, while the Latino population in the state grew by 70% between 2000 and 2014.

The median age of Puerto Ricans in Massachusetts for the year 2014 was 26.8 years, which was 2.1 years lower than

Graph 2.A: Puerto Rican Education Attainment, 25 years and over, 2014

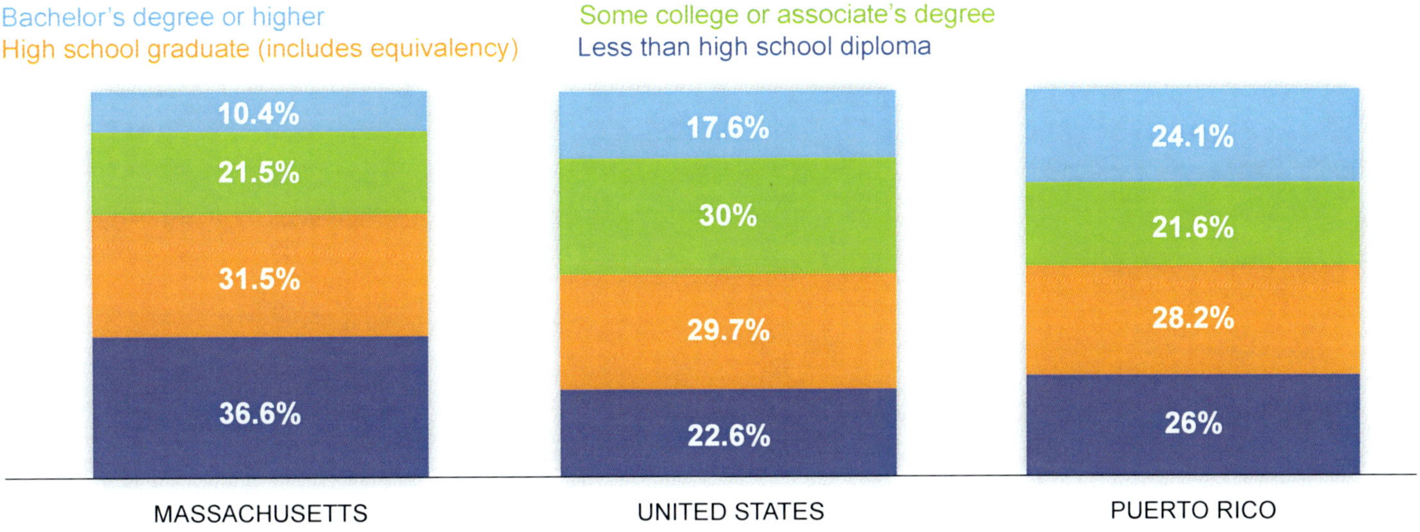

Table 2. Age, Education, and Language, 2014

Puerto Ricans	Massachusetts	United States	Puerto Rico*
TOTAL POPULATION	308,028	5,266,738	3,404,122
Median age (years)	26.8	28.9	38.9
62 years and over	7%	9.9%	21%
EDUCATIONAL ATTAINMENT			
Population 25 years and over			
Less than high school diploma	36.6%	22.6%	26%
High school graduate (includes equivalency)	31.5%	29.7%	28.2%
Some college or associate's degree	21.5%	30%	21.6%
Bachelor's degree or higher	10.4%	17.6%	24.1%
Male, bachelor's degree or higher	7.6%	15.6%	19.6%
Female, bachelor's degree or higher	12.9%	19.5%	28.1%
LANGUAGE SPOKEN AT HOME AND ABILITY TO SPEAK ENGLISH			
Population 5 years and over			
English only	27.2%	38.8%	5.3%
Language other than English	72.8%	61.2%	94.7%
Speak English less than "very well"	24.8%	17.3%	78.8%

Source: U.S. Census Bureau, 2014 American Community Survey 1-Year Estimates.
* Puerto Ricans only.

the median age for stateside Puerto Ricans of 28.9 and 12.1 years lower than the 38.9 median age in Puerto Rico. These differences in the age structure were evident in the percent of the population older than 62 years of age: 7% of Puerto Ricans in Massachusetts, which was lower than among stateside Puerto Ricans (9.9%) in this age group. With 21% of the population 62 years of age or older Puerto Rico had three times the percentage of its population aged 62 and older when compared to Puerto Ricans in Massachusetts.

Puerto Ricans in Massachusetts had different English fluency indicators than stateside Puerto Ricans. In Massachusetts, 27.2% of the population reported speaking only English at home, compared to 38.8% of stateside Puerto Ricans. One in four Puerto Ricans (24.8%) in Massachusetts reported speaking English less than "very well", more than the one in six average (17.3%) among stateside Puerto Ricans.

Puerto Ricans in Massachusetts had a significantly lower level of educational attainment, indicated by the low proportion of Puerto Ricans over the age of 25 holding a bachelor's degree or higher, 10.4%. This proportion was less than half of that of Puerto Ricans in Puerto Rico holding bachelor's degrees or above (24.1%). Among stateside Puerto Ricans this figure was 17.6%. Another indicator

Table 3. Employment and Occupations, 2014

Puerto Ricans	Massachusetts	United States	Puerto Rico*
EMPLOYMENT STATUS			
Population 16 years and over			
In labor force	58.2%	62.4%	43.7%
Civilian labor force	58.1%	61.6%	43.7%
Employed	48.5%	54.4%	35.4%
Unemployed	16.5%	11.6%	18.9%
Not in labor force	41.8%	37.6%	56.3%
Armed Forces	0%	0.8%	0%
OCCUPATION			
Civilian employed population 16 years and over			
Male	51,388	1,058,918	516,762
Management, business, science, and arts	16%	23.4%	23.9%
Service occupations	29.8%	22.5%	23%
Sales and office occupations	18.6%	19.6%	21.3%
Construction and maintenance	9.5%	13.8%	18%
Production, transportation, and moving	26.1%	20.7%	13.7%
Female	52,179	999,105	456,356
Management, business, science, and arts	26.3%	33.1%	39.7%
Service occupations	34.7%	24.4%	16.6%
Sales and office occupations	29.4%	35.7%	38.3%
Construction and maintenance	0.4%	0.6%	0.6%
Production, transportation, and moving	9.2%	6.2%	4.8%
CLASS OF WORKER			
Civilian employed population 16 years and over			
Private wage and salary workers	85.1%	82%	69%
Government workers	11.5%	14.8%	22.5%
Self-employed workers in own not incorporated business	3.2%	3.1%	8.3%
VETERAN STATUS			
Civilian population 18 years and over			
Civilian veteran	2.3%	6%	3.3%

Source: U.S. Census Bureau, 2014 American Community Survey 1-Year Estimates. * Puerto Ricans only.

of lower educational attainment among Massachusetts Puerto Ricans is the higher proportion of adults over age 25 without high school diplomas (36.6%) compared to the stateside average (22.6%) and island average (26%).

The data by major occupational category indicated that the structure of Puerto Rican employment in Massachusetts differed from that of other stateside Puerto Ricans and those in Puerto Rico. In Massachusetts the proportion of Puerto Rican males (16%) and females (26.3%) working in management, business, science, and arts was lower than among all stateside Puerto Ricans (23.4% and 33.1%, respectively) and those in Puerto Rico (23.9% and 39.7%, respectively). Puerto Ricans in Massachusetts also showed a greater proportion in production, transportation, and material moving occupations (17.6%) than the stateside Puerto Rican average (13.7%) or that of Puerto Ricans in Puerto Rico (9.5%).

The employment rate for Puerto Ricans in Massachusetts (48.5%) was lower than stateside Puerto Ricans overall (54.4%), as was their rate of labor force participation (58.2% and 62.4%, respectively). The employment rate of Massachusetts and stateside Puerto Ricans was between thirteen and nineteen percentage points higher than in Puerto Rico (35.4%). In 2014, the unemployment rate among Puerto Ricans in Massachusetts was 16.5%, more than two percentage points below Puerto Rico's unem-

Table 4. Income and Earnings, 2014

Puerto Ricans	Massachusetts	United States	Puerto Rico*
INCOME IN THE PAST 12 MONTHS (IN 2013 INFLATION-ADJUSTED DOLLARS)			
Households	97,301	1,635,808	1,175,297
Median household income (dollars)	$24,983	$39,322	$18,710
With earnings	68.3%	76.9%	54.7%
Mean earnings (dollars)	$48,194	$61,065	$36,407
With Social Security income	24.7%	24.1%	43.2%
Mean Social Security income (dollars)	$10,447	$13,727	$12,159
With Supplemental Security Income	25.9%	12.6%	0.4%
Mean Supplemental Security Income (dollars)	$9,010	$8,780	$10,025
With cash public assistance income	11%	6.9%	8.1%
Mean cash public assistance income (dollars)	$4,079	$3,441	$2,316
With retirement income	3.9%	10.1%	15.6%
Mean retirement income (dollars)	$18,728	$20,452	$15,387
With Food Stamp/SNAP benefits	55.1%	31.5%	39.7%
Families	64,099	1,114,628	830,807
Median family income (dollars)	$27,527	$44,499	$22,220
Married-couple family	37.5%	53.9%	56.1%
Median income (dollars)	$50,411	$67,129	$29,417
Male householder, no spouse present	11.2%	10.2%	9.5%
Median income (dollars)	$31,372	$37,513	$17,797
Female householder, no husband present	51.3%	35.9%	34.4%
Median income (dollars)	$20,697	$23,957	$13,554
Individuals	308,028	5,266,738	3,404,122
Per capita income (dollars)	$13,346	$18,457	$10,960
Mean earnings (dollars) for full-time, year-round workers:			
Male	$43,027	$50,756	$32,512
Female	$39,543	$42,263	$29,166

Source: U.S. Census Bureau, 2014 American Community Survey 1-Year Estimates.
* Puerto Ricans only.

ployment rate of 18.9% and 4.9 percentage points above the stateside average of 11.6%.

Average earnings of full-time, year-round Puerto Ricans in Massachusetts were $43,027 for men and $39,543 for women, lower than the stateside averages of $50,756 for men and $42,253 for women. Despite the average lower income when compared to all stateside Puerto Ricans, average earnings for Puerto Ricans in Massachusetts were higher than those in Puerto Rico, where men averaged $32,512 and women averaged $29,166 in earnings. The earnings gap between men and women was lower in Massachusetts and Puerto Rico, both less than $3,500, when compared to the stateside gender earnings gap among Puerto Ricans of about $8,500.

Household and family incomes are important indicators of economic well-being. These indicators were lower for Puerto Ricans in Massachusetts than for stateside Puerto Ricans, and slightly higher than in the island. Median household income was $24,983 for Puerto Ricans in Massachusetts and $39,322 for other stateside Puerto Ricans, but lower for the island at $18,710. There were also differences in the per capita income. In 2014, per capita income for Puerto Ricans in Massachusetts was $13,346 and $18,457 for other stateside Puerto Ricans, but only $10,960 for the island.

Graph 4.A: Mean Earnings for Full-Time, Year-Round Puerto Rican Workers, 2014

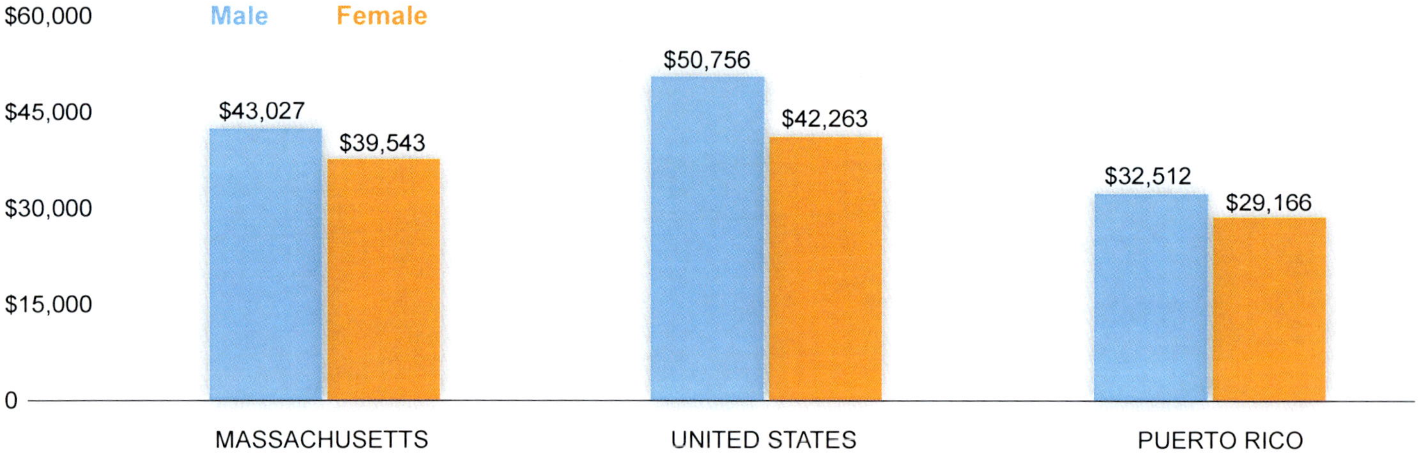

Graph 4.B: Puerto Rican Purchasing Power, in Billions, 2014

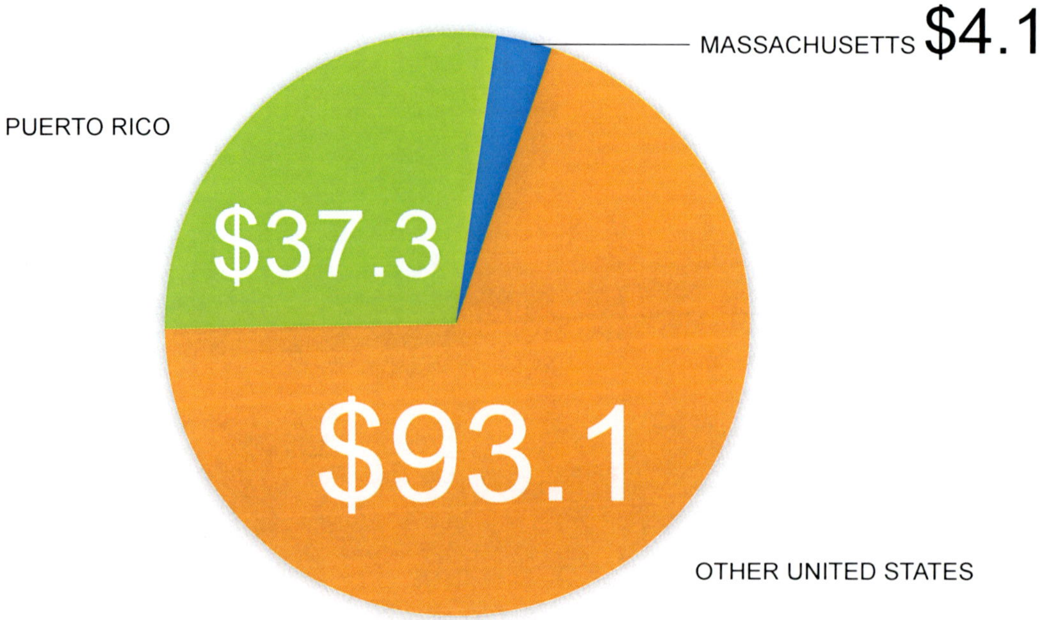

Puerto Rican Population by Counties in Massachusetts, 2014

Close to a third (30.6%) of all Massachusetts Puerto Ricans resided in Hampden County with high numbers in the cities of Springfield and Holyoke. Worcester County accounted for another 15.9% of Massachusetts's Puerto Ricans, the majority of which were found in or near the city of Worcester. Suffolk and Essex Counties, both included in the Boston metropolitan area, accounted for a combined 25.7% of all Massachusetts Puerto Ricans. Puerto Ricans were proportionately underrepresented in all other counties including Middlesex County, which accounted for only 11.4% of Massachusetts's Puerto Ricans compared to 23.1% of all Massachusetts residents. The sharpest difference between Puerto Ricans and other Latinos were in Hampden County where Puerto Ricans accounted for close to 90% of all Latinos in the county, and in Suffolk and Essex Counties which had higher proportions of Latinos than Puerto Ricans.

COUNTY	Puerto Rican Population	Percent	Latino Population	Percent	Total Population	Percent
Hampden County	86,946	30.6%	103,159	15.1%	466,447	7.0%
Worcester County	45,150	15.9%	80,488	11.8%	806,804	12.1%
Suffolk County	37,553	13.2%	156,323	22.9%	747,928	11.2%
Essex County	35,561	12.5%	133,486	19.6%	757,395	11.4%
Middlesex County	32,444	11.4%	108,884	16.0%	1,539,832	23.1%
Bristol County	22,277	7.8%	35,832	5.3%	551,065	8.3%
Plymouth County	8,234	2.9%	17,069	2.5%	500,772	7.5%
Norfolk County	8,064	2.8%	25,030	3.7%	682,860	10.3%
Hampshire County	3,697	1.3%	8,061	1.2%	160,328	2.4%
Berkshire County	1,635	0.6%	4,907	0.7%	130,064	2.0%
Barnstable County	1,573	0.6%	5,267	0.8%	215,167	3.2%
Franklin County	1,303	0.5%	2,502	0.4%	71,300	1.1%
Nantucket County	116	0%	753	0.1%	10,414	0.2%
Dukes County	12	0%	63	0%	16,915	0.3%
Total	**284,565**	**100%**	**681,824**	**100%**	**6,657,291**	**100%**

Sources: U.S. Census Bureau and 2014 American Community Survey 5-Year Estimates

Notes: Total counts for populations may differ depending on whether the estimates are derived from the five-year estimates or the one-year estimates of the American Community Survey.

PUERTO RICAN POPULATION BY COUNTIES IN MASSACHUSETTS, 2014

PUERTO RICAN POPULATION

● 1 dot = 100

'06-'14 PUERTO RICAN ARRIVALS

● 1 dot = 100

BOUNDARIES

County

City/Towns

Census Tracts

CONGRESSIONAL DISTRICT

Republican

Democrat

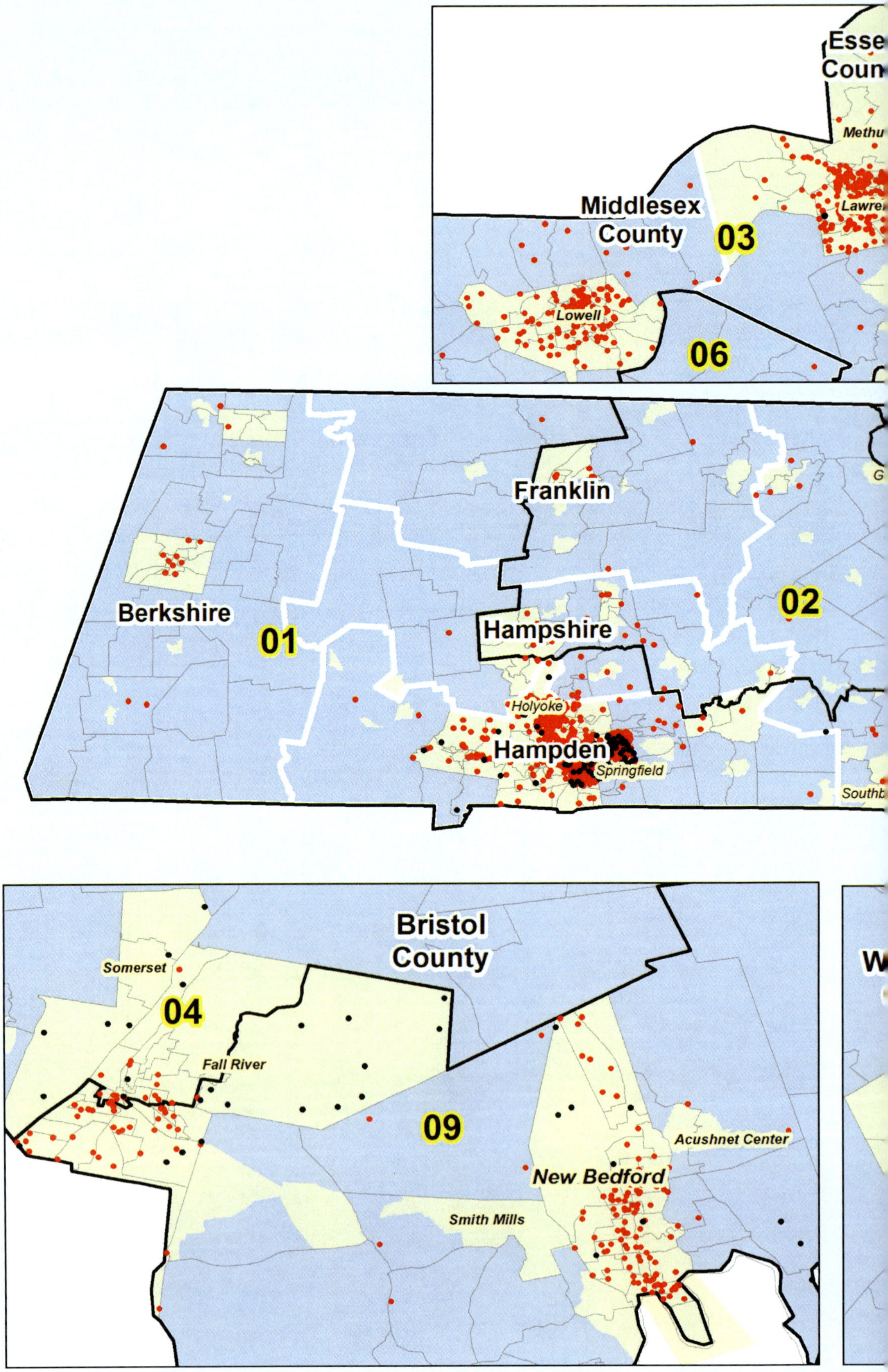

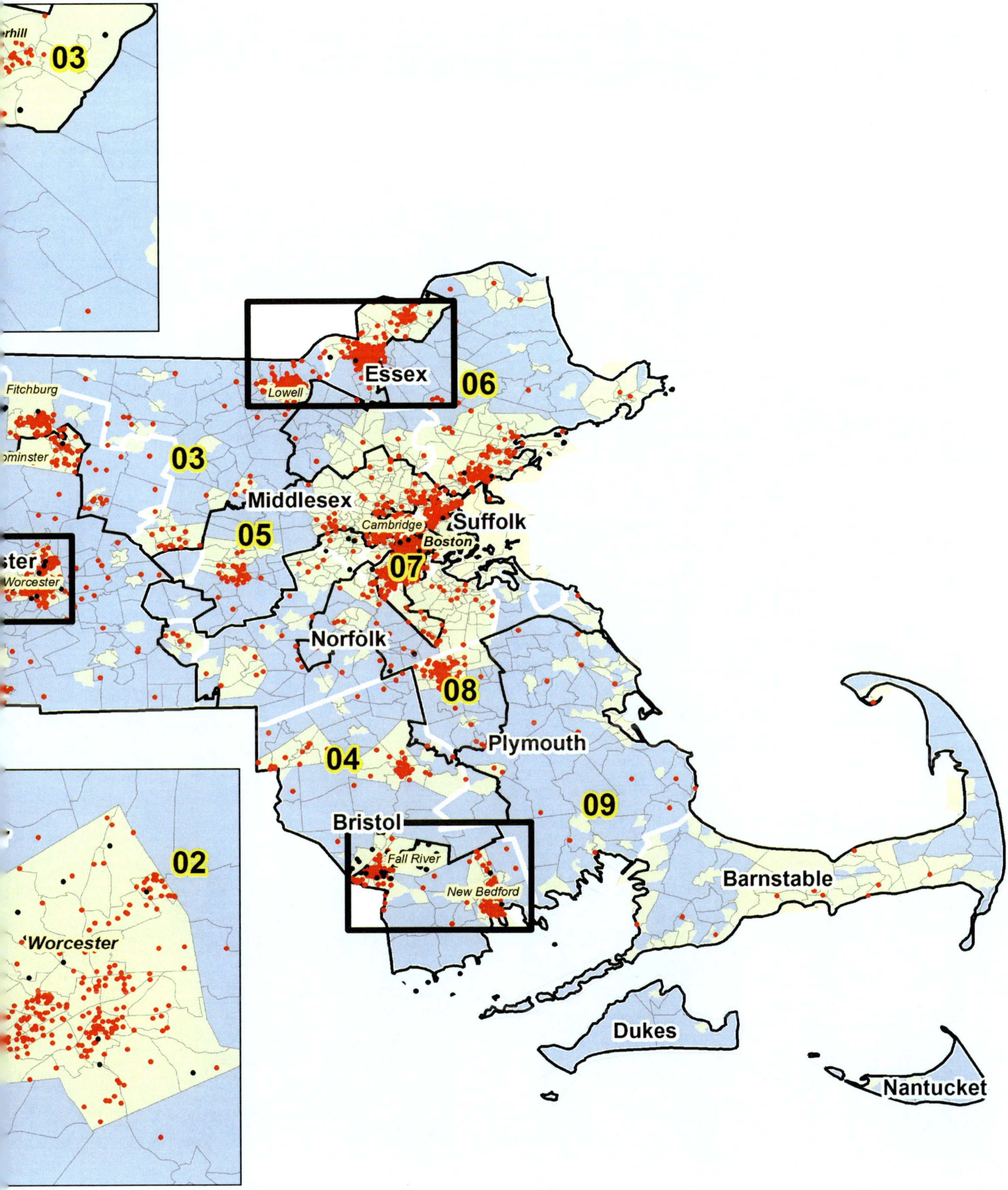
03
Fitchburg
03
Middlesex
05
Lowell
Essex
06
Cambridge
Suffolk
Boston
07
Worcester
Norfolk
08
Plymouth
04
09
Bristol
Fall River
New Bedford
02
Worcester
Barnstable
Dukes
Nantucket

PUERTO RICAN POPULATION BY COUNTIES IN MASSACHUSETTS, 2014

PUERTO RICAN POPULATION

● 1 dot = 100

'06-'14 PUERTO RICAN ARRIVALS

● 1 dot = 100

BOUNDARIES

County

City/Towns

Census Tracts

CONGRESSIONAL DISTRICT

Republican

Democrat

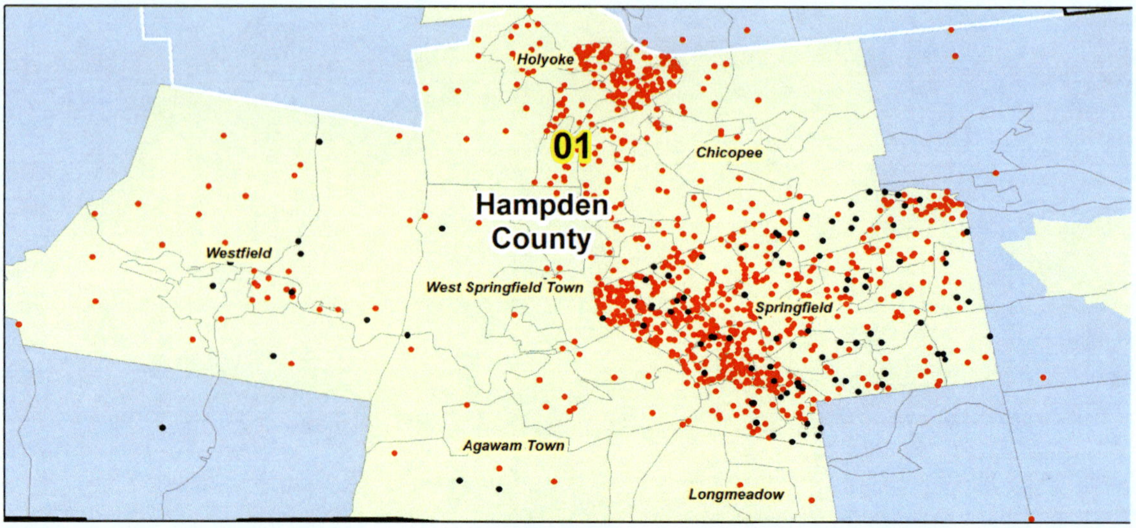

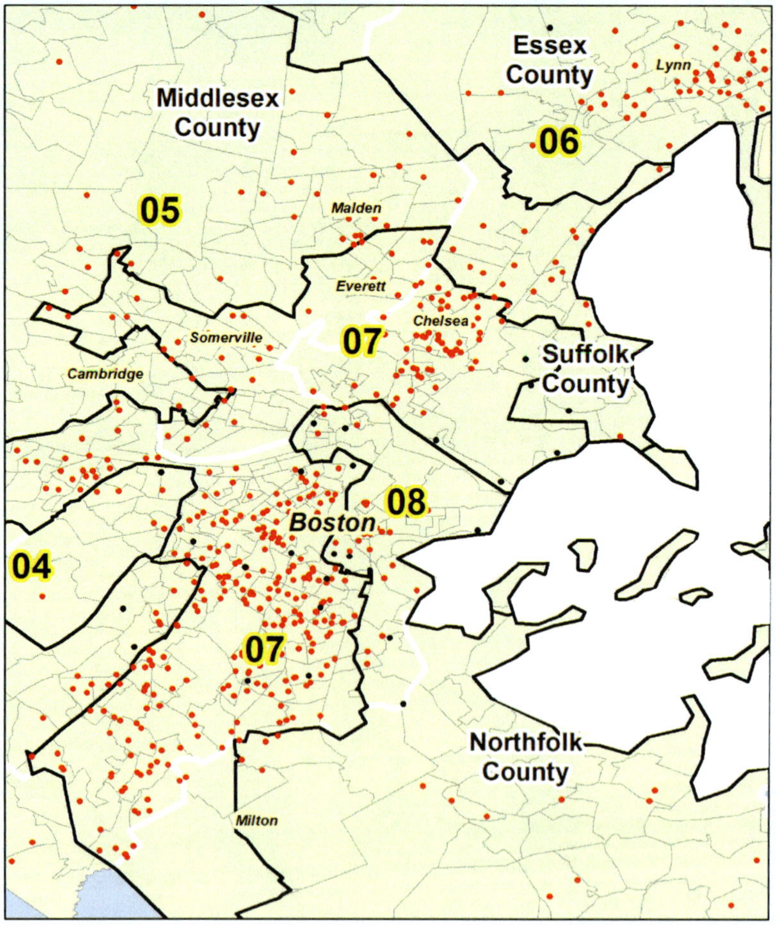

Graph 5.A: Poverty Rates, 2014

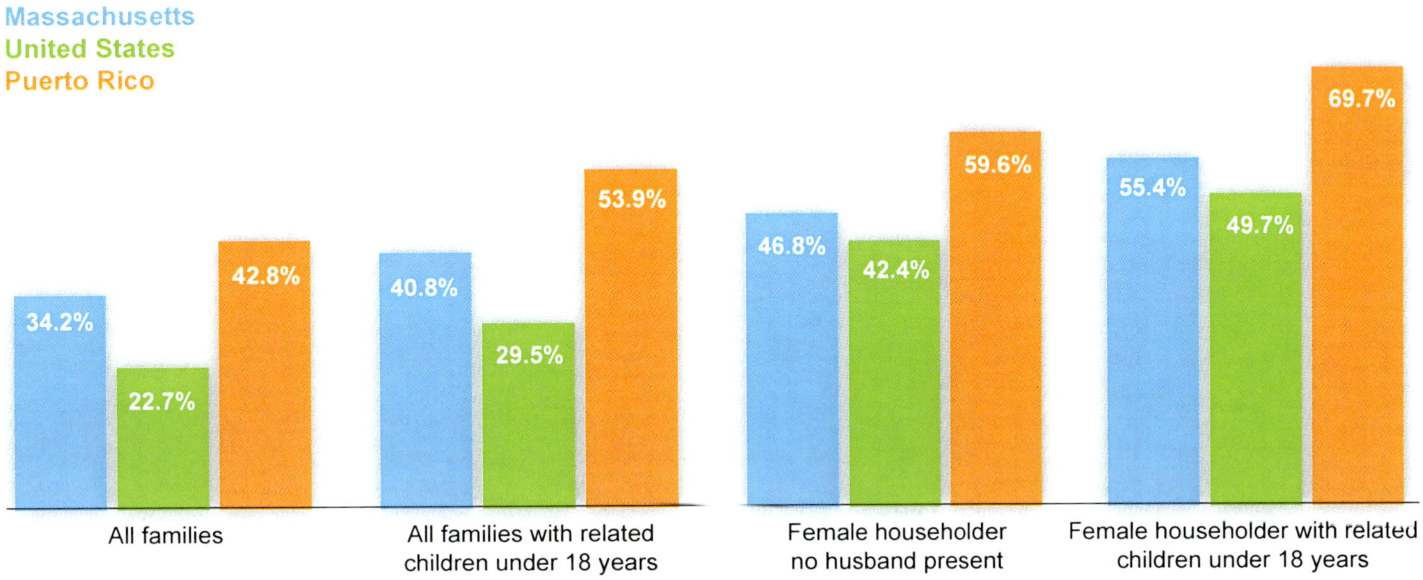

Table 5. Poverty, 2014

Puerto Ricans	Massachusetts	United States	Puerto Rico*
POVERTY RATES			
All families	34.2%	22.7%	42.8%
With related children under 18 years	40.8%	29.5%	53.9%
With related children under 5 years only	28.1%	24.6%	57.1%
Married-couple family	18.5%	9.7%	30.9%
With related children under 18 years	16.5%	11.3%	35.5%
With related children under 5 years only	5.9%	5.9%	33.9%
Female householder, no husband present, family	46.8%	42.4%	59.6%
With related children under 18 years	55.4%	49.7%	69.7%
With related children under 5 years only	47.8%	49.4%	75.7%
All people	38.3%	26.2%	46.6%
Under 18 years	46%	33.4%	58.7%
Related children under 18 years	45.9%	33.1%	58.6%
Related children under 5 years	50.2%	34.7%	62.8%
Related children 5 to 17 years	44.2%	32.4%	57.3%
18 years and over	34.3%	22.8%	43.2%
18 to 64 years	33.3%	22.8%	43.8%
65 years and over	45.5%	22.4%	41%
People in families	35%	23.6%	44.6%
Unrelated individuals 15 years and over	52.2%	38.5%	58.6%

Source: U.S. Census Bureau, 2014 American Community Survey 1-Year Estimates.
* Puerto Ricans only.

Puerto Ricans in Massachusetts, had $4.1 billion in purchasing power. From an economic perspective, stateside Puerto Ricans represented 72.3% of the $134.5 billion total purchasing power of the entire Puerto Rican population, whether in the United States or in Puerto Rico, in the year 2014. Purchasing power is defined simply as per capita income multiplied by the Puerto Rican population. Stateside Puerto Ricans had 2.6 times the total purchasing power of Puerto Ricans in Puerto Rico of $37.3 billion.

A higher proportion of Puerto Rican families in Massachusetts fall under the poverty rate (34.2%) than among stateside Puerto Rican families overall (22.7%). Despite the higher rate of poverty in Massachusetts, it is still below the island Puerto Rican proportion of 42.8%. Although this hierarchy of poverty rates is observed in almost all subgroups the poverty rates among families with female householders and children are alarmingly high in Massachusetts at 55.4%, among stateside Puerto Ricans at 49.7%, and in Puerto Rico at 69.7%. These are inordinately high poverty rates by any measure or comparative context.

In 2014, the proportion of households that received cash public assistance income was 11% for Puerto Ricans in Massachusetts, 6.9% for other stateside Puerto Ricans, and 8.1% in Puerto Rico. In other words, a higher percentage of Puerto Ricans families in Massachusetts received public assistance than in Puerto Rico. In addition, the average amount of money that the households received by public assistance were higher for Puerto Ricans in Massachusetts ($4,079) when compared to the amount received in Puerto Rico ($2,316). The propor tion of Puerto Rican households in Massachusetts receiving benefits through the Supplemental Nutrition Assistance Program (SNAP) was 55.1% in 2014, 23.6 percentage points higher than the 31.5% rate for Puerto Rican households in the U.S. as a whole and 15.4 percentage points higher than the 39.7% for Puerto Rico. The available data suggests that Puerto Ricans living in Massachusetts received in a higher proportion and higher amounts in welfare benefits than their counterparts in Puerto Rico, even though Puerto Ricans in Massachusetts exhibit lower poverty rates than in Puerto Rico.

Housing is a primary determinant of the cost of living. In general, the Northeast has a higher cost of home ownership than the South or other parts of the country. The median value of owner-occupied housing for Puerto Ricans in Massachusetts was $213,300, compared to $175,900 for other stateside Puerto Ricans, and $119,500 in Puerto Rico. The median monthly owner costs with a mortgage were $1,658 for Puerto Ricans in Massachusetts and $1,545 for other stateside Puerto Ricans. A comparable cost was $873 in Puerto Rico. These relative prices and ownership costs, along with income levels, were reflected in home ownership rates. Puerto Ricans in Massachusetts had lower rates of home ownership than Puerto Ricans in Puerto Rico or even among other stateside Puerto Ricans. Puerto Ricans in Massachusetts had a 17% rate of owner-occupied housing units, while the comparable rate for stateside Puerto Ricans was twice as high (36%). The home ownership rate in Puerto Rico was much higher, at 68.7%. Among Puerto Ricans in Massachusetts, housing costs were relatively higher than for other Puerto Ricans in the United States. Puerto Ricans in Massachusetts had higher median costs associated with home ownership ($1,658) than stateside Puerto Rican median homeownership costs ($1,545) and those in Puerto Rico ($873).

Table 6. Housing and Health Insurance, 2014

Puerto Ricans	Massachusetts	United States	Puerto Rico*
HOUSING			
Owner-occupied housing units	17%	36%	68.7%
Monthly owner costs as a percentage of household income in the past 12 months			
Less than 30 percent	67.8%	62.8%	52.6%
30 percent or more	32.2%	37.2%	47.4%
Owner-occupied housing units			
Median value (dollars)	$213,300	$175,900	$119,500
Median selected monthly owner costs with a mortgage (dollars)	$1,658	$1,545	$873
HEALTH INSURANCE COVERAGE			
Civilian noninstitutionalized population			
With private health insurance	33%	51.6%	38%
With public coverage	68.1%	43.5%	62.9%
No health insurance coverage	4.4%	11.5%	5.5%

Source: U.S. Census Bureau, 2014 American Community Survey 1-Year Estimates. * Puerto Ricans only.

Puerto Ricans in Connecticut, 2014

In 2014, Connecticut was the 6th state with most Puerto Ricans (301,182) in the United States. In 2014, the Puerto Rican population in Connecticut was 8.4% of the total state population. This is an increase from years 2000 (5.7%) and 2010 (7.1%). Employment rate of Puerto Ricans in Connecticut was 55%, not much different than the 54.4% average for stateside Puerto Ricans overall, but was nearly 20 percentage points higher than the 35.4% employment rate in Puerto Rico.

Graph 1.A: Latino Population Connecticut, 2014

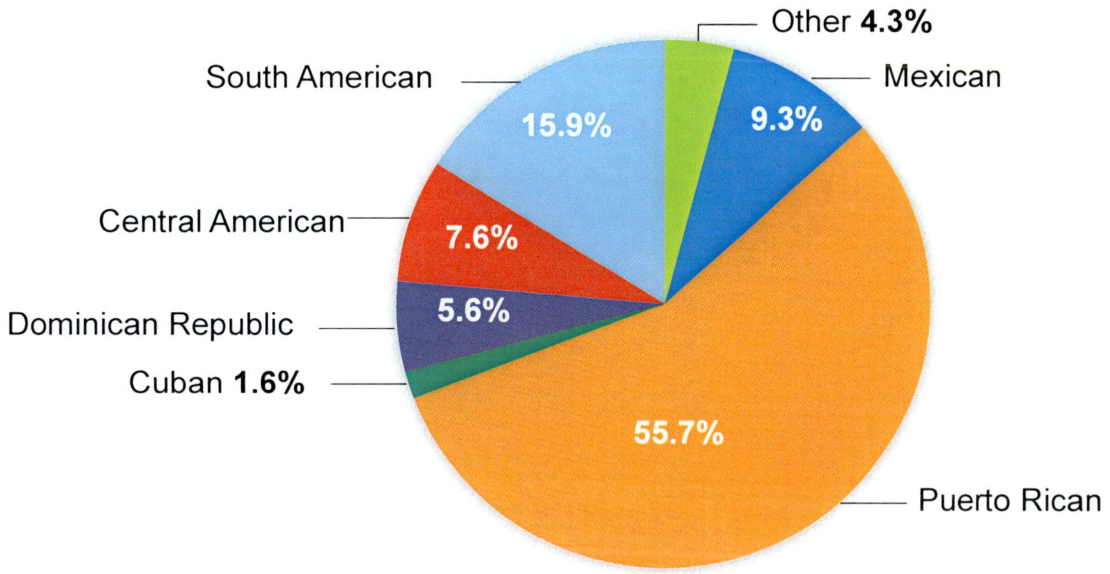

Table 1. Puerto Rican and Latino Population in Connecticut

	2000		2010		2014	
Total	3,405,565	100%	3,574,097	100%	3,596,677	100%
Not Hispanic or Latino	3,085,242	90.6%	3,095,010	86.6%	3,055,524	85%
Hispanic or Latino	320,323	9.4%	479,087	13.4%	541,153	15%
Mexican	23,484	0.7%	50,658	1.4%	50,382	1.4%
Puerto Rican	194,443	5.7%	252,972	7.1%	301,182	8.4%
Cuban	7,101	0.2%	9,490	0.3%	8,657	0.2%
Dominican Republic	9,546	0.3%	26,093	0.7%	30,408	0.8%
Central American	12,987	0.4%	35,023	1%	41,011	1.1%
South American	31,310	0.9%	71,355	2.0%	86,003	2.4%
Other	41,452	1.2%	33,496	0.9%	23,510	0.7%

Sources: U.S. Census Bureau, Census 2000 Summary File 1, 2010 Census. Summary File 1, and 2014 American Community Survey 1-Year Estimates.

The median age of Puerto Ricans in Connecticut in 2014 was 26.4 years, which was slightly lower than for all stateside Puerto Ricans at 28.9 years, but more than 10 years lower than Puerto Rico's median age of 38.9 years. These differences in the age structure were evident in the proportion of the population older than 62 years: only 7.8% of Puerto Ricans in Connecticut were over 61 years, compared to 9.9% of all stateside Puerto Ricans and 21% of Puerto Ricans in Puerto Rico.

Puerto Ricans in Connecticut had slightly lower English-fluency indicators than national indicators for stateside Puerto Ricans. In Connecticut, 32.9% of Puerto

Graph 2.A: Puerto Rican Education Attainment, 25 years and over, 2014

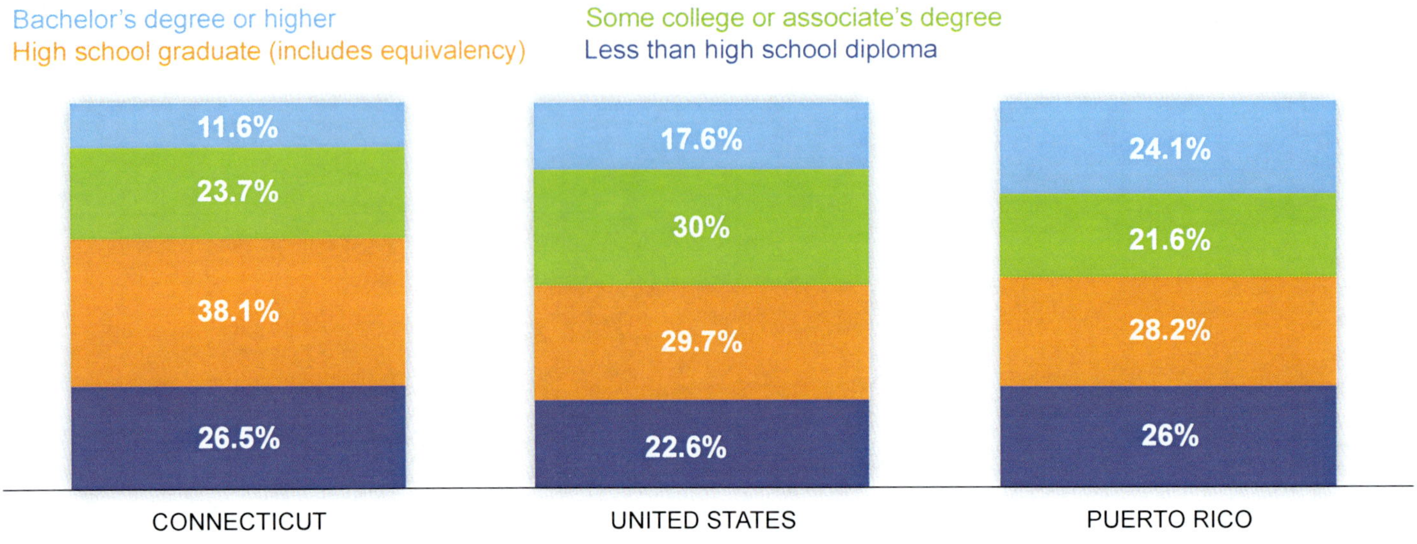

Table 2. Age, Education, and Language

	2014		
Puerto Ricans	**Connecticut**	**United States**	**Puerto Rico***
TOTAL POPULATION	301,182	5,266,738	3,404,122
Median age (years)	26.4	28.9	38.9
62 years and over	7.8%	9.9%	21%
EDUCATIONAL ATTAINMENT			
Population 25 years and over			
Less than high school diploma	26.5%	22.6%	26%
High school graduate (includes equivalency)	38.1%	29.7%	28.2%
Some college or associate's degree	23.7%	30%	21.6%
Bachelor's degree or higher	11.6%	17.6%	24.1%
Male, bachelor's degree or higher	10.1%	15.6%	19.6%
Female, bachelor's degree or higher	13%	19.5%	28.1%
LANGUAGE SPOKEN AT HOME AND ABILITY TO SPEAK ENGLISH			
Population 5 years and over			
English only	32.9%	38.8%	5.3%
Language other than English	67.1%	61.2%	94.7%
Speak English less than "very well"	20.9%	17.3%	78.8%

Source: U.S. Census Bureau, 2014 American Community Survey 1-Year Estimates.
* Puerto Ricans only.

Ricans reported speaking only English at home, compared to 38.8% of Puerto Ricans in other states. Conversely, 61.2% of stateside Puerto Ricans reported speaking a language other than English at home compared to 67.1% of Puerto Ricans in Connecticut. About one in five Connecticut Puerto Ricans declared that they speak English at a less than "very well" fluency level, slightly higher than the rate for stateside Puerto Ricans of about one in six.

Ricans in Connecticut had a bachelor's degree or above, compared to 28.1% in Puerto Rico and the national 19.5% rate for stateside Puerto Ricans. Although not as drastic of a disparity, the proportion of males with bachelor's degrees was also lower in Connecticut at 10.1% than the 19.6% in Puerto Rico and 15.6% for other stateside Puerto Rican males.

Besides education, it is also important to examine the occupational distribution of Puerto Ricans in various regions of the country and the island. The data by major occupational category indicated that male Puerto Rican employment in Connecticut was notably lower in the management, business, science, and arts sector at 15.4%. This figure was significantly lower than the proportion of stateside Puerto Ricans, 23.4%, and Puerto Ricans in Puerto Rico, 23.9%, working in the management sector. Almost one in four (24.3%) Puerto Rican males in Con-

Table 3. Employment and Occupations, 2014

Puerto Ricans	Connecticut	United States	Puerto Rico*
EMPLOYMENT STATUS			
Population 16 years and over			
In labor force	64.6%	62.4%	43.7%
Civilian labor force	64.5%	61.6%	43.7%
Employed	55%	54.4%	35.4%
Unemployed	14.8%	11.6%	18.9%
Not in labor force	35.4%	37.6%	56.3%
Armed Forces	0.1%	0.8%	0%
OCCUPATION			
Civilian employed population 16 years and over			
Male	56,911	1,058,918	516,762
Management, business, science, and arts	15.4%	23.4%	23.9%
Service occupations	26.6%	22.5%	23%
Sales and office occupations	17.3%	19.6%	21.3%
Construction and maintenance	16.4%	13.8%	18%
Production, transportation, and moving	24.3%	20.7%	13.7%
Female	57,290	999,105	456,356
Management, business, science, and arts	29.2%	33.1%	39.7%
Service occupations	27%	24.4%	16.6%
Sales and office occupations	32.9%	35.7%	38.3%
Construction and maintenance	0.7%	0.6%	0.6%
Production, transportation, and moving	10.3%	6.2%	4.8%
CLASS OF WORKER			
Civilian employed population 16 years and over			
Private wage and salary workers	83.5%	82%	69%
Government workers	14.3%	14.8%	22.5%
Self-employed workers in own not incorporated business	2%	3.1%	8.3%
VETERAN STATUS			
Civilian population 18 years and over			
Civilian veteran	3.3%	6%	3.3%

Source: U.S. Census Bureau, 2014 American Community Survey 1-Year Estimates.
* Puerto Ricans only.

necticut worked in the production and transportation sector, notably higher than the stateside Puerto Rican average of 20.7% and 13.7% rate of those in Puerto Rico.

Three out of ten (29.2%) Puerto Rican women in Connecticut worked in the management, business, science, and arts sector, compared to four out of ten women in Puerto Rico. Also notable is that 27% of Puerto Rican women in Connecticut worked in the service industry, higher than the stateside average of 24.4%, and more than ten percentage points higher than the 16.6% rate in Puerto Rico.

Unemployment was higher for Connecticut Puerto Ricans, at 14.8%, than the average for all stateside Puerto Ricans of 11.6%. The employment rate of stateside and Connecticut Puerto Ricans (54.4% and 55%, respectively) was nearly 20 percentage points higher than the similar rate in Puerto Rico of 35.4%. The disparity in unemployment was equally significant. In 2014, the unemployment rate in Puerto Rico stood at 18.9%. Despite having a higher than average unemployment rate for Puerto Ricans, Connecticut's Puerto Ricans exhibited a higher rate of employment than island residents.

Besides better employment opportunities, differences in earnings are an important factor inducing migration to the United States from Puerto Rico or interstate mobility among Puerto Ricans. The average earnings of full-time, year-round working Puerto Rican men in

Table 4. Income and Earnings, 2014

Puerto Ricans	Connecticut	United States	Puerto Rico*
INCOME IN THE PAST 12 MONTHS (IN 2013 INFLATION-ADJUSTED DOLLARS)			
Households	91,505	1,635,808	1,175,297
Median household income (dollars)	$29,323	$39,322	$18,710
With earnings	73.3%	76.9%	54.7%
Mean earnings (dollars)	$55,839	$61,065	$36,407
With Social Security income	20.3%	24.1%	43.2%
Mean Social Security income (dollars)	$11,647	$13,727	$12,159
With Supplemental Security Income	15.6%	12.6%	0.4%
Mean Supplemental Security Income (dollars)	$8,194	$8,780	$10,025
With cash public assistance income	13.4%	6.9%	8.1%
Mean cash public assistance income (dollars)	$4,799	$3,441	$2,316
With retirement income	7.1%	10.1%	15.6%
Mean retirement income (dollars)	$14,010	$20,452	$15,387
With Food Stamp/SNAP benefits	50.4%	31.5%	39.7%
Families	62,780	1,114,628	830,807
Median family income (dollars)	$37,203	$44,499	$22,220
Married-couple family	41.3%	53.9%	56.1%
Median income (dollars)	$67,328	$67,129	$29,417
Male householder, no spouse present	13.1%	10.2%	9.5%
Median income (dollars)	$38,130	$37,513	$17,797
Female householder, no husband present	45.7%	35.9%	34.4%
Median income (dollars)	$21,131	$23,957	$13,554
Individuals	301,182	5,266,738	3,404,122
Per capita income (dollars)	$16,501	$18,457	$10,960
Mean earnings (dollars) for full-time, year-round workers:			
Male	$50,423	$50,756	$32,512
Female	$42,813	$42,263	$29,166

Source: U.S. Census Bureau, 2014 American Community Survey 1-Year Estimates. * Puerto Ricans only.

Puerto Rican Population by Counties in Connecticut, 2014

Puerto Ricans in Connecticut are concentrated in Hartford County (37%) and New Haven County (31%), accounting for two-thirds (68%) of Connecticut's Puerto Rican population. By way of comparison about half of the general Connecticut population lives in these two counties. Fairfield County, the southernmost and most populated county in Connecticut, with just over a quarter of the general population, accounted for 20% of the Puerto Rican population. The majority of Latinos, one in three, in Connecticut were also located in Fairfield County; and like Puerto Ricans, close to 90% of the Latino population was concentrated in Hartford, New Haven, and Fairfield counties. In all other counties, except for Windham County, the proportion of Connecticut Puerto Ricans present was below the proportion of the general population present in said county indicating that Puerto Ricans are underrepresented in those counties.

COUNTY	Puerto Rican Population	Percent	Latino Population	Percent	Total Population	Percent
Hartford County	100,998	37%	145,270	28%	897,374	25%
New Haven County	84,672	31%	137,844	27%	863,148	24%
Fairfield County	55,536	20%	167,047	33%	934,215	26%
New London County	13,861	5%	25,384	5%	274,071	8%
Windham County	8,331	3%	12,070	2%	117,918	3%
Tolland County	4,456	2%	7,157	1%	152,251	4%
Middlesex County	4,441	2%	8,726	2%	165,534	5%
Litchfield County	3,261	1%	9,297	2%	187,542	5%
Total	**275,556**	**100%**	**512,795**	**100%**	**3,592,053**	**100%**

Sources: U.S. Census Bureau and 2014 American Community Survey 5-Year Estimates
Notes: Total counts for populations may differ depending on whether the estimates are derived from the five-year estimates or the one-year estimates of the American Community Survey

PUERTO RICAN POPULATION BY COUNTIES IN CONNECTICUT, 2014

PUERTO RICAN POPULATION

1 dot = 200

'06-'14 PUERTO RICAN ARRIVALS

1 dot = 100

BOUNDARIES

County

City/Towns

Census Tracts

CONGRESSIONAL DISTRICT

Republican

Democrat

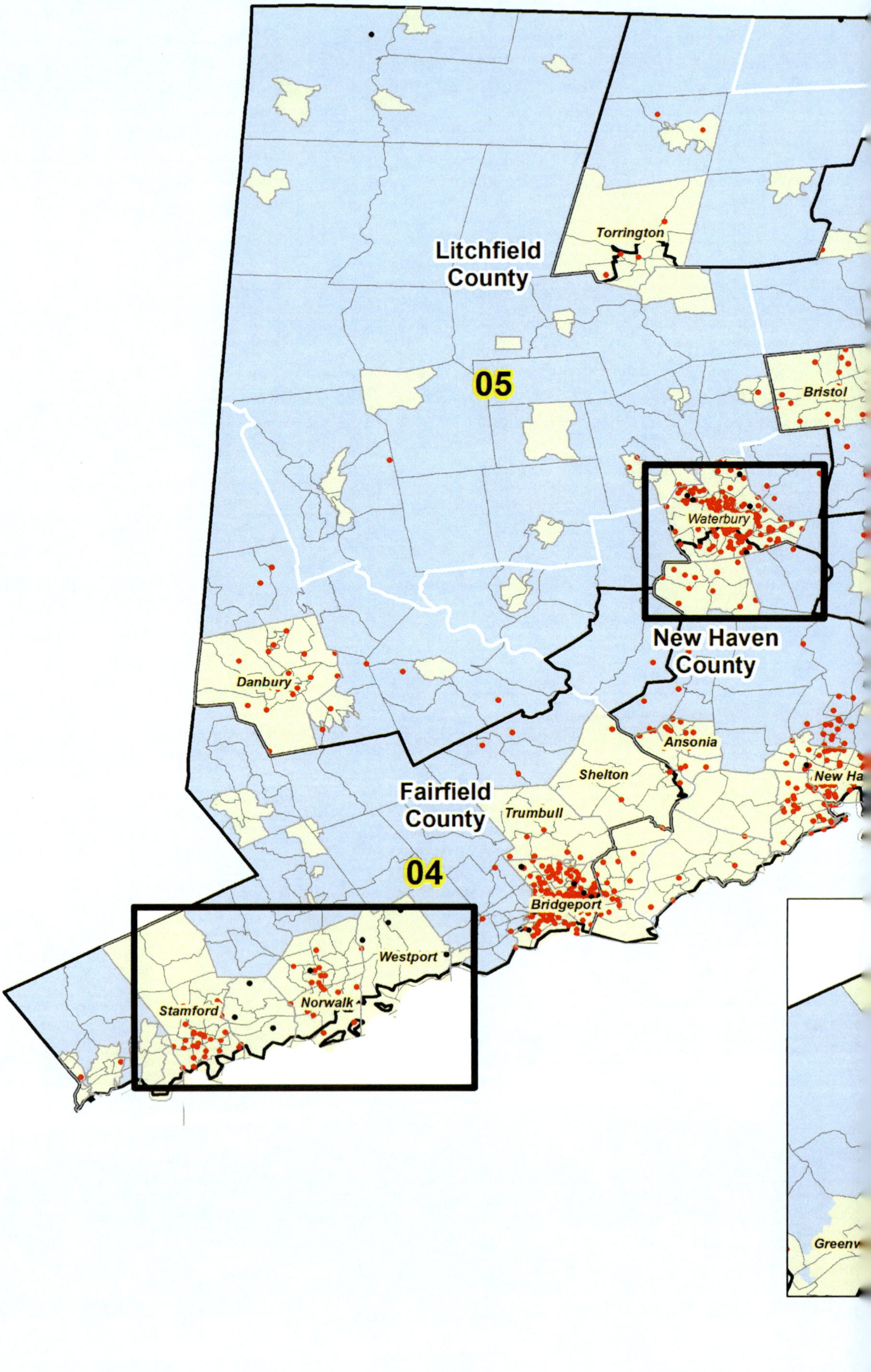

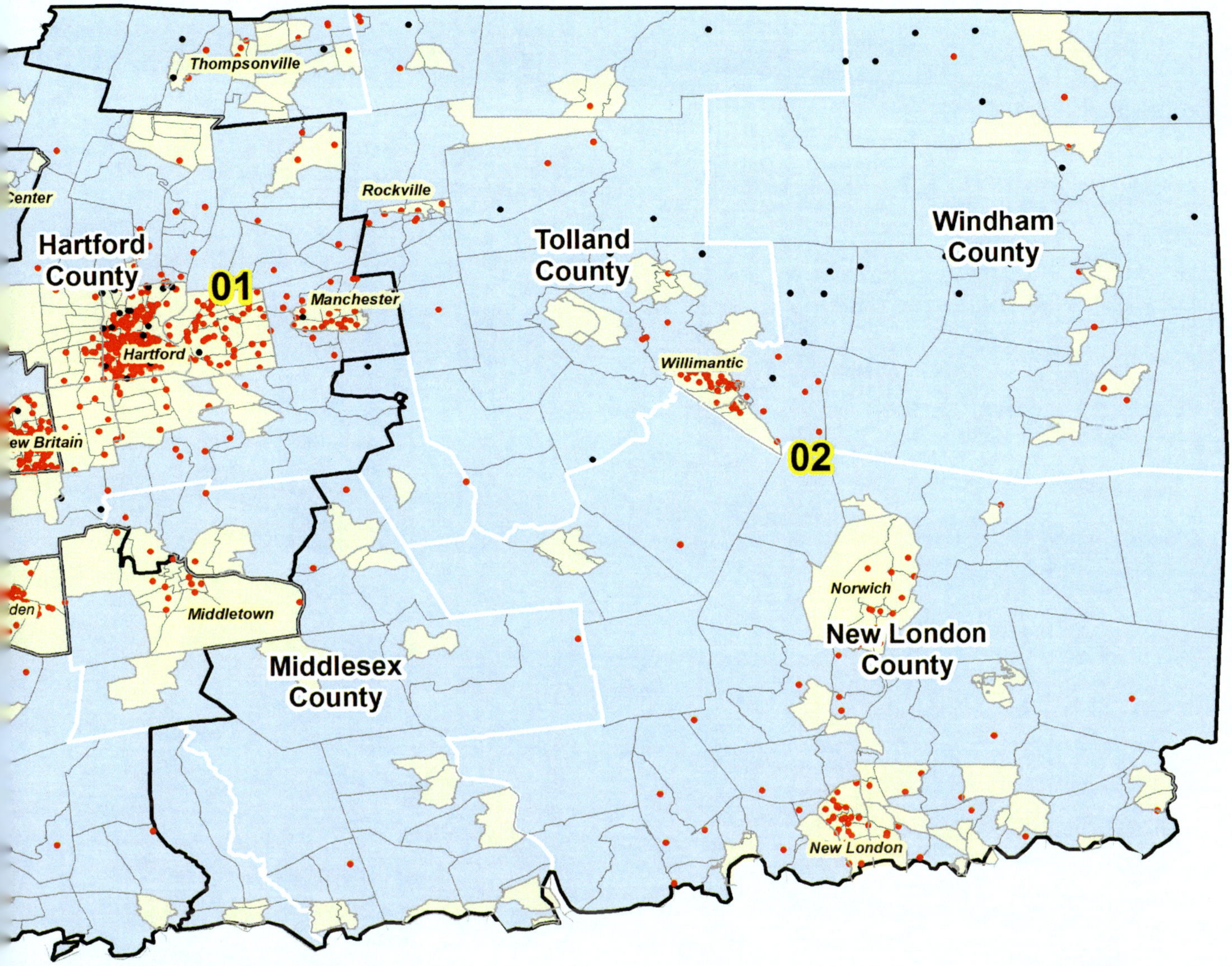
Thompsonville
Rockville
Center
Hartford County
01
Manchester
Hartford
Tolland County
Windham County
Willimantic
02
ew Britain
Middletown
den
Middlesex County
Norwich
New London County
New London

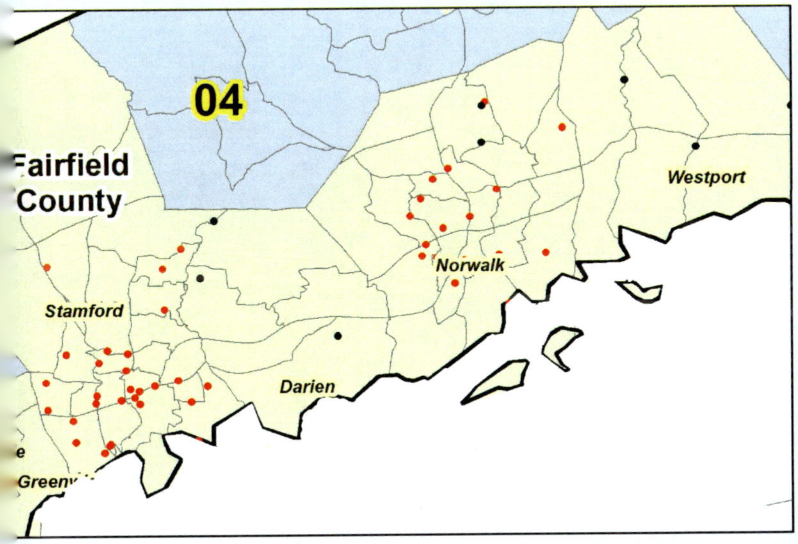
04
Fairfield County
Westport
Norwalk
Stamford
Darien

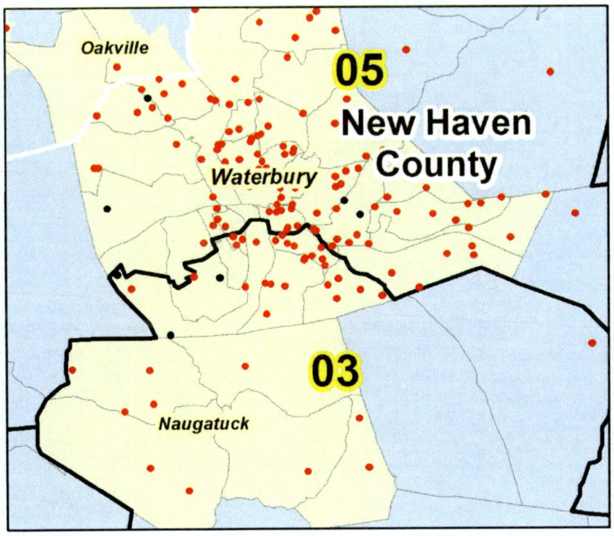
Oakville
05
New Haven County
Waterbury
03
Naugatuck

PUERTO RICAN POPULATION BY COUNTIES IN CONNECTICUT, 2014

PUERTO RICAN POPULATION

1 dot = 200

'06-'14 PUERTO RICAN ARRIVALS

1 dot = 100

BOUNDARIES

County

City/Towns

Census Tracts

CONGRESSIONAL DISTRICT

Republican

Democrat

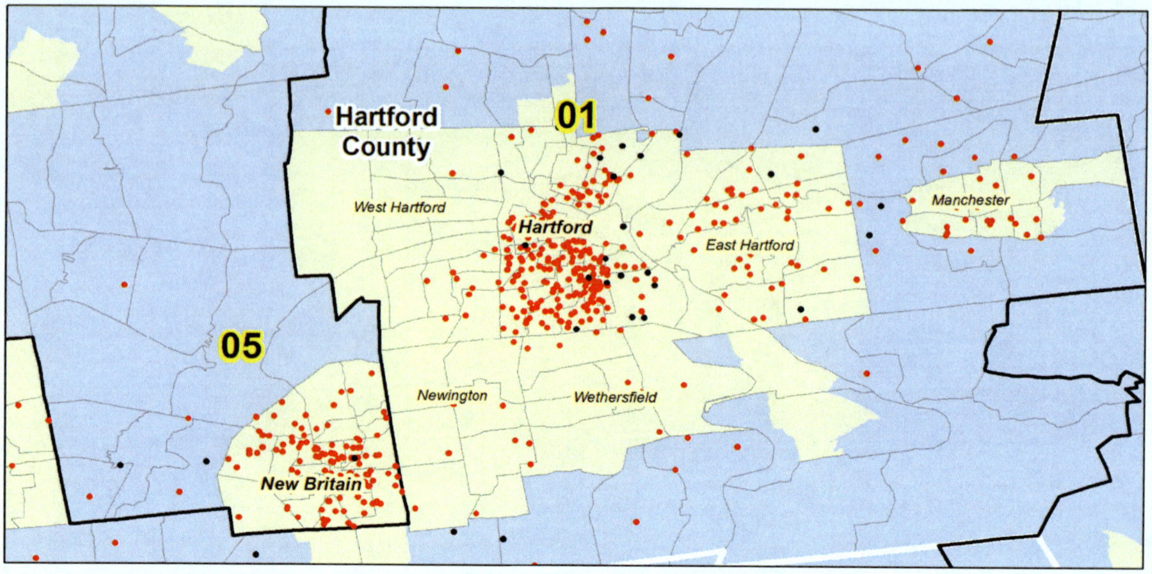

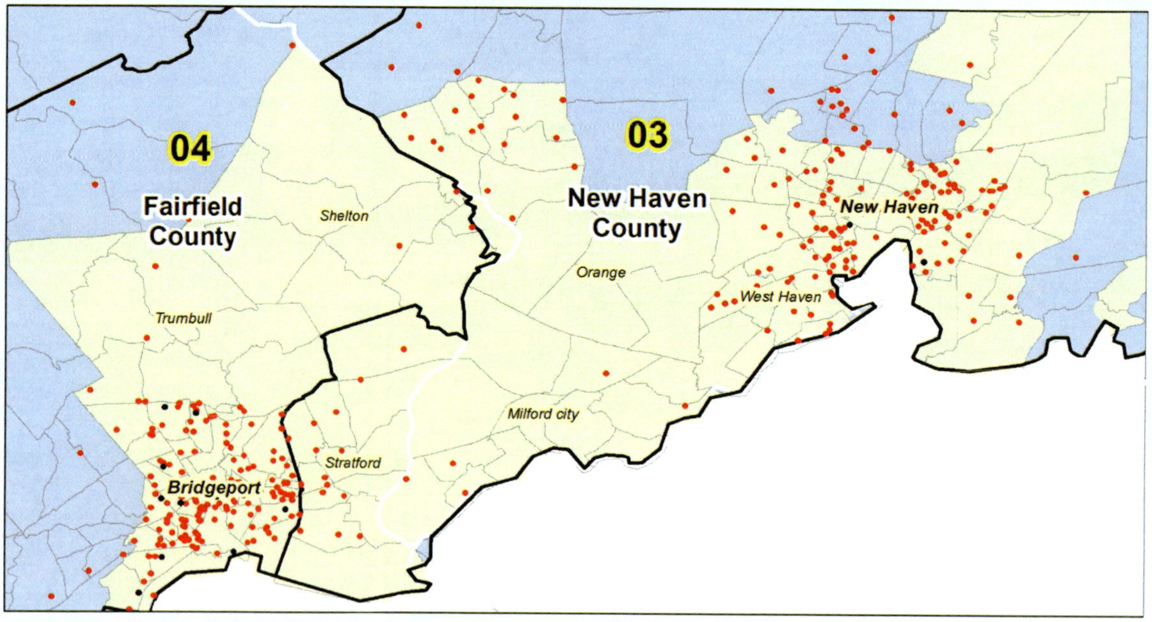

Connecticut of $50,423 were nearly equal to the state-side average of $50,756. Puerto Rican women in Connecticut averaged marginally higher earnings of $42,813 than all stateside Puerto Rican women who averaged $42,253. Earnings for Puerto Ricans in Connecticut were significantly higher than for Puerto Rico where full-time, year-round men in 2014 earned $32,512 and women earned $29,166.

Household and family incomes are important indicators of economic well-being. These indicators were much lower for Puerto Ricans in Connecticut than for stateside Puerto Ricans, but still more than 50 percent higher than the island median incomes. Median household income was $29,323 for Puerto Ricans in Connecticut, significantly less than the $39,322 stateside Puerto Rican average, but more than the $18,710 reported in Puerto Rico. These differences were also evident in per capita income, but to a lesser magnitude. In 2014, per capita income for Puerto Ricans in Connecticut was $16,501. This figure was lower than the stateside Puerto Rican average per capita income of $18,457, but higher than the $10,960 per capita income for Puerto Ricans living in Puerto Rico. Puerto Ricans in Connecticut are likely to earn more than they would in Puerto Rico, but still earn below the national average.

Puerto Ricans in Connecticut had $4.97 billion in purchasing power representing a significant potential market for

Graph 4.A: Mean Earnings for Full-Time Year-Round Puerto Rican Workers, 2014

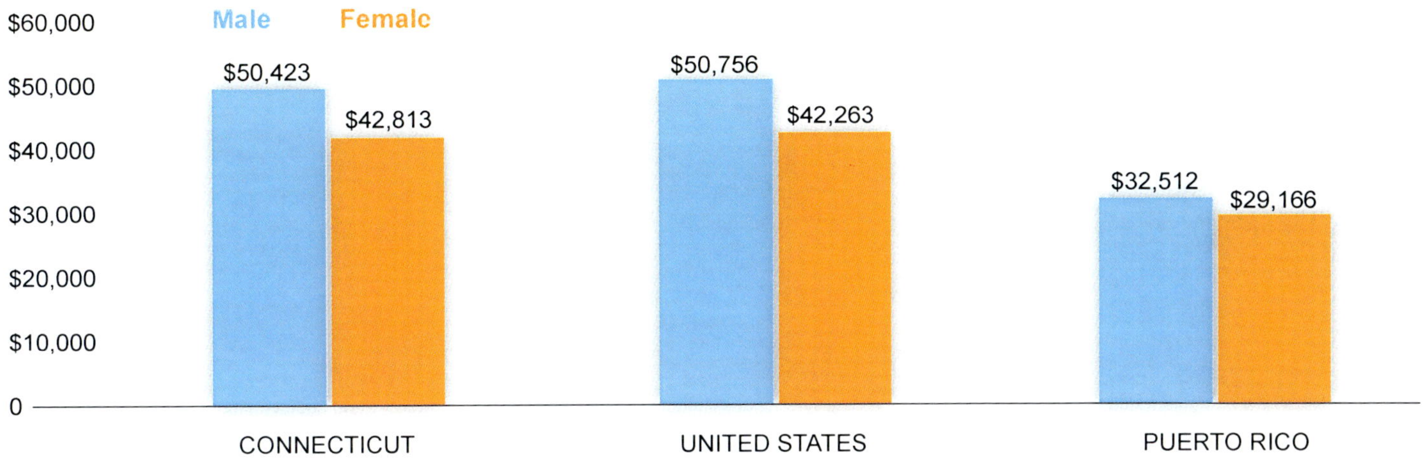

Graph 4.B: Puerto Rican Purchasing Power in Billions of Dollars, 2014

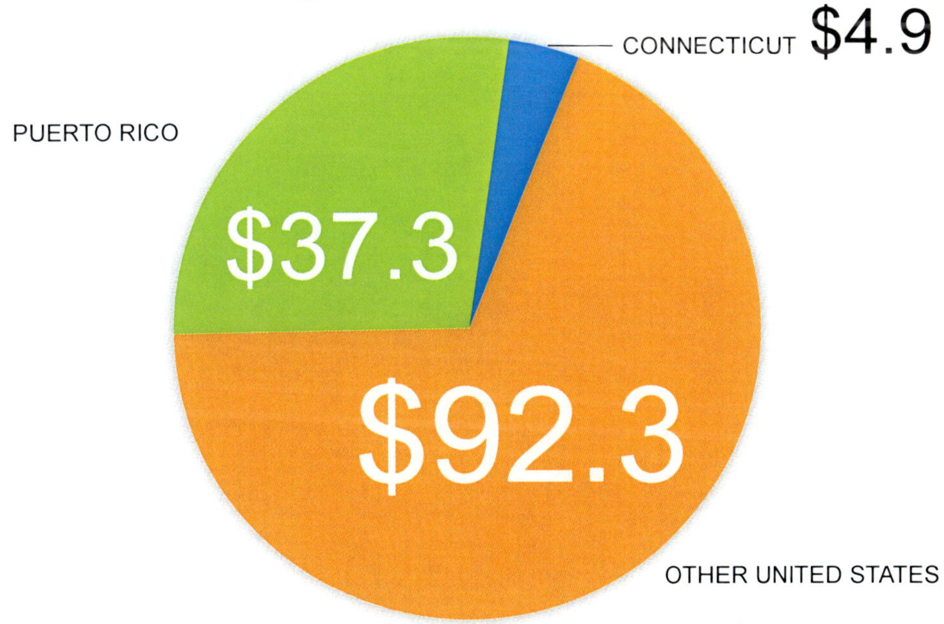

Graph 5.A: Poverty Rates, 2014

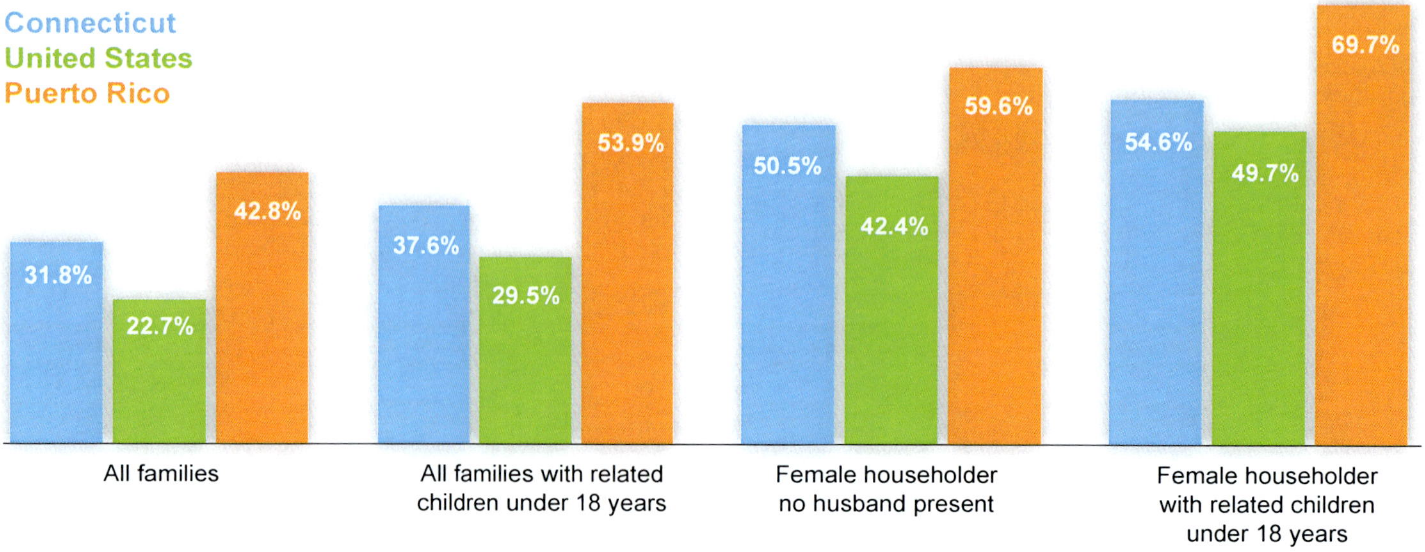

Table 5. Poverty, 2014

Puerto Ricans	Connecticut	United States	Puerto Rico*
POVERTY RATES			
All families	31.8%	22.7%	42.8%
With related children under 18 years	37.6%	29.5%	53.9%
With related children under 5 years only	29.6%	24.6%	57.1%
Married-couple family	13.2%	9.7%	30.9%
With related children under 18 years	14.4%	11.3%	35.5%
With related children under 5 years only	N/A	5.9%	33.9%
Female householder, no husband present, family	50.5%	42.4%	59.6%
With related children under 18 years	54.6%	49.7%	69.7%
With related children under 5 years only	58.5%	49.4%	75.7%
All people	33.1%	26.2%	46.6%
Under 18 years	38.4%	33.4%	58.7%
Related children under 18 years	38%	33.1%	58.6%
Related children under 5 years	41.4%	34.7%	62.8%
Related children 5 to 17 years	36.6%	32.4%	57.3%
18 years and over	30.2%	22.8%	43.2%
18 to 64 years	29.7%	22.8%	43.8%
65 years and over	35.7%	22.4%	41%
People in families	30%	23.6%	44.6%
Unrelated individuals 15 years and over	48.7%	38.5%	58%

Source: U.S. Census Bureau, 2014 American Community Survey 1-Year Estimates.
* Puerto Ricans only.

trade, investments, general and medical tourism, and other economic activities. From an economic perspective, all stateside Puerto Ricans represented 72.3% of the $134.5 billion total purchasing power of the entire Puerto Rican community in 2014. Stateside Puerto Ricans had more than double the total purchasing power of Puerto Ricans in Puerto Rico of $37.3 billion. Purchasing power is defined simply as per capita income multiplied by the Puerto Rican population.

The poverty rate for all Puerto Rican families was 31.8% in Connecticut, 22.7% for Puerto Ricans across the U.S., and 42.8% in Puerto Rico. Although Puerto Rico has higher poverty rates and thus a higher proportion of qualified recipients, Connecticut has higher enrollment in welfare assistance services. Families with female householder, no husband present and children under 18 years of age exhibited much higher incidence of poverty than the average family. For Puerto Rican female-headed families with children the rates were 54.6% in Connecticut, 49.7% for the rest of the U.S., and 69.7% in Puerto Rico. These are inordinately high poverty rates by any measure or comparative context.

In 2014, the proportion of households that received cash public assistance income of 13.4% was higher for Puerto Ricans in Connecticut than the 6.9% rate of all stateside Puerto Ricans, and 8.1% in Puerto Rico. The average amounts received by public assistance recipient households were higher for Connecticut Puerto Ricans ($4,799) than among all stateside Puerto Ricans ($3,441). The proportion of Puerto Rican households in Connecticut receiving benefits from the Food Stamp/SNAP program was 50.4% in 2014, 18.9 percentage points higher than the 31.5% rate for Puerto Rican households in other parts of the U.S. and 10.7 percent points higher than the 39.7% for Puerto Rico.

Housing is a primary determinant of the cost of living. The median value of owner-occupied housing for Puerto Ricans in Connecticut was $173,600, slightly lower than the $175,900 average for stateside Puerto Ricans, and $119,500 in Puerto Rico. The median monthly owner mortgage cost was $1,740 for Puerto Ricans in Connecticut, higher than the $1,545 for other stateside Puerto Ricans. A comparable cost was $873 in Puerto Rico. These relative prices and ownership costs, coupled with income data, were reflected in ownership rates. Puerto Ricans in Connecticut had lower rates of home ownership than Puerto Ricans in Puerto Rico or nationwide. The Census data revealed that Puerto Ricans in Connecticut had a 27.7% rate of owner-occupied housing units, less than the national average for Puerto Ricans of 36%. The home ownership rate in Puerto Rico was much higher at 68.7%.

Table 6. Housing and Health Insurance, 2014

Puerto Ricans	Connecticut	United States	Puerto Rico*
HOUSING			
Owner-occupied housing units	27.7%	36%	68.7%
Monthly owner costs as a percentage of household income in the past 12 months			
Less than 30 percent	56.5%	62.8%	52.6%
30 percent or more	43.5%	37.2%	47.4%
Owner-occupied housing units			
Median value (dollars)	$173,600	$175,900	$119,500
Median selected monthly owner costs with a mortgage (dollars)	$1,740	$1,545	$873
HEALTH INSURANCE COVERAGE			
Civilian noninstitutionalized population			
With private health insurance	39.4%	51.6%	38%
With public coverage	57.4%	43.5%	62.9%
No health insurance coverage	7.2%	11.5%	5.5%

Source: U.S. Census Bureau, 2014 American Community Survey 1-Year Estimates.
* Puerto Ricans only.

Puerto Ricans in Illinois, 2014

In 2014 Illinois had the 7th largest Puerto Rican population in the United States with 211,626 Puerto Ricans, comprising 1.6% of Illinois' almost 12.9 million residents. Between 2000 and 2014 the Puerto Rican population in Illinois grew from 157,851 to 211,626 individuals.

Graph 1.A: Latino Population Illinois, 2014

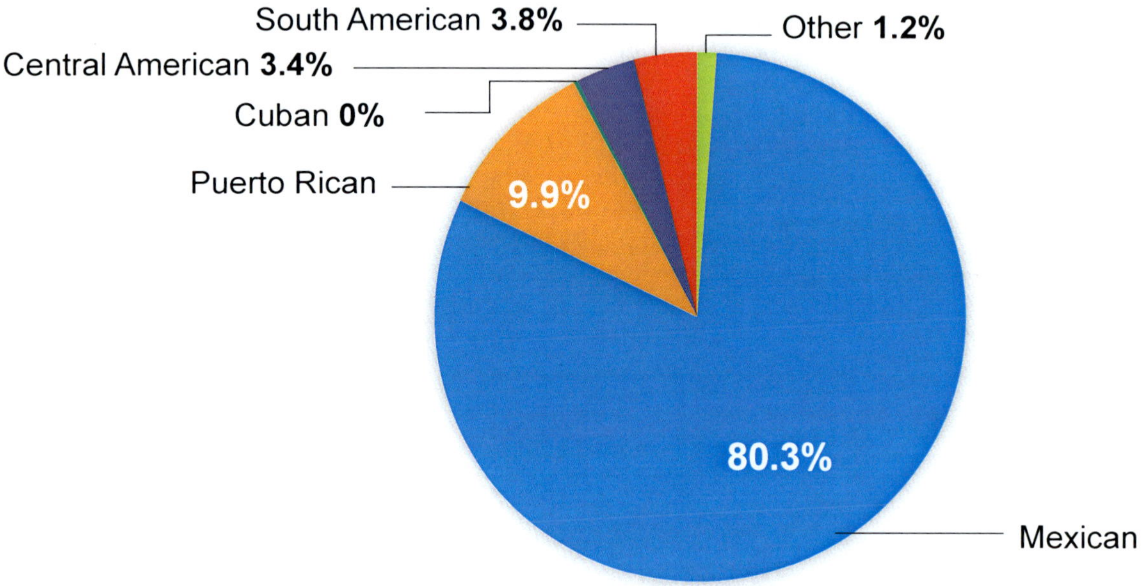

Table 1. Puerto Rican and Latino Population in Illinois

	2000		2010		2014	
Total	12,419,293	100%	12,830,632	100%	12,880,580	100%
Not Hispanic or Latino	10,889,031	88%	10,803,054	84%	10,729,074	83.3%
Hispanic or Latino	1,530,262	12%	2,027,578	16%	2,151,506	16.7%
Mexican	1,144,390	9.2%	1,602,403	12%	1,711,841	13.3%
Puerto Rican	157,851	1.3%	182,989	1%	211,626	1.6%
Cuban	18,438	0.1%	22,541	0%	22,566	0.2%
Dominican Republic	2,934	0.0%	5,691	0%	6,052	0.0%
Central American	39,377	0.3%	70,000	1%	73,255	0.6%
South American	38,676	0.3%	67,862	1%	80,048	0.6%
Other	128,596	1%	76,092	1%	46,118	0.4%

Sources: U.S. Census Bureau, Census 2000 Summary File 1, 2010 Census. Summary File 1, and 2014 American Community Survey 1-Year Estimates.

In 2014 Puerto Ricans accounted for almost 10% of Illinois' Latinos — a population characterized by the predominance of the Mexican origin population. In total, Latinos accounted for 2.6 million of Illinois' estimated 12.9 million residents, or proportionately, about 16.7% of the population. Puerto Ricans grew in total proportional representation from 1.3% of the total population in 2000 to 1.6% in 2014.

The median age of Puerto Ricans in Illinois in 2014 was 28 years, similar to the median age for stateside Puerto Ricans of 28.9 years. Both were more than a decade younger than

Graph 2.A: Puerto Rican Education Attainment, 25 years and over, 2014

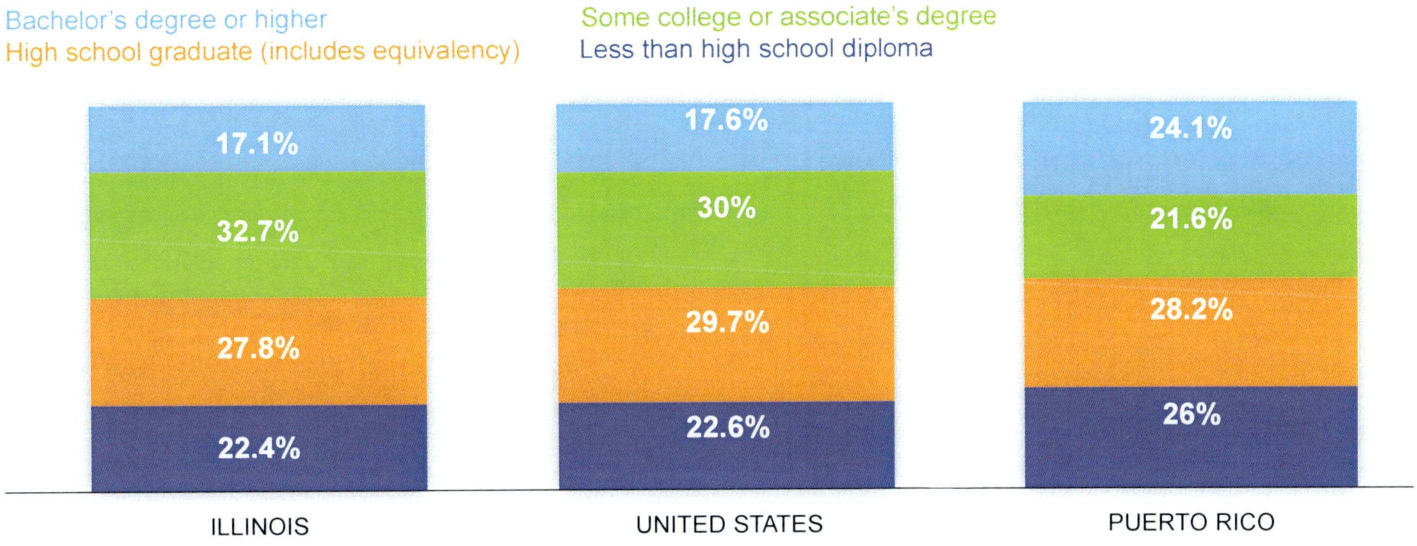

Table 2. Age, Education, and Language, 2014

Puerto Ricans	Illinois	United States	Puerto Rico*
TOTAL POPULATION	211,626	5,266,738	3,404,122
Median age (years)	28	28.9	38.9
62 years and over	9.5%	9.9%	21%
EDUCATIONAL ATTAINMENT			
Population 25 years and over			
Less than high school diploma	22.4%	22.6%	26%
High school graduate (includes equivalency)	27.8%	29.7%	28.2%
Some college or associate's degree	32.7%	30%	21.6%
Bachelor's degree or higher	17.1%	17.6%	24.1%
Male, bachelor's degree or higher	14.8%	15.6%	19.6%
Female, bachelor's degree or higher	19.1%	19.5%	28.1%
LANGUAGE SPOKEN AT HOME AND ABILITY TO SPEAK ENGLISH			
Population 5 years and over			
English only	40.3%	38.8%	5.3%
Language other than English	59.7%	61.2%	94.7%
Speak English less than "very well"	13.9%	17.3%	78.8%

Source: U.S. Census Bureau, 2014 American Community Survey 1-Year Estimates. * Puerto Ricans only.

Puerto Rico's median age of 38.9 years. The proportion of Puerto Ricans in Illinois 62 or older was also very similar to that of stateside Puerto Ricans, 9.5% and 9.9%, respectively. Both proportions are over ten percentage points below Puerto Rico's 21% of residents 62 or older.

Puerto Ricans in Illinois, while ostensibly bilingual, demonstrated a strong command of English via fluency indicators. Two out of five Puerto Ricans in Illinois (40.3%) reported only speaking English at home, compared to 38.8% of stateside Puerto Ricans. However, the 13.9% of Illinois Puerto Ricans who responded as speaking English less than "very well" is lower than the 17.3% for stateside Puerto Ricans in general.

Puerto Ricans in Illinois over the age of 25 had educational attainment indicators similar to those of stateside Puerto Ricans. Although only 17.1% of Illinois Puerto Ricans age 25 and older possessed a bachelor's degree or above — a figure slightly below the stateside Puerto Rican average of 17.7%, a higher proportion had some college experience or an associate's degree (32.7%). Combining Puerto Ricans in Illinois with a bachelor's degree or above with those that possessed either some college experience or an asso-

Table 3. Employment and Occupations, 2014

Puerto Ricans	Illinois	United States	Puerto Rico*
EMPLOYMENT STATUS			
Population 16 years and over			
In labor force	65.8%	62.4%	43.7%
Civilian labor force	65.8%	61.6%	43.7%
Employed	58.6%	54.4%	35.4%
Unemployed	10.9%	11.6%	18.9%
Not in labor force	34.2%	37.6%	56.3%
Armed Forces	0%	0.8%	0%
OCCUPATION			
Civilian employed population 16 years and over			
Male	44,290	1,058,918	516,762
Management, business, science, and arts	22.4%	23.4%	23.9%
Service occupations	22.5%	22.5%	23%
Sales and office occupations	22%	19.6%	21.3%
Construction and maintenance	9%	13.8%	18%
Production, transportation, and moving	24%	20.7%	13.7%
Female	44,794	999,105	456,356
Management, business, science, and arts	31.5%	33.1%	39.7%
Service occupations	21.3%	24.4%	16.6%
Sales and office occupations	37.1%	35.7%	38.3%
Construction and maintenance	0.2%	0.6%	0.6%
Production, transportation, and moving	10%	6.2%	4.8%
CLASS OF WORKER			
Civilian employed population 16 years and over			
Private wage and salary workers	85%	82%	69%
Government workers	12.8%	14.8%	22.5%
Self-employed workers in own not incorporated business	2.1%	3.1%	8.3%
VETERAN STATUS			
Civilian population 18 years and over			
Civilian veteran	4%	6%	3.3%

Source: U.S. Census Bureau, 2014 American Community Survey 1-Year Estimates.* Puerto Ricans only.

Puerto Rican Population by Counties in Illinois, 2014

More than two thirds of Puerto Ricans in Illinois (71.8%) resided in Cook County. Surrounding Kane County (5.6%), Lake County (4.5%), DuPage County (3.9%), and Will County (3.6%) accounted for another 17.6% of the Puerto Rican population in Illinois. Despite the heavy Puerto Rican concentration in the northeast Illinois, in Chicago's metropolitan area, small population clusters were scattered in other metropolitan areas including Winnebago County (1.2%) to the west, St. Clair County to the southwest (0.6%), and Champaign County to the south (0.5%). Illinois' Latino population demonstrated a similar pattern of settlement with 61.1% residing in Cook County, but was overall slightly more dispersed than the Puerto Rican population.

COUNTY	Puerto Rican Population	Percent	Latino Population	Percent	Total Population	Percent
Cook County	141,928	71.8%	1,281,217	61.1%	5,227,827	40.6%
Kane County	10,984	5.6%	162,048	7.7%	521,874	4.1%
Lake County	8,833	4.5%	143,841	6.9%	703,170	5.5%
DuPage County	7,782	3.9%	127,142	6.1%	926,485	7.2%
Will County	7,212	3.6%	109,841	5.2%	682,108	5.3%
Winnebago County	2,361	1.2%	33,578	1.6%	292,026	2.3%
McHenry County	2,306	1.2%	36,623	1.7%	307,888	2.4%
Kendall County	1,969	1%	19,155	0.9%	118,194	0.9%
DeKalb County	1,145	0.6%	11,053	0.5%	104,919	0.8%
St. Clair County	1,108	0.6%	9,534	0.5%	268,415	2.1%
Champaign County	1,022	0.5%	11,165	0.5%	204,214	1.6%
Other Counties	10,977	5.6%	150,298	7.2%	3,511,120	27.3%
Total	**197,627**	**100%**	**2,095,495**	**100%**	**12,868,747**	**100%**

Sources: U.S. Census Bureau 2014 American Community Survey 5-Year Estimates

Notes: Total counts for populations may differ depending on whether the estimates are derived from the five-year estimates or the one-year estimates of the American Community Survey.

PUERTO RICAN POPULATION BY COUNTIES IN ILLINOIS, 2014

PUERTO RICAN POPULATION

1 dot = 500

'06-'14 PUERTO RICAN ARRIVALS

1 dot = 50

BOUNDARIES

County

City/Towns

Census Tracts

CONGRESSIONAL DISTRICT

Republican

Democrat

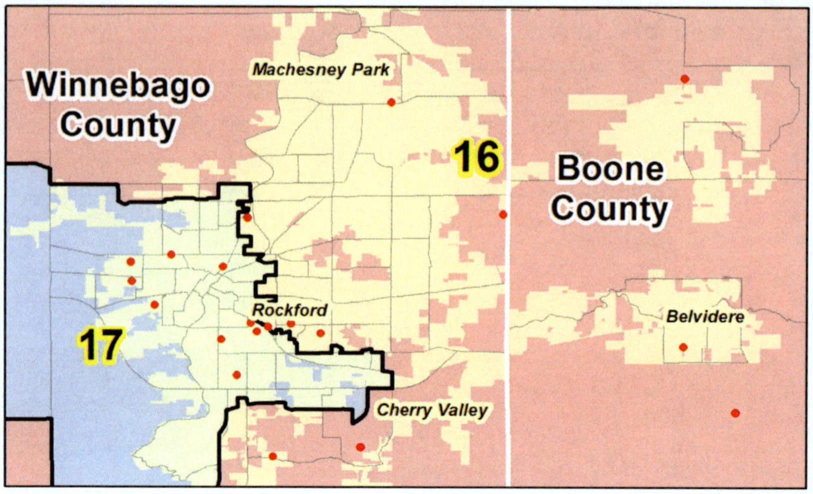

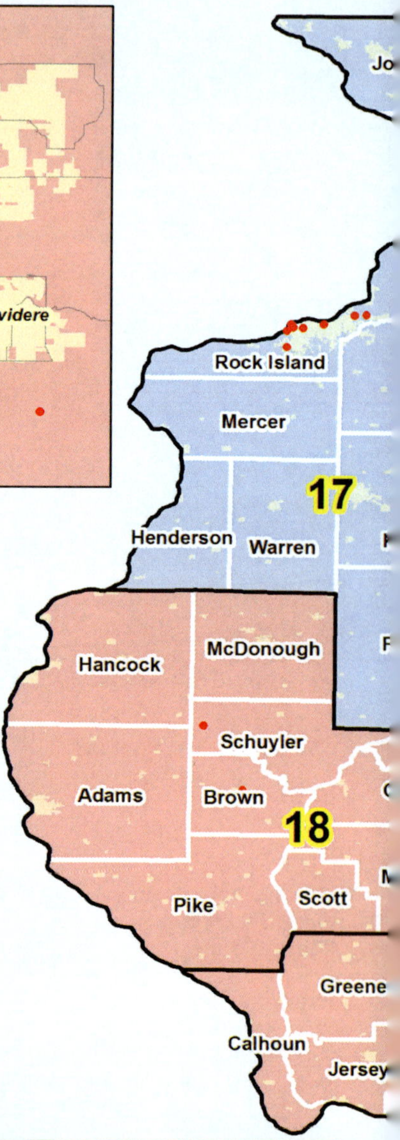

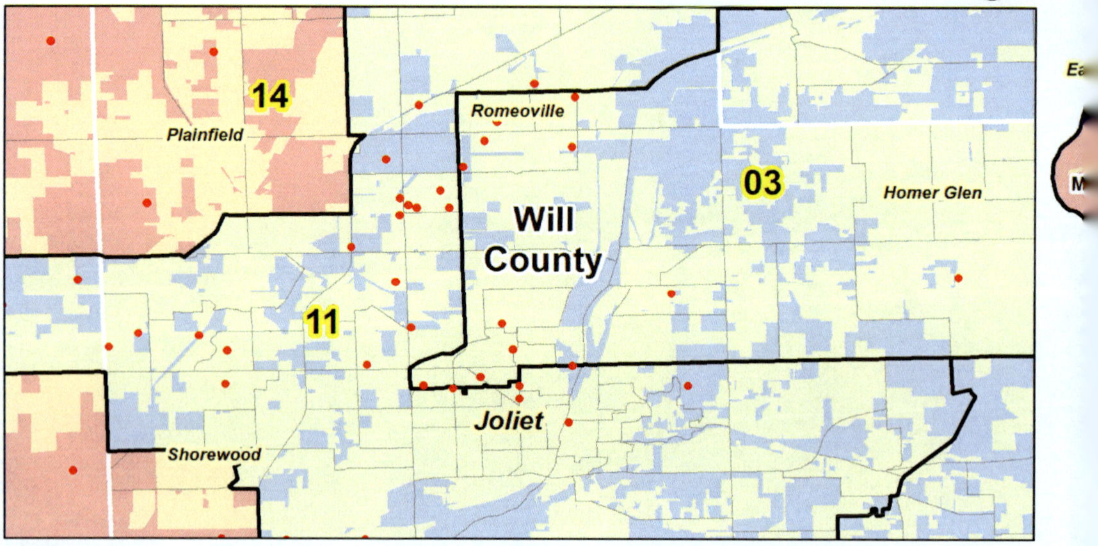

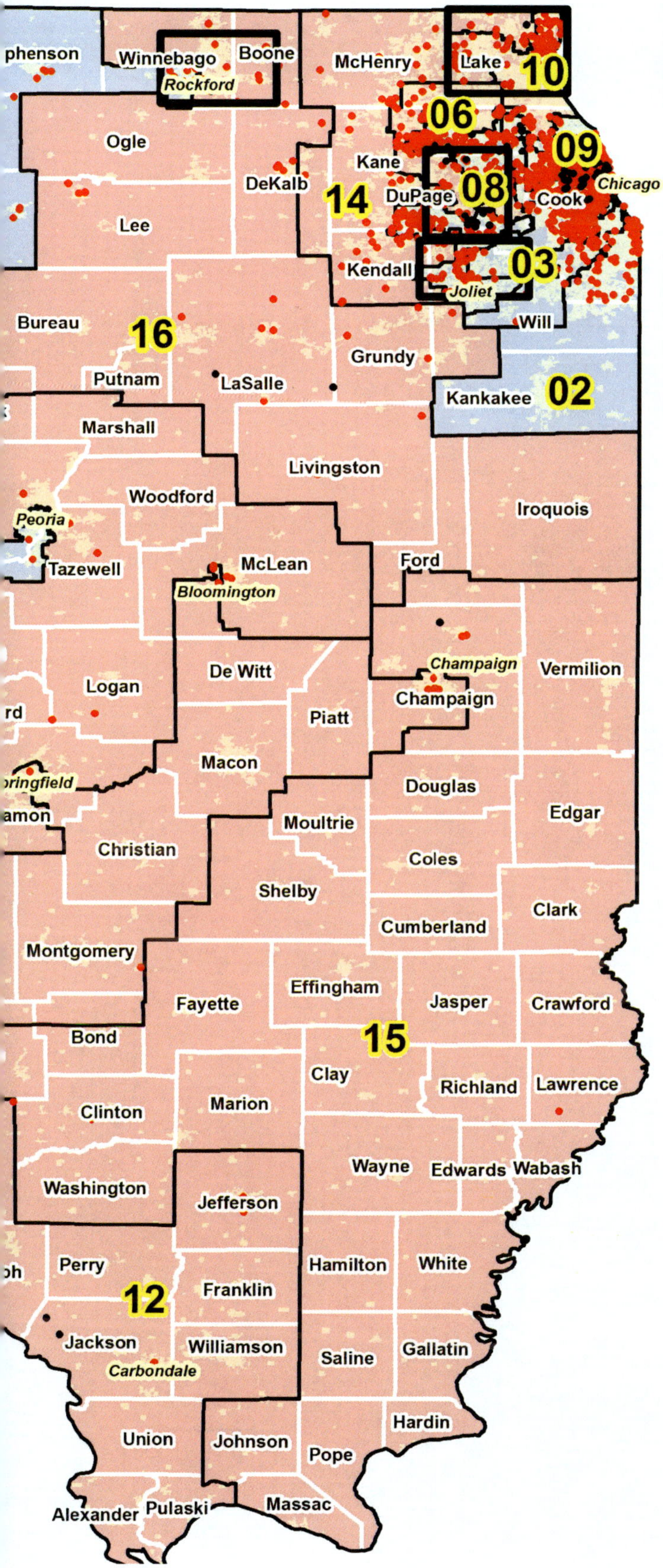

phenson
Winnebago
Boone
Rockford
McHenry
Lake
10
06
09
Ogle
Kane
Chicago
DeKalb
14
DuPage
08
Cook
Lee
Kendall
03
Joliet
Will
Bureau
16
Grundy
Putnam
LaSalle
Kankakee
02
Marshall
Livingston
Woodford
Iroquois
Peoria
Tazewell
McLean
Ford
Bloomington
Champaign
Vermilion
De Witt
Logan
Champaign
Piatt
Macon
Douglas
Edgar
Moultrie
Christian
Coles
Shelby
Clark
Cumberland
Montgomery
Effingham
Fayette
Jasper
Crawford
Bond
15
Clay
Richland
Lawrence
Clinton
Marion
Wayne
Edwards
Wabash
Washington
Jefferson
Perry
Hamilton
White
12
Franklin
Jackson
Williamson
Saline
Gallatin
Carbondale
Hardin
Union
Johnson
Pope
Alexander
Pulaski
Massac

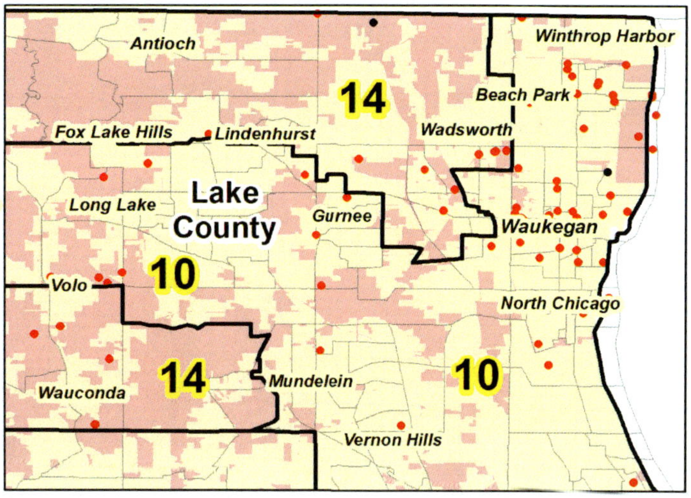

Antioch
Winthrop Harbor
14
Beach Park
Fox Lake Hills
Lindenhurst
Wadsworth
Lake County
Long Lake
Gurnee
Waukegan
10
Volo
North Chicago
14
Mundelein
10
Wauconda
Vernon Hills

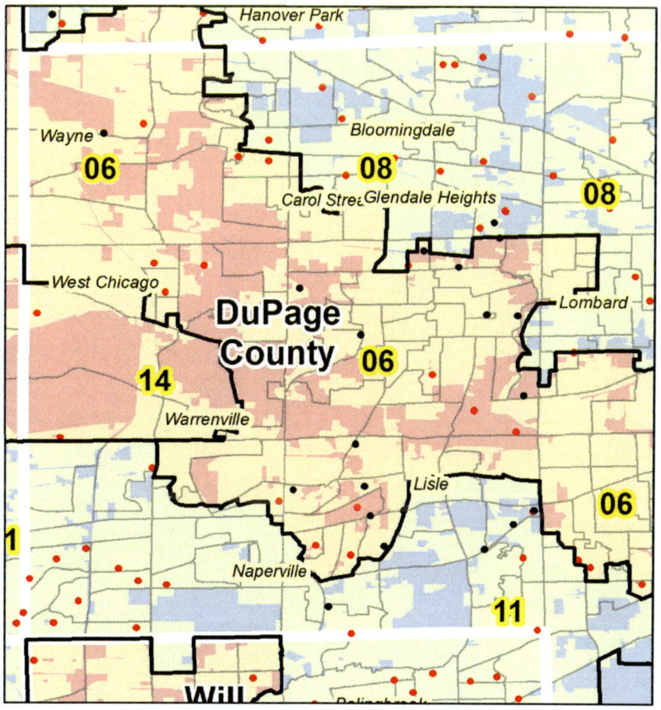

Hanover Park
Bloomingdale
Wayne
06
08
Carol Stre
Glendale Heights
08
West Chicago
Lombard
DuPage County
06
14
Warrenville
Lisle
06
Naperville
11
Will

PUERTO RICAN POPULATION BY COUNTIES IN ILLINOIS, 2014

PUERTO RICAN POPULATION

1 dot = 500

'06-'14 PUERTO RICAN ARRIVALS

1 dot = 50

BOUNDARIES

County

City/Towns

Census Tracts

CONGRESSIONAL DISTRICT

Republican

Democrat

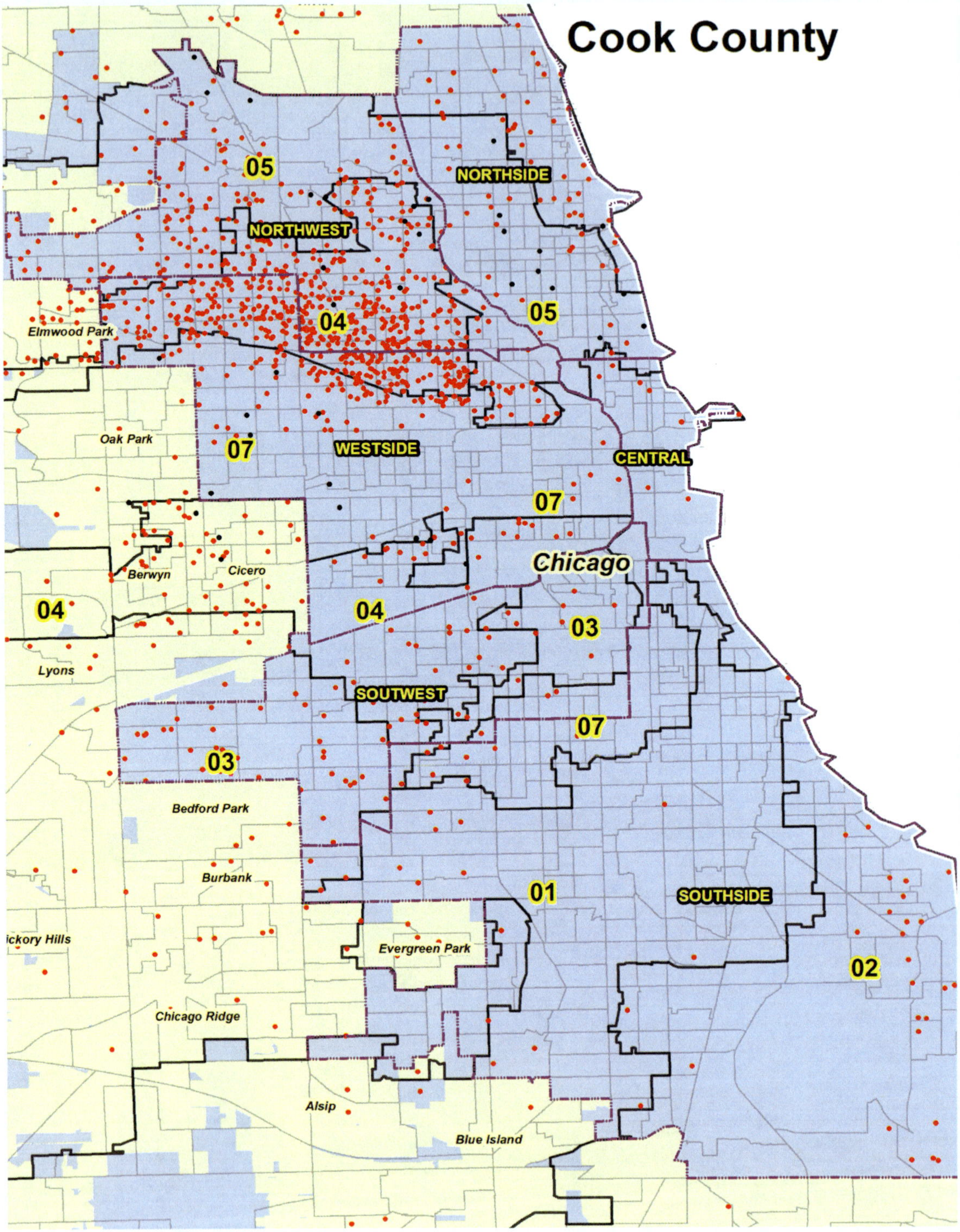

ciate's degree (49.8%) reveals a higher overall educational attainment when compared to all stateside Puerto Ricans (47.7%) and Puerto Ricans in Puerto Rico (45.7%).

Employment in the higher wage management, business, science, and arts occupational sector for Puerto Rican men and women in Illinois (22.4% and 31.5%, respectively) was consistent with stateside indicators for Puerto Rican men and women (23.4% and 33.1%, respectively). However, Puerto Rican women in Illinois were significantly less present in the management, science, business and arts sector compared to men and women in Puerto Rico (31.5% and 39.7%, respectively).

Illinois' working Puerto Rican population was very similar to those in other states, but had slightly better indicators regarding labor force participation and unemployment. Unemployment among Puerto Ricans in Illinois (10.9%) was slightly lower than the stateside Puerto Rican average (11.6%) and eight percentage points below Puerto Rico's 18.9% unemployment rate in 2014. Labor force participation in Illinois, 65.8%, was slightly higher than the stateside Puerto Rican rate of 61.6%. Both rates were approximately 20 percentage points higher than Puerto Rico's labor force participation rate of 43.7%.

Table 4. Income and Earnings, 2014

Puerto Ricans	Illinois	United States	Puerto Rico*
INCOME IN THE PAST 12 MONTHS (IN 2013 INFLATION-ADJUSTED DOLLARS)			
Households	60,793	1,635,808	1,175,297
Median household income (dollars)	$44,991	$39,322	$18,710
With earnings	79.4%	76.9%	54.7%
Mean earnings (dollars)	$68,143	$61,065	$36,407
With Social Security income	23.7%	24.1%	43.2%
Mean Social Security income (dollars)	$14,147	$13,727	$12,159
With Supplemental Security Income	10.1%	12.6%	0.4%
Mean Supplemental Security Income (dollars)	$9,598	$8,780	$10,025
With cash public assistance income	5.8%	6.9%	8.1%
Mean cash public assistance income (dollars)	$2,729	$3,441	$2,316
With retirement income	9.1%	10.1%	15.6%
Mean retirement income (dollars)	$18,882	$20,452	$15,387
With Food Stamp/SNAP benefits	26.8%	31.5%	39.7%
Families	42,313	111,4628	83,0807
Median family income (dollars)	$52,821	$44,499	$22,220
Married-couple family	53%	53.9%	56.1%
Median income (dollars)	$76,891	$67,129	$29,417
Male householder, no spouse present	12.6%	10.2%	9.5%
Median income (dollars)	$43,617	$37,513	$17,797
Female householder, no husband present	34.4%	35.9%	34.4%
Median income (dollars)	$29,656	$23,957	$13,554
Individuals	211,626	5,266,738	3,404,122
Per capita income (dollars)	$19,227	$18,457	$10,960
Mean earnings (dollars) for full-time, year-round workers:			
Male	$47,490	$50,756	$32,512
Female	$44,701	$42,263	$29,166

Source: U.S. Census Bureau, 2014 American Community Survey 1-Year Estimates.
* Puerto Ricans only.

Although full-time year-round Puerto Rican males earned about $3,000 less ($47,490) on average than Puerto Ricans in the U.S. as a whole ($50,756), women earned about $2,400 more ($44,701) in Illinois than the stateside average of $42,263. Incomes for Puerto Rican males and females in Illinois were substantially higher than in Puerto Rico ($32,512 and $29,166 for men and women respectively).

Household and family income is an important indicator of economic well-being. These indicators were moderately higher for Puerto Ricans in Illinois compared to stateside Puerto Ricans. Both were substantially higher than island residents. Median household income was $44,991 for Puerto Ricans in Illinois and $39,322 for other stateside Puerto Ricans, and $18,710 for the island. These differences were also evident in per capita income, but to a lesser magnitude. In 2014, per capita income for Puerto Ricans in Illinois was $19,227 and $18,457 for other stateside Puerto Ricans, and $10,960 for island residents.

Graph 4.A: Mean Earnings for Full-Time Year-Round Puerto Rican Workers, 2014

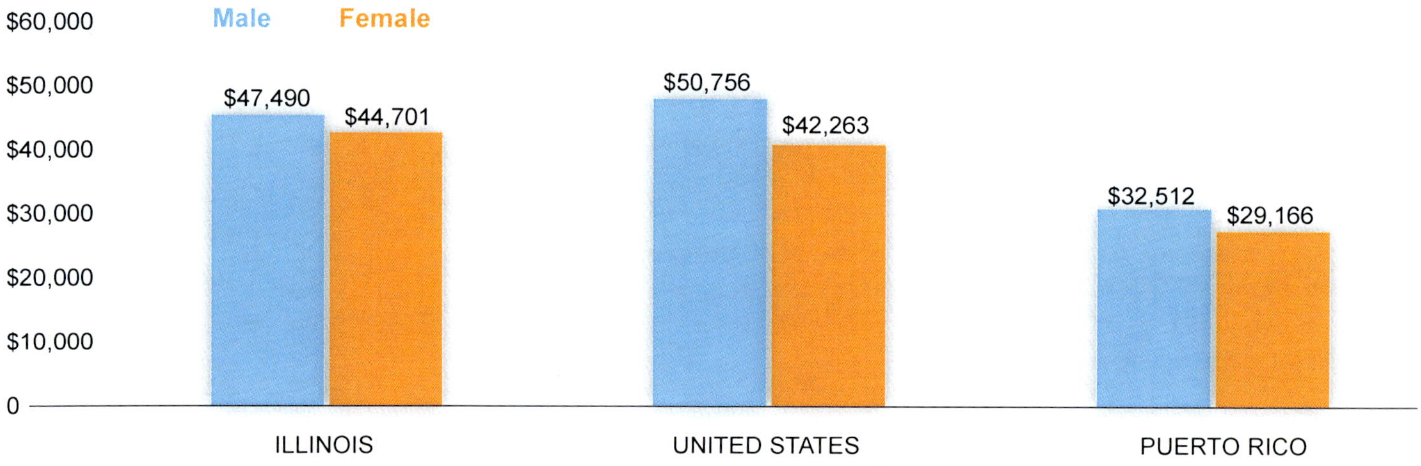

Graph 4.B: Puerto Rican Purchasing Power, in Billions, 2014

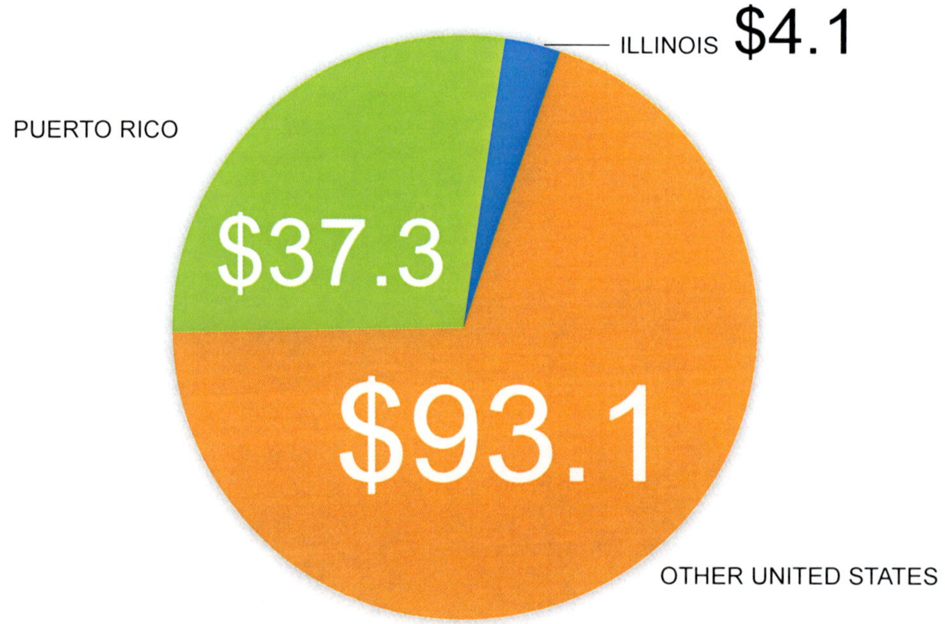

Graph 5.A: Poverty Rates, 2014

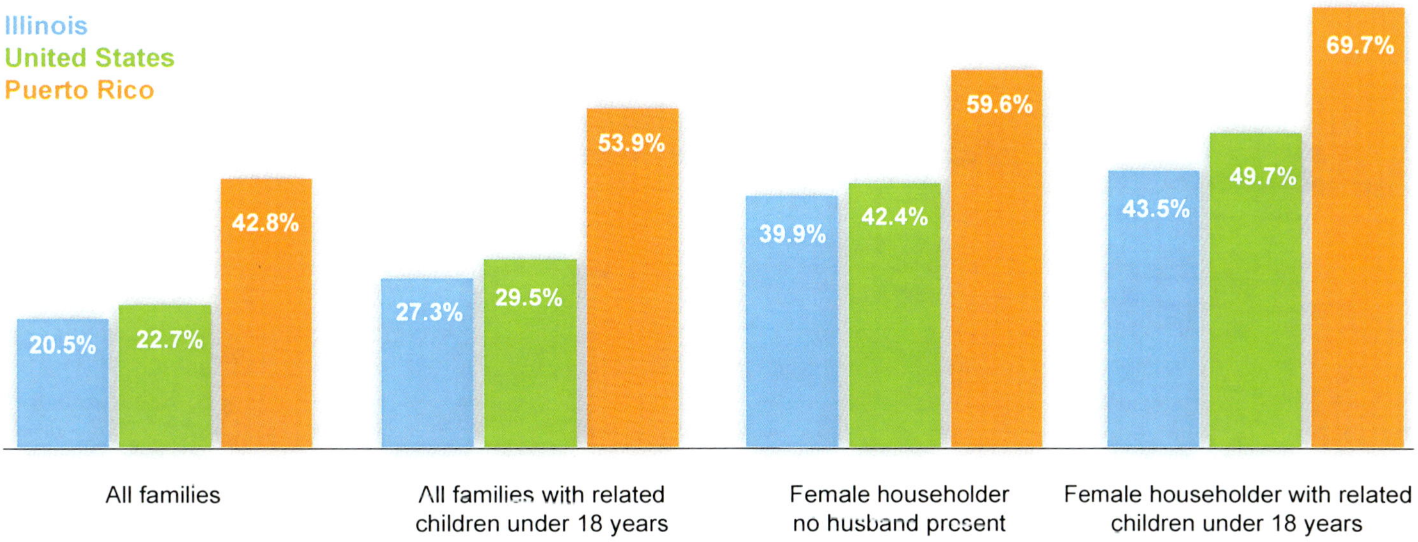

Table 5. Poverty, 2014

Puerto Ricans	Illinois	United States	Puerto Rico*
POVERTY RATES			
All families	20.5%	22.7%	42.8%
With related children under 18 years	27.3%	29.5%	53.9%
With related children under 5 years only	24.8%	24.6%	57.1%
Married-couple family	7.2%	9.7%	30.9%
With related children under 18 years	8.8%	11.3%	35.5%
With related children under 5 years only	N/A	5.9%	33.9%
Female householder, no husband present, family	39.9%	42.4%	59.6%
With related children under 18 years	43.5%	49.7%	69.7%
With related children under 5 years only	34.1%	49.4%	75.7%
All people	23%	26.2%	46.6%
Under 18 years	31.5%	33.4%	58.7%
Related children under 18 years	31.3%	33.1%	58.6%
Related children under 5 years	29.9%	34.7%	62.8%
Related children 5 to 17 years	31.8%	32.4%	57.3%
18 years and over	19%	22.8%	43.2%
18 to 64 years	19.1%	22.8%	43.8%
65 years and over	18.1%	22.4%	41%
People in families	21.6%	23.6%	44.6%
Unrelated individuals 15 years and over	30.4%	38.5%	58%

Source: U.S. Census Bureau, 2014 American Community Survey 1-Year Estimates.
* Puerto Ricans only.

Puerto Ricans in Illinois generated $4.1 billion in purchasing power, accounting for 4.2% of the $97.2 billion in purchasing power generated by all stateside Puerto Ricans in 2014.This share of Puerto Rican purchasing power in the U.S. is comparable to Illinois' share of the Puerto Rican population in the U.S., representing an even greater investment in Puerto Rico via trade, investment, and tourism. Purchasing power was defined simply as per capita income multiplied by the Puerto Rican population.

The poverty rate for all Puerto Rican families was 20.5% in Illinois, 22.7% for all stateside Puerto Rican families, and 42.8% for those in Puerto Rico. Though stateside Puerto Ricans' poverty rates where almost half of poverty rates in Puerto Rico, families with a female householder and no husband present with children under 18 years of age exhibited a much higher rate of poverty than the average Puerto Rican family. For Puerto Rican female-headed families with children the rates were 43.5% in Illinois, 49.7% throughout all stateside Puerto Ricans, and 69.7% in Puerto Rico. These are inordinately high poverty rates by any measure or comparative context.

In 2014, the proportion of households that received cash public assistance income of 5.8% was lower for Puerto Ricans in Illinois than the average of 6.9% for stateside Puerto Ricans, and 8.1% in Puerto Rico. The average amount households received from public assistance were higher for stateside Puerto Ricans overall ($3,441) than for Puerto Ricans in Illinois ($2,729). The proportion of Puerto Rican households in Illinois receiving benefits from the Supplemental Nutrition Assistance Program (SNAP) was 26.8% in 2014, 4.7 percentage points lower than the 31.5% average rate for stateside Puerto Rican households, and 15.8 percentage points lower than the 39.7% for Puerto Rico.

Housing is a primary determinant of the cost of living. In general, the Midwest has a lower cost of home ownership than coastal or Northeastern markets. However, the median value of owner-occupied housing for Puerto Ricans in Illinois was $195,400, compared to $175,900 for other stateside Puerto Ricans, and $119,500 in Puerto Rico. The median monthly owner cost associated with a mortgage was $1,692 for Puerto Ricans in Illinois, and $1,545 average for stateside Puerto Ricans. A comparable cost was $873 in Puerto Rico. Puerto Ricans in Illinois had higher rates of home ownership than Puerto Ricans in Puerto Rico. The Census data revealed that Puerto Ricans in Illinois had a 42.6% rate of owner-occupied housing units, while the comparable rate for stateside Puerto Ricans was 36%. The home ownership rate in Puerto Rico was much higher at 68.7%.

Table 6. Housing and Health Insurance, 2014

Puerto Ricans	Illinois	United States	Puerto Rico*
HOUSING			
Owner-occupied housing units	42.6%	36%	68.7%
Monthly owner costs as a percentage of household income in the past 12 months			
Less than 30 percent	62.3%	62.8%	52.6%
30 percent or more	37.7%	37.2%	47.4%
Owner-occupied housing units			
Median value (dollars)	$195,400	$175,900	$119,500
Median selected monthly owner costs with a mortgage (dollars)	$1,692	$1,545	$873
HEALTH INSURANCE COVERAGE			
Civilian noninstitutionalized population			
With private health insurance	53.2%	51.6%	38%
With public coverage	40.8%	43.5%	62.9%
No health insurance coverage	10.3%	11.5%	5.5%

Source: U.S. Census Bureau, 2014 American Community Survey 1-Year Estimates.
* Puerto Ricans only.

Puerto Ricans in California, 2014

In 2014, an estimated 200,000 Puerto Ricans lived in California, accounting for four percent of all Puerto Ricans living in the United States. Hispanics represented 38.6 percent of California's population, but Puerto Ricans accounted for only 0.5 percent of California's total population. Despite the relatively low proportion of Puerto Ricans, California had the eighth highest number of Puerto Ricans in the United States. California's Puerto Rican population has grown in the past 14 years representing

Graph 1.A: Latino Population California, 2014

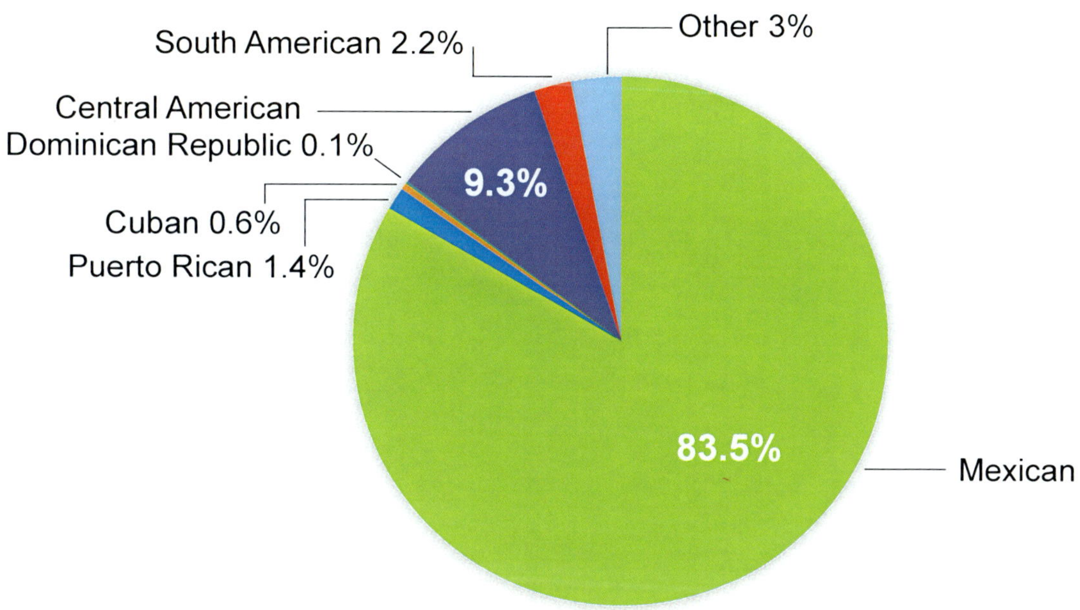

Table 1. Puerto Rican and Latino Population in California

	2000		2010		2014	
Total	33,871,648	100%	37,253,956	100%	38,802,500	100%
Not Hispanic or Latino	22,905,092	67.6%	23,240,237	62.4%	23,813,730	61.4%
Hispanic or Latino	10,966,556	32.4%	14,013,719	37.6%	14,988,770	38.6%
Mexican	8,455,926	25.0%	11,423,146	30.7%	12,510,971	32.2%
Puerto Rican	140,570	0.4%	189,945	0.5%	207,565	0.5%
Cuban	72,286	0.2%	88,607	0.2%	86,727	0.2%
Dominican Republic	5,047	0%	11,455	0%	15,157	0%
Central American	576,330	1.7%	1,132,520	3.0%	1,391,906	3.6%
South American	161,822	0.5%	293,880	0.8%	329,012	0.8%
Other	1,554,575	4.6%	874,166	2.3%	447,332	1.2%

Sources: U.S. Census Bureau, Census 2000 Summary File 1, 2010 Census. Summary File 1, and 2014 American Community Survey 1-Year Estimates.

The median age of Puerto Ricans in California was 29.1 years, close to the national average for Puerto Ricans at 28.9 years of age, and lower than the median among Puerto Ricans in Puerto Rico of 38.9 years. About one in ten Puerto Ricans in California (10.3%) were aged 62 years and older, a rate slightly higher than among all Puerto Ricans in the U.S. (9.9%), but less than half of Puerto Ricans in Puerto Rico (21%).

English fluency indicators for Puerto Ricans in California were higher than for all stateside Puerto Ricans. More than half of Puerto Ricans in California (58.2%) reported

Graph 2.A: Puerto Rican Education Attainment, 25 years and over, 2014

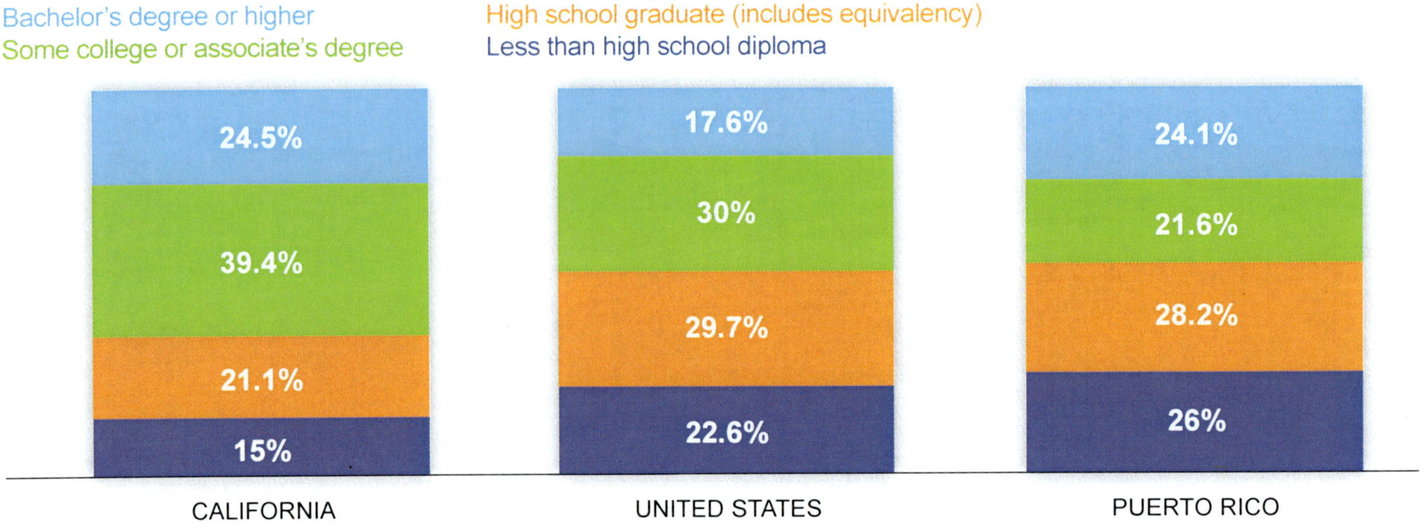

Table 2. Age, Education, and Language, 2014

Puerto Ricans	California	United States	Puerto Rico*
TOTAL POPULATION	207,565	5,266,738	3,404,122
Median age (years)	29.1	28.9	38.9
62 years and over	10.3%	9.9%	21%
EDUCATIONAL ATTAINMENT			
Population 25 years and over			
Less than high school diploma	15%	22.6%	26%
High school graduate (includes equivalency)	21.1%	29.7%	28.2%
Some college or associate's degree	39.4%	30%	21.6%
Bachelor's degree or higher	24.5%	17.6%	24.1%
Male, bachelor's degree or higher	23.8%	15.6%	19.6%
Female, bachelor's degree or higher	25.2%	19.5%	28.1%
LANGUAGE SPOKEN AT HOME AND ABILITY TO SPEAK ENGLISH			
Population 5 years and over			
English only	58.2%	38.8%	5.3%
Language other than English	41.8%	61.2%	94.7%
Speak English less than "very well"	8%	17.3%	78.8%

Source: U.S. Census Bureau, 2014 American Community Survey 1-Year Estimates.
* Puerto Ricans only.

speaking English in the home, a rate nearly 20 percentage points higher than among all Puerto Ricans in the U.S. (38.8%). Only 8 percent of Puerto Ricans in California reported speaking English less than "very well," less than half the rate among all Puerto Ricans in the U.S. (17.3%).

Puerto Ricans in California were generally more educated than Puerto Ricans throughout the U.S. or in Puerto Rico. Approximately a quarter (24.5%) of Puerto Ricans in California aged 25 or older had earned a bachelor's degree or higher, compared to 17.6 percent of stateside Puerto Ricans, and 24.1 percent of Puerto Ricans in Puerto Rico. A breakdown of the education demographics by sex indicates greater equality in educational attainment among Puerto Rican men and women in California than in either the United States or Puerto Rico. Among Puerto Ricans in California, 23.8 percent of men and 25.2 percent of women held a bachelor's degree or higher, compared to 15.6 percent of all Puerto Rican males and 19.5 percent of all Puerto Rican females age 25 and older in the U.S. In Puerto Rico, the disparity of men and women holding a bachelor's degree or higher was greatest, with 28.1 percent of Puerto Rican women having earned a bachelor's degree or higher, compared to 19.6 percent of males aged 25 and older.

Table 3. Employment and Occupations, 2014

Puerto Ricans	California	United States	Puerto Rico*
EMPLOYMENT STATUS			
Population 16 years and over			
In labor force	70%	62.4%	43.7%
Civilian labor force	68.1%	61.6%	43.7%
Employed	59.6%	54.4%	35.4%
Unemployed	12.4%	11.6%	18.9%
Not in labor force	30%	37.6%	56.3%
Armed Forces	1.9%	0.8%	0%
OCCUPATION			
Civilian employed population 16 years and over			
Male	48,280	1,058,918	516,762
Management, business, science, and arts	34.7%	23.4%	23.9%
Service occupations	18.2%	22.5%	23%
Sales and office occupations	20%	19.6%	21.3%
Construction and maintenance	13.5%	13.8%	18%
Production, transportation, and moving	13.7%	20.7%	13.7%
Female	41,316	999,105	456,356
Management, business, science, and arts	41.5%	33.1%	39.7%
Service occupations	19.8%	24.4%	16.6%
Sales and office occupations	34.6%	35.7%	38.3%
Construction and maintenance	0.5%	0.6%	0.6%
Production, transportation, and moving	3.5%	6.2%	4.8%
CLASS OF WORKER			
Civilian employed population 16 years and over			
Private wage and salary workers	77.2%	82%	69%
Government workers	16.2%	14.8%	22.5%
Self-employed workers in own not incorporated business	6.5%	3.1%	8.3%
VETERAN STATUS			
Civilian population 18 years and over			
Civilian veteran	9.8%	6%	3.3%

Source: U.S. Census Bureau, 2014 American Community Survey 1-Year Estimates.
* Puerto Ricans only.

Puerto Rican participation in California's labor force (70%) was seven percentage points higher than the rate among all stateside Puerto Ricans (62.4%), and twenty six percentage points above the rate in Puerto Rico (43.7%). The unemployment rate among the Puerto Rican civilian labor force in California was 12.4 percent, a rate higher than among all Puerto Ricans in the U.S. (11.6%), but lower than those in Puerto Rico (18.9%).

Proportionately, more Puerto Ricans in California worked in the higher wage management, business, science, and arts sector than among Puerto Ricans in the U.S. and those in Puerto Rico. More than a third of Puerto Rican men (34.7%) and women (41.5%) worked in the management, business, science, and arts sector compared to 23.4 percent and 33.1 percent to Puerto Rican men and women, respectively, in the U.S. The second occupational sector among Puerto Ricans in California was the sales and office occupations sector, representing 20 percent and 34.6 percent of men and women, respectively.

The average earnings of full-time, year-round Puerto Rican men and women in California, $62,132 and $54,608, respectively, were higher than the average for stateside Puerto Ricans of $50,756 and $42,623 for men and women, respectively. These earnings for Puerto Ricans in California far exceeded those of Puerto Ricans in Puerto Rico of $32,512 and $29,166.

Table 4. Income and Earnings, 2014

Puerto Ricans	California	United States	Puerto Rico*
INCOME IN THE PAST 12 MONTHS			
(IN 2013 INFLATION-ADJUSTED DOLLARS)			
Households	63,266	1,635,808	1,175,297
Median household income (dollars)	$60,273	$39,322	$18,710
With earnings	85%	76.9%	54.7%
Mean earnings (dollars)	$81,487	$61,065	$36,407
With Social Security income	21.9%	24.1%	43.2%
Mean Social Security income (dollars)	$16,277	$13,727	$12,159
With Supplemental Security Income	7.6%	12.6%	0.4%
Mean Supplemental Security Income (dollars)	$8,990	$8,780	$10,025
With cash public assistance income	6.2%	6.9%	8.1%
Mean cash public assistance income (dollars)	$3,860	$3,441	$2,316
With retirement income	13.3%	10.1%	15.6%
Mean retirement income (dollars)	$21,137	$20,452	$15,387
With Food Stamp/SNAP benefits	12.1%	31.5%	39.7%
Families	42,694	1,114,628	830,807
Median family income (dollars)	$70,463	$44,499	$22,220
Married-couple family	67.3%	53.9%	56.1%
Median income (dollars)	$85,243	$67,129	$29,417
Male householder, no spouse present	10%	10.2%	9.5%
Median income (dollars)	$41,137	$37,513	$17,797
Female householder, no husband present	22.7%	35.9%	34.4%
Median income (dollars)	$33,306	$23,957	$13,554
Individuals	207,565	5,266,738	3,404,122
Per capita income (dollars)	$24,519	$18,457	$10,960
Mean earnings (dollars) for full-time, year-round workers:			
Male	$62,132	$50,756	$32,512
Female	$54,608	$42,263	$29,166

Source: U.S. Census Bureau, 2014 American Community Survey 1-Year Estimates. * Puerto Ricans only.

Puerto Rican Population by Counties in California, 2014

More than three-fourths (76%) of the Puerto Rican population in California were mainly concentrated in five of the state's metropolitan areas: Los Angeles-Long Beach-Anaheim (30%), Riverside-San Bernardino-Ontario (15%), San Francisco-Oakland-Hayward (14%), San Diego-Carlsbad (11%), and Sacramento-Roseville-Arden-Arcade (7%); the remaining 25 percent were dispersed throughout the state. Puerto Ricans' largest concentrated settlements were in southern California in Los Angeles County (23.3%) and the Orange County (6.2%). These two counties are part of the Los Angeles-Long Beach-Anaheim metropolitan. The proportion of Puerto Ricans settled in Los Angeles and Orange counties was lower than for Latinos overall (33% in Los Angeles and 7.2% in Orange County) there, or among the state's overall population (26.2% in Los Angeles and 8.1% in Orange County). Part of the San Diego-Carlsbad metropolitan area, San Diego County, located in the southwestern region of the state, contained the second largest Puerto Rican (10.9%) concentration. The presence of U.S. military bases was a major influential factor in Puerto Rican settlement in the metropolitan area. Furthermore, Puerto Ricans in San Diego County (10.9%) showed a higher proportion (by 3.7 percentage points) more than settlement for Latinos overall (7.2%) and 2.5 percentage points more than the state's overall population (8.4%). San Bernardino County, located adjacent to Los Angeles County and at least 100 miles north of San Diego County, was the third county with the largest Puerto Rican community (8%) in California. San Bernardino (8%) and Riverside (6.8%) counties comprised Riverside-San Bernardino-Ontario metropolitan area and accounted close to 15 percent of Puerto Ricans in the state. Lastly, one in seven (14%) Puerto Ricans in California lived in San Francisco-Oakland-Hayward metropolitan area, included the following counties Alameda (5.1%), Contra Costa (3.8%), San Francisco (2.2%), San Mateo (2%), and Marin (1%). Puerto Rican settlement patterns consisted of general two settlement trends: first, they were largely settled around U.S. military bases and, secondly, in terms of proportions, Puerto Rican concentration in counties outside the Los Angeles-Long Beach-Anaheim metropolitan area exceeded that of Latinos overall. In other words, Puerto Ricans settlement did not reflect or follow settlement patterns of overall Hispanic population in California, but approximated the settlement of the state's overall population.

COUNTY	Puerto Rican Population	Percent	Latino Population	Percent	Total Population	Percent
Los Angeles County	48,333	23.3%	4,800,491	33%	9,974,203	26.2%
San Diego County	22,746	10.9%	1,039,752	7.2%	3,183,143	8.4%
San Bernardino County	16,723	8%	1,050,173	7.2%	2,078,586	5.5%
Riverside County	14,180	6.8%	1,055,027	7.3%	2,266,899	6%
Orange County	12,883	6.2%	1,050,771	7.2%	3,086,331	8.1%
Sacramento County	11,215	5.4%	319,934	2.2%	1,450,277	3.8%
Alameda County	10,645	5.1%	352,500	2.4%	1,559,308	4.1%
Contra Costa County	7,841	3.8%	267,859	1.8%	1,081,232	2.8%
Santa Clara County	7,700	3.7%	492,546	3.4%	1,841,569	4.8%
San Joaquin County	5,743	2.8%	278,523	1.9%	701,050	1.8%
San Francisco County	4,527	2.2%	126,524	0.9%	829,072	2.2%
Kern County	4,488	2.2%	432,370	3%	857,730	2.3%
Solano County	4,393	2.1%	104,865	0.7%	421,624	1.1%
San Mateo County	4,244	2%	187,635	1.3%	739,837	1.9%
Ventura County	3,776	1.8%	344,520	2.4%	835,790	2.2%
Fresno County	3,694	1.8%	485,914	3.3%	948,844	2.5%
Stanislaus County	3,265	1.6%	225,013	1.5%	522,794	1.4%
Monterey County	2,343	1.1%	239,901	1.7%	424,927	1.1%
Sonoma County	2,025	1%	125,674	0.9%	491,790	1.3%
Santa Barbara County	2,019	1%	188,743	1.3%	431,555	1.1%
Other Counties	15,095	7.3%	1,365,714	9%	4,340,359	11%
Total	**207,878**	**100%**	**14,534,449**	**100%**	**38,066,920**	**100%**

Sources: U.S. Census Bureau 2014 American Community Survey 5-Year Estimates Notes: Total counts for populations may differ depending on whether the estimates are derived from the five-year estimates or the one-year estimates of the American Community Survey.

PUERTO RICAN POPULATION IN CALIFORNIA, 2014

PUERTO RICAN POPULATION

🔴 1 dot = 100

'06-'14 PUERTO RICAN ARRIVALS

⚫ 1 dot = 100

BOUNDARIES

- County
- City/Towns
- Census Tracts

CONGRESSIONAL DISTRICT

- Republican
- Democrat

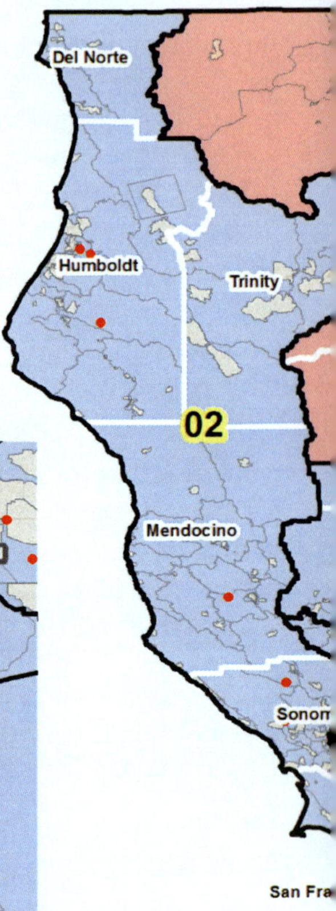

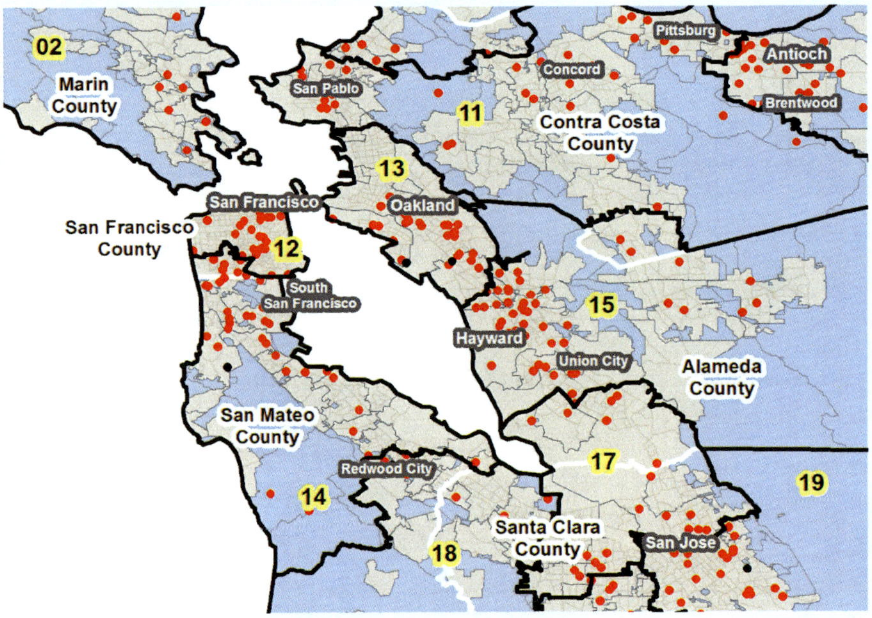

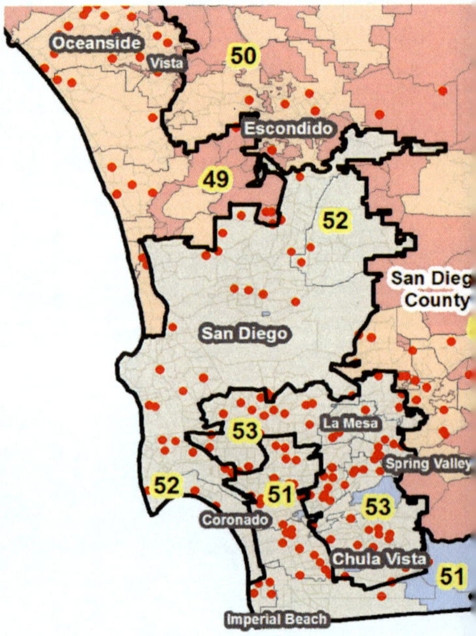

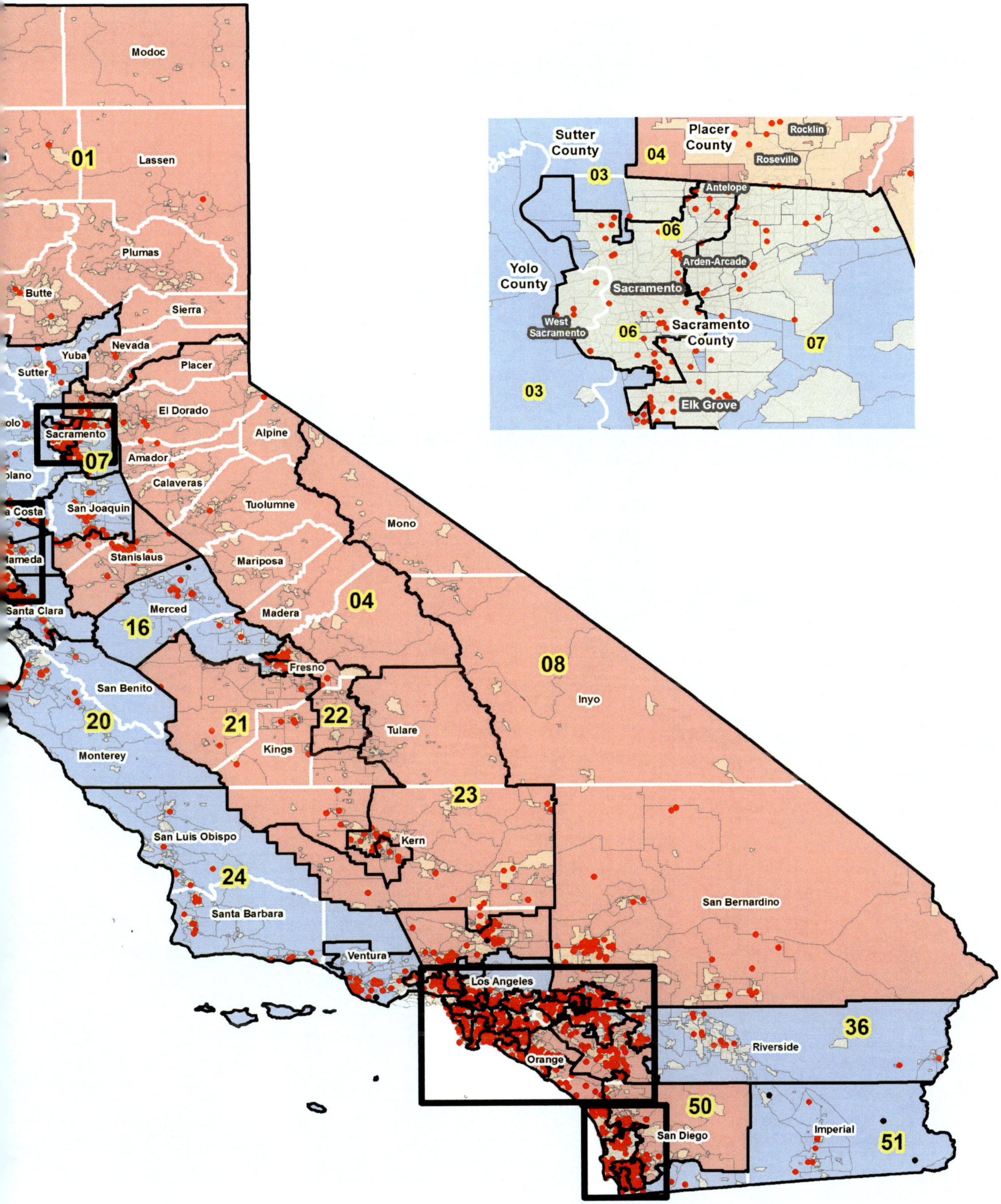
Sutter
County
Placer
County
Rocklin
Roseville
04
03
Antelope
06
Arden-Arcade
Yolo
County
Sacramento
West
Sacramento
06
Sacramento
County
07
03
Elk Grove
Modoc
01
Lassen
Plumas
Butte
Sierra
Nevada
Yuba
Sutter
Placer
El Dorado
Sacramento
07
Alpine
Amador
Calaveras
San Joaquin
Tuolumne
Mono
Stanislaus
Mariposa
Merced
16
Madera
04
Santa Clara
Fresno
08
San Benito
22
Inyo
20
21
Tulare
Kings
Monterey
23
Kern
San Luis Obispo
24
Santa Barbara
San Bernardino
Ventura
Los Angeles
36
Riverside
Orange
50
San Diego
Imperial
51

PUERTO RICAN POPULATION IN CALIFORNIA, 2014

PUERTO RICAN POPULATION

● 1 dot = 100

'06-'14 PUERTO RICAN ARRIVALS

● 1 dot = 100

BOUNDARIES

County

City/Towns

Census Tracts

CONGRESSIONAL DISTRICT

Republican

Democrat

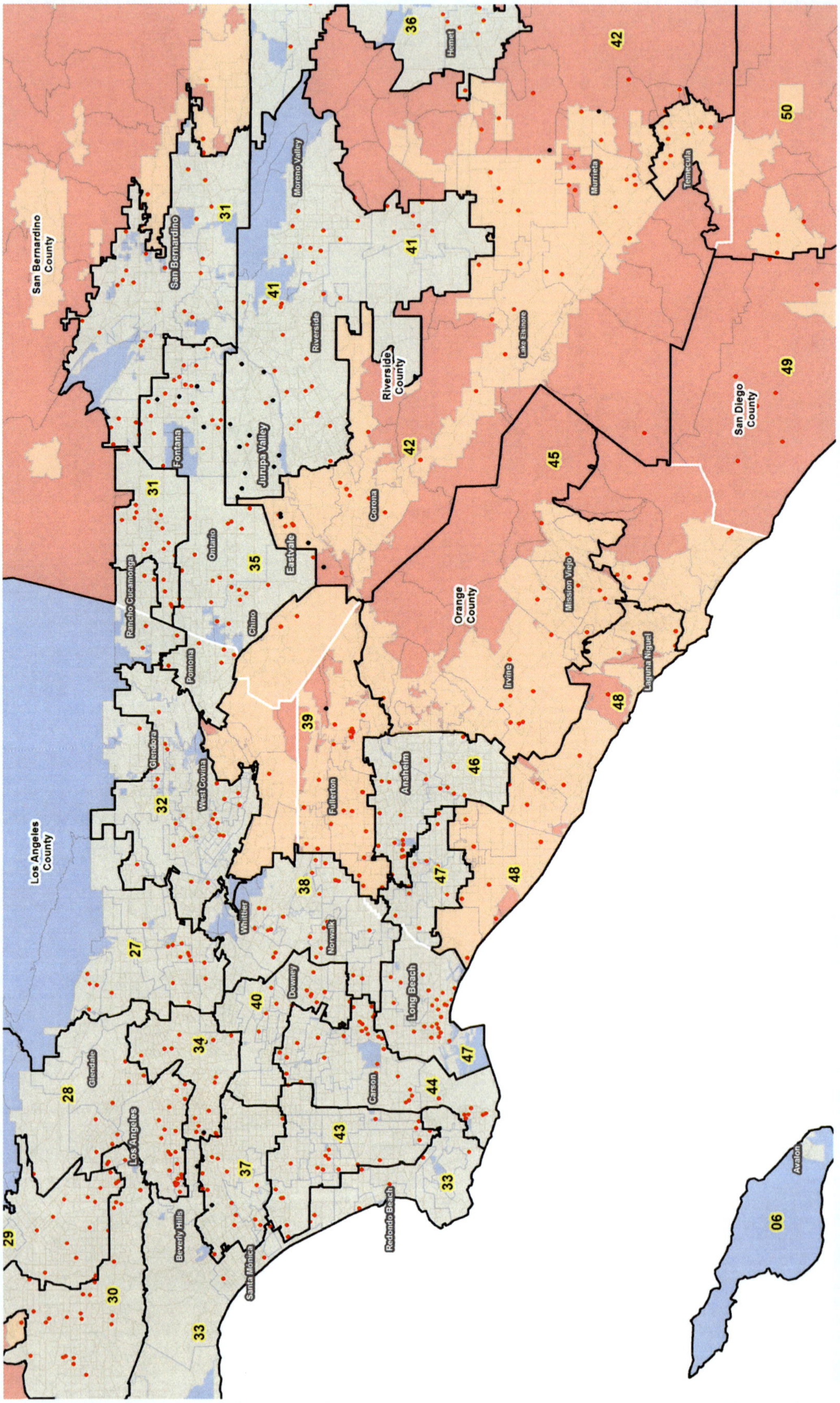

Household and family incomes are important indicators of economic well-being. These indicators were higher for Puerto Ricans in California than for stateside Puerto Ricans and those in Puerto Rico. The median household income was $60,273 for Puerto Rican households in California, more than twenty-thousand dollars higher than among all stateside Puerto Ricans ($39,322) and more than three times the median household income of Puerto Rican households in Puerto Rico ($18,710). Per capita incomes among Puerto Ricans in California ($24,519) were higher than among all stateside Puerto Ricans ($18,457) and more than double that of Puerto Ricans in Puerto Rico ($10, 960).

Puerto Ricans in California had $5.1 billion in purchasing power. From an economic perspective, stateside Puerto

Graph 4.A: Mean Earnings for Full-Time Year-Round Puerto Rican Workers, 2014

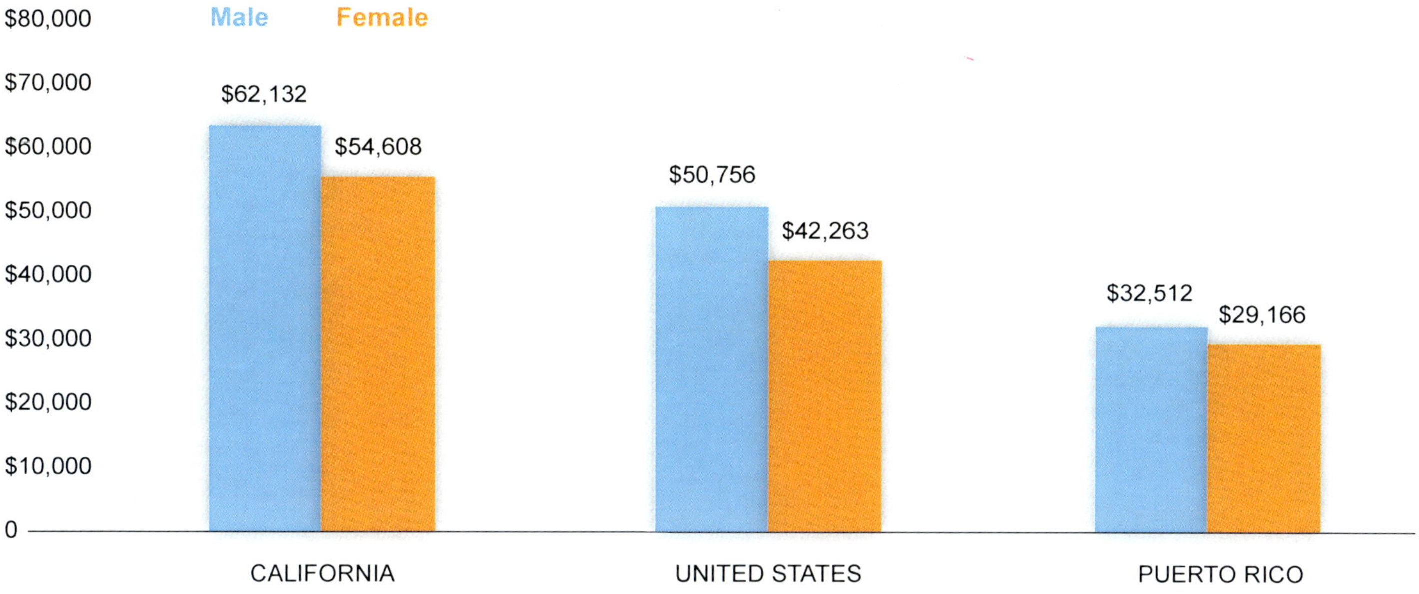

Graph 4.B: Puerto Rican Purchasing Power, in Billions, 2014

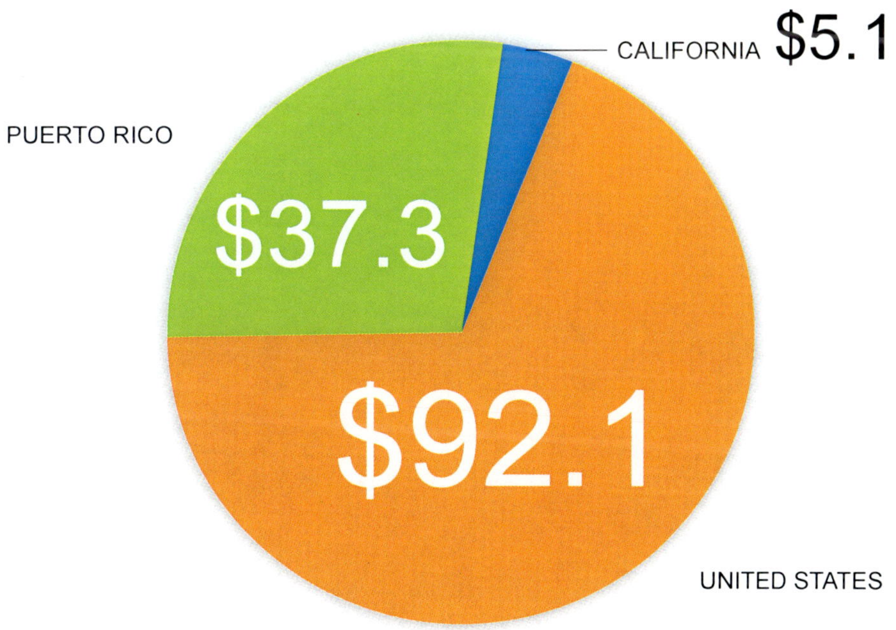

Graph 5.A: Poverty Rates, 2014

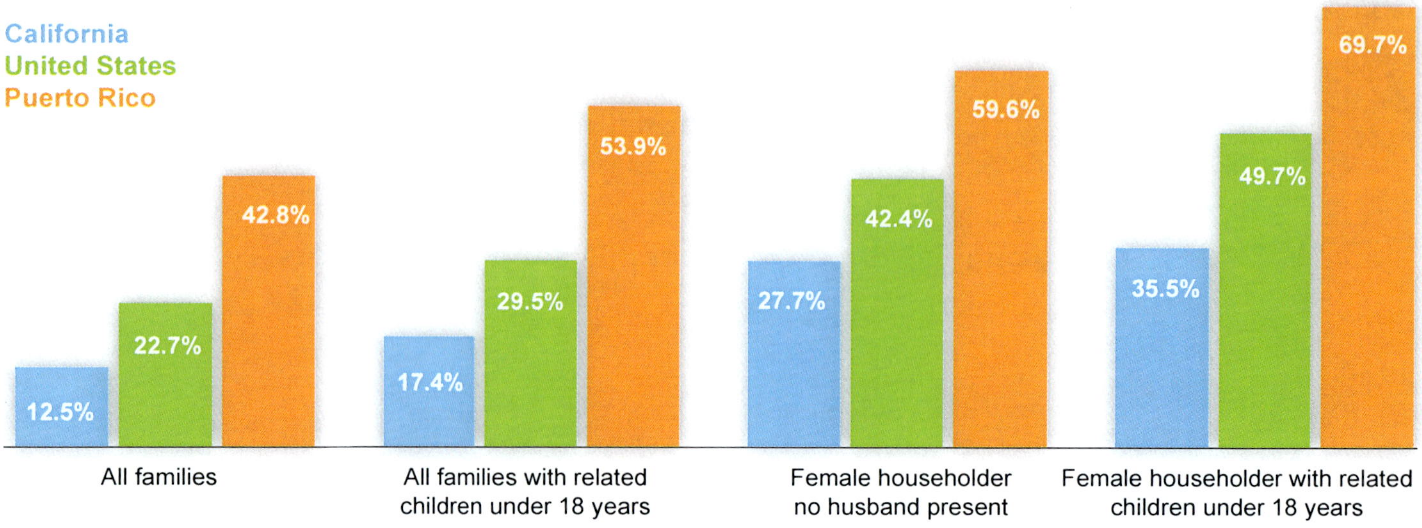

Table 5. Poverty, 2014

Puerto Ricans	California	United States	Puerto Rico*
POVERTY RATES			
All families	12.5%	22.7%	42.8%
With related children under 18 years	17.2%	29.5%	53.9%
With related children under 5 years only	15.4%	24.6%	57.1%
Married-couple family	6.1%	9.7%	30.9%
With related children under 18 years	7.1%	11.3%	35.5%
With related children under 5 years only	N	5.9%	33.9%
Female householder, no husband present, family	27.7%	42.4%	59.6%
With related children under 18 years	35.5%	49.7%	69.7%
With related children under 5 years only	42.3%	49.4%	75.7%
All people	16.9%	26.2%	46.6%
Under 18 years	20.7%	33.4%	58.7%
Related children under 18 years	20.2%	33.1%	58.6%
Related children under 5 years	19.7%	34.7%	62.8%
Related children 5 to 17 years	20.5%	32.4%	57.3%
18 years and over	15.1%	22.8%	43.2%
18 to 64 years	15.8%	22.8%	43.8%
65 years and over	10.3%	22.4%	41%
People in families	12.9%	23.6%	44.6%
Unrelated individuals 15 years and over	34.4%	38.5%	58.6%

Source: U.S. Census Bureau, 2014 American Community Survey 1-Year Estimates. * Puerto Ricans only.

Ricans represented 72.3 percent of the $134.5 billion total purchasing power of the entire Puerto Rican community in the year 2014. Purchasing power is defined simply as per capita income multiplied by the Puerto Rican population. Stateside Puerto Ricans had more than double the total Purchasing power of Puerto Ricans in Puerto Rico of $37.3 billion.

The poverty rate for all Puerto Rican families in California was 12.5 percent, lower than among all Puerto Rican families in the U.S. (22.7 percent) and those in Puerto Rico (42.8 percent). As seen in other states and in Puerto Rico, female headed households with children had the highest rates of poverty with 27.7 percent of those in California registering below the poverty rate. The poverty rates among female headed householders in the U.S. and Puerto Rico were 42.4 percent and 59.6 percent, respectively. Regardless of context, these rates of poverty are alarmingly high. Although California had considerably lower levels of poverty, the distribution among different types of households mirrored that of Puerto Rican families in the U.S. and in Puerto Rico.

Public assistance income participation in California (6.2 percent) was lower than among all Puerto Ricans in the U.S. (6.9 percent) and those in Puerto Rico (8.1 percent). Food stamp/SNAP (Supplementary Nutrition Assistance Program) participation among Puerto Ricans in California was 12.1 percent, less than half that among all stateside Puerto Ricans (31.5 percent), and less than a third among those in Puerto Rico (39.7 percent).

Housing is a primary determinant of the cost of living. The median value of owner-occupied housing for Puerto Ricans in California was $377,100, a price more than double the median value of owner-occupied housing for all stateside Puerto Ricans ($175,900) and more than triple in Puerto Rico ($119,500). Although this discrepancy in home values maybe affected largely by the higher costs of living in California, it is also likely linked to the higher wages and higher presence of the Puerto Rican labor force in higher wage sectors. The median monthly owner cost associated with a mortgage was $1,964 for Puerto Ricans in California, $1,545 for those in the U.S., and $873 for those in Puerto Rico. Despite the higher costs of home ownership, Puerto Ricans in California had higher rates of home ownership (39.6%) than the stateside average (36%). Both rates were considerably below that of Puerto Ricans in Puerto Rico (68.7%). Similarly, despite the higher cost of home ownership, the proportion of Puerto Rican home owners in California spending more than 30 percent of their income (36.9%) on housing was lower than among stateside Puerto Ricans (37.2%) and those in Puerto Rico (47.4%).

Table 6. Housing and Health Insurance, 2014

Puerto Ricans	California	United States	Puerto Rico*
HOUSING			
Owner-occupied housing units	39.6%	36%	68.7%
Monthly owner costs as a percentage of household income in the past 12 months			
Less than 30 percent	63.1%	62.8%	52.6%
30 percent or more	36.9%	37.2%	47.4%
Owner-occupied housing units			
Median value (dollars)	$377,100	$175,900	$119,500
Median selected monthly owner costs with a mortgage (dollars)	$1,964	$1,545	$873
HEALTH INSURANCE COVERAGE			
Civilian noninstitutionalized population			
With private health insurance	63.8%	51.6%	38%
With public coverage	32.9%	43.5%	62.9%
No health insurance coverage	11.3%	11.5%	5.5%

Source: U.S. Census Bureau, 2014 American Community Survey 1-Year Estimates.
* Puerto Ricans only.

Puerto Ricans in Texas, 2014

In 2014, there were approximately 177,448 Puerto Ricans living in Texas, making it home to the ninth largest Puerto Rican population in the United States. The number of Puerto Ricans in Texas more than doubled from 69,504 in 2000, but still accounted for less than 1% of Texas' total population of almost 27 million.

Graph 1.A: Latino Population Texas, 2014

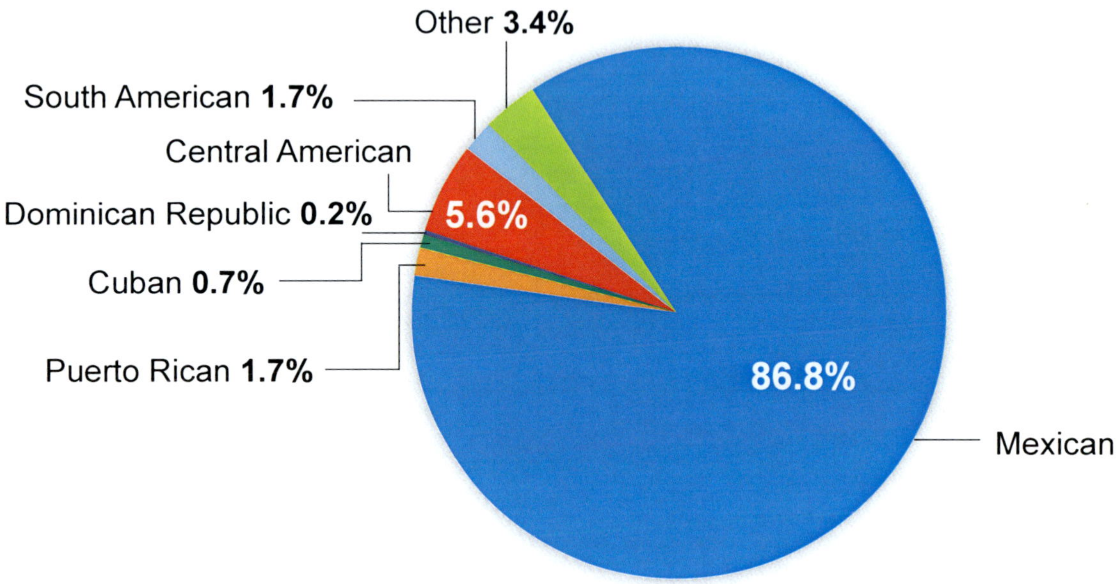

Table 1. Puerto Rican and Latino Population in Texas

	2000		2010		2014	
Total	20,851,820	100%	25,145,561	100%	26,956,958	100%
Not Hispanic or Latino	14,182,154	68%	15,684,640	62.4%	16,548,720	61.4%
Hispanic or Latino	6,669,666	32%	9,460,921	37.6%	10,408,238	38.6%
Mexican	5,071,963	24.3%	7,951,193	31.6%	9,032,310	33.5%
Puerto Rican	69,504	0.3%	130,576	0.5%	177,448	0.7%
Cuban	25,705	0.1%	46,541	0.2%	70,160	0.3%
Dominican Republic	4,296	0.0%	13,353	0.1%	21,482	0.1%
Central American	146,723	0.7%	420,683	1.7%	581,030	2.2%
South American	79,204	0.4%	222,599	0.9%	301,799	1.1%
Other	51,428	0.2%	133,808	0.5%	173,854	0.6%

Sources: U.S. Census Bureau, Census 2000 Summary File 1, 2010 Census. Summary File 1, and 2014 American Community Survey 1-Year Estimates.

Puerto Ricans constituted 1.7% of Texas' total Latino population and 0.7% of the total populaton. The Latino population in Texas was primarily of Mexican descent (86.8%). However, the Puerto Rican population in Texas more than doubled between 2000 and 2014 from 69,504 in 2000 to 130,576 in 2010 to 177,448 in 2014.

The median age of Puerto Ricans in Texas (28 years) was slightly below the median age of all stateside Puerto Ricans (28.9 years), and more than a decade younger than those in Puerto Rico (38.9 years). Despite the proximity in age, the proportion of Puerto Ricans in Texas age 62 and older was less at 7.1% than

Graph 2.A: Puerto Rican Education Attainment, 25 years and over, 2014

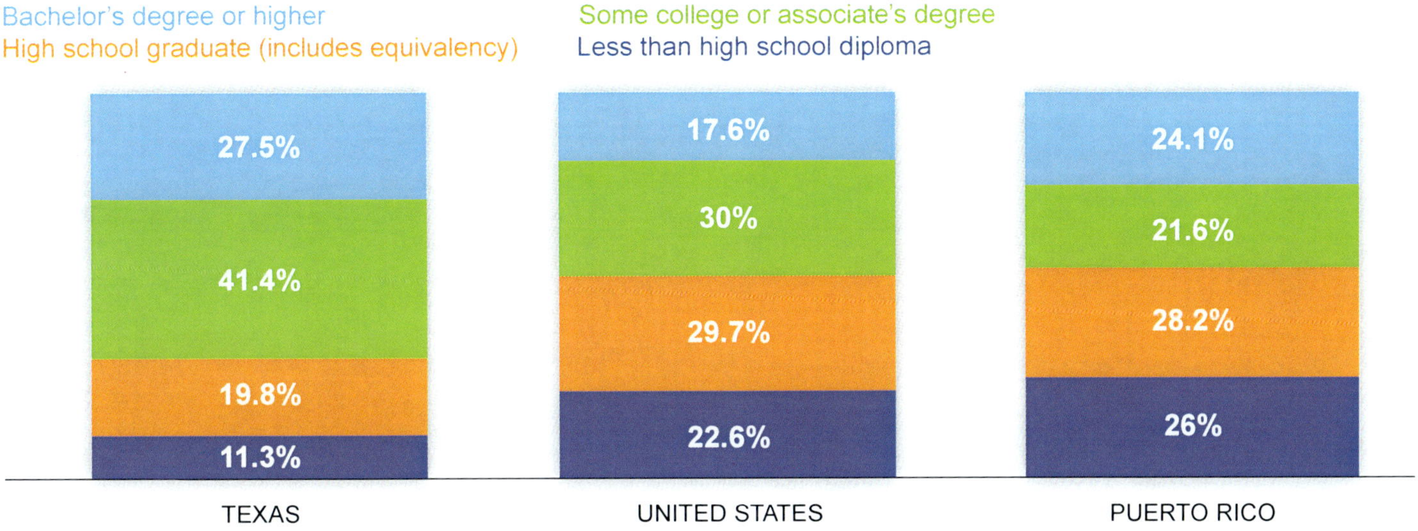

Table 2. Age, Education, and Language, 2014

Puerto Ricans	Texas	United States	Puerto Rico*
TOTAL POPULATION	117,448	5,266,738	3,404,122
Median age (years)	28	28.9	38.9
62 years and over	7.1%	9.9%	21%
EDUCATIONAL ATTAINMENT			
Population 25 years and over			
Less than high school diploma	11.3%	22.6%	26%
High school graduate (includes equivalency)	19.8%	29.7%	28.2%
Some college or associate's degree	41.4%	30%	21.6%
Bachelor's degree or higher	27.5%	17.6%	24.1%
Male, bachelor's degree or higher	23.4%	15.6%	19.6%
Female, bachelor's degree or higher	31.8%	19.5%	28.1%
LANGUAGE SPOKEN AT HOME AND ABILITY TO SPEAK ENGLISH			
Population 5 years and over			
English only	39.4%	38.8%	5.3%
Language other than English	60.6%	61.2%	94.7%
Speak English less than "very well"	17%	17.3%	78.8%

Source: U.S. Census Bureau, 2014 American Community Survey 1-Year Estimates.
* Puerto Ricans only.

the stateside Puerto Rican proportion of 9.9%. The Texas proportion of Puerto Ricans 62 and older was almost a third of the 21% in Puerto Rico.

English fluency among Texas Puerto Ricans was on par with the stateside averages for Puerto Ricans. 39.4% of Texas Puerto Ricans reported only speaking English in their home, compared to 38.8% of all stateside Puerto Ricans. Likewise, 17.3% of all stateside Puerto Ricans indicated speaking English less than "very well", compared to 17% of Texas Puerto Ricans.

A higher proportion of Texas Puerto Ricans aged 25 and older held a bachelor's degree or above (27.5%) than the proportion of all Puerto Ricans in the United States (17.7%) and those in Puerto Rico (24.1%). Texas also had a far higher proportion of Puerto Ricans with an associate's degree or some college experience, totaling to a 68.9% proportion with more than a high school diploma. Among stateside Puerto Ricans this total proportion was 47.7% and 45.7% for those in Puerto Rico. Texas also had a lower proportion of Puerto Ricans without a high school diploma (11.3%) than

Table 3. Employment and Occupations, 2014

Puerto Ricans	Texas	United States	Puerto Rico*
EMPLOYMENT STATUS			
Population 16 years and over			
In labor force	72.8%	62.4%	43.7%
Civilian labor force	69.7%	61.6%	43.7%
Employed	64%	54.4%	35.4%
Unemployed	8.2%	11.6%	18.9%
Not in labor force	3.2%	37.6%	56.3%
Armed Forces	27.2%	0.8%	0%
OCCUPATION			
Civilian employed population 16 years and over			
Male	44,236	1,058,918	516,762
Management, business, science, and arts	31.8%	23.4%	23.9%
Service occupations	14.9%	22.5%	23%
Sales and office occupations	17.8%	19.6%	21.3%
Construction and maintenance	17.6%	13.8%	18%
Production, transportation, and moving	17.8%	20.7%	13.7%
Female	35,103	999,105	456,356
Management, business, science, and arts	46.9%	33.1%	39.7%
Service occupations	18.7%	24.4%	16.6%
Sales and office occupations	31.5%	35.7%	38.3%
Construction and maintenance	0.4%	0.6%	0.6%
Production, transportation, and moving	2.4%	6.2%	4.8%
CLASS OF WORKER			
Civilian employed population 16 years and over			
Private wage and salary workers	79.2%	82%	69%
Government workers	18.2%	14.8%	22.5%
Self-employed workers in own not incorporated business	2.6%	3.1%	8.3%
VETERAN STATUS			
Civilian population 18 years and over			
Civilian veteran	12.9%	6%	3.3%

Source: U.S. Census Bureau, 2014 American Community Survey 1-Year Estimates.
* Puerto Ricans only.

Puerto Rican Population by Counties in Texas, 2014

Puerto Ricans in Texas resided in the most populous counties in the largest metropolitan areas. Harris County, in the Houston metropolitan area, accounted for 15.7% of all Puerto Ricans in Texas. Bexar County (13.3%), Bell County (8.4%), and El Paso County (5.4%) accounted for another 27.1% of the Texan Puerto Rican population. All three counties had a disproportionate amount of Puerto Ricans relative to the general population and all three counties contained large military installations. Tarrant County (10.6%) and Dallas County (7.8%), in the Dallas-Fort Worth metropolitan area, accounted for another 18.2% of Puerto Ricans in Texas.

COUNTY	Puerto Rican Population	Percent	Latino Population	Percent	Total Population	Percent
Harris County	24,510	15.7%	1,766,483	17.7%	4,269,608	16.4%
Bexar County	20,675	13.3%	1,055,568	10.6%	1,789,088	6.9%
Tarrant County	16,515	10.6%	513,740	5.2%	1,881,469	7.2%
Bell County	13,053	8.4%	73,126	0.7%	321,591	1.2%
Dallas County	12,150	7.8%	950,159	9.5%	2,448,943	9.4%
El Paso County	8,407	5.4%	670,946	6.7%	823,862	3.2%
Travis County	6,784	4.4%	368,010	3.7%	1,092,810	4.2%
Denton County	4,806	3.1%	132,267	1.3%	708,627	2.7%
Collin County	4,473	2.9%	125,023	1.3%	836,947	3.2%
Fort Bend County	3,757	2.4%	151,616	1.5%	632,946	2.4%
Galveston County	3,017	1.9%	70,050	0.7%	302,276	1.2%
Williamson County	2,896	1.9%	108,082	1.1%	457,218	1.8%
Montgomery County	1,966	1.3%	105,626	1.1%	487,028	1.9%
Coryell County	1,950	1.3%	13,005	0.1%	76,276	0.3%
Hidalgo County	1,921	1.2%	733,179	7.4%	806,447	3.1%
Nueces County	1,725	1.1%	214,573	2.2%	348,130	1.3%
McLennan County	1,559	1%	58,550	0.6%	239,717	0.9%
Brazoria County	1,547	1%	92,992	0.9%	325,477	1.2%
Guadalupe County	1,501	1%	50,790	0.5%	139,709	0.5%
Webb County	1,428	0.9%	247,596	2.5%	259,471	1%
Hays County	1,113	0.7%	61,863	0.6%	170,410	0.7%
Other Counties	20,060	12.9%	2,399,399	24.1%	18,418,050	29.4%
Total	**155,813**	**100%**	**9,962,643**	**100%**	**26,092,033**	**100%**

Sources: U.S. Census Bureau 2014 American Community Survey 5-Year Estimates
Notes: Total counts for populations may differ depending on whether the estimates are derived from the five-year estimates or the one-year estimates of the American Community Survey

PUERTO RICAN POPULATION BY COUNTIES IN TEXAS, 2014

PUERTO RICAN POPULATION

● 1 dot = 100

'06-'14 PUERTO RICAN ARRIVALS

● 1 dot = 100

BOUNDARIES

County

City/Towns

Census Tracts

CONGRESSIONAL DISTRICT

Republican

Democrat

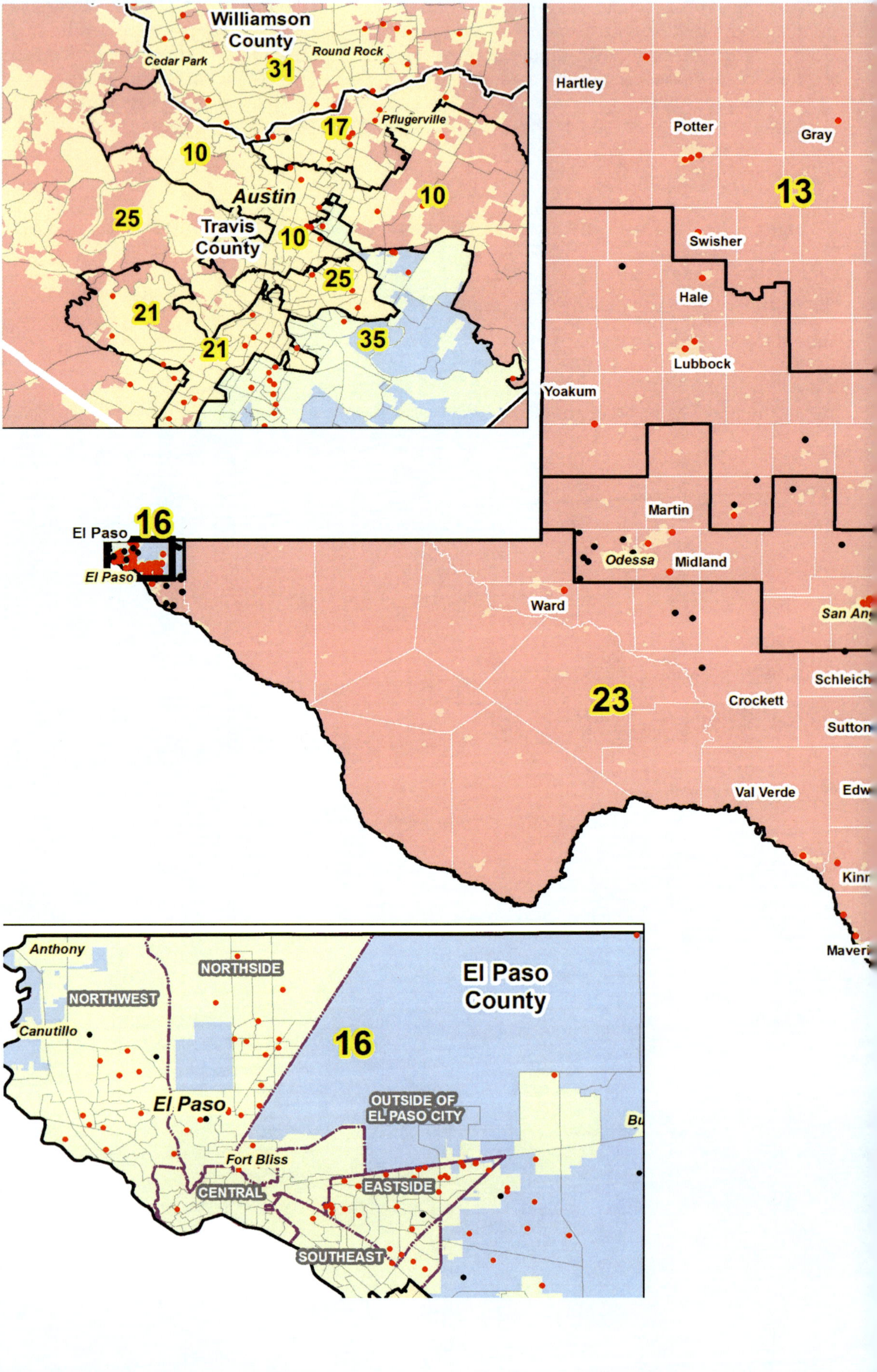

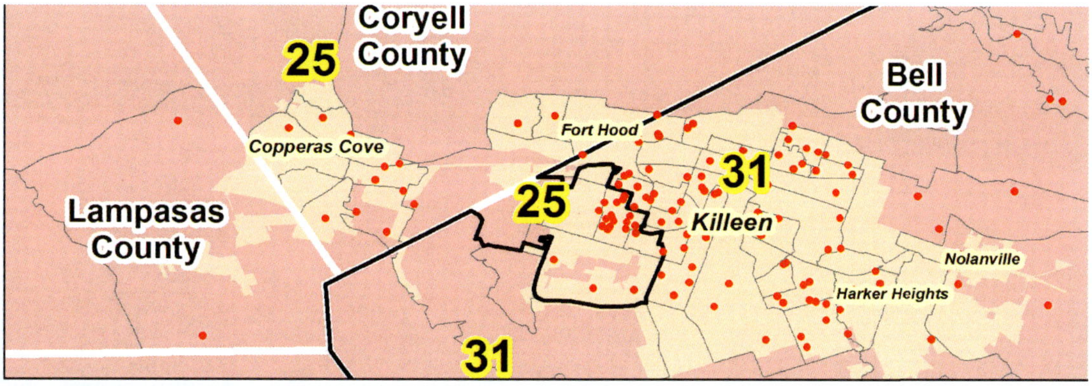
Coryell County
25
Bell County
Fort Hood
Copperas Cove
31
25
Lampasas County
Killeen
Nolanville
Harker Heights
31

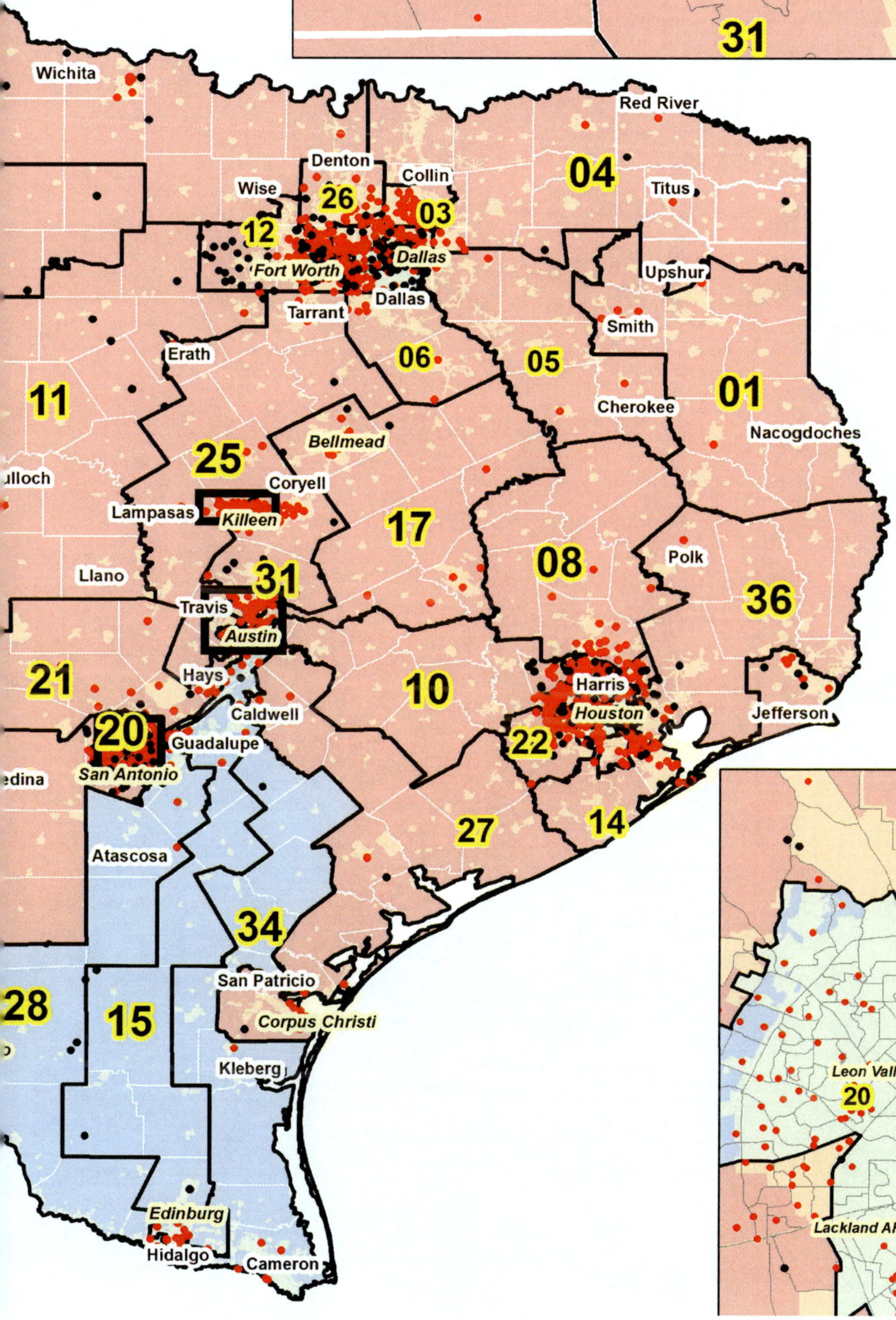
Wichita
Red River
Denton
Collin
04
Titus
Wise
26
03
12
Fort Worth
Dallas
Upshur
Dallas
Tarrant
Smith
Erath
06
05
11
Cherokee
01
Nacogdoches
Bellmead
25
ulloch
Coryell
Lampasas
Killeen
17
08
Polk
Llano
31
Travis
36
Austin
21
Hays
Harris
10
Caldwell
Houston
Jefferson
20
Guadalupe
22
San Antonio
edina
27
14
Atascosa
34
San Patricio
28
15
Corpus Christi
Kleberg
Edinburg
Hidalgo
Cameron

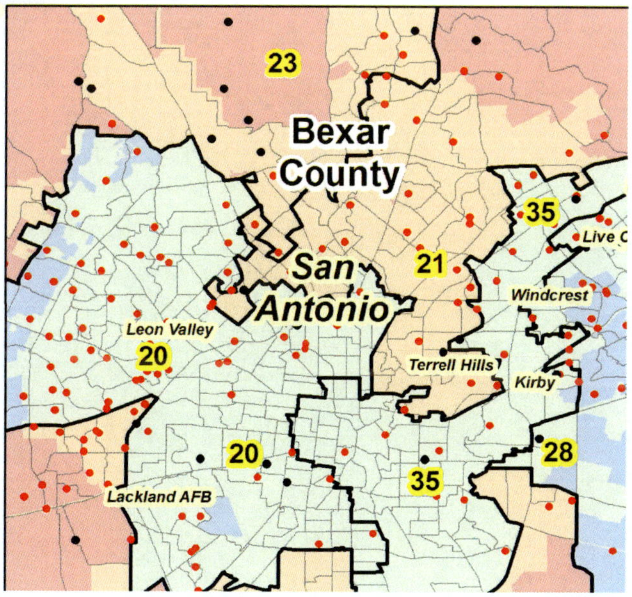
23
Bexar County
35
Live O
San Antonio
21
Windcrest
Leon Valley
20
Terrell Hills
Kirby
20
28
35
Lackland AFB

PUERTO RICAN POPULATION BY COUNTIES IN TEXAS, 2014

PUERTO RICAN POPULATION

1 dot = 100

'06-'14 PUERTO RICAN ARRIVALS

1 dot = 100

BOUNDARIES

County

City/Towns

Census Tracts

CONGRESSIONAL DISTRICT

Republican

Democrat

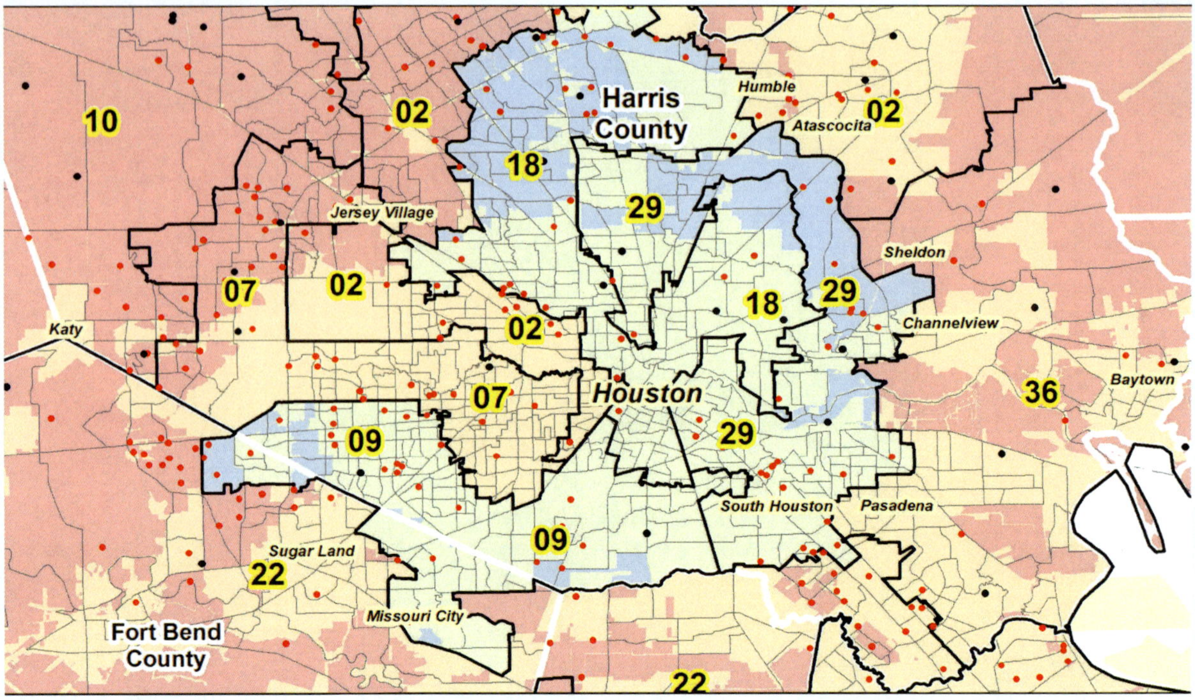

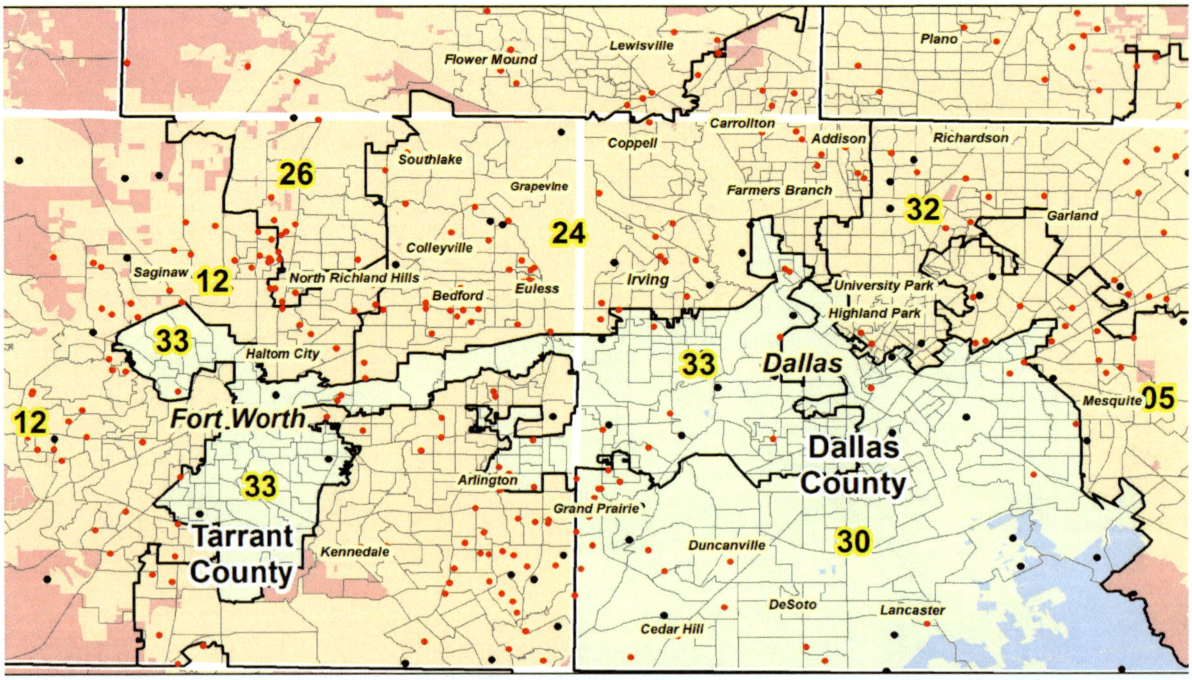

that of all stateside Puerto Ricans (11.3%) and those in Puerto Rico (26%).

Labor force participation for Texas Puerto Ricans was ten percentage points higher (72.8%) than the stateside Puerto Rican average (62.4%). An examination of unemployment rates reveals the rate of unemployment for Puerto Ricans in Texas as 8.3% to be more than three-percentage points below the stateside Puerto Rican average (11.6%) and less than half what it is in Puerto Rico (18.9%). Not only did Texan Puerto Ricans participate more in the economy, but they were also less likely to be unemployed.

Another notable characteristic among Texas Puerto Ricans is their greater representation in the Armed Forces. Approximately 3.2% of all Texas Puerto Ricans were serving in the armed forces in 2014, four times the rate among stateside Puerto Ricans of 0.8%. More than one in eight Puerto Ricans in Texas was a veteran (12.9%), a proportion more than double that of all stateside Puerto Ricans (6%) and almost four times as high as in Puerto Rico (3.3%).

By far the most common occupational sector for Puerto Rican males and females in Texas was the management, business, science and arts occupational sector account-

Table 4. Income and Earnings, 2014

Puerto Ricans	Texas	United States	Puerto Rico*
INCOME IN THE PAST 12 MONTHS (IN 2013 INFLATION-ADJUSTED DOLLARS)			
Households	56,709	1,635,808	1,175,297
Median household income (dollars)	$53,565	$39,322	$18,710
With earnings	89.4%	76.9%	54.7%
Mean earnings (dollars)	$68,833	$61,065	$36,407
With Social Security income	14.5%	24.1%	43.2%
Mean Social Security income (dollars)	$14,148	$13,727	$12,159
With Supplemental Security Income	3.7%	12.6%	0.4%
Mean Supplemental Security Income (dollars)	$9,401	$8,780	$10,025
With cash public assistance income	1.5%	6.9%	8.1%
Mean cash public assistance income (dollars)	$1,203	$3,441	$2,316
With retirement income	11.3%	10.1%	15.6%
Mean retirement income (dollars)	$19,875	$20,452	$15,387
With Food Stamp/SNAP benefits	15.8%	31.5%	39.7%
Families	39,287	111,4628	83,0807
Median family income (dollars)	$61,566	$44,499	$22,220
Married-couple family	64.9%	53.9%	56.1%
Median income (dollars)	$74,444	$67,129	$29,417
Male householder, no spouse present	10.6%	10.2%	9.5%
Median income (dollars)	$39,474	$37,513	$17,797
Female householder, no husband present	24.4%	35.9%	34.4%
Median income (dollars)	$34,788	$23,957	$13,554
Individuals	177,448	5,266,738	3,404,122
Per capita income (dollars)	$22,997	$18,457	$10,960
Mean earnings (dollars) for full-time, year-round workers:			
Male	$52,203	$50,756	$32,512
Female	$46,635	$42,263	$29,166

Source: U.S. Census Bureau, 2014 American Community Survey 1-Year Estimates.
* Puerto Ricans only.

ing for 31.8% of male and 46.9% of female Texas Puerto Rican employment. Both these proportions exceed stateside Puerto Rican figures of 23.4% and 33.1%, respectively, as well as the island figures of 23.9% and 39.7%, respectively. Puerto Rican male employment in Texas was almost evenly distributed across other sectors, but the case was not the same for women. Puerto Rican women in Texas were also present in sales and office occupation sector (31.5%) and service occupation sector (18.7%), but much less represented in other sectors.

The Puerto Rican household median income was $53,565, more than $12,000 than the stateside Puerto Rican median household income of $39,322 and almost twice the $18,710 median Puerto Rican household income in Puerto Rico. Puerto Rican women in Texas in particular earned more than their island resident counterparts. Whereas the national average earnings for full-time, year-round female Puerto Rican stateside workers was only $42,263 ($13,097 more than the island resident female worker average of $29,166) the same demographic group in Texas earned $46,635 ($17,469 more than island resident counterparts). Despite the increased income, a noticeable pay gap between men and women persisted across all jurisdictions.

Graph 4.A: Mean Earnings for Full-Time Year-Round Puerto Rican Workers, 2014

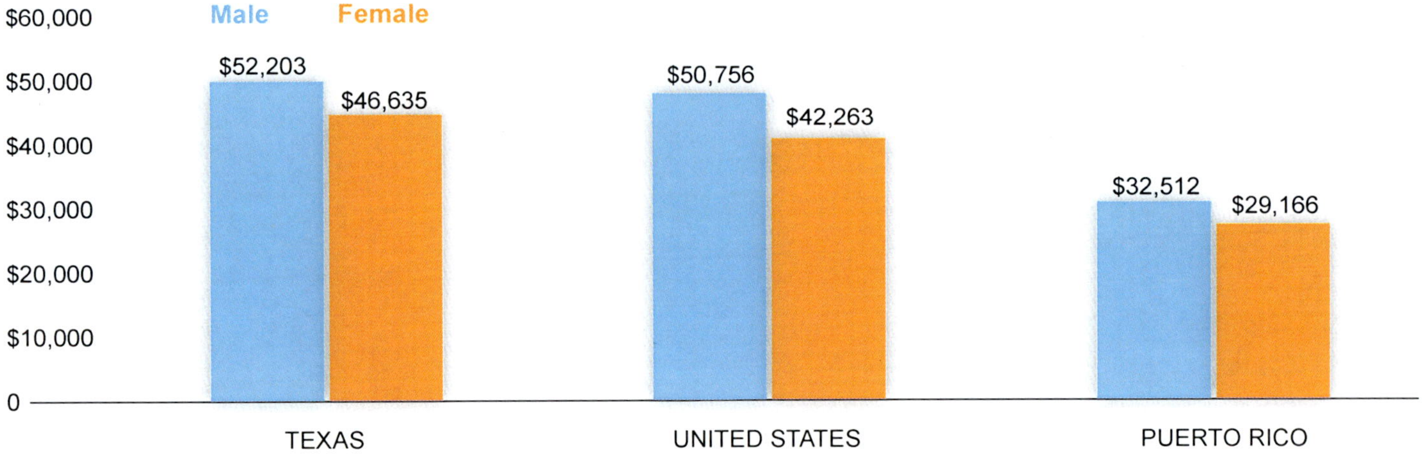

Graph 4.B: Puerto Rican Purchasing Power, in Billions, 2014

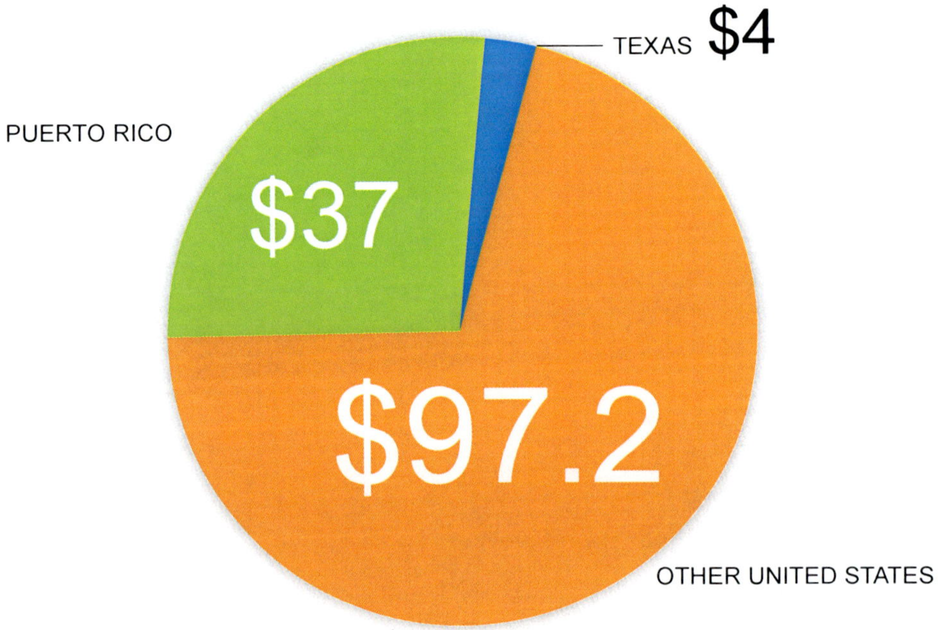

Graph 5.A: Poverty Rates, 2014

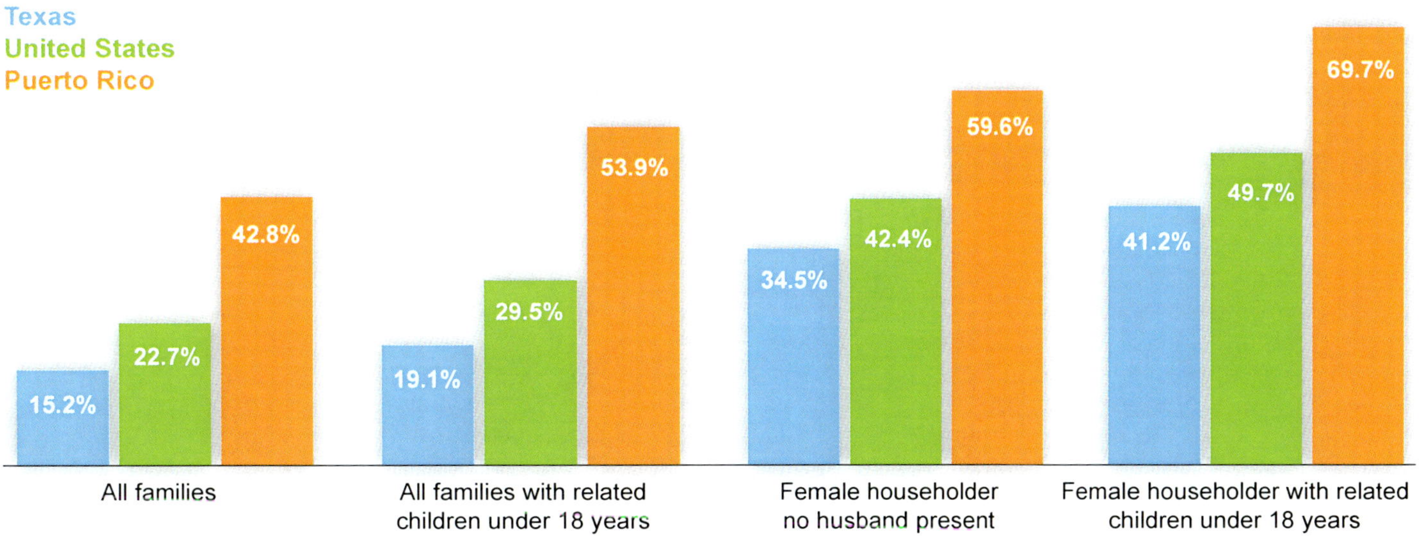

Table 5. Poverty, 2014

Puerto Ricans	Texas	United States	Puerto Rico*
POVERTY RATES			
All families	15.2%	22.7%	42.8%
With related children under 18 years	19.1%	29.5%	53.9%
With related children under 5 years only	33.6%	24.6%	57.1%
Married-couple family	7.7%	9.7%	30.9%
With related children under 18 years	8.7%	11.3%	35.5%
With related children under 5 years only	N/A	5.9%	33.9%
Female householder, no husband present, family	34.5%	42.4%	59.6%
With related children under 18 years	41.2%	49.7%	69.7%
With related children under 5 years only	84.8%	49.4%	75.7%
All people	16%	26.2%	46.6%
Under 18 years	20.9%	33.4%	58.7%
Related children under 18 years	20.8%	33.1%	58.6%
Related children under 5 years	24%	34.7%	62.8%
Related children 5 to 17 years	19.4%	32.4%	57.3%
18 years and over	13.6%	22.8%	43.2%
18 to 64 years	13.1%	22.8%	43.8%
65 years and over	18.9%	22.4%	41%
People in families	14.8%	23.6%	44.6%
Unrelated individuals 15 years and over	22.6%	38.5%	58%

Source: U.S. Census Bureau, 2014 American Community Survey 1-Year Estimates.
* Puerto Ricans only.

Puerto Ricans in Texas had $4 billion in purchasing power, constituting about 4.1% of the $97.2 in spending power generated by Puerto Ricans in the United States. This purchasing power represents a significant market for economic activity with and in Puerto Rico including tourism, both traditional and medical, investment, and trade. Purchasing power is defined simply as per capita income multiplied by the Puerto Rican population.

In 2014 only 1.5% of Puerto Ricans in Texas received cash public assistance, compared to 6.9% of all stateside Puerto Ricans and 8.1% of island residents. In Texas this assistance averaged $1,203 — just about a third of the average assistance received by stateside Puerto Ricans ($3,441) and just over half of that received by island residents ($2,316). Supplemental Nutrition Assistance Program (SNAP) benefit recipient rates were also lower for Texas Puerto Ricans at 15.8% compared to the 31.5% stateside Puerto Rican proportion and 39.7% proportion among those in Puerto Rico.

Puerto Rican families in Texas had a considerably lower rate of poverty (15.2%) than all stateside Puerto Rican families (22.7%) or those in Puerto Rico (42.8%). As seen in other states, the rate of poverty doubled for female led households without a husband to 34.5%, compared to 42.4% for stateside Puerto Ricans and 59.6% for island residents. For female households with related children under 18 years of age, the poverty levels are higher, at 41.2%, for Texas Puerto Ricans. However, a particularly vulnerable demographic in both Texas and Puerto Rico were female Puerto Rican households with related children under 5. In Texas this demographic exhibited a poverty rate of 84.8%, almost ten percentage points higher than the 75.7% rate in Puerto Rico and 35 percentage points higher than for all Puerto Ricans in the U.S. These poverty rates demonstrate that Puerto Rican families with absent husbands and children are particularly vulnerable to poverty.

Housing is a primary determinant of the cost of living. In general, the U.S. Southwest has a lower cost of home ownership than the Northeast or coastal parts of the country. The median value of owner-occupied housing for Puerto Ricans in Texas was $144,100, compared to $175,900 average for stateside Puerto Ricans, and $119,500 in Puerto Rico. The median monthly owner cost associated with a mortgage was $1,365 for Puerto Ricans in Texas, and $1,545 for other stateside Puerto Ricans. This cost was $873 in Puerto Rico. Puerto Ricans in Texas had lower rates of home ownership than Puerto Ricans in Puerto Rico, but higher than in the U.S. as a whole. The Census data revealed that Puerto Ricans in Texas had a 47.1% rate of owner-occupied housing units, higher than stateside Puerto Ricans at 36%. The home ownership rate in Puerto Rico was much higher 68.7%.

Table 6. Housing and Health Insurance, 2014

Puerto Ricans	Texas	United States	Puerto Rico*
HOUSING			
Owner-occupied housing units	47.1%	36%	68.7%
Monthly owner costs as a percentage of household income in the past 12 months			
Less than 30 percent	75.7%	62.8%	52.6%
30 percent or more	24.3%	37.2%	47.4%
Owner-occupied housing units			
Median value (dollars)	$144,100	$175,900	$119,500
Median selected monthly owner costs with a mortgage (dollars)	$1,365	$1,545	$873
HEALTH INSURANCE COVERAGE			
Civilian noninstitutionalized population			
With private health insurance	64.1%	51.6%	38%
With public coverage	27.6%	43.5%	62.9%
No health insurance coverage	15.3%	11.5%	5.5%

Source: U.S. Census Bureau, 2014 American Community Survey 1-Year Estimates.
* Puerto Ricans only.

Puerto Ricans in Ohio, 2014

In 2014, Ohio had the tenth largest number of Puerto Ricans in the United States with 108,174 residents, accounting for less than 1% of Ohio's 11.6-milion population, but 2.1% of all Puerto Ricans in the U.S. Despite the low proportion of the total Ohio population Puerto Ricans represented, this number has grown from 66,269 in 2000 to 108,174 in 2014 — an increase of more than 60%. Puerto Ricans in Ohio were most present in Lorain and Cuyahoga Counties.

Graph 1.A: Latino Population Ohio, 2014

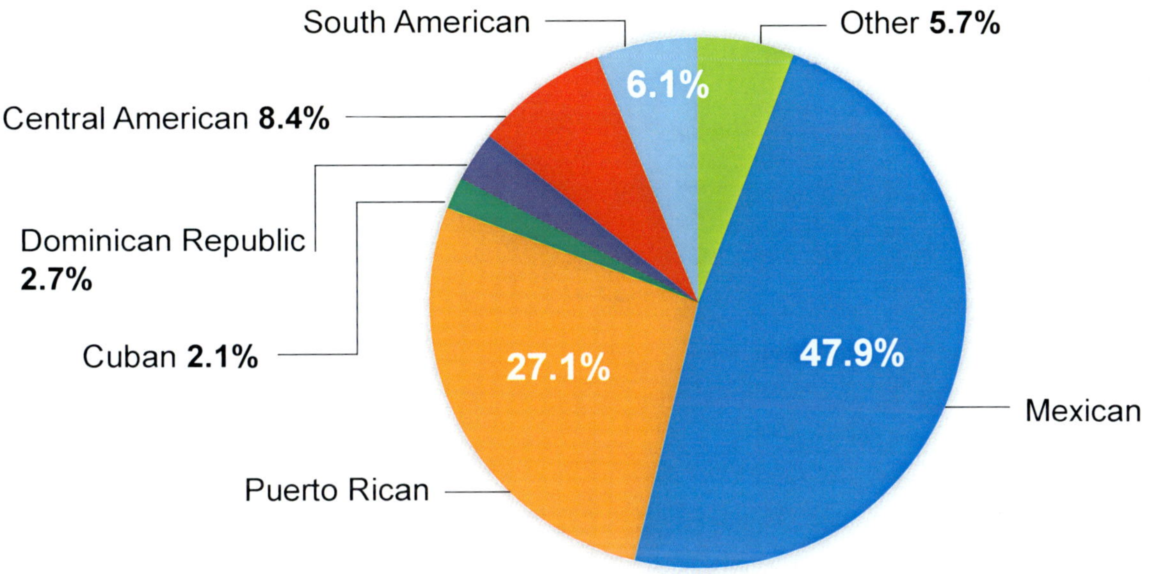

Table 1. Puerto Rican and Latino Population in Ohio

	2000		2010		2014	
Total	11,353,140	100%	11,536,504	100%	11,594,163	100%
Not Hispanic or Latino	11,136,017	98%	11,181,830	96.9%	11,195,457	96.6%
Hispanic or Latino	217,123	2%	354,674	3.1%	398,706	3.4%
Mexican	90,663	0.8%	172,029	1.5%	190,835	1.6%
Puerto Rican	66,269	0.6%	94,965	0.8%	108,174	0.9%
Cuban	5,152	0.0%	7,523	0.1%	8,544	0.1%
Dominican Republic	1,968	0.0%	6,453	0.1%	10,591	0.1%
Central American	6,577	0.1%	22,756	0.2%	33,564	0.3%
South American	7,539	0.1%	17,571	0.2%	24,244	0.2%
Other	38,955	0.3%	33,377	0.3%	22,754	0.2%

Sources: U.S. Census Bureau, Census 2000 Summary File 1, 2010 Census. Summary File 1, and 2014 American Community Survey 1-Year Estimates.

The next two largest Latino groups in Ohio were South and Central Americans, representing less than 15%, indicating that by and large, the Latino population is dominated by the Mexican and Puerto Rican presence.

The median age of Puerto Ricans in Ohio was 26.3 years, younger than both the national average for Puerto Ricans at 29.8 years of age and island residents at 38.9 years. These differences in the age structure were evident in the percent of the population aged 62 years or older; only 6% of Puerto Ricans in Ohio were 62 years of age or older compared to the 9.9% rate for all Puerto Ricans living stateside. With 21% of the population 62 years of

Graph 2.A: Puerto Rican Education Attainment, 25 years and over, 2014

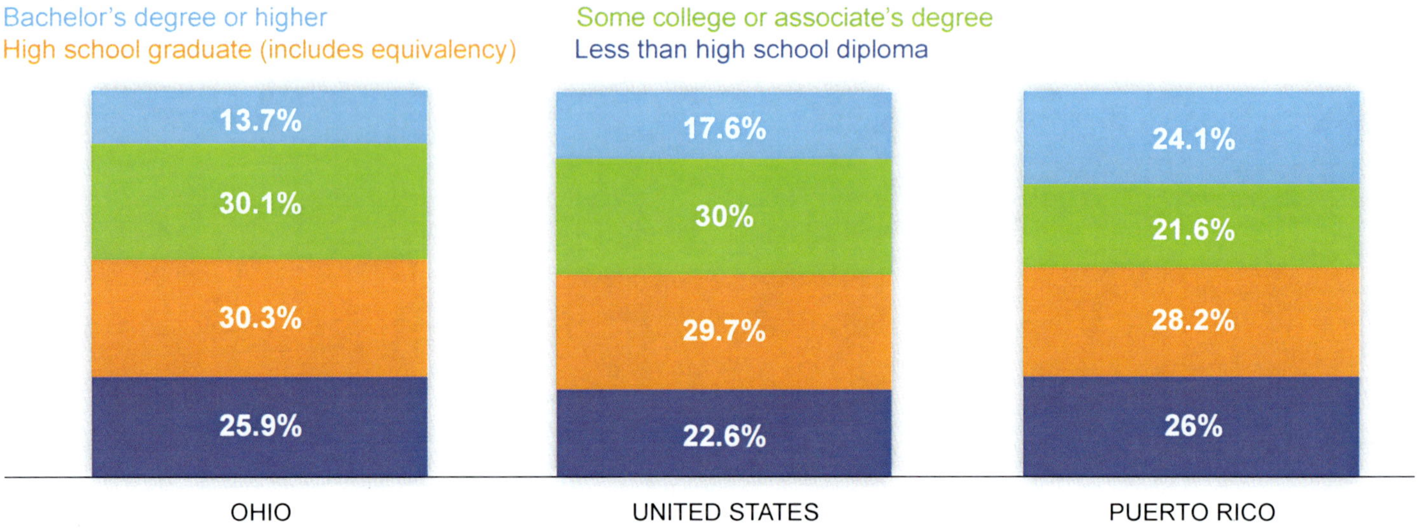

Table 2. Age, Education, and Language, 2014

Puerto Ricans	Ohio	United States	Puerto Rico*
TOTAL POPULATION	108,174	5,266,738	3,404,122
Median age (years)	26.3	28.9	38.9
62 years and over	6%	9.90%	21%
EDUCATIONAL ATTAINMENT			
Population 25 years and over			
Less than high school diploma	25.9%	22.6%	26%
High school graduate (includes equivalency)	30.3%	29.7%	28.2%
Some college or associate's degree	30.1%	30%	21.6%
Bachelor's degree or higher	13.7%	17.6%	24.1%
Male, bachelor's degree or higher	10.4%	15.6%	19.6%
Female, bachelor's degree or higher	16.8%	19.5%	28.1%
LANGUAGE SPOKEN AT HOME AND ABILITY TO SPEAK ENGLISH			
Population 5 years and over			
English only	45.3%	38.8%	5.3%
Language other than English	54.7%	61.2%	94.7%
Speak English less than "very well"	18.7%	17.3%	78.8%

Source: U.S. Census Bureau, 2014 American Community Survey 1-Year Estimates.
* Puerto Ricans only.

age or older in Puerto Rico, Ohio had a significantly lower proportion of the population in this age group.

English-fluency indicators for Puerto Ricans in Ohio were slightly higher than those for all stateside Puerto Ricans. Nearly half of Puerto Rican households in Ohio (45.3%) reported speaking only English, compared to the stateside Puerto Rican average of 38.8%. Only 18.7% of Puerto Ricans in Ohio reported speaking English less than "very well," slightly higher than the average for Puerto Ricans in the U.S. of 17.3%.

Puerto Ricans in Ohio were generally less educated than Puerto Ricans throughout the U.S. or in Puerto Rico. Only 13.7% of Puerto Ricans in Ohio had earned a bachelor's degree or higher, compared to 17.6% of stateside Puerto Ricans and 24.1% of Puerto Ricans in Puerto Rico. A gender breakdown of the education demographics indicates that Puerto Rican women in Ohio maintain a higher level of education attainment with 16.8% having attained a bachelor's degree or higher. This rate is much lower than Puerto Rico's 28.1%, and slightly lower than the stateside average of 19.5% for Puerto Rican women. Only 10.4% of Puerto Rican men in Ohio attained a bachelor's degree or higher compared to 19.6% in Puerto Rican average of 15.6%.

Table 3. Employment and Occupations, 2014

Puerto Ricans	Ohio	United States	Puerto Rico*
EMPLOYMENT STATUS			
Population 16 years and over			
In labor force	67.1%	62.4%	43.7%
Civilian labor force	66.8%	61.6%	43.7%
Employed	58.1%	54.4%	35.4%
Unemployed	13%	11.6%	18.9%
Not in labor force	32.9%	37.6%	56.3%
Armed Forces	0.2%	0.8%	0%
OCCUPATION			
Civilian employed population 16 years and over			
Male	23,257	1,058,918	516,762
Management, business, science, and arts	16.9%	23.4%	23.9%
Service occupations	18.4%	22.5%	23%
Sales and office occupations	15.6%	19.6%	21.3%
Construction and maintenance	17.1%	13.8%	18%
Production, transportation, and moving	32.1%	20.7%	13.7%
Female	20,058	999105	456356
Management, business, science, and arts	25.9%	33.1%	39.7%
Service occupations	29%	24.4%	16.6%
Sales and office occupations	29.5%	35.7%	38.3%
Construction and maintenance	1.6%	0.6%	0.6%
Production, transportation, and moving	14%	6.2%	4.8%
CLASS OF WORKER			
Civilian employed population 16 years and over			
Private wage and salary workers	84%	82%	69%
Government workers	13.5%	14.8%	22.5%
Self-employed workers in own not incorporated business	2.6%	3.1%	8.3%
VETERAN STATUS			
Civilian population 18 years and over			
Civilian veteran	4.9%	6%	3.3%

Source: U.S. Census Bureau, 2014 American Community Survey 1-Year Estimates.
* Puerto Ricans only.

Puerto Rican participation in the Ohio labor force (67.1%) was almost five percentage points higher than the figure reported for all stateside Puerto Ricans (62.4%), and more than 20 percentage points higher than Puerto Rico's 43.7%. Puerto Ricans in Ohio have an unemployment rate of 13%, 1.4 percentage points higher than national Puerto Rican unemployment rate of 11.6%, but 5.9 percentage points below Puerto Rico's 18.9% unemployment rate.

Proportionately, less Puerto Ricans in Ohio worked in the higher-wage management, business, science, and arts sector than stateside Puerto Ricans overall and those in Puerto Rico. Only 16.9% of Puerto Rican males in Ohio worked in the management sector, lower than the 23.4% stateside Puerto Rican male average and 23.9% rate in Puerto Rico. A greater disparity was seen in women's employment; although one out of four (25.9%) Puerto Rican women in Ohio worked in the management sector, this percentage is below the national rate of one in three (33.1%) and almost fifteen percentage points below the percentage of Puerto Rican women employed in Puerto Rico's management sector (39.7%).

For Puerto Rican males in Ohio, the most common occupational sector was the production, transportation, and material moving category accounting for 32.1% of labor

Table 4. Income and Earnings, 2014

Puerto Ricans	Ohio	United States	Puerto Rico*
INCOME IN THE PAST 12 MONTHS (IN 2013 INFLATION-ADJUSTED DOLLARS)			
Households	32,426	1,635,808	1,175,297
Median household income (dollars)	$34,862	$39,322	$18,710
With earnings	82.7%	76.9%	54.7%
Mean earnings (dollars)	$53,211	$61,065	$36,407
With Social Security income	18.7%	24.1%	43.2%
Mean Social Security income (dollars)	$12,560	$13,727	$12,159
With Supplemental Security Income	11%	12.6%	0.4%
Mean Supplemental Security Income (dollars)	$8,094	$8,780	$10,025
With cash public assistance income	6.8%	6.9%	8.1%
Mean cash public assistance income (dollars)	$2,835	$3,441	$2,316
With retirement income	6.6%	10.1%	15.6%
Mean retirement income (dollars)	$19,664	20,452	15,387
With Food Stamp/SNAP benefits	35.2%	31.5%	39.7%
Families	23,543	1,114,628	830,807
Median family income (dollars)	$35,538	$44,499	$22,220
Married-couple family	56.5%	53.9%	56.1%
Median income (dollars)	$58,825	$67,129	$29,417
Male householder, no spouse present	7.6%	10.2%	9.5%
Median income (dollars)	$42,896	$37,513	$17,797
Female householder, no husband present	35.9%	35.9%	34.4%
Median income (dollars)	$16,745	$23,957	$13,554
Individuals	108,174	5,266,738	3,404,122
Per capita income (dollars)	$15,117	$18,457	$10,960
Mean earnings (dollars) for full-time, year-round workers:			
Male	$45,521	$50,756	$32,512
Female	$36,970	$42,263	$29,166

Source: U.S. Census Bureau, 2014 American Community Survey 1-Year Estimates.
* Puerto Ricans only.

Puerto Rican Population by Counties in Ohio, 2014

The majority of Puerto Ricans in Ohio live in Cuyahoga and Lorain Counties. More than one in three Puerto Ricans (38.4%) in Ohio resided in Cuyahoga County within the Cleveland metro area. Lorain County accounted for another 16.9% of Ohio's Puerto Rican population. In both these counties, Puerto Ricans accounted for the majority of Latinos present, 61.3% in Cuyahoga and 66.5% in Loraine. Franklin County, which contains the city of Columbus, accounted for another 7.2% of Ohio Puerto Ricans, and Mahoning County, with Youngstown as its main urban center, accounted for another 6.9% of Ohio Puerto Ricans. With the exception of Ashtabula County, which accounted for 2.1% of the Ohio Puerto Rican population but only 0.9% of the total Ohio population, Puerto Ricans tended to be disproportionately underrepresented in other counties.

COUNTY	Puerto Rican Population	Percent	Latino Population	Percent	Total Population	Percent
Cuyahoga County	39,538	38.4%	64,518	17%	1,267,513	11%
Lorain County	17,437	16.9%	26,637	7%	302,465	2.6%
Franklin County	7,430	7.2%	59,157	15.6%	1,197,592	10.4%
Mahoning County	7,136	6.9%	11,861	3.1%	235,809	2%
Lucas County	3,018	2.9%	28,129	7.4%	438,167	3.8%
Summit County	2,699	2.6%	9,586	2.5%	541,464	4.7%
Ashtabula County	2,166	2.1%	3,625	1%	100,346	0.9%
Hamilton County	2,112	2%	21,969	5.8%	803,272	6.9%
Butler County	2,093	2%	15,699	4.1%	371,154	3.2%
Montgomery County	2,086	2%	13,098	3.5%	534,801	4.6%
Lake County	1,347	1.3%	8,504	2.2%	229,602	2%
Stark County	1,096	1.1%	6,596	1.7%	375,090	3.2%
Medina County	1,055	1%	3,066	0.8%	174,091	1.5%
Other Counties	13,877	13.5%	107,097	28.2%	4,989,014	43.2%
Total	**103,090**	**100%**	**379,542**	**100%**	**11,560,380**	**100%**

Sources: U.S. Census Bureau and 2014 American Community Survey 5-Year Estimates
Notes: Total counts for populations maydiffer depending on whether the estimates are derived from the five-year estimates or the one-year estimates of the American Community Survey Not all counties with Puerto Ricans in Ohio were included; the above table only accounts for 86.5% of the total Puerto Rican population as all other counties in Ohio failed to meet a 1% population threshold. Please contact Centro with any questions regarding methods or data sources.

PUERTO RICAN POPULATION BY COUNTIES IN OHIO, 2014

PUERTO RICAN POPULATION

1 dot = 50

'06-'14 PUERTO RICAN ARRIVALS

1 dot = 50

BOUNDARIES

County

City/Towns

Census Tracts

CONGRESSIONAL DISTRICT

Republican

Democrat

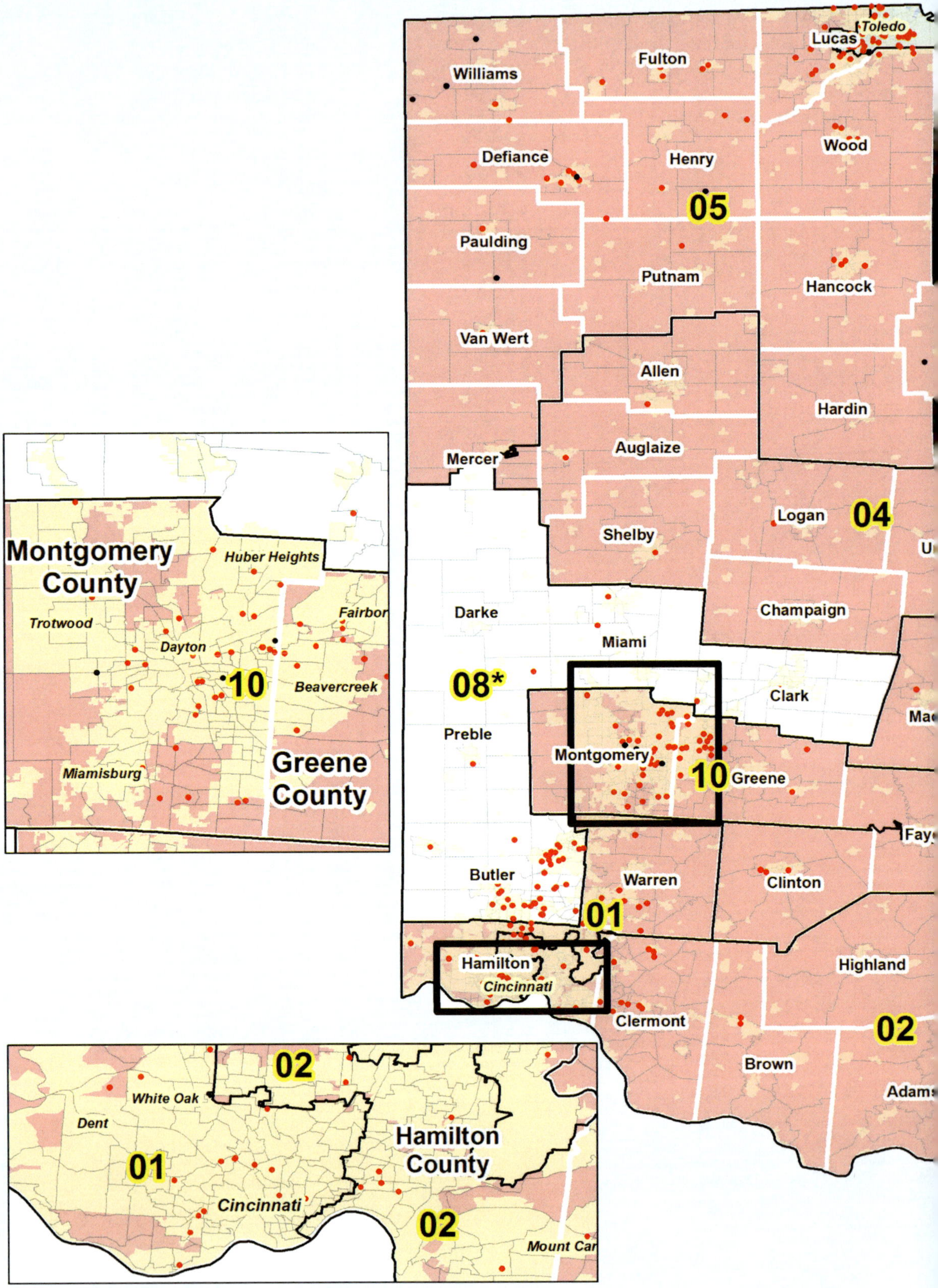

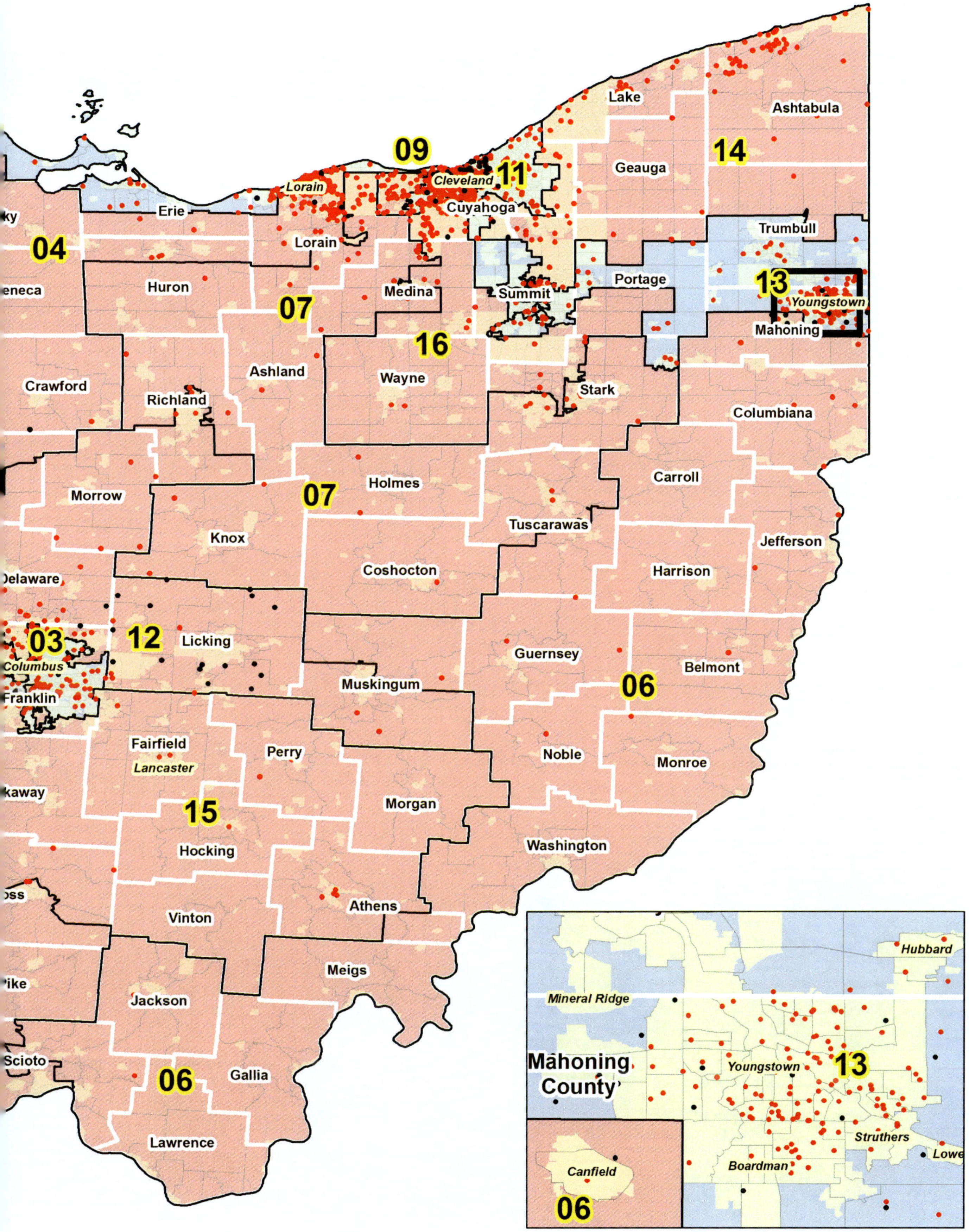

09
11
14
04
07
16
13
12
03
15
06
Lake
Ashtabula
Geauga
Lorain
Cleveland
Cuyahoga
Erie
Trumbull
Huron
Medina
Summit
Portage
Youngstown
Mahoning
Ashland
Wayne
Crawford
Richland
Stark
Columbiana
Morrow
Holmes
Carroll
Tuscarawas
Knox
Jefferson
Coshocton
Harrison
Licking
Columbus
Franklin
Guernsey
Belmont
Muskingum
Fairfield
Lancaster
Perry
Noble
Monroe
Morgan
Hocking
Washington
Athens
Vinton
Meigs
Jackson
Gallia
Lawrence
Scioto
Hubbard
Mineral Ridge
Mahoning County
Struthers
Boardman
Canfield

PUERTO RICAN POPULATION BY COUNTIES IN OHIO, 2014

PUERTO RICAN POPULATION

● 1 dot = 50

'06-'14 PUERTO RICAN ARRIVALS

● 1 dot = 50

BOUNDARIES

County

City/Towns

Census Tracts

CONGRESSIONAL DISTRICT

Republican

Democrat

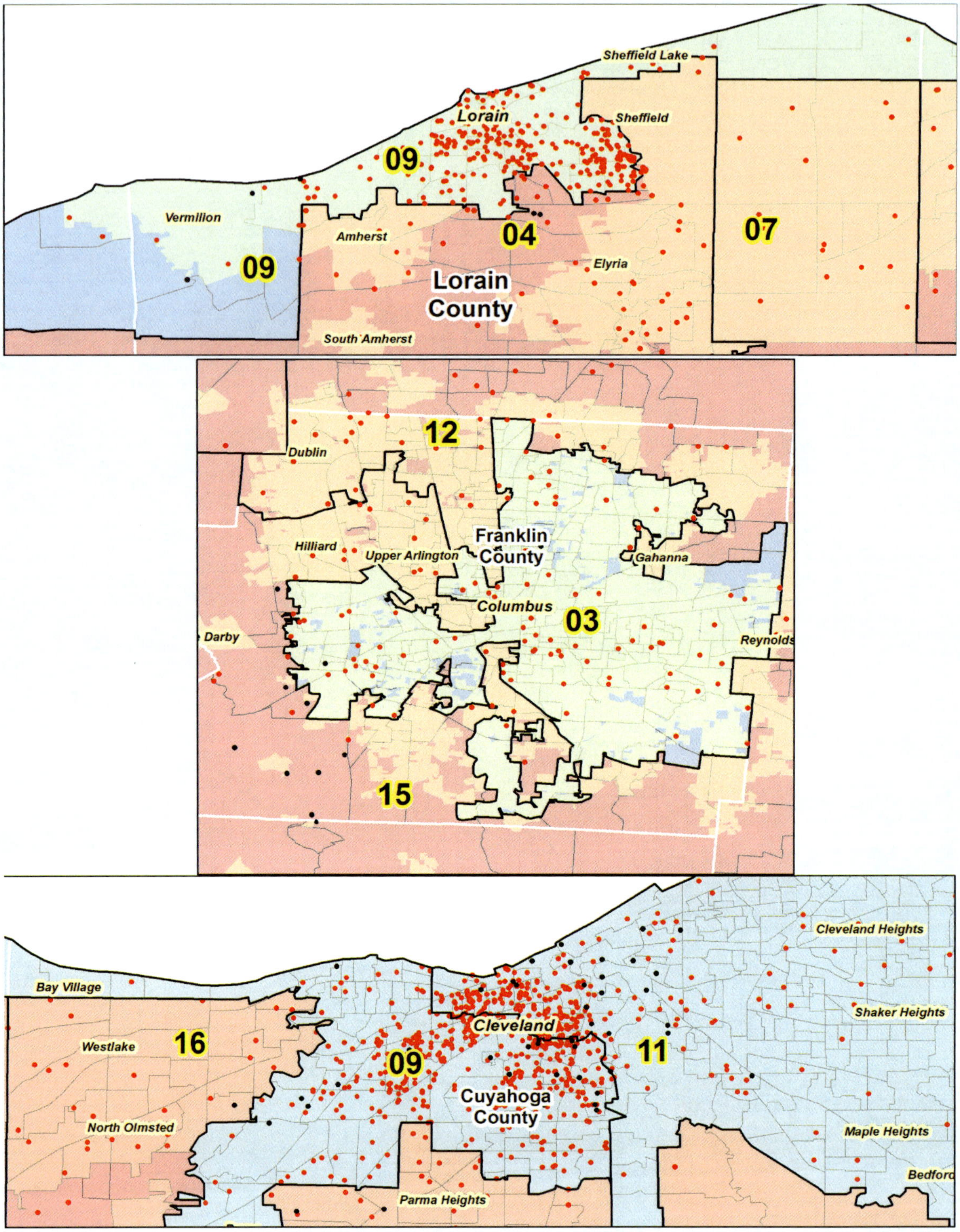

compared to 13.7% for island residents, and 20.7% for other stateside Puerto Rican residents.

The average earnings of full-time, year-round of Puerto Rican men and women in Ohio, $45,521 and $36,970, respectively, were lower than the average for stateside Puerto Ricans of $50,756 for men and $42,263 for women. Earnings for Puerto Ricans in Ohio were still higher than for island residents, where full-time, year-round Puerto Rican men and women averaged $32,512 and $29,166 in 2014.

Household and family incomes are important indicators of economic well-being. These indicators were lower for Puerto Ricans in Ohio than for stateside Puerto Ricans overall, but were higher than island figures. Median household income was $34,862 for Puerto Ricans in Ohio and $39,322 for other stateside Puerto Ricans, and $18,710 for the island. These differences were also evident in per capita income. In 2014, per capita income for Puerto Ricans in Ohio was $15,117 and $18,457 for other stateside Puerto Ricans, and $10,960 for the island.

Puerto Ricans in Ohio had $1.6 billion in purchasing power. From an economic perspective, stateside Puerto Ricans represented 72.3% of the $134.5 billion total purchasing power of the entire Puerto Rican community in the year 2014. Purchasing power is defined simply as

Graph 4.A: Mean Earnings for Full-Time Year-Round Puerto Rican Workers, 2014

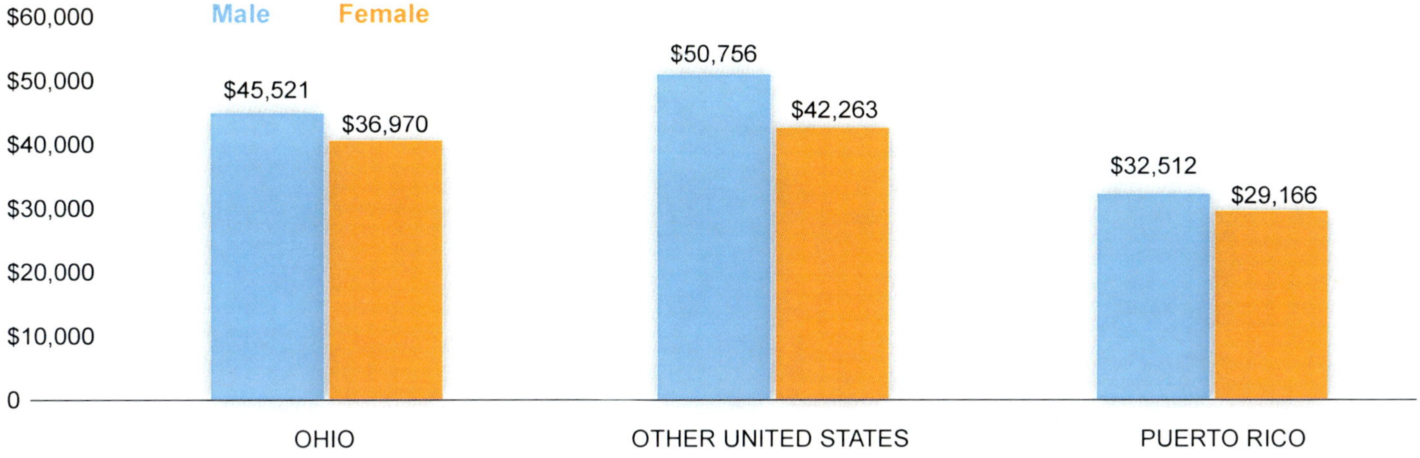

Graph 4.B: Puerto Rican Purchasing Power, in Billions, 2014

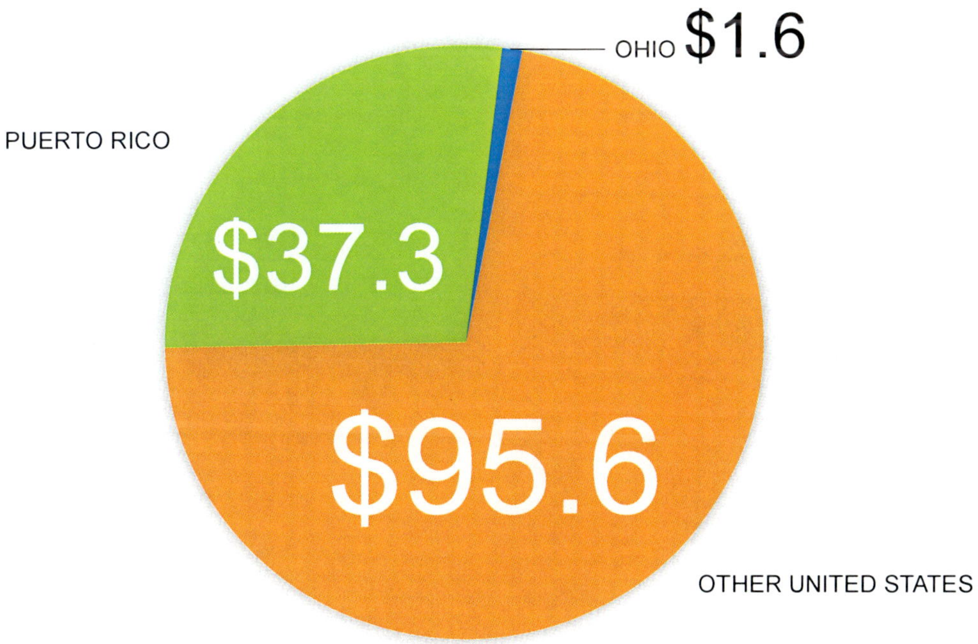

Graph 5.A: Poverty Rates, 2014

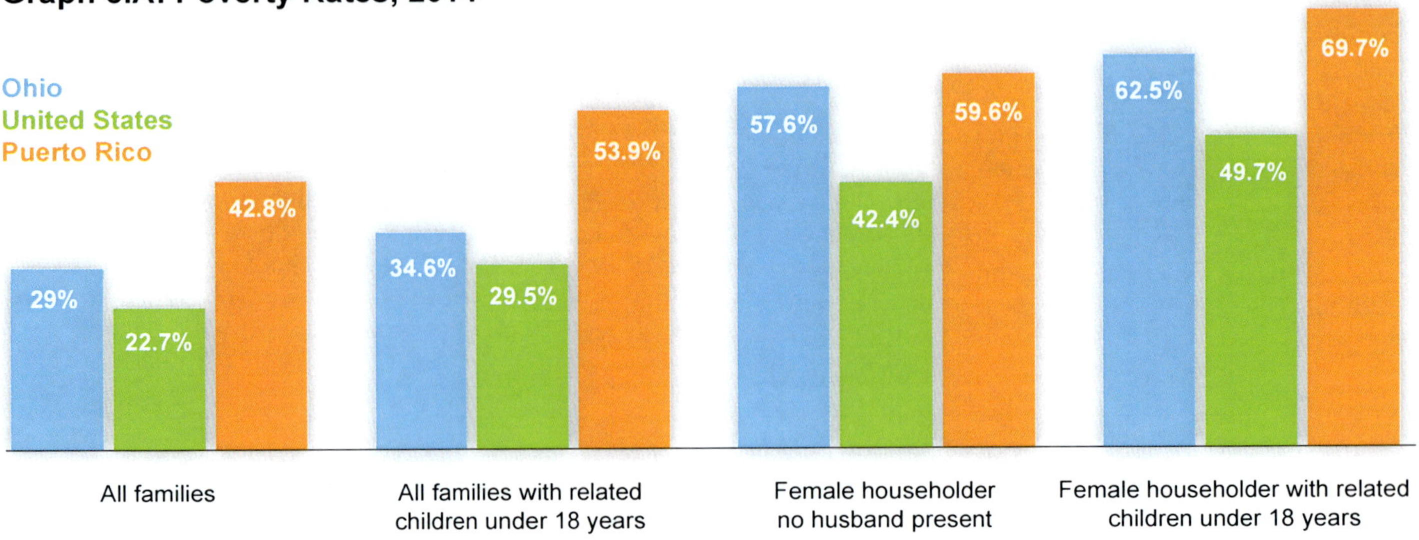

Table 5. Poverty, 2014

Puerto Ricans	Ohio	United States	Puerto Rico*
POVERTY RATES			
All families	29%	22.7%	42.8%
With related children under 18 years	34.6%	29.5%	53.9%
With related children under 5 years only	22.1%	24.6%	57.1%
Married-couple family	13.2%	9.7%	30.9%
With related children under 18 years	14.9%	11.3%	35.5%
With related children under 5 years only	N/A	5.9%	33.9%
Female householder, no husband present, family	57.6%	42.4%	59.6%
With related children under 18 years	62.5%	49.7%	69.7%
With related children under 5 years only	49.2%	49.4%	75.7%
All people	33.3%	26.2%	46.6%
Under 18 years	41.9%	33.4%	58.7%
Related children under 18 years	41.7%	33.1%	58.6%
Related children under 5 years	44.1%	34.7%	62.8%
Related children 5 to 17 years	40.9%	32.4%	57.3%
18 years and over	28.5%	22.8%	43.2%
18 to 64 years	28.3%	22.8%	43.8%
65 years and over	31.2%	22.4%	41%
People in families	32.3%	23.6%	44.6%
Unrelated individuals 15 years and over	38.4%	38.5%	58%

Source: U.S. Census Bureau, 2014 American Community Survey 1-Year Estimates.
* Puerto Ricans only.

per capita income multiplied by the Puerto Rican population. Stateside Puerto Ricans had more than double the total purchasing power of Puerto Ricans in Puerto Rico of $37.3 billion.

Puerto Ricans in Ohio have a higher incidence of public assistance recipients due to higher poverty rates and thus a higher proportion of qualified recipients. The poverty rate for all Puerto Rican families in Ohio was 29% compared to the national Puerto Rican average of 22.7%, and 42.8% in Puerto Rico. Though stateside Puerto Ricans' rates were about half, or less, than poverty rates in Puerto Rico, families with female householder, no husband present and children under 18 years of age exhibited much higher incidence of poverty than the average family. For Puerto Rican female-headed families with children the rates were 62.5% in Ohio, 49.7% in the U.S. overall, and 69.7% in Puerto Rico. These rates of poverty are alarmingly high.

In 2014, the proportion of households that received cash public assistance income of 6.8% was almost equal for Puerto Ricans in Ohio than a comparable rate of 6.9% for other stateside Puerto Ricans, and 8.1% in Puerto Rico. A higher proportion of Puerto Ricans received cash public assistance income in Puerto Rico than in either Ohio or as indicated by the total stateside data. In addition, the differences in the amount that the households received by public assistance were higher for stateside Puerto Ricans ($3,441) than for Puerto Ricans in Ohio ($2,835). The proportion of Puerto Rican households in Ohio receiving benefits from the Supplemental Nutrition Assistance Program (SNAP) was 35.2% in 2014, 3.7 percentage points higher than the 31.5% average stateside Puerto Rican household rate, but lower than the 39.7% rate for Puerto Rico's island residents.

Housing is a primary determinant of the cost of living. In general, the Rust Belt has a lower cost of home ownership than the Northeast or coastal parts of the country. The median value of owner-occupied housing for Puerto Ricans in Ohio was $103,100, compared to $175,900 average for stateside Puerto Ricans, and $119,500 in Puerto Rico. The median monthly owner cost associated with a mortgage was $1,117 for Puerto Ricans in Ohio, and $1,545 for other stateside Puerto Ricans. This cost was $873 in Puerto Rico. Puerto Ricans in Ohio had lower rates of home ownership than Puerto Ricans in Puerto Rico, but higher than in the U.S. as a whole. Puerto Ricans in Ohio had a 41% rate of owner-occupied housing units, higher than stateside Puerto Ricans at 36%. The home ownership rate in Puerto Rico was much higher, at 68.7%.

Table 6. Housing and Health Insurance, 2014

Puerto Ricans	Ohio	United States	Puerto Rico*
HOUSING			
Owner-occupied housing units	41%	36%	68.7%
Monthly owner costs as a percentage of household income in the past 12 months			
Less than 30 percent	74.8%	62.8%	52.6%
30 percent or more	25.2%	37.2%	47.4%
Owner-occupied housing units			
Median value (dollars)	$103,100	$175,900	$119,500
Median selected monthly owner costs with a mortgage (dollars)	$1,117	$1,545	$873
HEALTH INSURANCE COVERAGE			
Civilian noninstitutionalized population			
With private health insurance	46.8%	51.6%	38%
With public coverage	49.2%	43.5%	62.9%
No health insurance coverage	10.2%	11.5%	5.5%

Source: U.S. Census Bureau, 2014 American Community Survey 1-Year Estimates.
* Puerto Ricans only.

Puerto Ricans in Virginia, 2014

In 2014, Virginia had the 11th largest Puerto Rican population in the United States with 92,319 Puerto Ricans, accounting for 1.8 percent of all Puerto Ricans living in the United States. From 2000 to 2014, the number of Puerto Ricans in Virginia more than doubled from 41,131 to 92,319.

Graph 1.A: Puerto Rican and Latino Population in Virginia, 2014

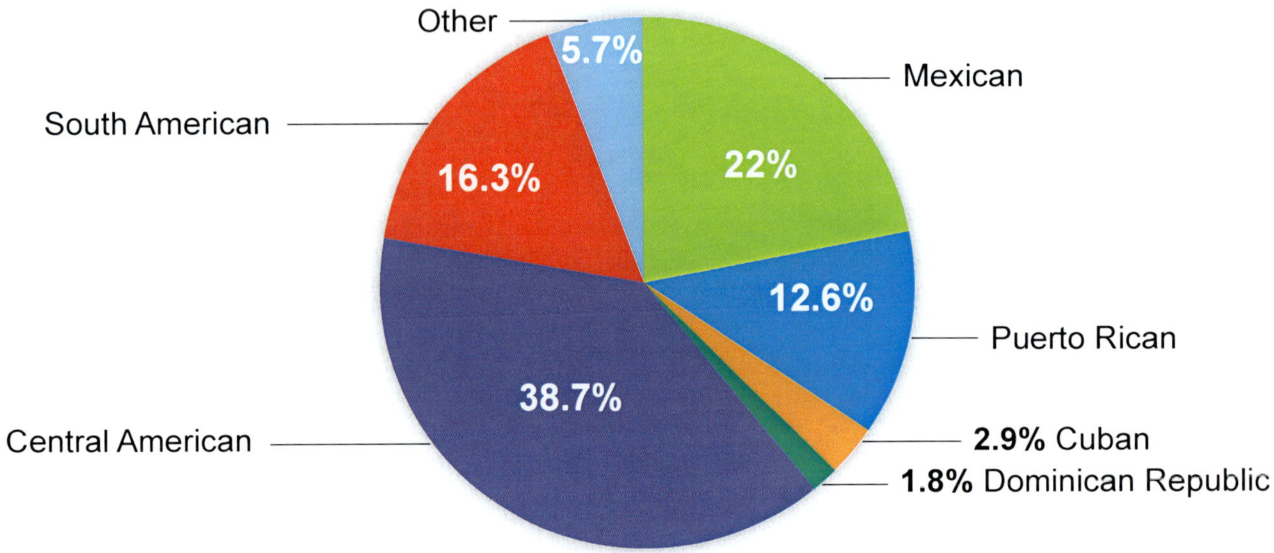

Table 1. Puerto Rican and Latino Population in Virginia

	2000		2010		2014	
Total	7,078,515	100%	8,001,024	100%	8,326,289	100%
Not Hispanic or Latino	6,748,975	9.6%	7,369,199	92.1%	7,594,318	91.2%
Hispanic or Latino	329,540	4.7%	631,825	7.9%	731,971	8.8%
Mexican	73,979	1%	155,067	1.9%	160,772	1.9%
Puerto Rican	41,131	0.6%	73,958	0.9%	92,319	1.1%
Cuban	8,332	0.1%	15,229	0.2%	21,399	0.3%
Dominican Republic	3,497	0%	10,504	0.1%	13,372	0.2%
Central American	73,140	1%	206,568	2.6%	283,403	3.4%
South American	39,841	0.6%	101,480	1.3%	119,236	1.4%
Other	89,620	1.3%	69,019	0.9%	41,470	0.5%

Sources: U.S. Census Bureau, Census 2000 Summary File 1, 2010 Census. Summary File 1, and 2014 American Community Survey 1-Year Estimates.

The median age of Puerto Ricans in Virginia was 27.3 years, which is below the national median for Puerto Ricans (28.9) more than ten years lower than the median age among Puerto Ricans in Puerto Rico of 38.9 years. The proportion of Puerto Ricans age 62 years and older is lower in Virginia (5.6%) relative to their representation in the total stateside Puerto Rican population (9.9%) and in Puerto Rico (21%).

English fluency indicators for Puerto Ricans in Virginia were higher than for all stateside Puerto Ricans. Nearly half of Puerto Ricans in Virginia (48.6%) reported speaking only English in the home, a rate about ten percentage points higher than among all Puerto Ricans in the U.S. (38.8%). Only 11.3 percent of Puerto Ricans in Virginia reported speaking English less than "very

Graph 2.A: Puerto Rican Education Attainment, 25 years and over, 2014

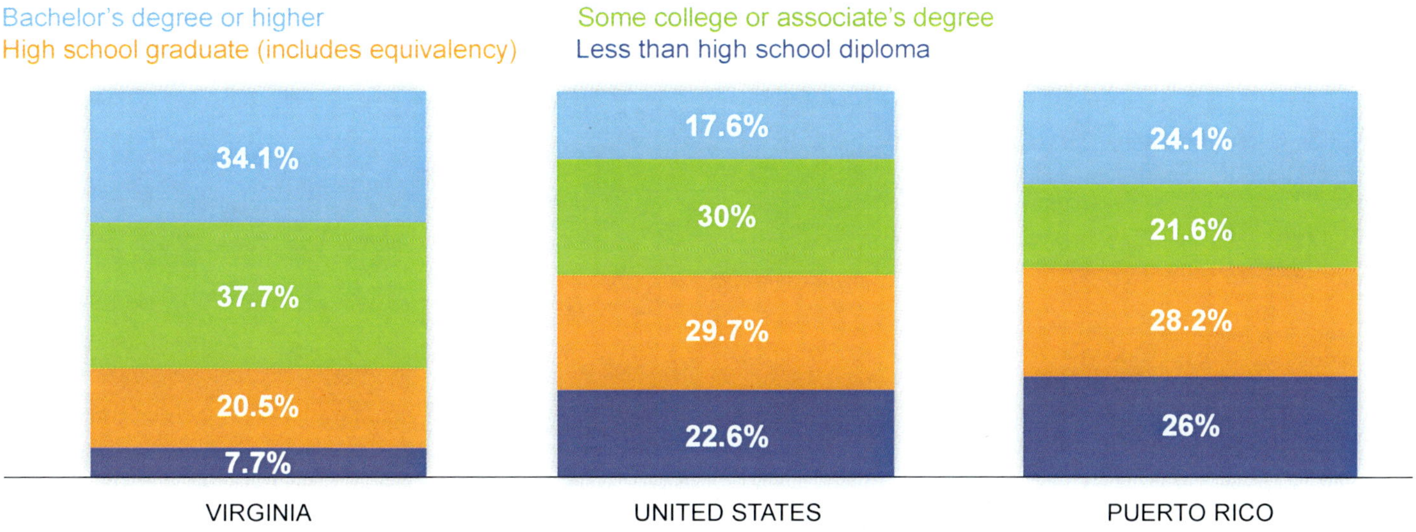

Table 2. Age, Education, and Language, 2014

Puerto Ricans	Virginia	United States	Puerto Rico*
TOTAL POPULATION	92,319	5,266,738	3,404,122
Median age (years)	27.3	28.9	38.9
62 years and over	5.6%	9.9%	21%
EDUCATIONAL ATTAINMENT			
Population 25 years and over			
Less than high school diploma	7.7%	22.6%	26%
High school graduate (includes equivalency)	20.5%	29.7%	28.2%
Some college or associate's degree	37.7%	30%	21.6%
Bachelor's degree or higher	34.1%	17.6%	24.1%
Male, bachelor's degree or higher	34.5%	15.6%	19.6%
Female, bachelor's degree or higher	33.8%	19.5%	28.1%
LANGUAGE SPOKEN AT HOME AND ABILITY TO SPEAK ENGLISH			
Population 5 years and over			
English only	48.6%	38.8%	5.3%
Language other than English	51.4%	61.2%	94.7%
Speak English less than "very well"	11.3%	17.3%	78.8%

Source: U.S. Census Bureau, 2014 American Community Survey 1-Year Estimates.
* Puerto Ricans only.

well," six-percentage points lower than the rate among all Puerto Ricans in the U.S. (17.3%).

Puerto Ricans in Virginia were generally more educated than Puerto Ricans throughout the U.S. or in Puerto Rico. More than a third (34.1%) of Puerto Ricans age 25 or older had earned a bachelor's degree or higher, compared 17.6 percent of all stateside Puerto Ricans and 24.1 percent of those in Puerto Rico. A breakdown of the education demographics by sex indicates that men had a higher proportion of having a bachelor's degree or higher (34.5%) than women (33.8%) in Virginia. However, this was different for Puerto Ricans in the U.S. and in Puerto Rico where women (19.5% and 28.1%, respectively) had a higher proportion of having a bachelor's degree or higher than men (15.6% and 19.6%, respectively).

Puerto Rican participation in Virginia's civilian labor force (66.2%) was slightly higher than among the entire U.S. (61.6%), and both were almost 20 percentage points higher than the labor force participation in Puerto Rico (43.7%). The unemployment rate among Puerto Ricans in Virginia was 8.7 percent, about three-percentage points below the national Puerto Rican average (11.6%) and less than half than those in Puerto Rico (18.9%).

Table 3. Employment and Occupations, 2014

Puerto Ricans	Virginia	United States	Puerto Rico*
EMPLOYMENT STATUS			
Population 16 years and over			
In labor force	70.3%	62.4%	43.7%
Civilian labor force	66.2%	61.6%	43.7%
Employed	60.4%	54.4%	35.4%
Unemployed	8.7%	11.6%	18.9%
Not in labor force	29.7%	37.6%	56.3%
Armed Forces	4.1%	0.8%	0%
OCCUPATION			
Civilian employed population 16 years and over			
Male	20,632	1,058,918	516,762
Management, business, science, and arts	41.6%	23.4%	23.9%
Service occupations	14.5%	22.5%	23%
Sales and office occupations	15.6%	19.6%	21.3%
Construction and maintenance	17%	13.8%	18%
Production, transportation, and moving	11.2%	20.7%	13.7%
Female	18,272	999,105	456,356
Management, business, science, and arts	42.1%	33.1%	39.7%
Service occupations	18.7%	24.4%	16.6%
Sales and office occupations	35.7%	35.7%	38.3%
Construction and maintenance	0.8%	0.6%	0.6%
Production, transportation, and moving	2.8%	6.2%	4.8%
CLASS OF WORKER			
Civilian employed population 16 years and over			
Private wage and salary workers	69.7%	82%	69%
Government workers	28.9%	14.8%	22.5%
Self-employed workers in own not incorporated business	1.2%	3.1%	8.3%
VETERAN STATUS			
Civilian population 18 years and over			
Civilian veteran	17.1%	6%	3.3%

Source: U.S. Census Bureau, 2014 American Community Survey 1-Year Estimates. * Puerto Ricans only.* Puerto Ricans only.

Proportionately, more Puerto Ricans males and females in Virginia worked in the higher wage management, business, science, and arts sector than among Puerto Ricans in the U.S. and those in Puerto Rico. More than two in five Puerto Rican males (41.6%) and females (42.1%) living in Virginia worked in the higher wage management, business, science, and arts sector compared to 23.4 percent of Puerto Rican males and 33.1 percent of Puerto Rican females in the U.S.

Puerto Ricans actively serving in the Armed Forces accounted for 3.7 percent of Puerto Ricans in Virginia, five times the rate of armed services participation than Puerto Ricans in the U.S. overall (0.8%). Similarly, 17.1 percent of the total Puerto Rican population were veterans; this number was more than double the national rate (6%) and more than five times the rate in Puerto Rico (3.3%).

The average earnings of full-time, year-round Puerto Rican men and women in Virginia, $69,680 and $49,393, demonstrating a higher disparity than at the national level of $50,756 and $42,623 for Puerto Rican men and women, respectively. Puerto Rican men in Virginia earned almost twenty thousand dollars more than at the national level while Puerto Rican women in Virginia earned about seven thousand dollars more than at the

Table 4. Income and Earnings, 2014

Puerto Ricans	Virginia	United States	Puerto Rico*
INCOME IN THE PAST 12 MONTHS (IN 2013 INFLATION-ADJUSTED DOLLARS)			
Households	25,640	1,635,808	1,175,297
Median household income (dollars)	$68,383	$39,322	$18,710
With earnings	89.7%	76.9%	54.7%
Mean earnings (dollars)	$86,762	$61,065	$36,407
With Social Security income	14.4%	24.1%	43.2%
Mean Social Security income (dollars)	$15,876	$13,727	$12,159
With Supplemental Security Income	3.5%	12.6%	0.4%
Mean Supplemental Security Income (dollars)	$10,585	$8,780	$10,025
With cash public assistance income	3.8%	6.9%	8.1%
Mean cash public assistance income (dollars)	$2,848	$3,441	$2,316
With retirement income	17.4%	10.1%	15.6%
Mean retirement income (dollars)	$19,997	$20,452	$15,387
With Food Stamp/SNAP benefits	13.6%	31.5%	39.7%
Families	19,381	1,114,628	830,807
Median family income (dollars)	$70,563	$44,499	$22,220
Married-couple family	68.8%	53.9%	56.1%
Median income (dollars)	$96,211	$67,129	$29,417
Male householder, no spouse present	4.3%	10.2%	9.5%
Median income (dollars)	$61,872	$37,513	$17,797
Female householder, no husband present	26.9%	35.9%	34.4%
Median income (dollars)	$37,866	$23,957	$13,554
Individuals	92,319	5,266,738	3,404,122
Per capita income (dollars)	$26,532	$18,457	$10,960
Mean earnings (dollars) for full-time, year-round workers:			
Male	$69,680	$50,756	$32,512
Female	$49,393	$42,263	$29,166

Source: U.S. Census Bureau, 2014 American Community Survey 1-Year Estimates.
* Puerto Ricans only.

national level. Compared to Puerto Rico, where average full-time, year round Puerto Rican earnings were $32,512 and $29,166 for men and women, respectively, Puerto Ricans in Virginia and the U.S. as a whole earned more on average.

Household and family incomes are important indicators of economic well-being. These indicators were higher for Puerto Ricans in Virginia than for stateside Puerto Ricans and those in Puerto Rico. The median household income was $68,383 for Puerto Rican households in Virginia, nearly thirty thousand dollars higher than among all stateside Puerto Ricans ($39,322) and more than three times greater than the median household income of Puerto Rican households in Puerto Rico ($18,710). Per capita incomes among Puerto Ricans in Virginia

Graph 4.A: Mean Earnings for Full-Time Year-Round Puerto Rican Workers, 2014

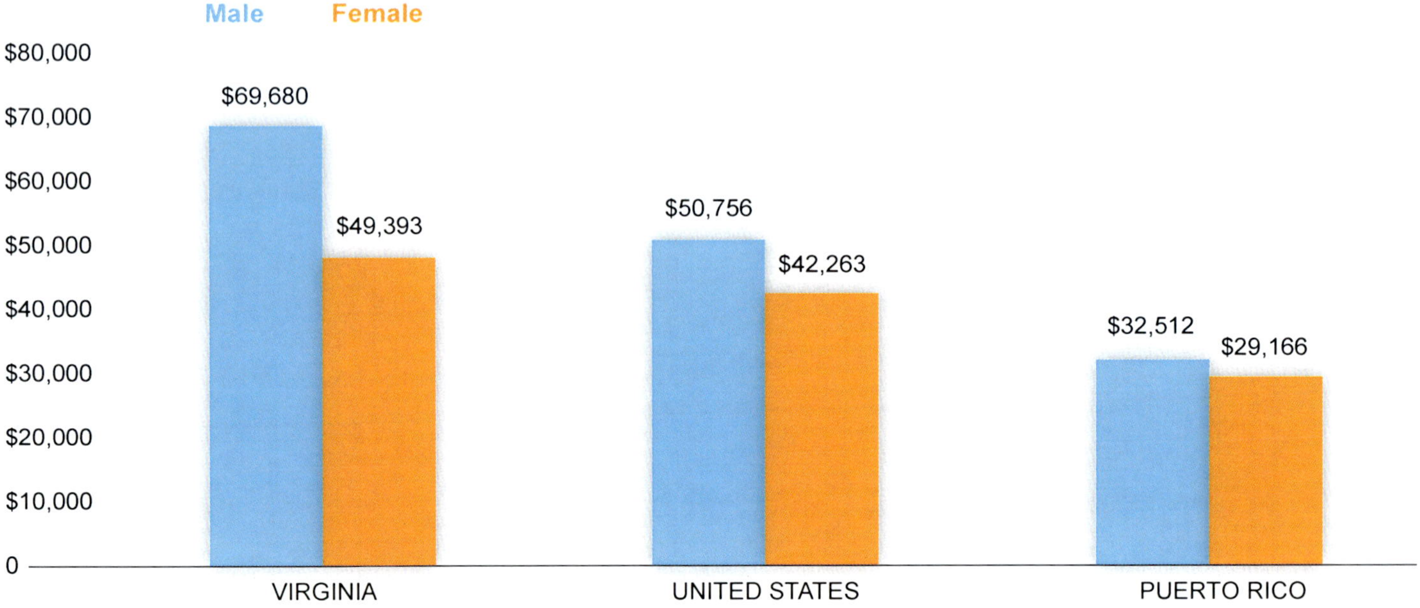

Graph 4.B: Puerto Rican Purchasing Power, in Billions, 2014

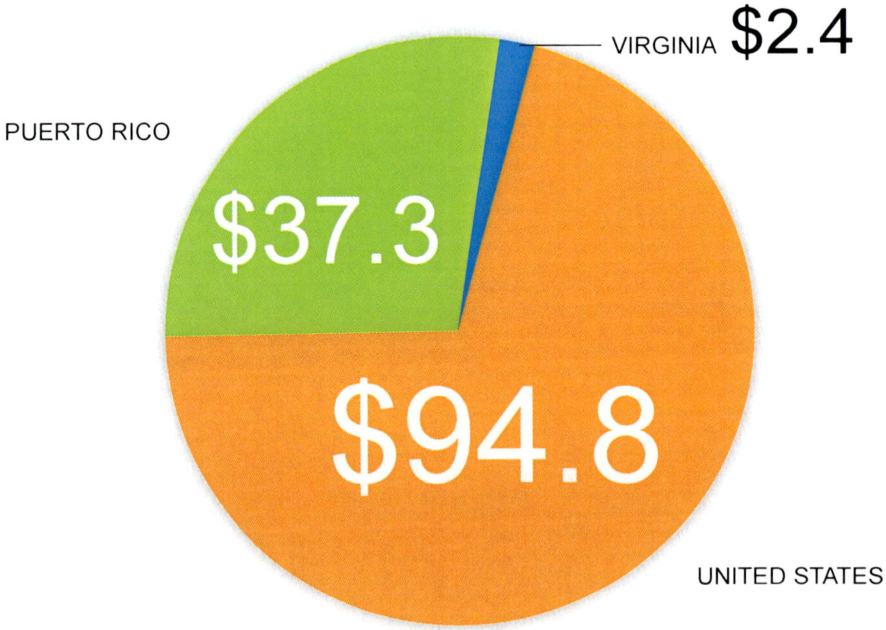

Puerto Rican Population by Counties in Virginia, 2014

Puerto Ricans accounted for about 1.1 percent of Virginia's total population and were most concentrated in Washington-Arlington-Alexandria, DC-VA-MD-WV (43%) and Virginia Beach-Norfolk-Newport News, VA-NC (35%) metropolitan areas. One in seven (14.6%) Puerto Ricans in Virginia lived in Fairfax County compared to about one in four Latinos (26%). Other counties within the Washington-Arlington-Alexandria, DC-VA-MD-WV metropolitan area included Prince William (8.9%), Loudoun (4.4%), Stafford (3.2%), Arlington (2.8%), Spotsylvania (2.5%), Alexandria City (1.8%), and the remaining 19.4 of Puerto Ricans resided in the neighboring counties within the metro area. Virginia Beach-Norfolk-Newport News, VA-NC metropolitan area, located in the southeastern region, was the second largest area of Puerto Rican concentration in Virginia. Counties within this metro area included Virginia Beach City (12%), Norfolk City (5.3%), Newport News City (4.8%), Hampton City (3.6%), Chesapeake City (3.3%), York (1.2%), James City (1.2%) and the remaining 3.6 percent of the Puerto Rican population were dispersed in other counties within the metro area. The proportion of the Puerto Rican population (35%) residing in the Virginia Beach metro area was greater than the proportion of Latinos overall (15%) and the state's overall population (22%). Lastly, the Richmond metropolitan area, also known as the 'Greater Richmond Region', located northwest of Virginia Beach, contained the third largest Puerto Rican settlement (13%). Chesterfield County accounted 4.2 percent of the Puerto Rican population within the Richmond metro area followed by 1.3 percent in Richmond City, 2.7 percent in Henrico County, and the remaining 4.8 percent resided in other counties in the metro area. Puerto Rican presence (13%) was overrepresented in counties within the Richmond metro area compared to the Latino population (10%). In all, Puerto Ricans in Virginia showed two types of settlement patterns: first, large concentrations surrounding U.S. military bases (located in the top 3 metropolitan areas) and, secondly, pockets of Puerto Rican communities in the state's western region such as Spotsylvania, Harrisonburg, Waynesboro, and Roanoke counties.

COUNTY	Puerto Rican Population	Percent	Latino Population	Percent	Total Population	Percent
Fairfax County	11,843	14%	33,555	4%	324,002	3%
Virginia Beach city	10,222	12%	32,158	4.7%	445,623	5.4%
Prince William County	7,582	8.9%	90,746	13.2%	428,772	5.2%
Norfolk city	4,507	5.3%	17,351	2.5%	244,745	3%
Newport News city	4,068	4.8%	14,546	2.1%	181,362	2.2%
Loudoun County	3,741	4.4%	44,028	6.4%	338,916	4.1%
Chesterfield County	3,548	4.2%	24,629	3.6%	324,337	4%
Hampton city	3,080	3.6%	6,848	1%	136,904	1.7%
Chesapeake city	2,813	3.3%	11,089	1.6%	228,168	2.8%
Stafford County	2,719	3.2%	13,644	2%	134,672	1.6%
Arlington County	2,359	2.8%	34,014	4.9%	220,173	2.7%
Henrico County	2,302	2.7%	16,303	2.4%	314,878	3.8%
Spotsylvania County	2,088	2.5%	10,236	1.5%	126,200	1.5%
Alexandria city	1,492	1.8%	24,112	3.5%	146,422	1.8%
Harrisonburg city	1,261	1.5%	8,790	1.3%	50,821	0.6%
Richmond city	1,126	1.3%	13,508	2%	211,063	2.6%
York County	1,047	1.2%	3,367	0.5%	65,808	0.8%
James City County	1,043	1.2%	3,562	0.5%	69,832	0.9%
Hopewell city	814	1%	1,508	0.2%	22,375	0.3%
Other Counties	16,676	19.7%	137,904	20.1%	3,376,988	41.4%
Total	**84,905**	**100%**	**687,265**	**100%**	**8,185,131**	**100%**

Sources: U.S. Census Bureau 2014 American Community Survey 5-Year Estimates Notes: Total counts for populations may differ depending on whether the estimates are derived from the five-year estimates or the one-year estimates of the American Community Survey.

PUERTO RICAN POPULATION BY COUNTIES IN VIRGINIA, 2014

PUERTO RICAN POPULATION

1 dot = 50

'06-'14 PUERTO RICAN ARRIVALS

1 dot = 50

BOUNDARIES

County

City/Towns

Census Tracts

CONGRESSIONAL DISTRICT

Republican

Democrat

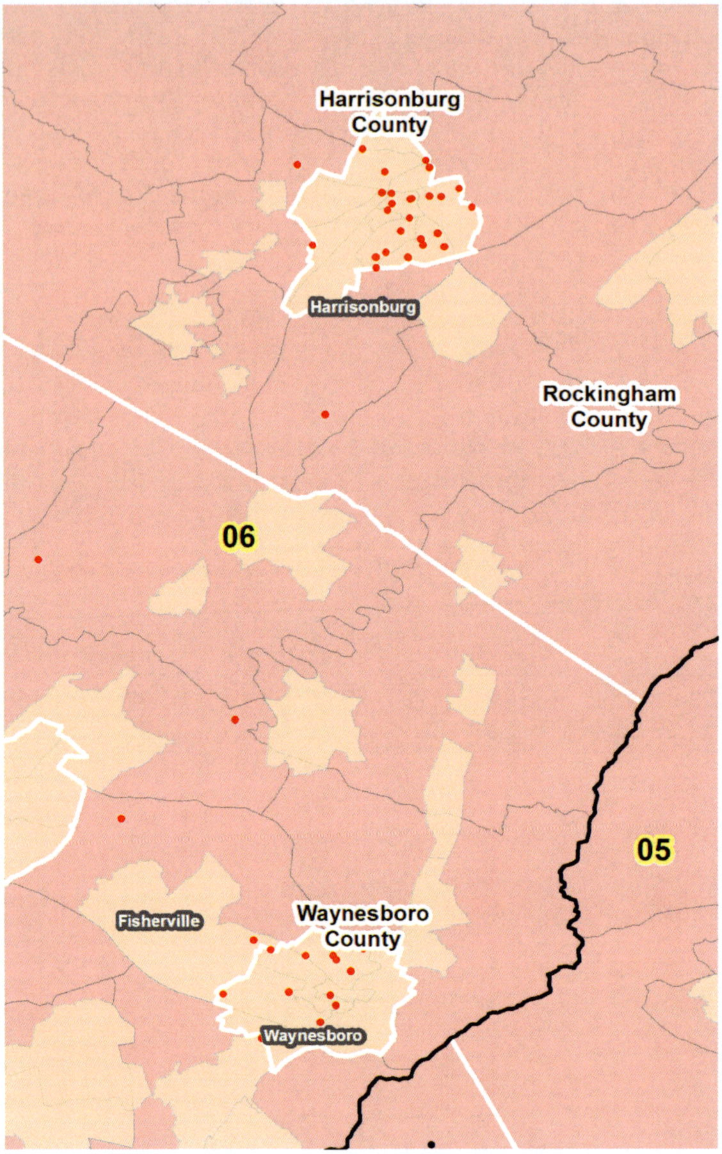

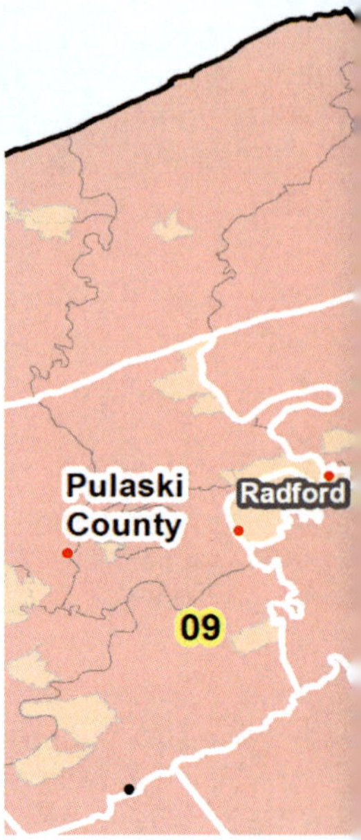

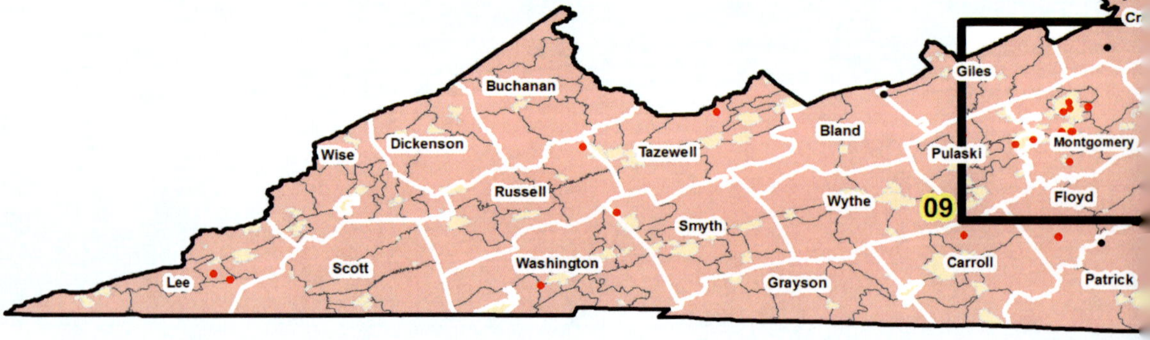

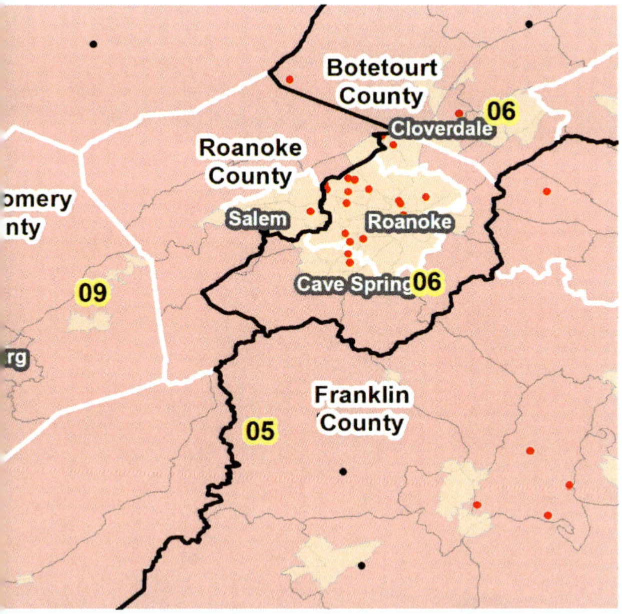
Botetourt County
06
Cloverdale
Roanoke County
omery
nty
Salem
Roanoke
Cave Spring
06
09
rg
Franklin County
05

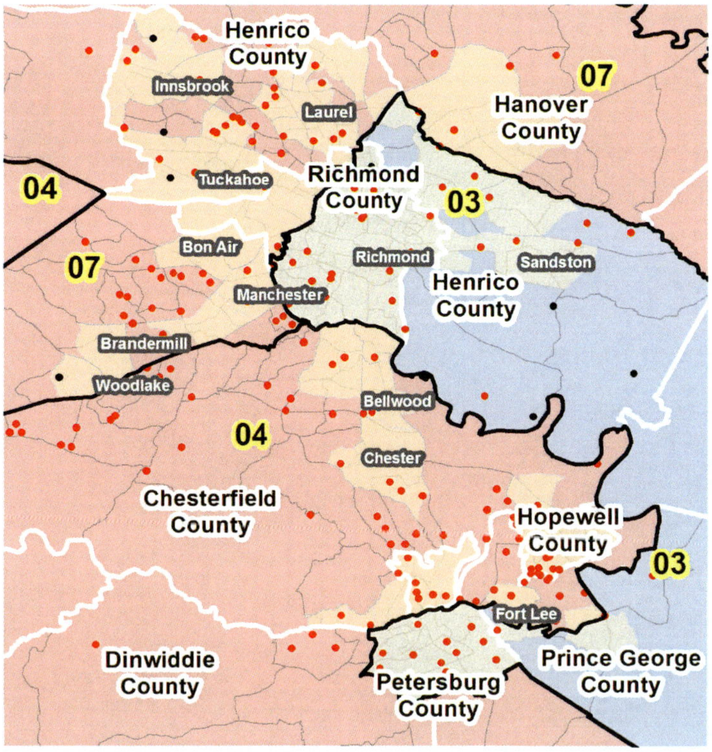
Henrico County
Innsbrook
Laurel
07
Hanover County
04
Tuckahoe
Richmond County
03
Bon Air
Richmond
Sandston
07
Henrico County
Manchester
Brandermill
Woodlake
Bellwood
04
Chester
Chesterfield County
Hopewell County
03
Fort Lee
Dinwiddie County
Petersburg County
Prince George County

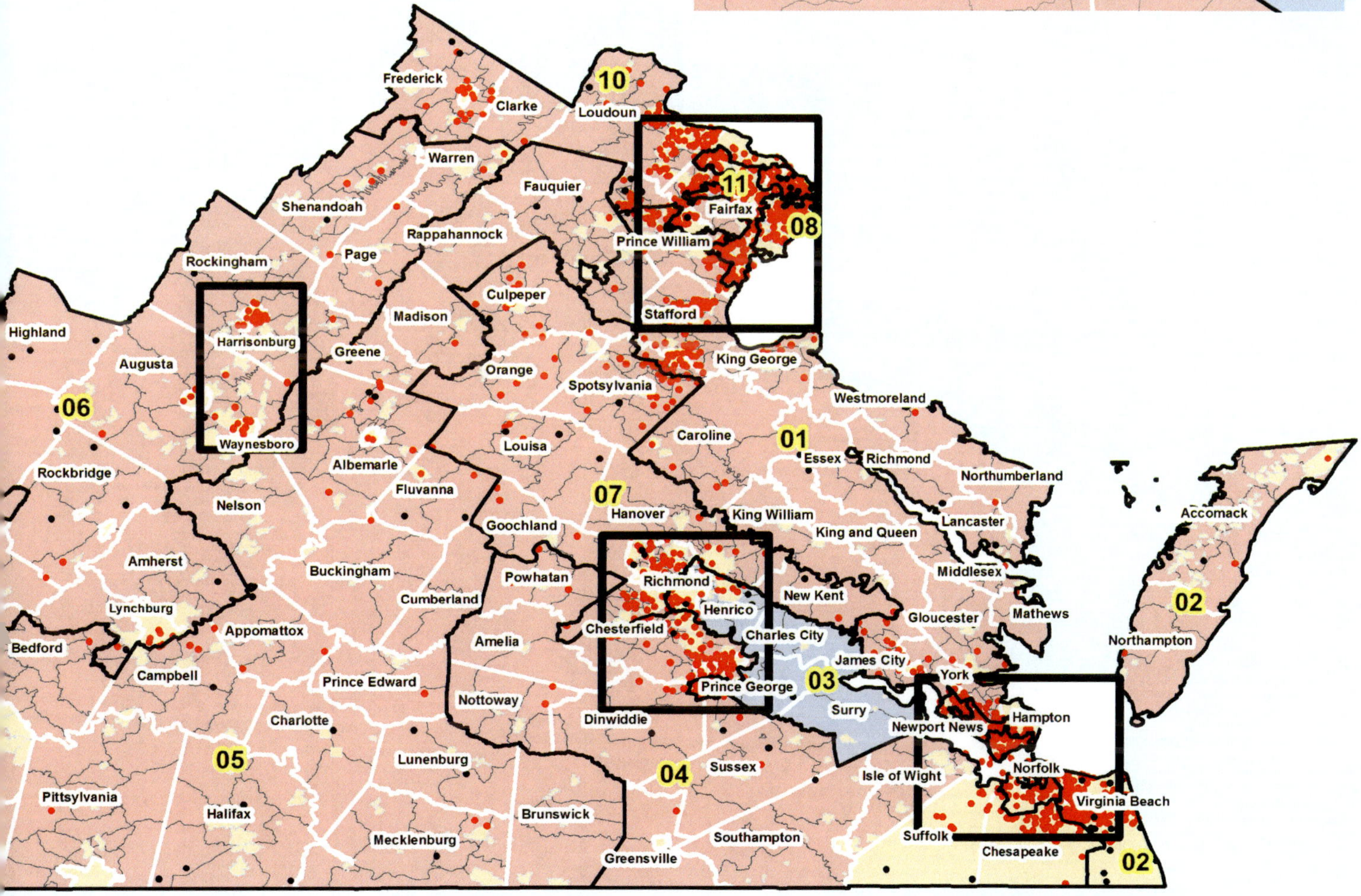
Frederick
10
Clarke
Loudoun
Warren
11
Fauquier
Shenandoah
Fairfax
08
Rappahannock
Prince William
Rockingham
Page
Culpeper
Madison
Stafford
Highland
Harrisonburg
Greene
Augusta
Orange
King George
Spotsylvania
06
Westmoreland
Waynesboro
Caroline
01
Louisa
Essex
Richmond
Rockbridge
Albemarle
Northumberland
Fluvanna
07
Nelson
Hanover
King William
Goochland
King and Queen
Lancaster
Accomack
Amherst
Powhatan
Middlesex
Buckingham
Richmond
Cumberland
New Kent
Henrico
Mathews
02
Lynchburg
Gloucester
Appomattox
Chesterfield
Amelia
Charles City
Northampton
Bedford
James City
Campbell
Prince George
03
York
Prince Edward
Nottoway
Surry
Hampton
Charlotte
Dinwiddie
Newport News
05
Lunenburg
Norfolk
04
Sussex
Isle of Wight
Pittsylvania
Virginia Beach
Halifax
Brunswick
Mecklenburg
Southampton
Suffolk
Chesapeake
Greensville
02

PUERTO RICAN POPULATION BY COUNTIES IN VIRGINIA, 2014

PUERTO RICAN POPULATION

1 dot = 50

'06-'14 PUERTO RICAN ARRIVALS

1 dot = 50

BOUNDARIES

County

City/Towns

Census Tracts

CONGRESSIONAL DISTRICT

Republican

Democrat

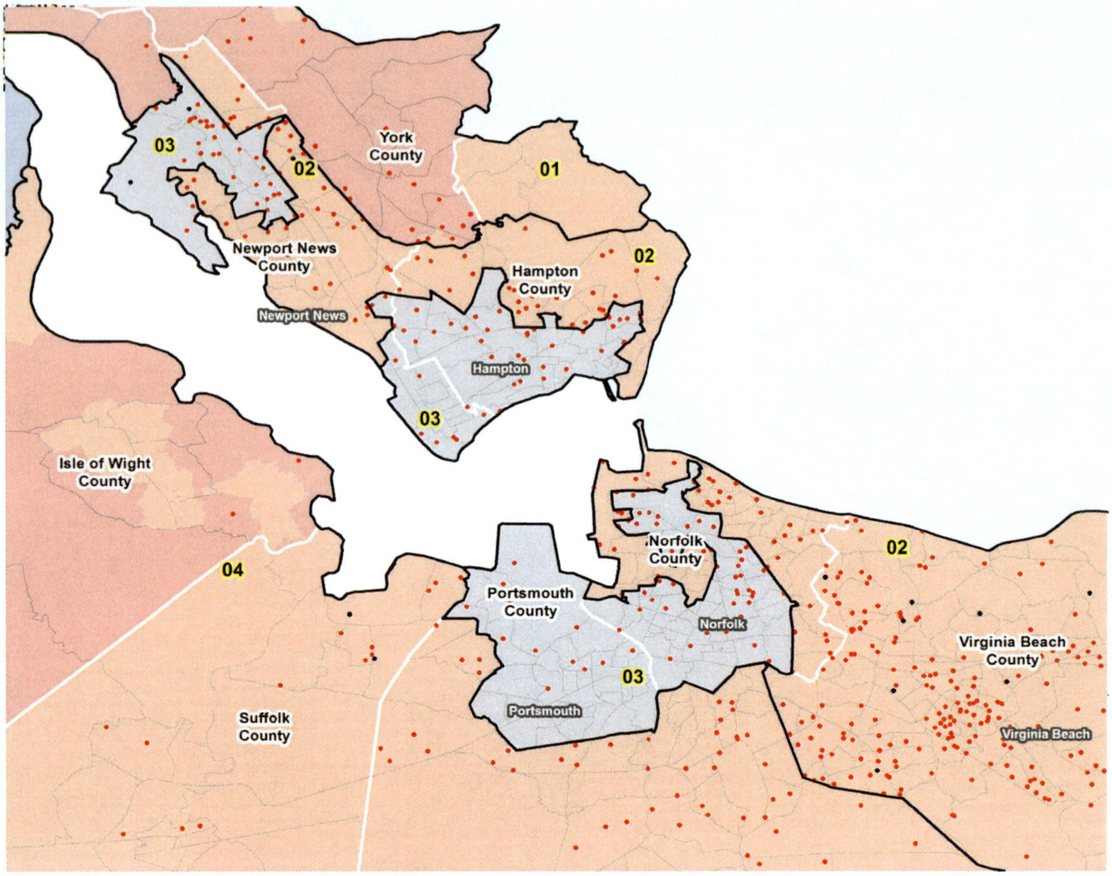

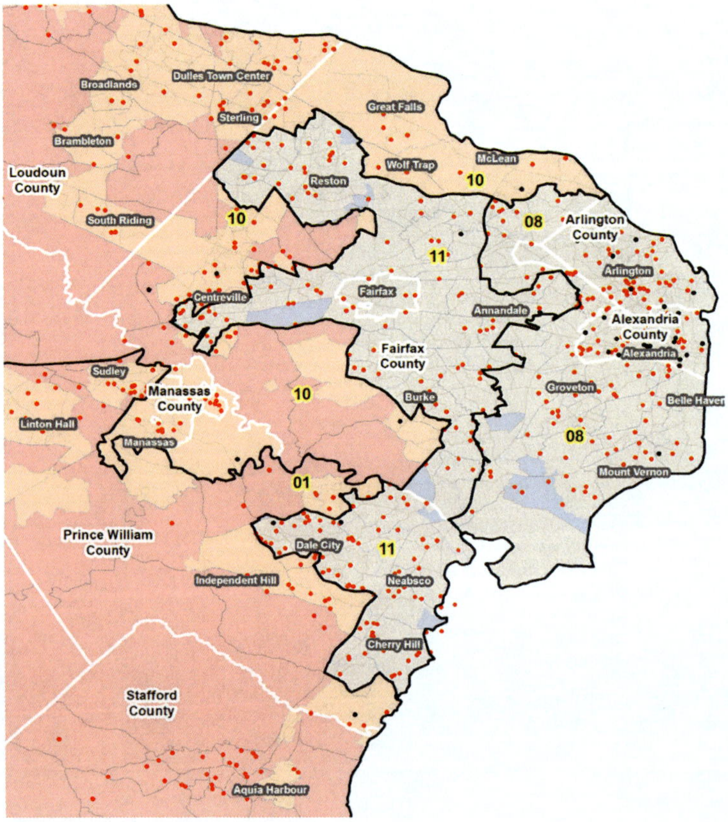

Graph 5.A: Poverty Rates, 2014

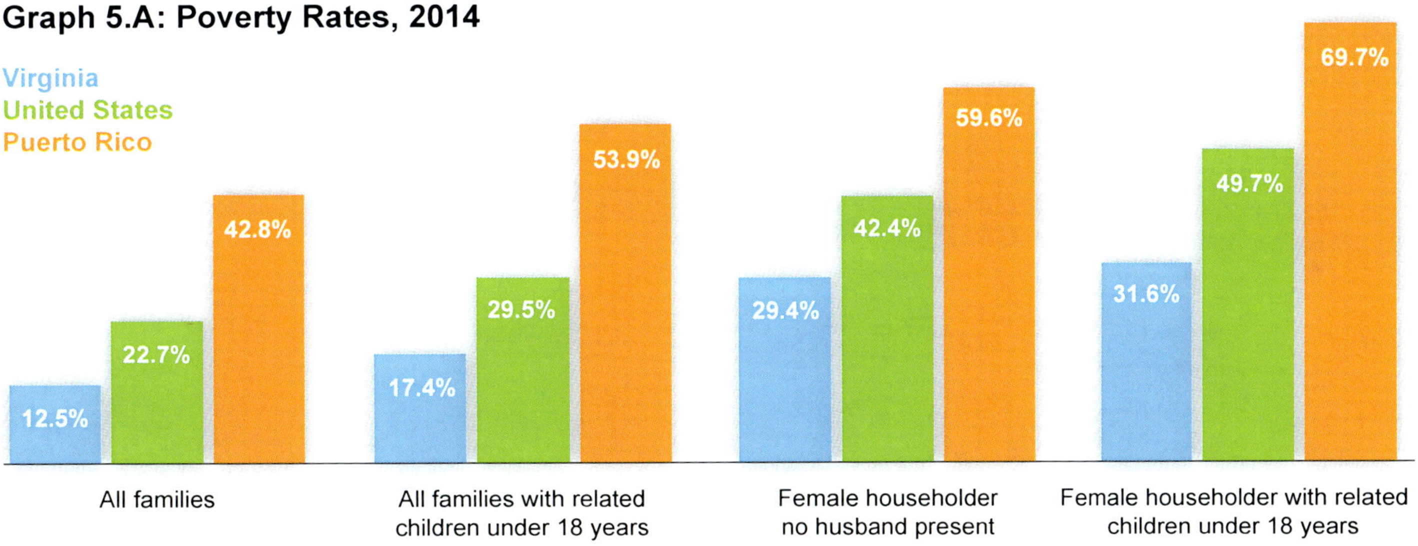

Table 5. Poverty, 2014

Puerto Ricans	Virginia	United States	Puerto Rico*
POVERTY RATES			
All families	12.5%	22.7%	42.8%
With related children under 18 years	17.4%	29.5%	53.9%
With related children under 5 years only	N	24.6%	57.1%
Married-couple family	6.7%	9.7%	30.9%
With related children under 18 years	11.2%	11.3%	35.5%
With related children under 5 years only	N	5.9%	33.9%
Female householder, no husband present, family	29.4%	42.4%	59.6%
With related children under 18 years	31.6%	49.7%	69.7%
With related children under 5 years only	51.2%	49.4%	75.7%
All people	15.4%	26.2%	46.6%
Under 18 years	19%	33.4%	58.7%
Related children under 18 years	18%	33.1%	58.6%
Related children under 5 years	17.6%	34.7%	62.8%
Related children 5 to 17 years	18.2%	32.4%	57.3%
18 years and over	13.5%	22.8%	43.2%
18 to 64 years	13.9%	22.8%	43.8%
65 years and over	8.8%	22.4%	41%
People in families	13%	23.6%	44.6%
Unrelated individuals 15 years and over	31.3%	38.5%	58.6%

Source: U.S. Census Bureau, 2014 American Community Survey 1-Year Estimates.
* Puerto Ricans only. N = No Observations.

were higher ($26,532) than among all stateside Puerto Ricans ($18,457) and those in Puerto Rico ($10,960).

Puerto Ricans in Virginia had $2.4 billion purchasing power, representing 3.3 percent of Puerto Rican purchasing power in the U.S. From an economic perspective, stateside Puerto Ricans represented 72.3 percent of the $134.5 billion total purchasing power of the entire Puerto Rican community in the year 2014. Purchasing power is defined simply as per capita income multiplied by the Puerto Rican population. Stateside Puerto Ricans had more than double the total purchasing power of Puerto Ricans in Puerto Rico of $37.3 billion.

The poverty rate for all Puerto Rican families in Virginia was 12.5 percent, lower than among all Puerto Rican families in the U.S. (22.7%) and those in Puerto Rico (42.8%). As seen in other states and in Puerto Rico, Puerto Rican households with a female householder, no husband, and children under 18 years (31.6%) had a higher rate of poverty compared to married-couple family households with children under 18 years (11.2%) and all families with children under 18 years (17.4%). In Virginia, 31.6 percent of Puerto Rican households with a female householder, no husband, and with children under 18 years reported living in poverty, compared to 49.7 percent across the U.S. and 69.7 in Puerto Rico. Regardless of context, these poverty rates are alarmingly high.

Although there were generally fewer Puerto Rican families in poverty in Virginia relative to Puerto Rican families in the United States and in Puerto Rico, the patterns of poverty in specific types of households mirrored that of other states.

Public assistance income participation rates for Puerto Rican families in Virginia (3.8%) were less than half the national level (6.9%) and in Puerto Rico (8.1%). Although food stamp/SNAP (Supplementary Nutrition Assistance Program) participation among Puerto Rican families in Virginia was 13.6%, it was considerably lower than the national level (31.5%) and in Puerto Rico (39.7%).

Housing is a primary determinant of the cost of living. The median value of owner-occupied housing for Puerto Ricans in Virginia was $278,400, over $100,000 more than the median value of owner-occupied housing for all Puerto Ricans in the U.S. ($175,900) and Puerto Rico ($119,500). The median monthly owner cost associated with a mortgage was $1,905 for Puerto Ricans in Virginia, $1,545 for those in the U.S., and $873 for those in Puerto Rico. More than a third (34.1%) of Puerto Ricans in Virginia who own home pay more than 30 percent of their income in monthly owner costs. This rate is rate is lower than the national (37.2%) level and in Puerto Rico (47.4%). Virginia has considerably higher rates of home ownership (46.6%) among Puerto Rican households when compared to the national level (36%).

Table 6. Housing and Health Insurance, 2014

Puerto Ricans	Virginia	United States	Puerto Rico*
HOUSING			
Owner-occupied housing units	46.6%	36%	68.7%
Monthly owner costs as a percentage of household income in the past 12 months			
Less than 30 percent	65.9%	62.8%	52.6%
30 percent or more	34.1%	37.2%	47.4%
Owner-occupied housing units			
Median value (dollars)	$278,400	$175,900	$119,500
Median selected monthly owner costs with a mortgage (dollars)	$1,905	$1,545	$873
HEALTH INSURANCE COVERAGE			
Civilian noninstitutionalized population			
With private health insurance	72.6%	51.6%	38%
With public coverage	24.5%	43.5%	62.9%
No health insurance coverage	11.6%	11.5%	5.5%

Source: U.S. Census Bureau, 2014 American Community Survey 1-Year Estimates.
* Puerto Ricans only.

Puerto Ricans in Georgia, 2014

In 2014, an estimated 89,462 Puerto Ricans lived in Georgia and accounted for 1.7 percent of all Puerto Ricans living in the United States. Georgia had the 13th largest Puerto Rican population in the United States. The number of Puerto Ricans in Georgia more than doubled from 35,532 in the year 2000 to 89,462 in 2014.

Graph 1.A: Puerto Rican and Latino Population in Georgia, 2014

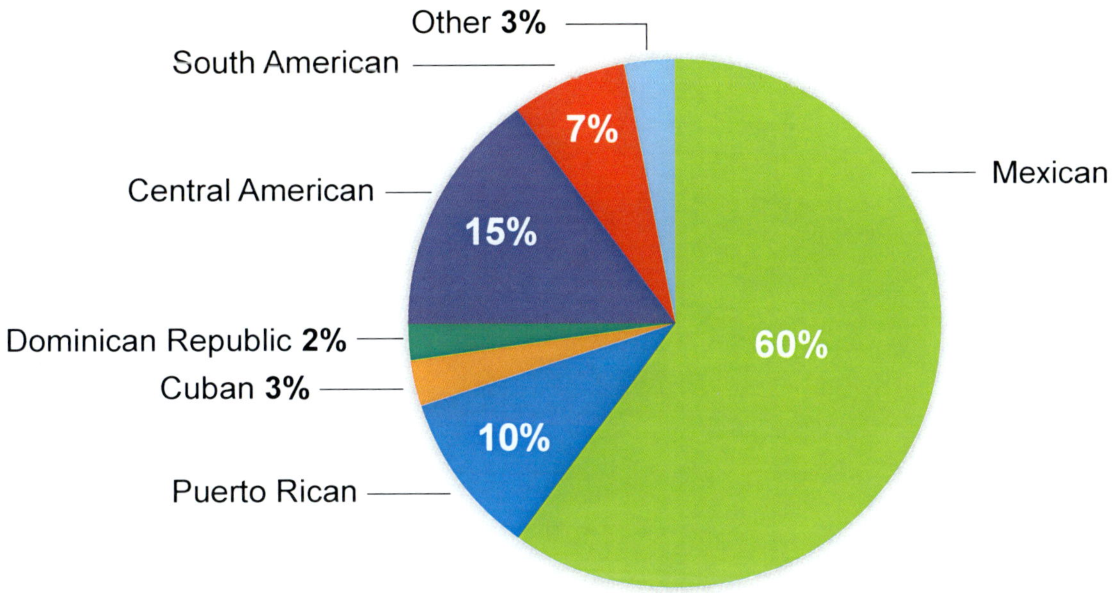

Table 1. Puerto Rican and Latino Population in Georgia

	2000		2010		2014	
Total	8,186,453	100%	9,687,653	100%	10,097,343	100%
Not Hispanic or Latino	7,751,226	94.7%	8,833,964	91.2%	9,175,228	90.9%
Hispanic or Latino	435,227	5.3%	853,689	8.8%	922,115	9.1%
Mexican	275,288	3.4%	519,502	5.4%	557,780	5.5%
Puerto Rican	35,532	0.4%	71,987	0.7%	89,462	0.9%
Cuban	12,536	0.2%	25,048	0.3%	28,543	0.3%
Dominican Republic	3,233	0%	14,941	0.2%	19,014	0.2%
Central American	31,813	0.4%	106,987	1.1%	134,276	1.3%
South American	19,496	0.2%	57,707	0.6%	68,288	0.7%
Other	57,329	0.7%	57,517	0.6%	24,752	0.2%

Sources: U.S. Census Bureau, Census 2000 Summary File 1, 2010 Census. Summary File 1, and 2014 American Community Survey 1-Year Estimates.

The median age of Puerto Ricans in Georgia was 27 years old, below the national median for Puerto Ricans of 28.9 years of age, and more than ten years lower than the median age among Puerto Ricans in Puerto Rico (38.9 years). The proportion of Puerto Ricans aged 62 years and older in Georgia was 6.4 percent, lower than for Puerto Ricans across the United States (9.9%) and less than a third of those in Puerto Rico (21%).

English fluency indicators for Puerto Ricans in Georgia were higher than for stateside Puerto Ricans overall. About half of Puerto Ricans in Georgia (51.9%) reported speaking

Graph 2.A: Puerto Rican Education Attainment, 25 years and over, 2014

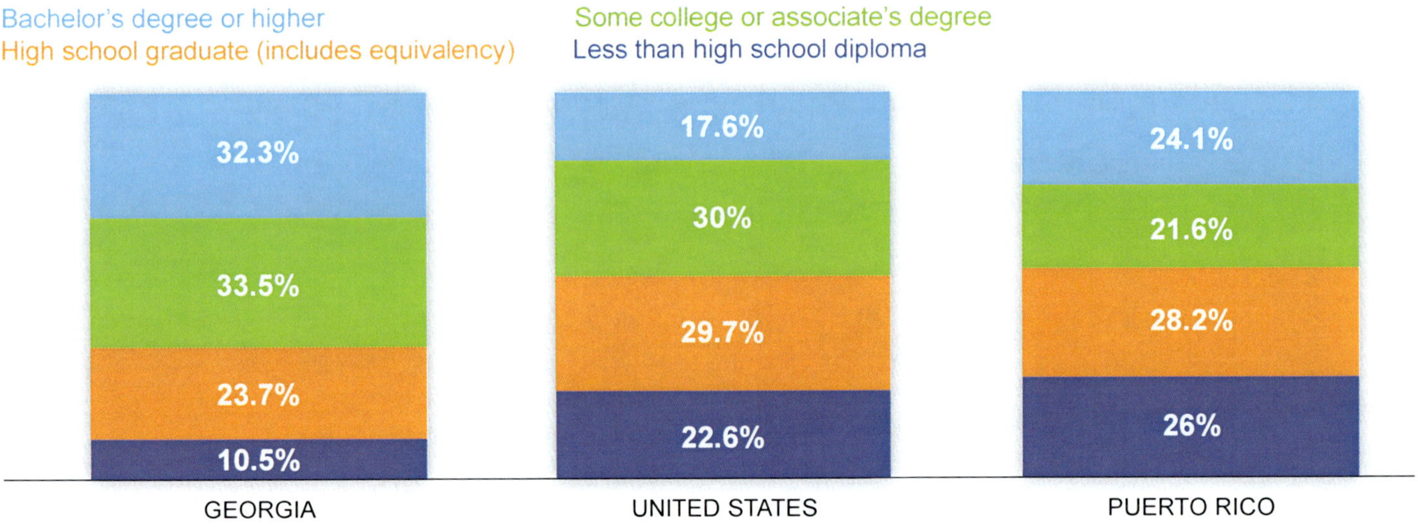

Table 2. Age, Education, and Language, 2014

Puerto Ricans	Georgia	United States	Puerto Rico*
TOTAL POPULATION	89,462	5,266,738	3,404,122
Median age (years)	27	28.9	38.9
62 years and over	6.4%	9.9%	21%
EDUCATIONAL ATTAINMENT			
Population 25 years and over			
Less than high school diploma	10.5%	22.6%	26%
High school graduate (includes equivalency)	23.7%	29.7%	28.2%
Some college or associate's degree	33.5%	30%	21.6%
Bachelor's degree or higher	32.3%	17.6%	24.1%
Male, bachelor's degree or higher	29.5%	15.6%	19.6%
Female, bachelor's degree or higher	35.2%	19.5%	28.1%
LANGUAGE SPOKEN AT HOME AND ABILITY TO SPEAK ENGLISH			
Population 5 years and over			
English only	51.9%	38.8%	5.3%
Language other than English	48.1%	61.2%	94.7%
Speak English less than "very well"	10.3%	17.3%	78.8%

Source: U.S. Census Bureau, 2014 American Community Survey 1-Year Estimates.
* Puerto Ricans only.

only English in the home, a rate more than ten percentage points higher than among all Puerto Ricans in the U.S. (38.8%). Only 10.3 percent of Puerto Ricans in Georgia reported speaking English less than "very well," less than half the rate among all Puerto Ricans in the U.S. (17.3%).

Puerto Ricans in Georgia were generally more educated than Puerto Ricans throughout the U.S. or in Puerto Rico. About a third (32.3%) of Puerto Ricans aged 25 or older had earned a bachelor's degree or higher, compared 17.6 percent of all stateside Puerto Ricans and 24.1 percent of those in Puerto Rico. A breakdown of the education demographics by sex indicates that a higher proportion of women (35.2%) had earned a bachelor's degree or higher, than men (29.5%) in Georgia. This pattern was also observed among stateside Puerto Ricans as a whole and those in Puerto Rico.

Puerto Rican participation in Georgia's civilian labor force (63.4%) was slightly higher than among the entire U.S. (61.6%), and both rates were almost 20 percentage points higher than the labor force participation in Puerto Rico (43.7%). The unemployment rate among Puerto Ricans in Georgia was 9.8 percent, lower than the stateside

Table 3. Employment and Occupations, 2014

Puerto Ricans	Georgia	United States	Puerto Rico*
EMPLOYMENT STATUS			
Population 16 years and over			
In labor force	67.2%	62.4%	43.7%
Civilian labor force	63.4%	61.6%	43.7%
Employed	57.2%	54.4%	35.4%
Unemployed	9.8%	11.6%	18.9%
Not in labor force	32.8%	37.6%	56.3%
Armed Forces	3.7%	0.8%	0%
OCCUPATION			
Civilian employed population 16 years and over	19,456	1,058,918	516,762
Male	31.9%	23.4%	23.9%
Management, business, science, and arts	16%	22.5%	23%
Service occupations	23.6%	19.6%	21.3%
Sales and office occupations	12.7%	13.8%	18%
Construction and maintenance	15.8%	20.7%	13.7%
Production, transportation, and moving	16,235	999,105	456,356
Female	35.6%	33.1%	39.7%
Management, business, science, and arts	17.7%	24.4%	16.6%
Service occupations	39.1%	35.7%	38.3%
Sales and office occupations	0.9%	0.6%	0.6%
Construction and maintenance	6.7%	6.2%	4.8%
Production, transportation, and moving	9.5%	6.4%	5.4%
CLASS OF WORKER			
Civilian employed population 16 years and over			
Private wage and salary workers	79.8%	82%	69%
Government workers	17.3%	14.8%	22.5%
Self-employed workers in own not incorporated business	2.9%	3.1%	8.3%
VETERAN STATUS			
Civilian population 18 years and over			
Civilian veteran	11.6%	6%	3.3%

Source: U.S. Census Bureau, 2014 American Community Survey 1-Year Estimates.
* Puerto Ricans only.

Puerto Rican unemployment rate (11.6%) and less than a third than in Puerto Rico (18.9%).

Proportionately, more Puerto Ricans in Georgia worked in the higher wage management, business, science, and arts sector than among all Puerto Ricans in the U.S. and those in Puerto Rico. A third (33.6%) of Puerto Ricans in Georgia worked in the higher wage management, business, science, and arts sector compared to 28.1 percent of Puerto Ricans in the U.S. and 31.3 percent in Puerto Rico. Proportionately, Puerto Rican women were more present than men in in the management, business, science, and arts sector. In Georgia, 35.6 percent of Puerto Rican women worked in this sector, compared to 31.9 percent of Puerto Rican men. In the United States these proportions were 33.1 percent and 23.4 percent respectively, and in Puerto Rico were 39.7 percent and 23.9 percent respectively. The second most common occupational sector was the sales and office occupations sector accounting for 30.7 percent of Puerto Rican employment in Georgia.

Puerto Ricans actively serving in the Armed Forces accounted for 3.7 percent of Puerto Ricans in Georgia. Similarly, over one in ten (11.6%) Puerto Ricans in Georgia was a veteran, almost double the national rate (6%) and more than three times the rate in Puerto Rico (3.3%). Puerto

Table 4. Income and Earnings, 2014

Puerto Ricans	Georgia	United States	Puerto Rico*
INCOME IN THE PAST 12 MONTHS (IN 2013 INFLATION-ADJUSTED DOLLARS)			
Households	27,272	1,635,808	1,175,297
Median household income (dollars)	$52,661	$39,322	$18,710
With earnings	90.2%	76.9%	54.7%
Mean earnings (dollars)	$63,939	$61,065	$36,407
With Social Security income	16.7%	24.1%	43.2%
Mean Social Security income (dollars)	$15,926	$13,727	$12,159
With Supplemental Security Income	4.6%	12.6%	0.4%
Mean Supplemental Security Income (dollars)	$9,666	$8,780	$10,025
With cash public assistance income	2.7%	6.9%	8.1%
Mean cash public assistance income (dollars)	$2,798	$3,441	$2,316
With retirement income	10.8%	10.1%	15.6%
Mean retirement income (dollars)	$21,806	$20,452	$15,387
With Food Stamp/SNAP benefits	17.3%	31.5%	39.7%
Families	18,792	1,114,628	830,807
Median family income (dollars)	$61,150	$44,499	$22,220
Married-couple family	72.2%	53.9%	56.1%
Median income (dollars)	$75,072	$67,129	$29,417
Male householder, no spouse present	12.1%	10.2%	9.5%
Median income (dollars)	$37,169	$37,513	$17,797
Female householder, no husband present	15.7%	35.9%	34.4%
Median income (dollars)	$28,834	$23,957	$13,554
Individuals	89,462	5,266,738	3,404,122
Per capita income (dollars)	$20,552	$18,457	$10,960
Mean earnings (dollars) for full-time, year-round workers:			
Male	$56,304	$50,756	$32,512
Female	$40,374	$42,263	$29,166

Source: U.S. Census Bureau, 2014 American Community Survey 1-Year Estimates.
* Puerto Ricans only.

Puerto Rican Population by Counties in Georgia, 2014

Most Puerto Ricans in Georgia (45.8%) were settled in the northwestern region of the state, particularly in the Atlanta-Sandy Springs-Roswell metropolitan area. The remaining 54.2 percent of the Puerto Rican population are dispersed throughout the state, yet there are small areas of concentration in the northeast (Whitfield County), parts of the east (Richmond, Liberty, Chatham Counties), and southwest (Muscogee County) regions of the state. The largest area of Puerto Rican settlement was found in the nine counties of Atlanta-Sandy Springs-Roswell metropolitan area: Gwinnett (15.6%), Cobb (8.5%), Fulton (7.3%), DeKalb (4.8%), Henry (3%), Clayton (2.6%), Coweta (1.6%), Douglas (1.2%), and Fayette (1%). The second largest Puerto Rican concentration outside of Atlanta metropolitan area was in Richmond County (Augusta City) and in Columbia County, and both areas accounted for 7.4 percent of the state's Puerto Rican population. Muscogee County (Columbus City) located in the southwest region and Chatham County (Savannah city) located in the southeast region of the state both accounted 7.8 percent of the Puerto Rican population. At least 30 miles west of Chatham County is another Puerto Rican community located in Liberty County and contains 3.4 percent of the population. Latinos as a whole show a similarly settlement pattern in Georgia as Puerto Ricans, with nearly one-fifth (19.1%) of Latinos settled in Gwinnet County and the remainder distributed in lower concentration throughout the state. Puerto Rican presence was overrepresented in counties outside of the Atlanta-Sandy Springs-Roswell metropolitan area compared to the Latino population in Georgia. In all, Puerto Rican communities tend to reflect the location of U.S. military bases located throughout the state.

COUNTY	Puerto Rican Population	Percent	Latino Population	Percent	Total Population	Percent
Gwinnett County	13,263	15.6%	171,142	19.1%	842,091	8.5%
Cobb County	7,240	8.5%	88,665	9.9%	708,920	7.2%
Fulton County	6,197	7.3%	74,583	8.3%	967,100	9.8%
DeKalb County	4,047	4.8%	65,649	7.3%	707,185	7.1%
Richmond County	3,608	4.3%	8,889	1%	201,244	2%
Muscogee County	3,340	3.9%	14,018	1.6%	198,247	2%
Chatham County	3,267	3.9%	15,990	1.8%	275,303	2.8%
Liberty County	2,896	3.4%	7,176	0.8%	64,489	0.7%
Columbia County	2,657	3.1%	7,508	0.8%	132,362	1.3%
Henry County	2,582	3%	12,788	1.4%	209,069	2.1%
Cherokee County	2,258	2.7%	21,900	2.4%	221,951	2.2%
Clayton County	2,226	2.6%	35,231	3.9%	264,221	2.7%
Paulding County	1,726	2%	7,807	0.9%	145,565	1.5%
Houston County	1,690	2%	9,262	1%	145,622	1.5%
Whitfield County	1,563	1.8%	33,644	3.8%	103,132	1%
Forsyth County	1,426	1.7%	18,184	2%	189,314	1.9%
Coweta County	1,344	1.6%	8,833	1%	131,419	1.3%
Lowndes County	1,235	1.5%	5,863	0.7%	112,515	1.1%
Camden County	1,168	1.4%	2,925	0.3%	51,193	0.5%
Douglas County	1,004	1.2%	11,740	1.3%	135,037	1.4%
Other Counties	20,021	23.6%	274,920	30.7%	4,101,777	41.4%
Total	**84,758**	**100%**	**896,717**	**100%**	**9,907,756**	**100%**

Sources: U.S. Census Bureau and 2014 American Community Survey 5-Year Estimates
Notes: Total counts for populations may differ depending on whether the estimates are derived from the five-year estimates or the one-year estimates of the American Community Survey. Counties with less than 1% of the total Puerto Rican population were omitted.

PUERTO RICAN POPULATION BY COUNTIES IN GEORGIA, 2014

PUERTO RICAN POPULATION

1 dot = 50

'06-'14 PUERTO RICAN ARRIVALS

1 dot = 50

BOUNDARIES

County

City/Towns

Census Tracts

CONGRESSIONAL DISTRICT

Republican

Democrat

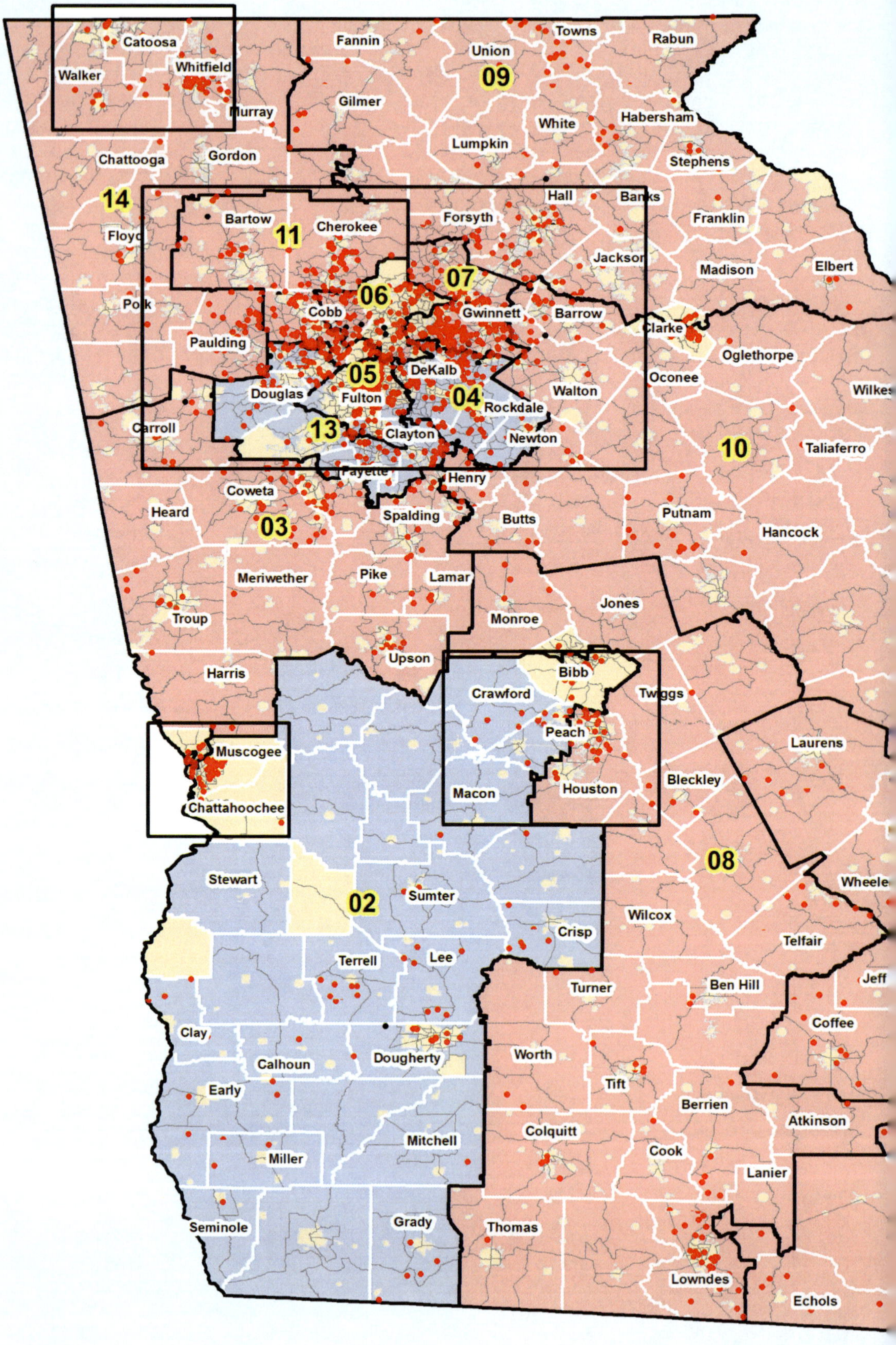

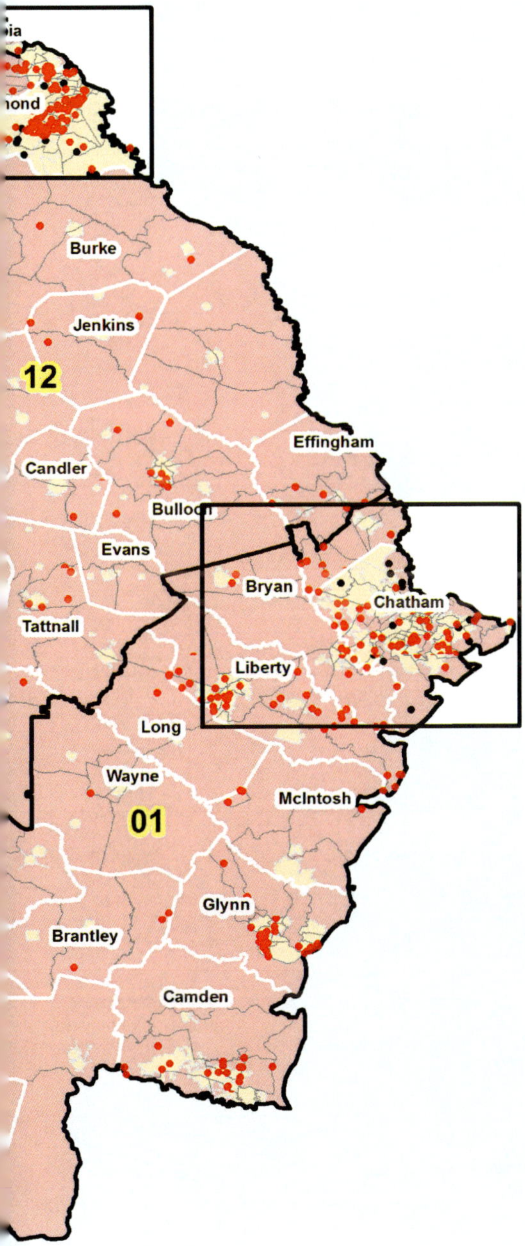

Burke
Jenkins
12
Candler
Effingham
Bulloch
Evans
Bryan
Chatham
Tattnall
Liberty
Long
Wayne
McIntosh
01
Glynn
Brantley
Camden

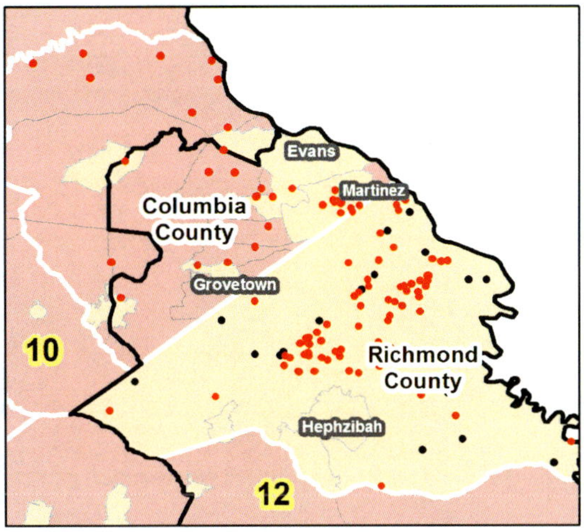

Evans
Martinez
Columbia County
Grovetown
10
Richmond County
Hephzibah
12

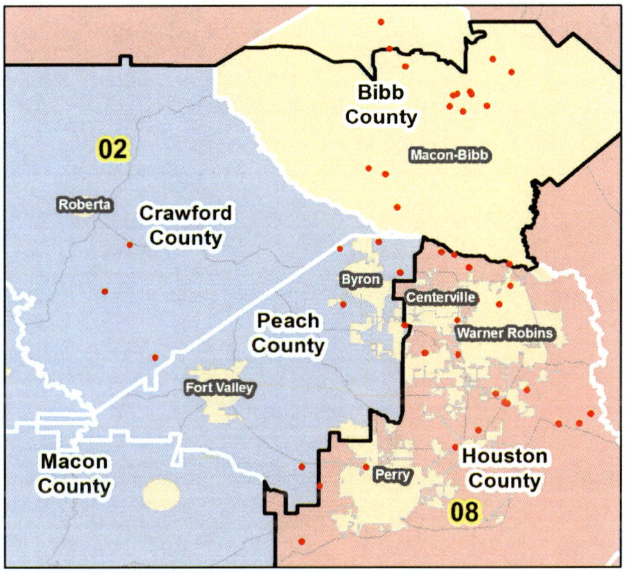

Bibb County
Macon-Bibb
02
Roberta
Crawford County
Byron
Centerville
Warner Robins
Peach County
Fort Valley
Macon County
Perry
Houston County
08

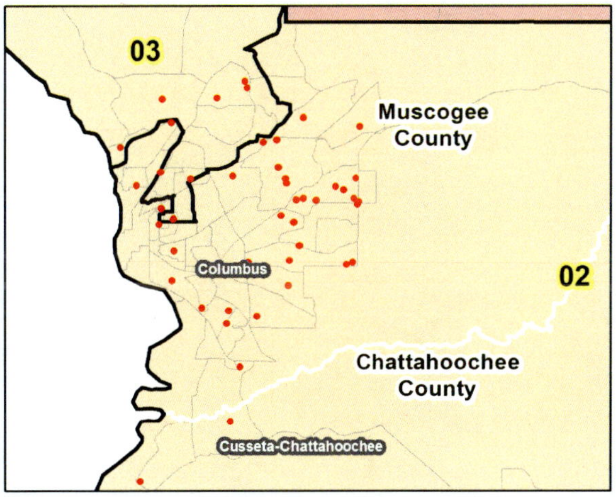

03
Muscogee County
Columbus
02
Chattahoochee County
Cusseta-Chattahoochee

PUERTO RICAN POPULATION BY COUNTIES IN GEORGIA, 2014

PUERTO RICAN POPULATION

1 dot = 50

'06-'14 PUERTO RICAN ARRIVALS

1 dot = 50

BOUNDARIES

County

City/Towns

Census Tracts

CONGRESSIONAL DISTRICT

Republican

Democrat

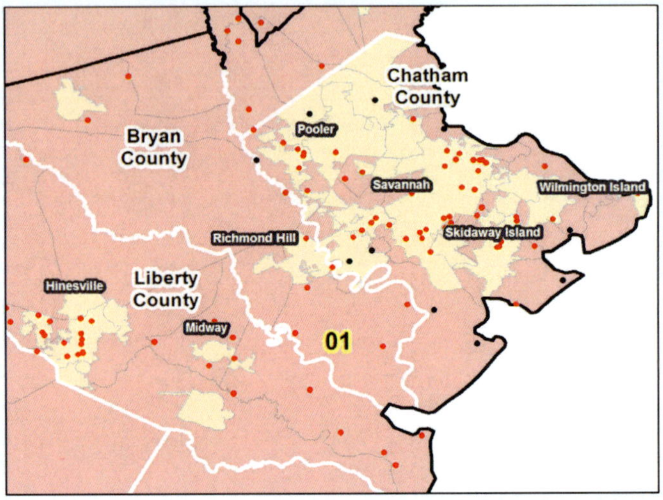

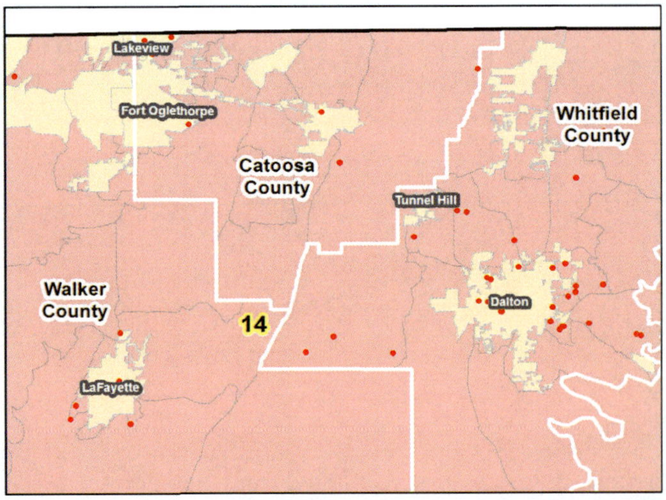

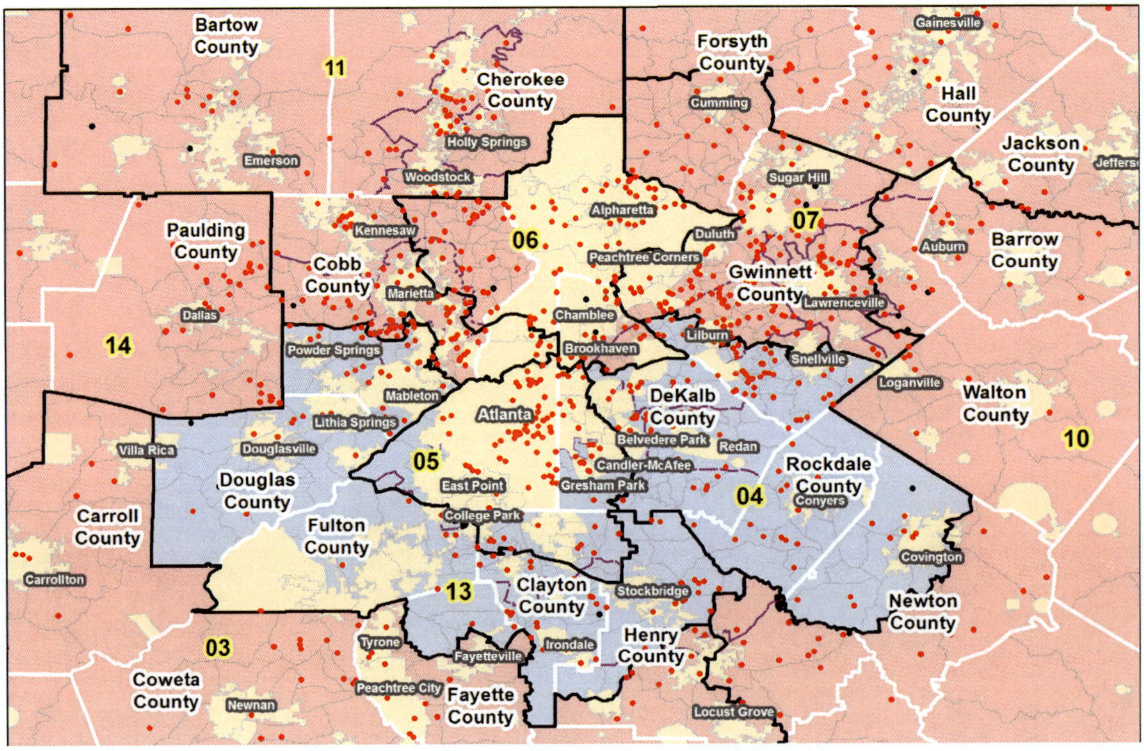

Ricans in Georgia also work in the government sector at a higher rate (17.3%) than Puerto Ricans across the country as a whole, though lower than in Puerto Rico (22.5%)

The average earnings of full-time, year-round Puerto Rican men and women in Georgia, $56,304 and $40,374, demonstrated a higher disparity (nearly $16,000) than at the national level of $50,756 and $42,623 (about $8,000) for Puerto Rican men and women, respectively. Although Puerto Rican men in Georgia earned almost six thousand dollars more than at the national level, Puerto Rican women in Georgia earned about two thousand dollars less than at the national level. Compared to Puerto Rico where average full-time, year round Puerto Rican earnings were $32,512 and $29,166 for men and women respectively, Puerto Ricans in Georgia and the U.S. as a whole earn more on average.

Household and family incomes are important indicators of economic well-being. These indicators were higher for Puerto Ricans in Georgia than for stateside Puerto Ricans and those in Puerto Rico. The median income was $52,661 for Puerto Rican households in Georgia, more than ten thousand dollars higher than among all stateside Puerto

Graph 4.A: Mean Earnings for Full-Time Year-Round Puerto Rican Workers, 2014

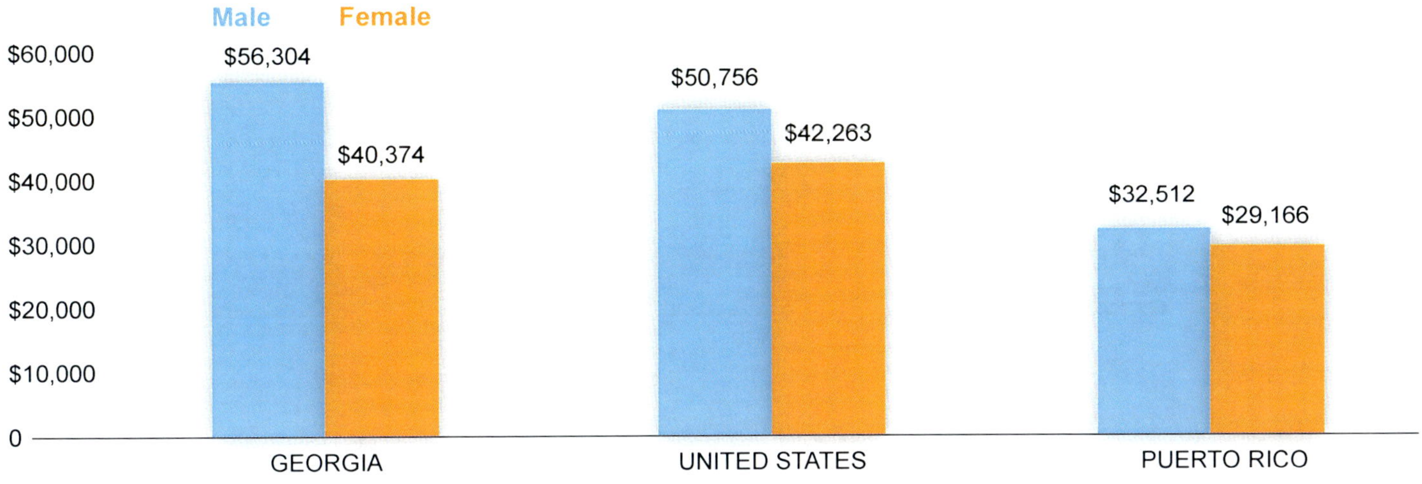

Graph 4.B: Puerto Rican Purchasing Power, in Billions, 2014

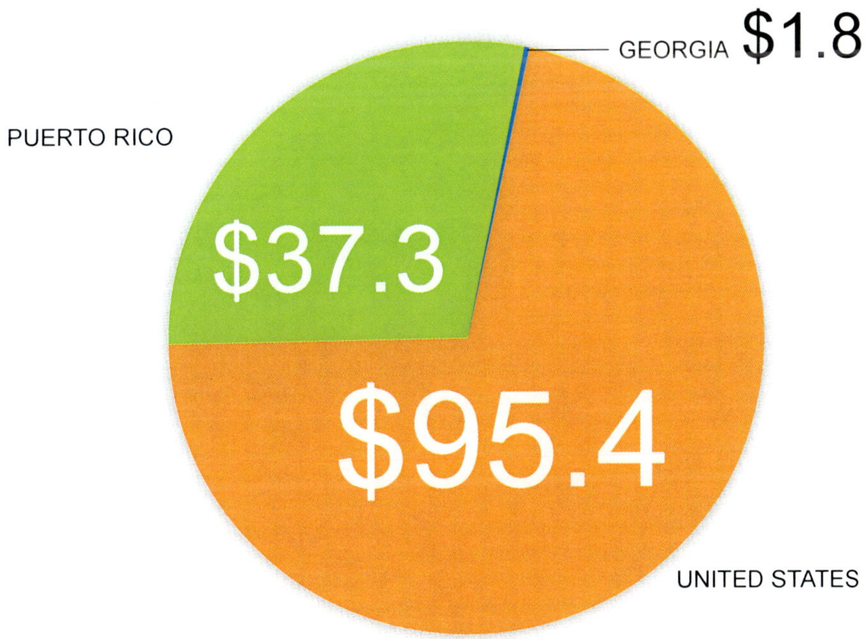

Graph 5.A: Poverty Rates, 2014

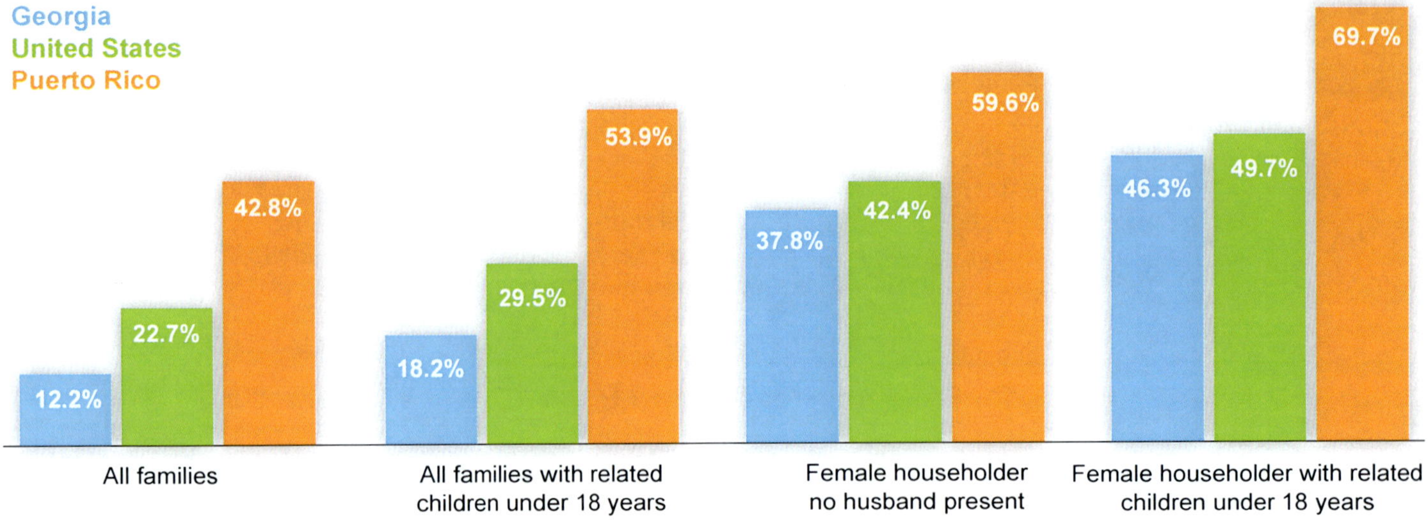

Table 5. Poverty, 2014

Puerto Ricans	Georgia	United States	Puerto Rico*
POVERTY RATES			
All families	12.2%	22.7%	42.8%
With related children under 18 years	18.2%	29.5%	53.9%
With related children under 5 years only	N	24.6%	57.1%
Married-couple family	5.5%	9.7%	30.9%
With related children under 18 years	N	11.3%	35.5%
With related children under 5 years only	N	5.9%	33.9%
Female householder, no husband present, family	37.8%	42.4%	59.6%
With related children under 18 years	46.3%	49.7%	69.7%
With related children under 5 years only	N	49.4%	75.7%
All people	18.3%	26.2%	46.6%
Under 18 years	23.6%	33.4%	58.7%
Related children under 18 years	23.6%	33.1%	58.6%
Related children under 5 years	27.3%	34.7%	62.8%
Related children 5 to 17 years	21.7%	32.4%	57.3%
18 years and over	15.4%	22.8%	43.2%
18 to 64 years	16.6%	22.8%	43.8%
65 years and over	3%	22.4%	41%
People in families	15.6%	23.6%	44.6%
Unrelated individuals 15 years and over	32.3%	38.5%	58.6%

Source: U.S. Census Bureau, 2014 American Community Survey 1-Year Estimates.
* Puerto Ricans only. N = No Observations.

Ricans ($39,322) and more than double the median income of Puerto Rican households in Puerto Rico ($18,710). Per capita incomes among Puerto Ricans in Georgia were higher ($20,552) than among all stateside Puerto Ricans ($18,457) and those in Puerto Rico ($10,960).

Puerto Ricans in Georgia had $1.8 billion purchasing power. From an economic perspective, stateside Puerto Ricans represented 72.3 percent of the $134.5 billion total purchasing power of the entire Puerto Rican community in the year 2014. Purchasing power is defined simply as per capita income multiplied by the Puerto Rican population. Stateside Puerto Ricans had more than double the total purchasing power of Puerto Ricans in Puerto Rico of $37.3 billion.

The poverty rate for all Puerto Rican families in Georgia (12%) was ten-percent points lower than among all Puerto Rican families in the U.S. (22.7%) and those in Puerto Rico (42.8%). As seen in other states and in Puerto Rico, Puerto Rican households with a female householder, no husband, and children under 18 had the highest rates of poverty. In Georgia, 46.3 percent of these households reported living in poverty, compared to 49.7 percent across the U.S. and 69.7 percent in Puerto Rico. Regardless of context, these poverty rates are alarmingly high. Although Georgia had overall less Puerto Rican households in poverty, the proportional frequency of poverty in specific types of households mirrored that of other states.

Public assistance income participation rates for Puerto Rican families in Georgia (2.7%) were less than half the national level (6.9%) and in Puerto Rico (8.1%). Although food stamp/SNAP (Supplementary Nutrition Assistance Program) participation among Puerto Rican families in Georgia was 17.3%, it was considerably below the national level (31.5%) and in Puerto Rico (39.7%).

Housing is a primary determinant of the cost of living. The median value of owner-occupied housing for Puerto Ricans in Georgia was $155,000, lower than the median value of owner-occupied housing for all stateside Puerto Ricans ($175,900), but higher than in Puerto Rico ($119,500). This discrepancy in home values may be affected largely by the lower costs of living in Georgia. Puerto Ricans in the state are generally making more money and more likely to be employed in higher wage sectors than at the national level, and could presumably afford more expensive homes. The median monthly owner cost associated with a mortgage was $1,317 for Puerto Ricans in Georgia, $1,545 for those in the U.S., and $873 for those in Puerto Rico. Less than a quarter (23%) of Puerto Ricans in Georgia who own a home pay more than 30 percent of their income in monthly owner costs. This rate is higher at the national (37.2%) level and in Puerto Rico (47.4%). Georgia has considerably higher rates of home ownership (48.6%) among Puerto Rican households when compared to the national level (36%). However, these rates are lower than in Puerto Rico (68.7%).

Table 6. Housing and Health Insurance, 2014

Puerto Ricans	Georgia	United States	Puerto Rico*
HOUSING			
Owner-occupied housing units	48.6%	36%	68.7%
Monthly owner costs as a percentage of household income in the past 12 months			
Less than 30 percent	77%	62.8%	52.6%
30 percent or more	23%	37.2%	47.4%
Owner-occupied housing units			
Median value (dollars)	$155,000	$175,900	$119,500
Median selected monthly owner costs with a mortgage (dollars)	$1,317	$1,545	$873
HEALTH INSURANCE COVERAGE Civilian noninstitutionalized population			
With private health insurance	65.7%	51.6%	38%
With public coverage	26.3%	43.5%	62.9%
No health insurance coverage	13.2%	11.5%	5.5%

Source: U.S. Census Bureau, 2014 American Community Survey 1-Year Estimates.
* Puerto Ricans only.

Puerto Ricans in North Carolina, 2014

In 2014 an estimated 89,212 Puerto Ricans lived in North Carolina and accounted for 1.7% of all Puerto Ricans living in the United States. The number of Puerto Ricans in North Carolina almost tripled from 31,117 in the year 2000 to 89,212 in 2014.

Graph 1.A: Puerto Rican and Latino Population in North Carolina, 2014

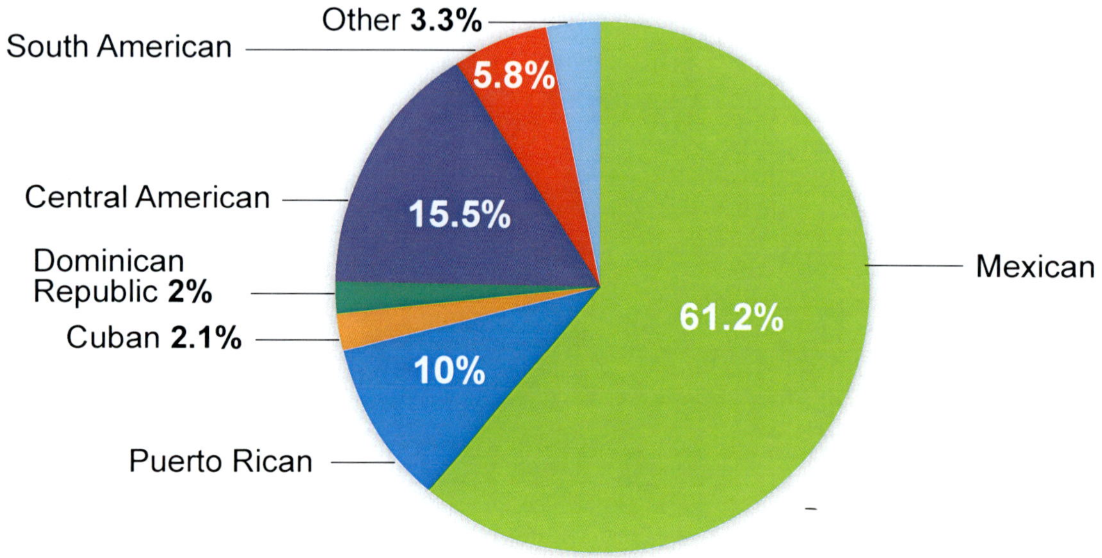

Table 1. Puerto Rican and Latino Population in North Carolina

	2000		2010		2014	
Total	8,049,313	100%	9,535,483	100%	9,943,964	100%
Not Hispanic or Latino	7,670,350	95.3%	8,735,363	91.6%	9,053,363	91%
Hispanic or Latino	378,963	4.7%	800,120	8.4%	890,601	9%
Mexican	246,545	3.1%	486,960	5.1%	545,340	5.5%
Puerto Rican	31,117	0.4%	71,800	0.8%	89,212	0.9%
Cuban	7,389	0.1%	18,079	0.2%	19,146	0.2%
Dominican Republic	2,865	0%	15,225	0.2%	17,977	0.2%
Central American	30,783	0.4%	105,066	1.1%	137,788	1.4%
South American	12,958	0.2%	46,307	0.5%	51,383	0.5%
Other	47,306	0.6%	56,683	0.6%	29,755	0.3%

Sources: U.S. Census Bureau, Census 2000 Summary File 1, 2010 Census. Summary File 1, and 2014 American Community Survey 1-Year Estimates.

The median age of Puerto Ricans in North Carolina was 25.3 years, below the national rate of Puerto Ricans of 28.9 years of age, and more than ten years lower than the median age among Puerto Ricans in Puerto Rico of 38.9 years. The proportion of Puerto Ricans aged 62 years and older in North Carolina was 7.1 percent, lower than for Puerto Ricans across the United States (9.9%) and a third less of those in Puerto Rico (21%).

English fluency indicators for Puerto Ricans in North Carolina were higher than for all stateside Puerto Ricans. Almost half of Puerto Ricans in North Carolina (48.2%) reported speaking only English at home, a rate almost ten percentage points higher than among all Puerto Ricans in the U.S. (38.8%). Puerto Ricans living in North Carolina that reported speaking English less than "very well" were 11.5%, which is less than the rate of all Puerto Ricans in the U.S. (17.3%).

Graph 2.A: Puerto Rican Education Attainment, 25 years and over, 2014

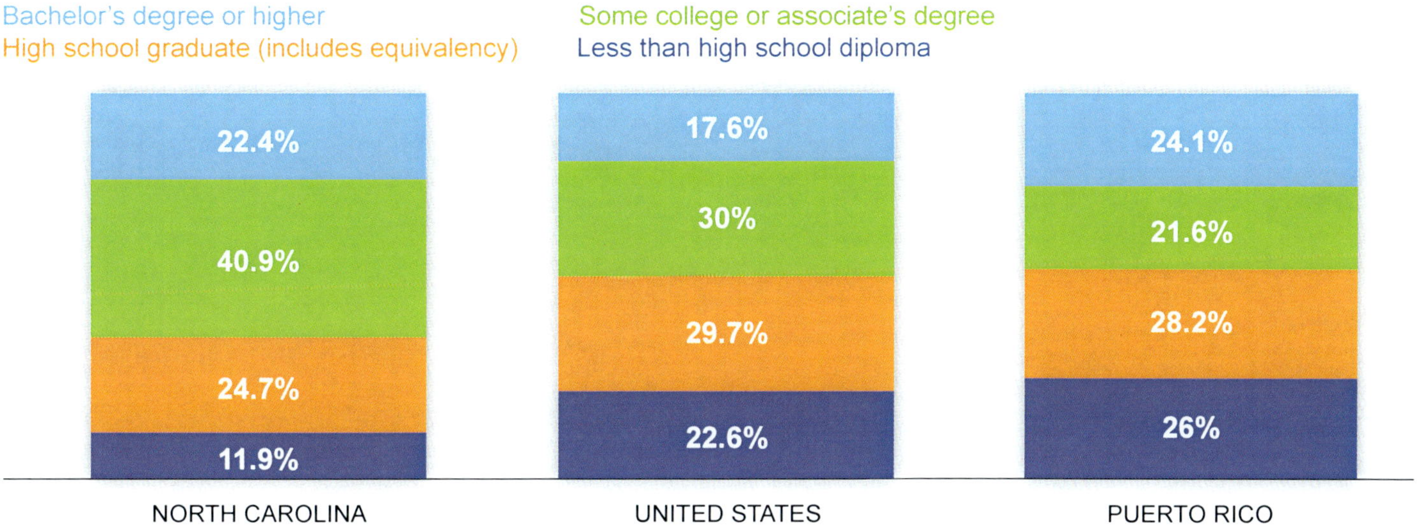

Table 2. Age, Education, and Language, 2014

Puerto Ricans	North Carolina	United States	Puerto Rico*
TOTAL POPULATION	89,212	5,266,738	3,404,122
Median age (years)	25.3	28.9	38.9
62 years and over	7.1%	9.9%	21%
EDUCATIONAL ATTAINMENT			
Population 25 years and over			
Less than high school diploma	11.9%	22.6%	26%
High school graduate (includes equivalency)	24.7%	29.7%	28.2%
Some college or associate's degree	40.9%	30%	21.6%
Bachelor's degree or higher	22.4%	17.6%	24.1%
Male, bachelor's degree or higher	15.6%	15.6%	19.6%
Female, bachelor's degree or higher	28.7%	19.5%	28.1%
LANGUAGE SPOKEN AT HOME AND ABILITY TO SPEAK ENGLISH			
Population 5 years and over			
English only	48.2%	38.8%	5.3%
Language other than English	51.8%	61.2%	94.7%
Speak English less than "very well"	11.5%	17.3%	78.8%

Source: U.S. Census Bureau, 2014 American Community Survey 1-Year Estimates.
* Puerto Ricans only.

Puerto Ricans in North Carolina were generally more educated than stateside Puerto Ricans. Nearly two-thirds (63.3%) of Puerto Ricans aged 25 years and older in North Carolina had some college or higher degrees, compared to stateside Puerto Ricans (46.7%) and Puerto Ricans in Puerto Rico (45.7%). A breakdown of the education by sex showed that Puerto Rican women (28.7%) in North Carolina earned almost doubled Puerto Rican men (15.6%) on attainment, having earned a bachelor's degree or higher. Stateside Puerto Rican women (19.5%) and those living in Puerto Rico (28.1%), also earned a higher proportion of bachelor's degree over Puerto Rican men in the U.S. and in Puerto Rico.

Puerto Ricans participation in North Carolina's civilian labor force (66.9%) was five percentage points higher than those among the U.S. (61.6%), and both were almost twenty percentage points more than the civilian labor force participation in Puerto Rico (43.7%). The unemployment rate in North Carolina was 11.1 percent, which is near the national Puerto Rican average (11.6%) and less than those living in Puerto Rico (18.9%).

Almost a third (29.2%) of Puerto Ricans in North Carolina worked at the management, business, science, and arts sector compared to 28.1 percent of Puerto Ricans in the

Table 3. Employment and Occupations, 2014

Puerto Ricans	North Carolina	United States	Puerto Rico*
EMPLOYMENT STATUS			
Population 16 years and over			
In labor force	72.6%	62.4%	43.7%
Civilian labor force	66.9%	61.6%	43.7%
Employed	59.5%	54.4%	35.4%
Unemployed	11.1%	11.6%	18.9%
Not in labor force	27.4%	37.6%	56.3%
Armed Forces	5.7%	0.8%	0%
OCCUPATION			
Civilian employed population 16 years and over			
Male	18,022	1,058,918	516,762
Management, business, science, and arts	25%	23.4%	23.9%
Service occupations	20.2%	22.5%	23%
Sales and office occupations	15.4%	19.6%	21.3%
Construction and maintenance	16.7%	13.8%	18%
Production, transportation, and moving	22.7%	20.7%	13.7%
Female	17,190	999,105	456,356
Management, business, science, and arts	33.5%	33.1%	39.7%
Service occupations	21.7%	24.4%	16.6%
Sales and office occupations	39.5%	35.7%	38.3%
Construction and maintenance	2.4%	0.6%	0.6%
Production, transportation, and moving	2.8%	6.2%	4.8%
CLASS OF WORKER			
Civilian employed population 16 years and over			
Private wage and salary workers	79.9%	82%	69%
Government workers	17.4%	14.8%	22.5%
Self-employed workers in own not incorporated business	2.7%	3.1%	8.3%
VETERAN STATUS			
Civilian population 18 years and over			
Civilian veteran	10.9%	6%	3.3%

Source: U.S. Census Bureau, 2014 American Community Survey 1-Year Estimates.
* Puerto Ricans only.

Puerto Rican Population by Counties in North Carolina, 2014

Puerto Ricans were mostly concentrated in North Carolina's central region and dispersed in parts of the state's southern region borderline. The majority of the Puerto Rican population (14%) resided in Cumberland County, followed by 12 percent in Wake County, both counties located in the state's central regional area. The proportion of Puerto Ricans in both these counties was greater than the proportion of Latinos overall (4% in Cumberland and 11% in Wake County) and the state's overall population (3% in Cumberland County and 10% in Wake County). Major cities like Fayetteville in Cumberland County and the high-tech community areas known as the Research Triangle in Wake County (includes Raleigh, Durham, and Chapel Hill cities) contains a quarter of the state's Puerto Rican population. The next two populous counties outside North Carolina's central area were Mecklenburg County (12%) and Onslow County (6%), both located in the state's south borderline. Lastly, Forsyth County (4%) and Guilford County (4%) both accounted for 8 percent of Puerto Ricans in north central region of North Carolina. In all, Puerto Rican settlement patterns closely reflected U.S. military bases located throughout the state and high-tech community area known as the 'Research Triangle' located in Raleigh-Durham-Cary-Chapel Hill combined statistical area (CSA).

COUNTY	Puerto Rican Population	Percent	Latino Population	Percent	Total Population	Percent
Cumberland County	11,843	14%	33,555	4%	324,002	3%
Wake County	10,293	12%	94,166	11%	952,513	10%
Mecklenburg County	9,934	12%	120,368	14%	968,500	10%
Onslow County	4,635	6%	20,552	2%	182,921	2%
Forsyth County	3,574	4%	43,929	5%	358,130	4%
Guilford County	3,459	4%	36,976	4%	500,899	5%
Harnett County	2,930	4%	13,858	2%	121,789	1%
Durham County	2,404	3%	37,889	4%	282,422	3%
Union County	1,957	2%	22,419	3%	209,387	2%
Buncombe County	1,936	2%	15,238	2%	244,599	3%
Hoke County	1,860	2%	6,199	1%	50,034	1%
Johnston County	1,726	2%	22,991	3%	175,343	2%
New Hanover County	1,657	2%	11,208	1%	209,586	2%
Cabarrus County	1,609	2%	17,927	2%	184,855	2%
Other Counties	22,954	28%	351,322	41%	4,985,425	51%
Total	**82,771**	**100%**	**848,597**	**100%**	**9,750,405**	**100%**

Sources: U.S. Census Bureau and 2014 American Community Survey 5-Year Estimates
Notes: Total counts for populations may differ depending on whether the estimates are derived from the five-year estimates or the one-year estimates of the American Community Survey. Counties with less than 1% of the total Puerto Rican population were omitted.

PUERTO RICAN POPULATION BY COUNTIES IN NORTH CAROLINA, 2014

PUERTO RICAN POPULATION

1 dot = 50

'06-'14 PUERTO RICAN ARRIVALS

1 dot = 50

BOUNDARIES

County

City/Towns

Census Tracts

CONGRESSIONAL DISTRICT

Republican

Democrat

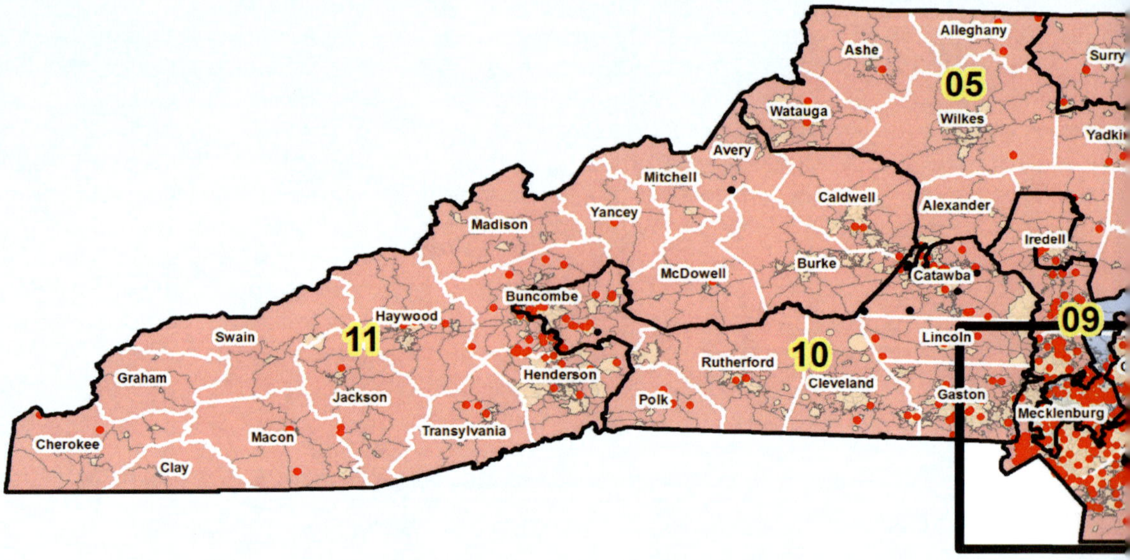

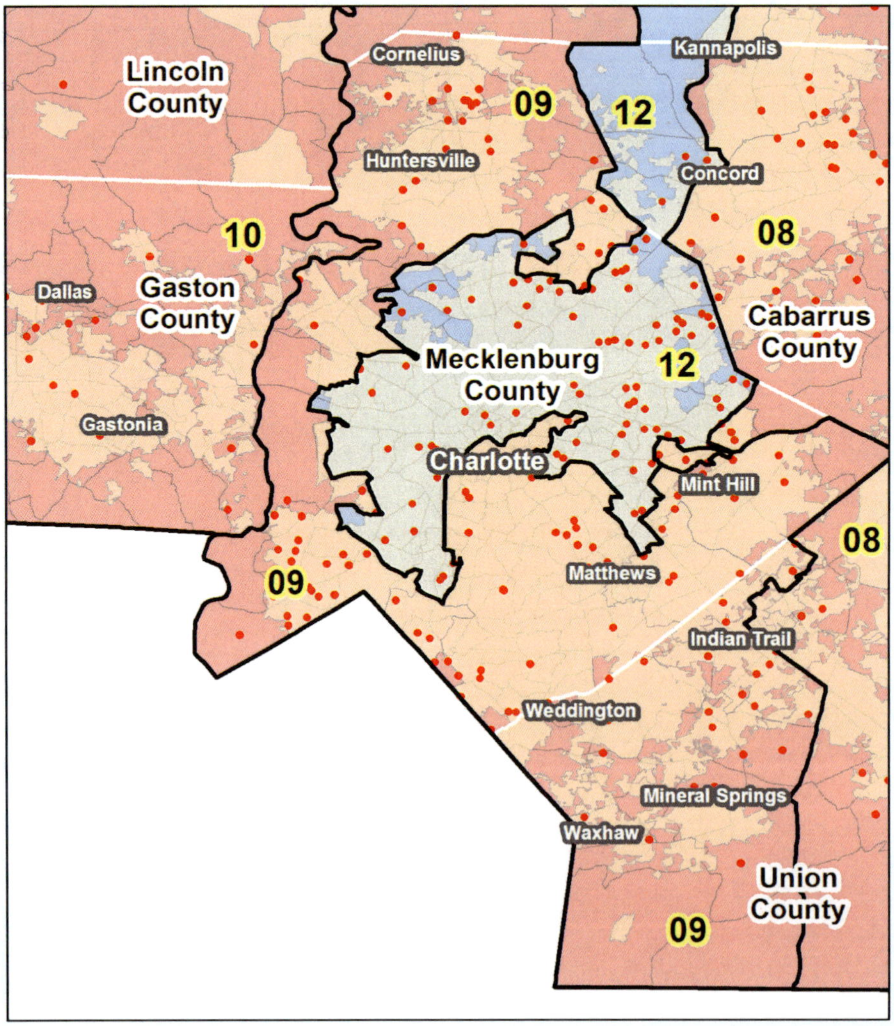

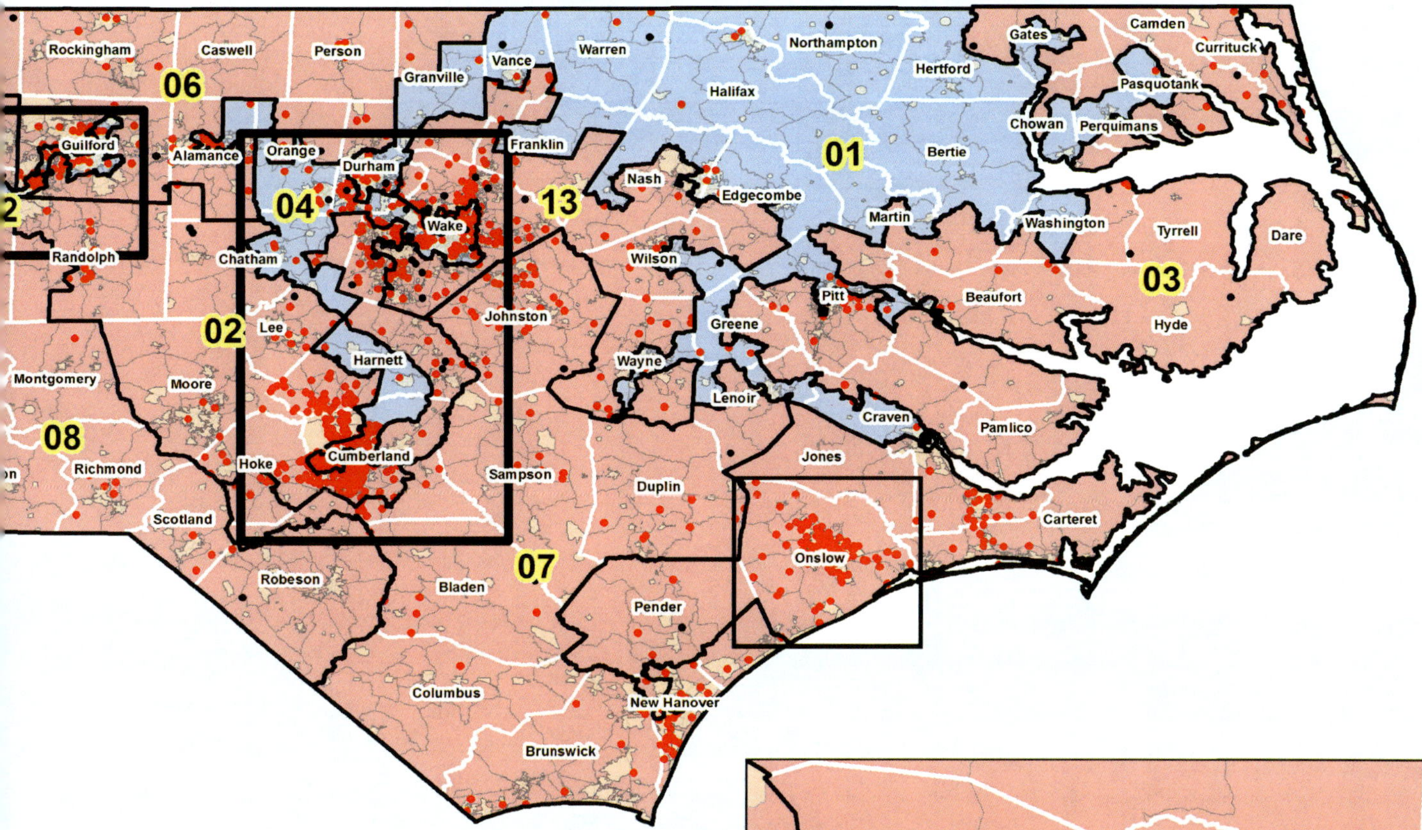
Rockingham
Caswell
Person
Granville
Vance
Warren
Northampton
Hertford
Gates
Camden
Currituck
Pasquotank
Perquimans
Chowan
Halifax
06
Guilford
Alamance
Orange
Durham
Franklin
01
Bertie
Nash
Edgecombe
04
13
Wake
Martin
Washington
Tyrrell
Dare
Randolph
Chatham
Wilson
03
Pitt
Beaufort
Johnston
Greene
Hyde
02
Lee
Montgomery
Moore
Harnett
Wayne
Lenoir
Craven
Pamlico
08
Richmond
Hoke
Cumberland
Jones
Sampson
Duplin
Carteret
Scotland
Onslow
07
Robeson
Bladen
Pender
Columbus
New Hanover
Brunswick

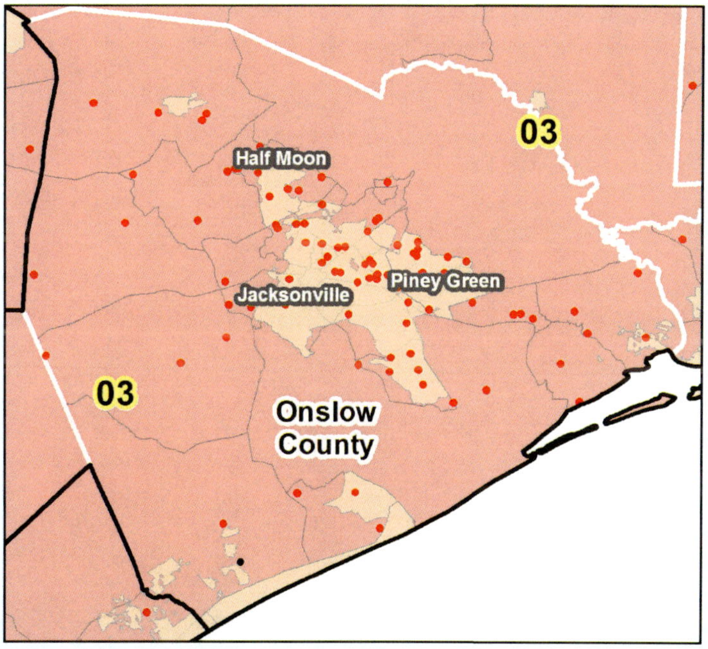
03
Half Moon
Jacksonville
Piney Green
03
Onslow
County

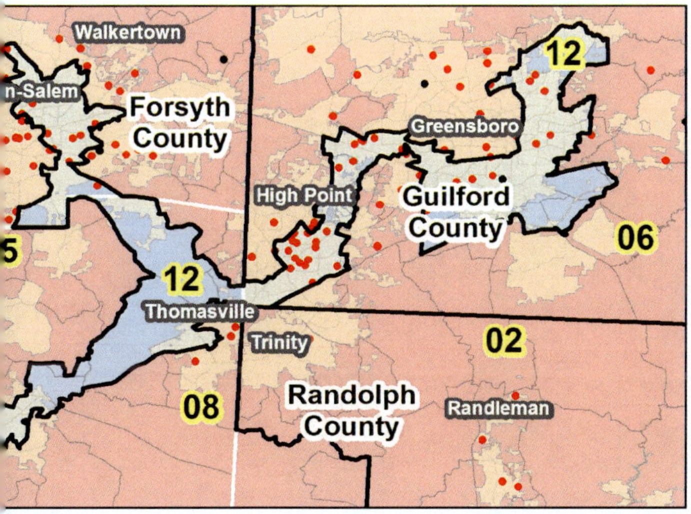
Walkertown
12
n-Salem
Forsyth
County
Greensboro
High Point
Guilford
County
06
12
Thomasville
Trinity
02
08
Randolph
County
Randleman

PUERTO RICAN POPULATION BY COUNTIES IN NORTH CAROLINA, 2014

PUERTO RICAN POPULATION

1 dot = 50

'06-'14 PUERTO RICAN ARRIVALS

1 dot = 50

BOUNDARIES

County

City/Towns

Census Tracts

CONGRESSIONAL DISTRICT

Republican

Democrat

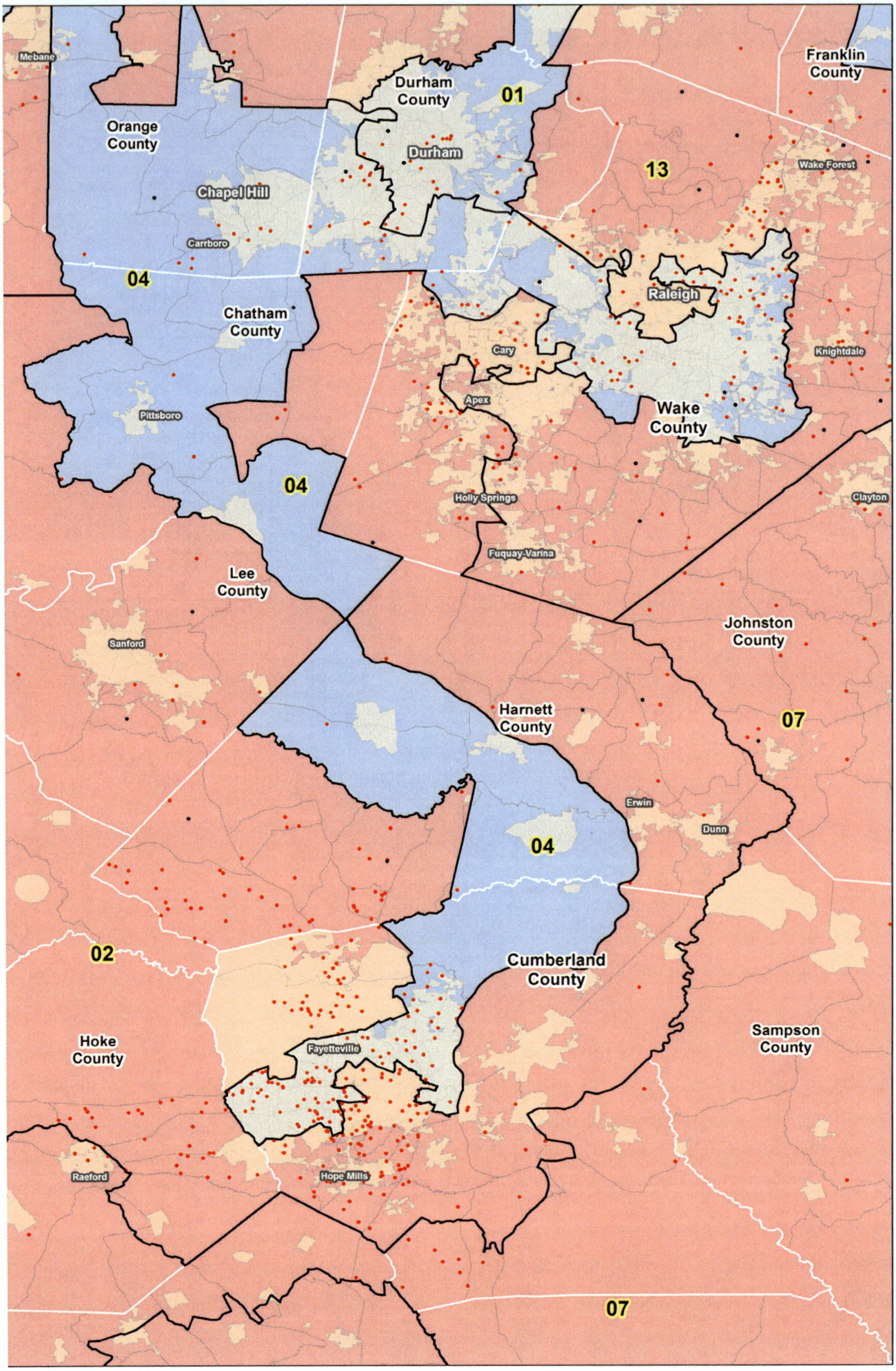

United States and 31.3 percent in Puerto Rico. Puerto Rican women had a greater percent in the management, business, science, and arts sector than Puerto Rican men. In North Carolina 33.5 percent of Puerto Rican women worked in this sector compared to 25 percent of Puerto Rican men. In the U.S. these proportions were 33.1 percent and 23.4 percent, respectively, and in Puerto Rico were 39.7 percent and 23.9 percent, respectively. The sales and office occupations sector followed with 27.5 percent of Puerto Rican employment in North Carolina.

Puerto Ricans serving in the Armed Forces accounted for 5.7 percent of its working age population in North Carolina, seven times higher than the proportion of Puerto Ricans in the U.S. overall (0.8%). A 10.9 percent of Puerto Ricans in North Carolina reported being veterans, nearly double the Puerto Rican national rate (6.0%) and more than three times the rate of those living in Puerto Rico.

The average earnings of full-time, year-round Puerto Rican men and women in North Carolina, $51,336 and $36,716, showed a slight disparity than at the national level of $50,756 for Puerto Rican men, but wider for women with $42,623 for Puerto Rican women. Although Puerto Rican men in North Carolina earned just a thousand dollars more than the Puerto Rican national level, Puerto Rican women earned about six thousand dollars less than Puerto Rican

Table 4. Income and Earnings, 2014

Puerto Ricans	North Carolina	United States	Puerto Rico*
INCOME IN THE PAST 12 MONTHS (IN 2013 INFLATION-ADJUSTED DOLLARS)			
Households	29,516	1,635,808	1,175,297
Median household income (dollars)	$37,238	$39,322	$18,710
With earnings	86.5%	76.9%	54.7%
Mean earnings (dollars)	$51,055	$61,065	$36,407
With Social Security income	18.1%	24.1%	43.2%
Mean Social Security income (dollars)	$15,098	$13,727	$12,159
With Supplemental Security Income	6%	12.6%	0.4%
Mean Supplemental Security Income (dollars)	$9,135	$8,780	$10,025
With cash public assistance income	2.7%	6.9%	8.1%
Mean cash public assistance income (dollars)	$3,185	$3,441	$2,316
With retirement income	9.5%	10.1%	15.6%
Mean retirement income (dollars)	$19,035	$20,452	$15,387
With Food Stamp/SNAP benefits	20.3%	31.5%	39.7%
Families	20,399	1,114,628	830,807
Median family income (dollars)	$41,431	$44,499	$22,220
Married-couple family	64.6%	53.9%	56.1%
Median income (dollars)	$55,059	$67,129	$29,417
Male householder, no spouse present	8.6%	10.2%	9.5%
Median income (dollars)	$40,288	$37,513	$17,797
Female householder, no husband present	26.8%	35.9%	34.4%
Median income (dollars)	$23,651	$23,957	$13,554
Individuals	89,212	5,266,738	3,404,122
Per capita income (dollars)	$17,427	$18,457	$10,960
Mean earnings (dollars) for full-time, year-round workers:			
Male	$51,336	$50,756	$32,512
Female	$36,716	$42,263	$29,166

Source: U.S. Census Bureau, 2014 American Community Survey 1-Year Estimates.
* Puerto Ricans only.

women at the Puerto Rican national level. Compared to Puerto Rico where full-time, year-round Puerto Rican workers earnings were $32,512 and $29,166 for men and women, respectively, Puerto Ricans in North Carolina and in the U.S. as a whole earn more on average.

The income in households and families is a strong indicator of economic stability. This (median income) indicator was higher for Puerto Ricans living in North Carolina ($37,238) than those in Puerto Rico ($18,710), but notably lower by two thousand dollars of the stateside Puerto Ricans ($39,322). Per capita income among Puerto Ricans in North Carolina ($17,427) were higher than those in Puerto Rico ($10,960) but lower than the stateside Puerto Ricans ($18,457) by one thousand dollars.

Puerto Ricans in North Carolina had a $1.6 billion dollars purchasing power. Stateside Puerto Ricans represented a 72.3 percent of the $134.5 billion dollars total purchasing power of the entire Puerto Rican community in 2014. Purchasing power is defined simply as per capita income multiplied by the Puerto Rican population. Stateside

Graph 4.A: Mean Earnings for Full-Time Year-Round Puerto Rican Workers, 2014

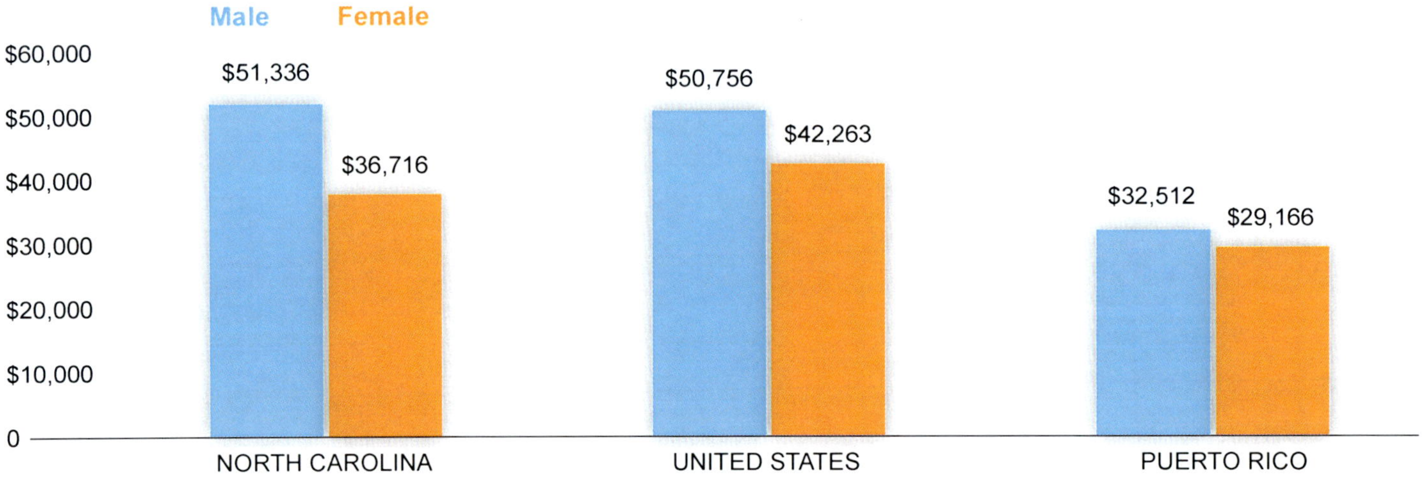

Graph 4.B: Puerto Rican Purchasing Power, in Billions, 2014

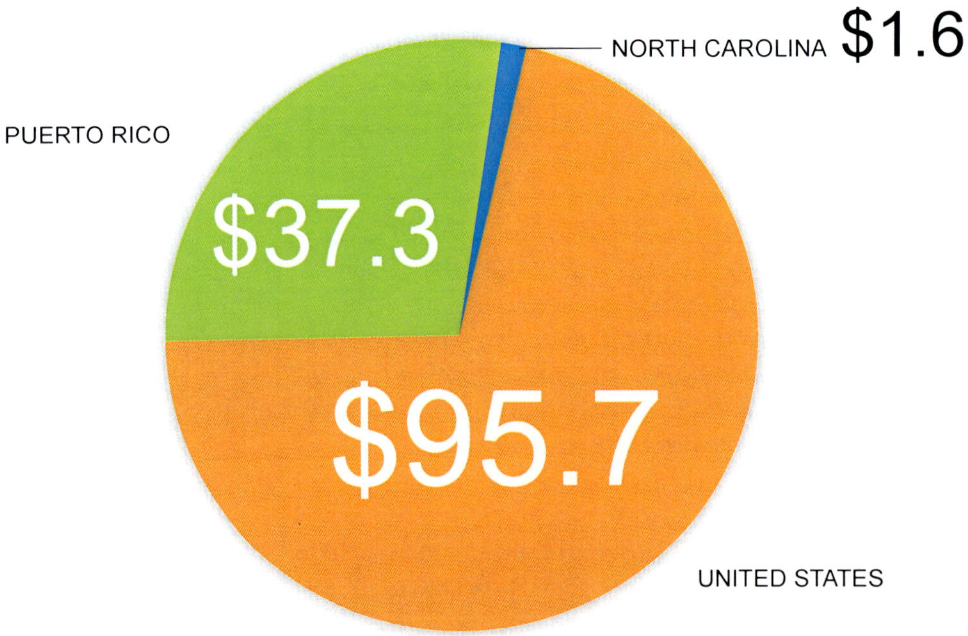

Graph 5.A: Poverty Rates, 2014

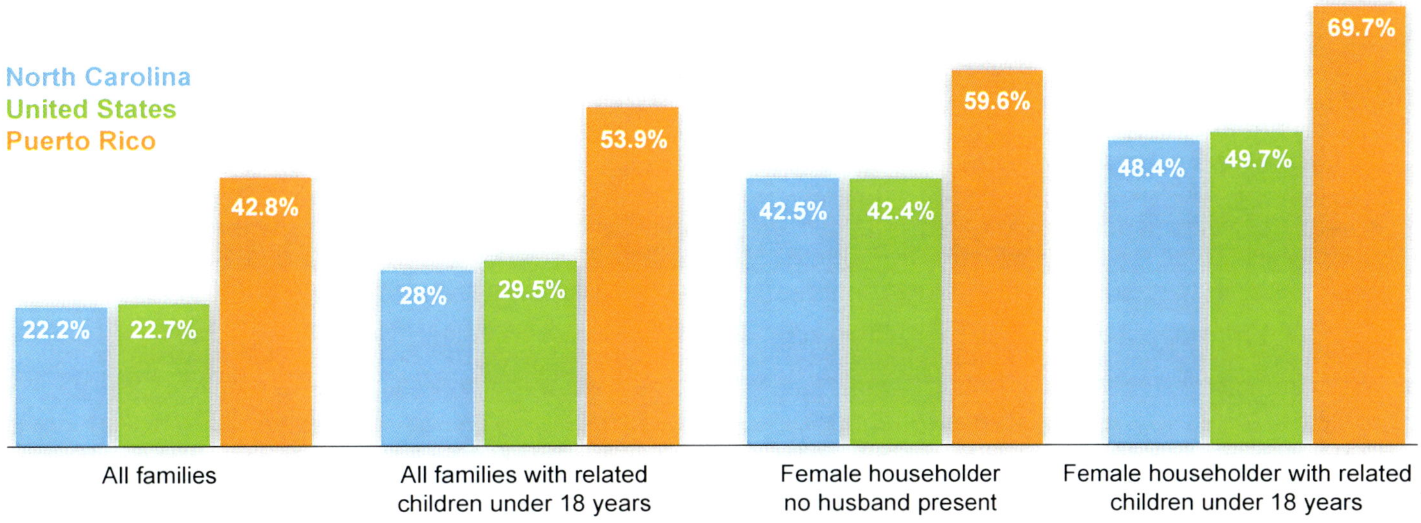

Table 5. Poverty, 2014

Puerto Ricans	North Carolina	United States	Puerto Rico*
POVERTY RATES			
All families	22.2%	22.7%	42.8%
With related children under 18 years	28%	29.5%	53.9%
With related children under 5 years only	33.7%	24.6%	57.1%
Married-couple family	13.9%	9.7%	30.9%
With related children under 18 years	14.2%	11.3%	35.5%
With related children under 5 years only	35.7%	5.9%	33.9%
Female householder, no husband present, family	42.5%	42.4%	59.6%
With related children under 18 years	48.4%	49.7%	69.7%
With related children under 5 years only	50.3%	49.4%	75.7%
All people	24.5%	26.2%	46.6%
Under 18 years	31%	33.4%	58.7%
Related children under 18 years	30.7%	33.1%	58.6%
Related children under 5 years	40.1%	34.7%	62.8%
Related children 5 to 17 years	26.4%	32.4%	57.3%
18 years and over	20.6%	22.8%	43.2%
18 to 64 years	20.8%	22.8%	43.8%
65 years and over	18%	22.4%	41%
People in families	21.9%	23.6%	44.6%
Unrelated individuals 15 years and over	38.5%	38.5%	58.6%

Source: U.S. Census Bureau, 2014 American Community Survey 1-Year Estimates.
* Puerto Ricans only.

Puerto Ricans more than doubled the purchasing power of those in Puerto Rico with $37.3 billion dollars.

The poverty rate for all Puerto Rican families in North Carolina was 22.2 percent, slightly lower than for stateside Puerto Rican families (22.7%), and less than half for those families living in Puerto Rico (42.8%). As seen in other states and in Puerto Rico, households with a female householder, no husband, with children under 18 years had the highest rates of poverty. In North Carolina, 48.4 percent of these households reported living in poverty, compared to 49.7 percent across the United States and 59.6 percent for those in Puerto Rico. These numbers on the poverty rate sound alarming and disturbing. North Carolina had a percent slightly less from the national number, but reflects what found in other states in terms of the poverty rates by specific types of households.

Public assistance income participation rates for Puerto Ricans families in North Carolina (2.7%) were less than half the national level (6.9%) and in Puerto Rico (8.1%). Although food stamps/SNAP (Supplementary Nutrition Assistance Program) participation among Puerto Rican families in North Carolina was 20.3 percent, it was considerably lower than stateside Puerto Rican families (31.5%) and those in Puerto Rico (39.7%).

North Carolina has considerably higher rates of home ownership (43.1%) among Puerto Ricans households in comparison to those Puerto Ricans living in the U.S. (36.0%).The median value of owner-occupied housing for Puerto Ricans in North Carolina was $160,000, a price below the median value of owner-occupied housing for all stateside Puerto Ricans ($175,900), but higher than in Puerto Rico ($119,500). This difference on home values may be affected by the lower costs of living in North Carolina Puerto Ricans in the state are earning more money and more likely to be employed in higher wage sectors than at the national level, and presumably can afford more expensive homes. The median monthly owner cost associated with a mortgage was $1,289 for Puerto Ricans in North Carolina, $1,545 for those living in the U.S., and $873 for those in Puerto Rico. This number was a percentage point higher than the national level percent (37.2%) of Puerto Ricans in the U.S., but is lower in Puerto Rico (47.4%).

Table 6. Housing and Health Insurance, 2014

Puerto Ricans	North Carolina	United States	Puerto Rico*
HOUSING			
Owner-occupied housing units	43.1%	36%	68.7%
Monthly owner costs as a percentage of household income in the past 12 months			
Less than 30 percent	61.8%	62.8%	52.6%
30 percent or more	38.2%	37.2%	47.4%
Owner-occupied housing units			
Median value (dollars)	$160,000	$175,900	$119,500
Median selected monthly owner costs with a mortgage (dollars)	$1,289	$1,545	$873
HEALTH INSURANCE COVERAGE			
Civilian noninstitutionalized population			
With private health insurance	60.5%	51.6%	38%
With public coverage	31.4%	43.5%	62.9%
No health insurance coverage	13.9%	11.5%	5.5%

Source: U.S. Census Bureau, 2014 American Community Survey 1-Year Estimates.
* Puerto Ricans only.

About the Data Center

The Data Center packages and disseminates the most current information about Puerto Ricans. This information is provided to present socioeconomic and demographic portraits of the Puerto Rican population, mostly in the United States. The purpose is to provide basic descriptive information to scholars, policy makers and the public in general. The sources for this information are publically available repositories, such as the U.S. Census Bureau.

Data Center Staff

Eric Franqui

Jennifer Hinojosa

Omari-Khalid Rahman

Rafael Pérez-Torres

Nashia Román

Carlos Vargas-Ramos, Coordinator

Made in United States
North Haven, CT
04 November 2026

21728942R10095